RESEARCH METHODS IN SPORT MANAGEMENT

RESEARCH METHODS IN SPORT MANAGEMENT

MING LI, ED.D.

Ohio University

BRENDA G. PITTS, ED.D.

Georgia State University

JEROME QUARTERMAN, PH.D.

Howard University

FITNESS INFORMATION TECHNOLOGY
A Division of the International Center
for Performance Excellence
West Virginia University
262 Coliseum, WVU-PE
PO Box 6116
Morgantown, WV 26506-6116

Library of Congress Card Catalog Number: 2008929366

$37.00

ISBN: 978-1-885693-85-3

Cover illustration: © Josh Rodriguez, bigstockphoto.com
Cover Composition: Bellerophon Productions
Typesetter: Bellerophon Productions
Production Editor: Valerie Gittings
Copyeditor: Anita Stanley
Proofreader: Maria E. denBoer
Printed by Sheridan Books

10 9 8 7 6 5 4 3 2 1

Fitness Information Technology
A Division of the International Center for Performance Excellence
West Virginia University
262 Coliseum, WVU-PE
PO Box 6116
Morgantown, WV 26506-6116
800.477.4348 (toll free)
304.293.6888 (phone)
304.293.6658 (fax)
Email: icpe@mail.wvu.edu
Website: www.fitinfotech.com

CONTENTS

DETAILED TABLE OF CONTENTS

CHAPTER 11—ETHICS IN SPORT MANAGEMENT RESEARCH AND PUBLICATIONS

CHAPTER 17—INTRODUCTION TO STATISTICAL DATA ANALYSIS IN SPORT MANAGEMENT RESEARCH

CHAPTER 18—DESCRIPTIVE STATISTICS IN SPORT MANAGEMENT RESEARCH

PREFACE

Over many years, we listened as numerous professors and students lamented that the field of sport management did not have its own research methods courses or book. Without such, our students were placed in courses on research methods in physical education, general education, or exercise science. These are good courses for students in those fields, but do not have the focus on the sport business industry that we need. Even as some of the professors of those courses assured us that they would include content about sport management, or allow the sport management students to focus their assignments on sport business, we knew the coverage would be just a scratch at the surface of what we needed for our students. Students constantly complained about having to take the course because of the lack of focus on the sport business field, feeling like they didn't fit in, the instructor's lack of knowledge of sport management, and the lack of a textbook about research in sport business. We certainly appreciate our colleagues making their attempts to provide space and content in their classrooms over the years.

Finally, the wait is over. We introduce to the field the first textbook on *Research Methods in Sport Management*. It is an attempt to help the field begin to address the need to have its own specialized materials in research methods in sport management. We hope also that the book will encourage instructors of any research methods course to have students of sport management use this book as their text for the class. Additionally, and perhaps more importantly, we hope that this book will encourage faculties in sport management to offer a course especially designed for research methods in sport management.

EXPERTISE OF THE AUTHORS. The authors of this book have the experience and credentials necessary to produce a book about research in sport management. First, *in conducting research*, each author has substantial depth and breadth of ex-

perience. Each one has an established reputation as an expert researcher in his or her specialization areas, with respected and substantial bodies of works. All three authors have years of experience in service as editorial reviewers for numerous research journals and for research conference programs, have served as major professors and advisors for numerous master's students thesis and doctoral students dissertation research, and have served as expert research reviewers for promotion cases for assistant, associate, and full professors.

Additionally, the authors all have experience in writing and editing textbooks—indeed, they are authors, editors, and development editors of more than 20 textbooks in sport management, most of which are in subsequent editions, many of which are distributed worldwide, and some of which have been translated into several different languages.

IN TEACHING ABOUT RESEARCH, all authors of this book teach research methods courses. Some of those courses have been the generic research methods in HPER course, filled with a mixture of students in different fields of study, and had to use the typical textbooks on research methods in HPER. A few, fortunately, have been courses with a specific focus on research methods in sport management. In order to provide specific content and material, we each supplemented heavily from many sources.

When we were approached to write a textbook, we were very happy—we could put all of our teaching notes, lecture notes, experience, and a plethora of supplemental materials into one source. Thus, we are very happy to produce this book and share it with our colleagues, many of whom have been awaiting its arrival!

STATE OF RESEARCH IN SPORT MANAGEMENT. Much has been written about the state of research in sport management. The consensus seems to be that research in our field is still in its infancy, awaiting growth in variety, depth, and breadth of both research methods and content focus.

Thankfully, in recent years, the field has realized an explosion of research journals, associations, and conferences in sport business. We believe that this growth is good for the field. The much-needed additional outlets for research will stimulate progress toward an expanding the methods utilized in research, and encourage broadening the scope of topics, content, subjects, and issues to be studied and contributed to the body of literature.

Now, what have we done? What's in this book that makes it unique to sport management and different from all the other books on research methods? In other words, why should you use it instead of what you are currently using? Let's provide for you an introduction and overview of the book, its unique features, and how to get the most out of it.

WHO CAN USE THIS BOOK? Anyone who teaches research methods courses who will need material specific to research in the sport business industry; students in any research methods course who needs research in sport management material; and, industry professionals who need a resource manual (a "how to" guide) on conducting research for their business.

INSTRUCTORS will find a book that is organized specifically for the introduction to research methods course. The book is designed to provide introductory content for a first course on research methods for senior level undergraduate or graduate students in sport management.

STUDENTS will have a book that speaks specifically to the field of sport management—a book full of content, examples, and methods of research in sport management.

INDUSTRY PROFESSIONALS will have a book that can serve as a "how to" guide on research. It offers basic information and guidelines on conducting research in numerous situations as may be needed by the business.

ORGANIZATION AND CONTENTS. This book is organized for an introduction to and overview of research methods in sport management. It can be used in a research methods in sport management course, or as a specialized content supplement book in other courses. By doing this, we fulfill your need for a book that provides comprehensive coverage of the research process specific to sport management, and also provides breadth and depth while serving as a valuable reference and resource.

Chapters contain examples and cases of real life research. Students will learn how research is used in the business to make decisions and provide solutions for practical problems and issues.

Content in the examples and throughout the chapters reflect the depth and breadth of the sport business industry, in relation to business type, sports, organization, gender, ethnicity, level, and many other characteristics that define our industry. That is, we know that the greatest portions of the industry are comprised of amateur participant sports and the multitudes of businesses that service them. This is where the majority of our students work. Therefore, the examples focus on real life problems in places where our students will be working and will need specific help.

FEATURES OF THIS FIRST EDITION

We are keenly aware that this book will need your input and help along the years as it matures into subsequent editions. We ask that you—instructors, students, and industry professionals—provide us with your ideas for improvements as you use this first edition. We want to point out some of the features and benefits that this first edition offers.

Professors will appreciate:

■ An organized presentation of research methods from the most basic to the complex.

- Presentation of practical applications in industry as well as applications and use of research in academia.
- Inclusion of timely issues of ethics in research practice and reporting.
- Emphasis on sound decision making in research practice
- A research process model that guides from question development through to research method and application.
- Topics and examples that cover the depth and breadth of the sport business industry.
- A set of instructor's materials such as Power-Point presentation slides, assignment and project ideas, and exam materials that can all be used to get you started.

Students will appreciate:

- A research methods book that is focused on their specific field of study
- A book written with their practical application uses in mind
- Practical and useful examples from the real world of sport business
- Sound guidelines to learning and building knowledge and skills in doing research
- A book that they can keep and use as a reference guide beyond the course and on the job

And Finally...

As we prepared this book, we were profoundly aware of the challenge we faced in our attempt to provide the field with its first book on research methods in sport management. We know that this book will provide a starting place for teaching research methods in sport management to our students. We are keenly aware that this first edition may be enhanced through additions and changes, so we ask for your feedback and ideas to improve it as we all use this valuable resource. As we said, this gives us all a starting place. Let's work together to make it better as we move forward in our young field.

Enjoy . . . and please let us hear from you.

Ming Li, Brenda Pitts, and Jerome Quarterman

CHAPTER 1
INTRODUCTION TO SPORT MANAGEMENT RESEARCH

OBJECTIVES FOR COMPLETING THIS
CHAPTER ARE THAT STUDENTS WILL
BE ABLE TO:

Define research and sport management research

Understand the role of research for sport business

Understand the role of research for the academic field
of sport management

Understand the value of research for students
in sport management

Understand the characteristics of sport
management research

Understand the purpose of sport management
research

Differentiate the philosophical approaches
to sport management research

Differentiate the applied sport management research
vs. basic sport management research

Describe each of the three types of sport management
research: exploratory research, descriptive research,
and causal research

Understand the evolution of sport
management research

Discuss the future of sport management research

THE PURPOSE OF THIS CHAPTER is to provide an overview of sport management research and its significance to the field of sport management and to the sport industry. Specifically, the chapter will first define sport management research and substantiate the importance of research to the academic field of sport management and to the sport industry. The chapter will then discuss the characteristics of sport management research and the different types of research that sport management researchers can use in solving their research problems. The evolution and future of sport management research will also be reviewed.

NATURE AND SCOPE OF SPORT MANAGEMENT RESEARCH

At its most basic level, the purpose of research is to generate information. This information will be used for a variety of purposes. Information is critical for making decisions and developing strategies in every part of the company. Research can provide basic answers to simple questions, and it can uncover information needed in complicated situations.

As an academic field of study, sport management is relatively new. Compare this field to such fields as law, medicine, or education. Yet, for all of millennia, sport management is an activity that humans have been doing ever since we started playing. That is, once a human started to play a game, someone was there to provide management. Even though sport management is something we have been doing forever, it is only recently that it is a labeled academic field of study. In fact, the first sport-related administration program has been traced to 1949 when Florida Southern University offered a curriculum titled "Baseball Business Administration" (Isaacs, 1964). The origins of the words used to describe this field have not yet been traced. However, the earliest use of the label "Sports Administration" comes from a book entitled *Careers and Opportunities in Sports*, in which a variety of jobs in sport business are presented and one chapter is labeled "Sports Administration." As a field of study in current decades, sports administration has been traced to a program at Ohio University in 1966.

Research in Our Daily Lives

Research touches us every day. Whether we reach for something in the fridge, get into our cars, turn on our cell phones, or put on our running shoes, each one of these items has been created, developed, manufactured, and marketed with the help of research.

Staying current with the knowledge of today is a demanding task. Information, old and new, is produced and flows at amazing speeds. When an incident happens on the other side of the world, we can read about it, hear about it, and see it within seconds. Additionally, information technology, the invention, production, and distribution of high technology equipment that allows us to access and manage information, improves daily at a blinding pace—we can surf the web, manage email, watch

Consumer	Demographics
	Psychographics
	Lifestyle
	Geodemographics
	Purchase behavior
Competitor	The industry and marketplace
	Product differentiation
	Pricing strategies
	Financial strategies
	Positioning
	Promotion strategies
Company	Mission & objectives
	Strengths
	Production
	Product management
	Distribution strategies
	Promotion strategies
	Weaknesses
Climate	Economic
	Legal
	Social and cultural
	Political
	Ethical
	Trends
	Technology
	Education
	Community
	Corporate

Source: Pitts, B. & Stotlar, D. (2007). *Fundamentals of sport marketing* (3rd ed.). Morgantown, WV: Fitness Information Technology.

FIGURE 1-1. The 4 Cs: What the Sport Business Must Study Constantly to Stay Informed and Make Good Decisions and Successful Strategies

TV or movies, listen to music, and check our GPS for directions on a gadget that fits in the palm of a hand. And, oh, by the way, it's also a phone.

In the world of sports, research affects every part of the industry. In sporting apparel, the athlete's clothing is lighter, warmer, faster, safer, and basically whatever the athlete needs to maximize performance. In goods, advances in equipment have caused many sports to change rules to either restrict the technology, or to embrace it. In golf, for instance, golf course designers have had to lengthen courses because the technology of golf clubs and golf balls allow the average player to hit the ball farther.

In every sport business, information is critical. Sport managers need information to make informed decisions and to generate strategies. The nature and scope of sport management research is limited only by one's definition of business and of research. Research provides information needed about the consumer, the competitor, the company, and the climate —the 4 Cs of marketing—as presented in Figure 1-1 (Pitts & Stotlar, 2007).

Sport Management Research Defined

How is "sport management research" defined? Sport management is the study and practice of all people, activities, businesses, or organizations involved in producing, facilitating, promoting, or organizing any sport-related business or product (Pitts & Stotlar, 2007). Research, at its most basic level, is the generation of information. Other common definitions of research are "to examine carefully to help build a scientific body of knowledge," "the systematic investigation of phenomena (behavior, events, people, things, etc.)," and "a diligent systematic inquiry or study to gain new knowledge or refine existing."

One of the most comprehensive definitions of research is offered by Kerlinger and Lee (2000). They regarded research as "a systematic, controlled, empirical, amoral, public, and critical investigation of natural phenomena. It is guided by theory and hypotheses about the presumed relations among such phenomena" (p. 14). McMillan and Schumacher (2006) defined research as "the systematic process of collecting and logically analyzing data for some purpose" (p. 9).

The authors of this book define sport management research as a scientific, purposeful, systematic and rigorous method of collecting, analyzing, and interpreting data objectively or subjectively about some characteristic (individual (s), group(s), organization(s), idea(s), demographic(s), concept(s), model(s), theory(ies), etc), in order to gain new knowledge or add to the existing knowledge base of the field of sport organization management studies. For the purpose of this book, sport management research is defined as *an orderly investigative process that involves purposeful and systematic collection, analysis, and interpretation of data (units of information) to gain new knowledge or to verify already existing knowledge within the specific domain of managing human and material resources in organizations of the sport industry.*

RESEARCH FOR THE BODY OF KNOWLEDGE IN SPORT MANAGEMENT

Sport management is an emerging and expanding field of study as a science. Science involves systematic study for the development of new information or ways to validate existing information. Such systematic study leads to the creation of a scientific body of knowledge for sport administration education. As shown in academic journals in the field, such as *Journal of Sport Management*, *Sport Marketing Quarterly*, and *International Journal of Sport Management*, there has been a refinement of a variety of field surveys within the past 10 years that has made the study of sport management more scientific.

The study of sport management still needs much progress before its academic scholars will be able to describe appropriate behaviors for all situations. However, by virtue of the advances already achieved by such scholars, sport management can be identified as a rapidly growing science.

Value of Research for Students in Sport Management

Students in sport management are in a unique position to learn the value of research, why to conduct research, and how to conduct research. Knowledge and skill to conduct basic research are valuable to organizations. When the students gain the knowledge and skill while in college, they attain a major skill-set that future employers will value. The following outlines the value of research to the student in sport management:

- It enhances the development of critical thinking of students for study of supervisory management of firms (enterprises) of the sport industry.
- It helps students to become more authoritative in research procedures for the study of supervisory management in the sport industry.
- It helps students to become authorities in their designated fields or options of study, (i.e., sport promotion, professional sport management, sporting goods manufacture, etc.)
- It helps students to identify problems that need to be investigated in their designated fields or options of study.
- It helps students to masterfully apply research findings to the practice of the sport business.
- It help students to share more research findings with their colleagues and instructors about the study of sport management in the sport industry
- It motivates students to become involved either as principal investigators or as participants in research about the study of sport management in the sport industry.

Value of Research for the Practice of Sport Management

As has already been established, research is needed for information purposes. In business, research is used in a number of ways to solve problems, answer queries, and develop strategies for the organization. The desired end result is to move the company forward to successful strategies for competitive advantage.

Characteristics of Sport Management Research

Van Doren, Holland, and Crompton (1984) identify a number of general characteristics of leisure research, based upon the analysis of articles published in six volumes of the *Journal of Leisure Research*

and *Leisure Sciences*. Using the same analogy, three general characteristics of sport management research are recognized:

Sport management research is interdisciplinary in nature. This characteristic implies that the foundation of sport management research is built upon several related disciplines including physical education, recreation, business management, public administration, hospitality management, sport psychology, and tourism. In addition, the behavioral sciences (psychology, sociology, social psychology, and anthropology) and social sciences (economics, political science, and history) also lend support for research in the new and emerging field of sport management.

A wide variety of topical specialty areas are included in published reports. Twenty-six different subject areas were found to exist, ranging from general leisure behavior (number one) to facility management and sports (the last two) (Pederson & Pitts, 2001).

Most of the studies conducted by sport management researchers are quantitative in nature. Quarterman, Jackson, Koo, Kim, Yoo, Prugger, and Han (2006) conducted a content analysis of the statistical data analysis techniques used in the *Journal of Sport Management (JSM)* from its starting issue in 1987 to the last issue of 2004. Quantitative research articles accounted for more than half (165 or 55.0%) of the articles published in *JSM*. Qualitative research articles accounted for 27 (9.0%) of the articles, and essay or conceptual articles accounted for 101 or one-third (34.0%) of such publications. Six (2.0%) of the studies used mixed methods, including both quantitative and qualitative research techniques. It was also reported in this study that 151 articles revealed that percentages and one-way ANOVA were the most frequent basic techniques used by sport management researchers; correlations and post-hoc multiple comparisons were the most frequently used intermediate techniques; and factor analysis was the single most advanced technique used.

A second study conducted by Quarterman,

Pitts, Jackson, Kim, and Kim (2005) showed that quantitative data-based articles accounted for nearly two-thirds (159 or 63.3%) of the articles published in the *Sport Marketing Quarterly (SMQ)* from its first issue in 1992 to the last issue of 2004. Qualitative data-based articles accounted for less than one tenth (6.4%) of the articles, and conceptual articles accounted for nearly one-third (29.5%) of such publications. It was also reported that, of the data analysis techniques used in 159 articles in the *Sport Marketing Quarterly*, half (50.6%) used descriptive statistics, more than one-third (41.7%) used parametric statistics, and less than one-tenth (7.7%) used nonparametric statistics.

Riddick, DeSchriver, and Weissinger (1984) found that more than 90% of reported research in the field used the survey research approach. At the same time, few experimental studies were published. As has been argued elsewhere (Iso-Ahola, 1986), this has largely been a result of research training of graduate students in sport management programs.

Major Purposes of Sport Management Research

Why is research important in sport management? At its most fundamental base, the purpose of sport management research is to generate information. Let's take this fundamental purpose and look at the detailed reasons for research in different settings.

The need for research in sport management has never been greater than it was during the 1990s. Several reasons can be listed to validate the importance of research in sport management. It is paradoxical that more than 200 colleges and universities offered undergraduate and graduate degrees in sport management and produced a large number of graduates, despite a limited amount of empirical data-based research directed at problems and issues occurring in the field itself.

The primary rationale for research is to explicate a scientific body of knowledge that will eventually define and describe sport management as a unique field of study. The problem is that sport management exists as a field of study and as a field of practice without a scientific heritage. Therefore, a scientific body of knowledge is needed to give autonomy and provide direction for the study and practice of sport management in such areas as intercollegiate athletics administration, the sporting goods industry, sports marketing, and so on.

There is need to expand the knowledge base through scientific studies about management processes, management skills, management roles, organizational structures, and organizational behavior that will help those who are now studying in undergraduate and graduate programs, as well as those who now practice leadership and management in the various segments of sport management.

A second reason for research is to substantiate a body of knowledge that will lend support for the development of ideas, concepts, and theories unique to the field of sport management. Currently, much of sport management education functions from an untested theoretical (atheoretical) base. At the time of this writing, there are no known theories unique to the field of sport management. All of the theories are borrowed from other fields and disciplines. The field is in poverty for conceptual and theoretical frameworks unique to sport management.

A third reason for research is to substantiate a body of knowledge that will lend support for teaching students in undergraduate and graduate degree programs. Too much of the literature utilized in classroom teaching is speculative and generally unsubstantiated by empirical evidence.

A fourth reason is to advance the emerging field of sport management as a credible practicing profession. As sport management strives to establish itself as a profession, it must develop, through empirical research, a unique body of knowledge—one of the primary criteria of a profession.

A fifth and final rationale for research is to ensure survival of sport management as a part of the higher education enterprise. Currently there are more than 200 sport management programs at the undergraduate level; therefore, more faculty find themselves challenged and encouraged to conduct research not only because of the demands of the evolving field of sport management, but also because of the promotion/tenure requirements of colleges and universities. Research is one way to ensure survival of the sport management programs of undergraduate and graduate programs in higher education.

PHILOSOPHICAL APPROACHES TO SPORT MANAGEMENT RESEARCH

The philosophical nature of research is captured under what is known as a paradigm. According to Patton (1990), a paradigm is a world view, a general perspective, a way of breaking down the complexity of the real world. Guba (1990) also told us that a paradigm is an interpretative framework, which is guided by "a set of beliefs and feelings about the world and how it should be understood and studied" (p. 17). This perspective is used as a way to guide research and practice in academics for the study of sport management.

There are two major research paradigms that guide the approach to inquiry in research: the positivist paradigm and the naturalistic paradigm (Creswell, 1994; 2005). It is important for sport management students to understand the assumptions of both paradigms. It is these two paradigms that provide the philosophical foundations and assumptions for the research process in the field of sport management. The two paradigms underlie psychological and sociological research and have different assumptions about the nature of reality as well as different research objectives. The logic of these paradigms provides direction for sport management research. Figure 1-2 and Figure 1-3 provide detailed explanations on the differences of these two philosophical approaches to sport management research.

Positivist Paradigm

The positivist paradigm refers to a philosophical doctrine that asserts that scientific knowledge is logically embedded in the traditional scientific method,

Positivist Paradigm	Naturalistic Paradigm
— Values objectivity; there are strategies to keep the researcher independent of the participant so as not to influence the findings (reality is objective and exists independently of human influence)	— Accepts subjectivity; it is recognized that the findings are created as a result of the researcher's and informants' interactions (reality is subject to human influence)
— Is rooted in deductive logic	— Is rooted in inductive logic
— Uses analysis of numerical data by statistical techniques for meaning	— Organizes narrative data into themes or conceptual models for meaning
— Utilizes quantitative research designs (experimental, quasi-experimental, non-experimental descriptive)	— Utilizes qualitative research designs (ethnography, phenomenology, grounded theory)
— Draws out quantitative (numeric) information	— Draws out qualitative (verbal) information
— Examines research from a general theory to determine how it applies to a specific area of interest	— Examines research about a specific phenomenon of interest to see how it applies to a larger conceptual or theoretical framework
— Utilizes quantitative statistical analysis tools and techniques	— Utilizes qualitative analysis tools and techniques (constant comparative procedures)

Sources:
Creswell, J. (1998). *Qualitative inquiry and research design.* Thousand Oaks, CA: Sage Publications.
Currier, D. P. (1990). Elements of research in physical therapy (3rd ed.) Baltimore, MD: Williams and Wilkins.
Lincoln, Y. S., & Guba, E. G. (1995). Naturalistic inquiry. Beverly Hills, CA: Sage Publications.
Morse, J. M. (Ed.) (1994). Critical issues in qualitative research methods. Thousand Oaks, CA: Sage Publications.
Robbins, S. P. (1996). Organizational behavior (7th ed.). Englewood Cliffs, NJ: Prentice Hall Publishers.

FIGURE 1-2. **Philosophical Assumptions of Sport Management Research**

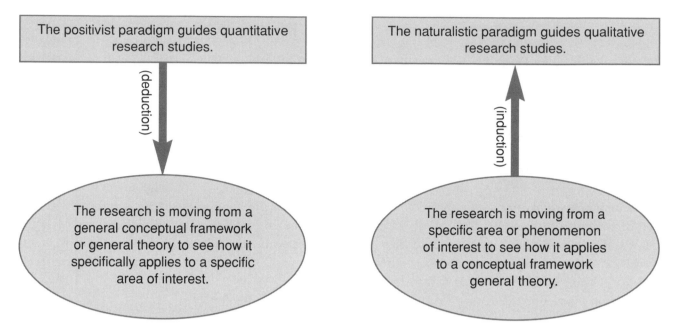

FIGURE 1-3. Positivist and Naturalistic Research Paradigms

and because of this it is the only kind of factual knowledge. The positivist paradigm is rooted in deductive logic. It is the process of using rigorous empirical tools and techniques to discover generalizable explanations. In other words, it takes the view that if something can't be proven in the laboratory or "field setting," it is not useful because it was not derived from scientific methods. Figure 1-4 shows deductive logic or reasoning.

The research that embraces this paradigm is often considered "hard science." The logic of the positivist paradigm underscores the premise that the quantity (numerical) of a measurable phenomenon gives rise to quantitative research. The positivist approach relies heavily on the quantitative research approach. The researcher is independent of what is being researched and does not influence the findings, Definitions are set at the beginning of the study, and deductive reasoning focuses on specific discrete concepts isolated before the inquiry.

Most research in sport management has embraced the research paradigm of positivists. The paradigm provides objective reality that allows for researchers in sport management to claim and ascertain truth.

Naturalistic Paradigm

The naturalistic paradigm refers to the subjective nature of research. The naturalists believe that there are multiple interpretations of reality, and the goal of researchers working within this perspective is to understand how individuals construct their own reali-

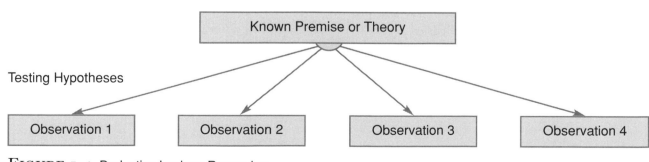

FIGURE 1-4. Deductive Logic or Reasoning

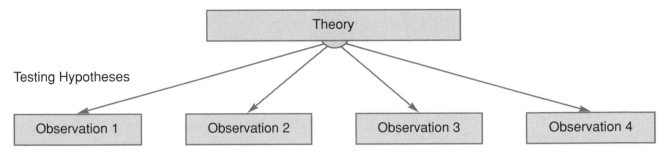

Testing Hypotheses

FIGURE 1-5. Inductive Logic or Reasoning

ties within their social contexts. It is logically embedded in a non-traditional approach to scientific inquiry and is primarily subjective in nature. The naturalist paradigm is primarily rooted in inductive logic. It is a complementary approach to positivism. It is often viewed as "soft science." Figure 1-5 demonstrates inductive logic or reasoning.

The naturalist paradigm underscores quality (nonnumerical) of phenomenon. As such, it relies heavily on the qualitative research approach. The researcher interacts with what is being researched; the interaction process creates the findings. Definitions evolve during the course of the study, and inductive reasoning focuses on the entire phenomena as they emerge during the inquiry.

MAJOR APPROACHES TO SPORT MANAGEMENT RESEARCH

Approaches to and methodologies of research consist of several methods. Not all research is conducted in a laboratory with chemicals. Much research is conducted in numerous settings and involves a variety of methods. This section provides an overview of research methodologies.

Basic and Applied Research in Sport Management

Basic research. Basic research (also known as pure research) is primarily theoretical in nature. Its primary purpose is the development of new knowledge or knowledge to validate existing knowledge for theory development. In other words, it aims at the "knowledge for the sake of knowledge." Basic research is the main vehicle to substantiate further research in sport manage-

ment. The results of this type of research have no immediate practical applications, and in fact it may be years before the results of basic research are used in practical applications (Baumgartner, Strong, & Hensley, 2002).

Applied research. Applied research is also known as practical research. It is primarily concerned with the development of new knowledge or with the validation of existing knowledge that can be applied immediately in practical settings in sport management. Unlike basic research, the primary purpose of applied research is the solution of an immediate practical problem. The results of applied research are less likely to be published in peer review or scholarly journals. Often the results are not published and a report is given to a committee or a board of directors. Unlike basic research, applied research is not conducted within an academic department of a college or university. It is usually conducted in the workplace, where immediate decisions can be made in terms of effective and efficient job satisfaction and work performance and production of goods and services. It really is "knowledge for the sake of practical application." For example, Zhang, Pease, Hui, and Michaud (1995) conducted an applied research to determine the variables affecting the spectators' decisions to attend NBA games. The major finding revealed that NBA teams should consider fans' sociodemographic backgrounds (age, economic, status, ethnicity, education, and occupation) when developing and implementing marketing strategies to lure spectators to the games.

Quantitative and Qualitative Research in Sport Management

Qualitative and quantitative are two distinctive and complementary approaches to research. Each has its own functions and characteristic activities. These approaches originate from different philosophical perspectives and use different methods for collection and analysis of data. Qualitative research is rooted in the fields of anthropology, sociology, and philosophy. Quantitative research is rooted in the fields of psychology, economics, and management. The differences between the two approaches are based on the extent to which the analysis can be done by converting observations into numbers or using narrative text to describe human experiences. It is best to think of the qualitative-quantitative distinction as dualistic in nature. Qualitative research is a method of research designed for discovery rather than verification; this type of research is used to explore little-known or ambiguous phenomena. Quantitative research uses numbers to measure variables and is a method to verify if there are differences or relationships about phenomena.

Quantitative research. Sport management research also can be classified as either qualitative research or quantitative research. Qualitative research is referred to the type of research methodology that attempts to explain the phenomenon to be investigated without the use of quantitative measurements to describe the phenomenon (e.g., its characteristics). Quantitative research, on the other hand, is a type of research practices that employ measurements and statistically analyses to explain the phenomenon that is under investigation. The contents of this book are arranged along this classification of research methods in sport management.

Since the 1980s quantitative research has been the predominant research methodology used in sport management research studies. Based on the positivist paradigm, this methodology emphasizes the search for the facts and causes of human behavior through objective, observable, and quantifiable data. The researcher is viewed as an objective scientist whose main tasks are to manipulate the external environment and observe the effects on the subjects (Stainback & Stainback, 1984). The field of sport management has been greatly influenced by the quantitative-positivist view of the world. For example, of 782 articles published in the *Journal of Sport Management, Sport Marketing Quarterly, International Journal of Sport Management,* and *European Sport Marketing Quarterly* from each of their initial issues to 1994, quantitative research articles accounted for more than half (440, or 56.26%) of the total articles. Conceptual articles accounted for the second highest amount of articles published in the four journals (249, or 31.84%). Seventy (8.95%) were classified as qualitative articles and 23 (2.04%) as mixed, including both quantitative and qualitative data analysis (Quarterman, 2006). This may be attributed to such reasons as those discussed here.

Sport management researchers adopted the prevailing quantitative-positivist model as the primary base for the research activities because they wanted to be accepted and respected by other academic fields in the higher education enterprise. Also, because almost all of such researchers were responsible for establishing the first doctoral programs in sport management, they instituted the quantitative positivist model as the primary research model within these programs. In addition, it may have been that the primary sport management research publication outlets would accept only quantitative research reports for publication. Federal funding for research projects was awarded only to quantitative research projects. Thus the quantitative approach is the most prominent research model within the field of sport management.

There is no debate of the fact that sport management researchers using quantitative research methodology have contributed greatly to the advancement of the field of sport management. However, in the past few years there has been increasing recognition in nursing and in other disciplines that relying solely on the quantitative approach to answer research questions has serious limitations. Sport management researchers have been frustrated and disenchanted with trying to use only quantitative methods to gain a better understanding of the sport management discipline and the sport industry. Leininger (1994) noted that individuals are not reducible and measurable objects that exist independently of their historical, cultural, and social contexts. To treat them as such, as quantitative research does, reduces them to machine-like figures that are only a sum of their parts. Sport management researchers are urged to think anew and to keep an open mind for new ways to collect, analyze, and interpret data for the betterment of the field of sport management.

Qualitative research. Qualitative research is another major research method for investigating diverse phenomena. Chapter 3 of this book provides a detailed description of this type of research method.

Qualitative research is a popular methodology and is being used with increasing frequency in sport management. The qualitative method, which has enjoyed a long and rich tradition in sociology and anthropology, is anchored theoretically in the naturalist paradigm (Creswell, 2005). Within the past two decades researchers have been challenged to guide research and sport management and have supported the use of qualitative methodologies to take research beyond the traditional quantitative designs (Paton, 1987; Olafson, 1990; Inglis, 1992). Qualitative studies are now appearing with increasing frequency in sport management research.

Exploratory, Descriptive, and Causal Research in Sport Management

Exploratory research. Exploratory research involves preliminary activities to find answers or to refine the problem or question into a researchable form. The purpose of this type of research is to progressively shape the scope of the research into a well-defined project with specific, measurable, and appropriate objectives.

Descriptive research. Descriptive research describes characteristics of a population or a phenomenon. A study conducted to acquire information about the season ticket holders in terms of their household income, education level, size of family, age, occupation, and so is a typical example of descriptive research. Data collection usually includes the use of surveys, interviews, or observations (Gay, 1992; McMillian & Shumacher, 2004). Descriptive research is commonly used to collect detailed descriptions about existing demographic variables such as age, sex, marital status, ethnicity, income, occupation, or religious status.

Descriptive research has a number of advantages. The major advantage is that it is used to describe the state of something. Often, descriptive research is needed as a base on which other research can be conducted. On the other hand, there are several noticeable disadvantages, including:

- independent variables cannot be manipulated the way they are in laboratory experiments,
- inappropriate wording or placement of questions within a questionnaire can bias results; and
- potential problem of talking to the wrong people (e.g., telephone studies).

Causal research. Causal research identifies cause-and-effect relationships among variables where the research problem has already been narrowly defined. A study conducted to examine ticket pricing and attendance or a study conducted to examine the effect of various marketing and promotion strategies on consumers' perception of an athletic product are good illustrations of causal research in sport management. If organizational commitment scores for African-American female office workers of the Nike Corporation are significantly different than those of white female office workers, a relationship exists between the two groups of workers and their commitment to the Nike Corporation.

The Evolution and Future of Sport Management Research

Over the last twenty years, there has been a tremendous growth of published research in the field of sport management in the U.S., Canada, Europe, Asia (South Korea, Japan) and Australia.

The quality of published research has also increased with journals being able to reject 65% of submitted articles. In other words, researchers are contributing many more papers than can be accepted for publication in journals; editors and their respective editorial boards can reject two-thirds or more of the manuscripts submitted. For example, the *Journal of Sport Management* receives well over 100 research manuscripts for possible publication annually, but only about 15% of them are accepted for publication. In addition, the North American Society for Sport Management Conference is held annually with over 100 research papers presented at each meeting.

To truly appreciate the growth of published research in the field of sport management, it is important to understand how fast it has evolved and grown over the past two decades.

Academic conferences and publications for sharing sport management research are relatively new. Sport management research in academia began with graduate theses and dissertations in the 1960s. Also, sport management-related manuscripts were initially published in academic journals primarily in the physical education field. On the other hand, trade conferences and publications for sport management have been around for much longer. For example, the NCAA began in 1910 and now hosts an annual convention for athletic directors; the *Sporting Goods Dealer* publication was first published in 1899.

The first academic organization for sport management started with the inception of the North American Society for Sport Management (NASSM) in 1985. During the 1985–1986 academic year, NASSM organized its first sport management conference, which was attended mainly by university and college personnel from the U.S. and Canada (Zeigler, 1987). In 1987, this organization launched its first academic publication, *Journal of Sport Management*. Since then, several journals published by other academic organizations have been established, including *Sport Management Review (1990)*, *European Journal of Sport Management (1992)*, and *Sport Marketing Quarterly (1992)*. Today, as you can see in Table 1-1, there are more than 20 academic journals specializing in the topic of sport management.

TABLE 1-1
Sport Management and Related Journals

Australian Leisure Management
Entertainment and Sports Law Forum
European Sport Management Quarterly (formerly the European Journal of Sport Management)
International Journal of Sport Management
International Sports Journal
Journal of Hospitality and Leisure Marketing
Journal of Issues in Intercollegiate Athletics
Journal of Legal Aspects of Sport and Physical Activity
Journal of Sports Economics
Journal of Sport Management
Journal of Sport Tourism
International Journal of Sports Marketing and Sponsorship
International Journal of Sport Management and Marketing
International Journal of Sport Finance
Japan Journal of the Sports Industry
Journal of Sports Engineering
Marquette Sport Law Journal
Seton Hall Journal of Sport Law
SMART Journal
Southern California Sports & Entertainment Law Journal
Sport Management Review
Sport Marketing Quarterly
The Sport Lawyer Journal
Women in Sport and Physical Activity Journal

Bicycle Retailer & Industry	Golf Retailer
Golf Marketing	Sporting Goods Business
Fitness Product News	Sports Executive Weekly

FIGURE 1-6. Examples of Sport Business Industry Trade Publications

Other academic organizations include the European Association for Sport Management and the Sport Management Association of Australia and New Zealand. Additionally, there are now organizations in many individual countries, such as China, France, Japan, Korea, Italy, Germany, and England. A new movement in academic associations is the organization of topical associations. Two examples include an organization for the study of sport law, the Sports Lawyers Association, and an organization for the study of sport marketing, the Sport Marketing Association.

In the sport industry, there are numerous outlets for research, primarily in trade publications and conventions. Some of these are shown in Figure 1-6.

There are some research companies that specialize in conducting research for companies, such as Joyce Julius & Associates, Boulder Sports Research, and Goliath's Sports Research Corporation. These companies and more will continue to provide valuable research for companies that want to outsource the research activity.

SUMMARY

The purpose of this chapter is to give students an introduction to sport management research. Sport management research is defined as *an orderly investigative process that involves purposeful and systematic collection, analysis, and interpretation of data (units of information) to gain new knowledge or to verify already existing knowledge within the specific domain of managing human and material resources in organizations of the sport industry.*

The three general characteristics of sport management research are: (a) it is interdisciplinary in nature; (b) a wide variety of topical specialty areas are included in published reports; and (c) most of the studies conducted by sport management researchers are quantitative in nature.

There is a need for research in sport management: (a) to explicate a scientific body of knowledge that will eventually define and describe sport management as a unique field of study; (b) to substantiate a body of knowledge that will lend support for the development of ideas, concepts, and theories unique to the field of sport management; (c) to substantiate a body of knowledge that will lend support for teaching students in undergraduate and graduate degree programs; (d) to advance the emerging field of sport management as a credible practicing profession; and (e) to ensure survival of sport management as a part of the higher education enterprise.

The two major research paradigms that guide research inquiry in sport management are the positivist paradigm and the naturalistic paradigm. In general, sport management research can be classified in three different ways. First, they are either basic or applied research. Second, they are either quantitative or qualitative research. Third, they are exploratory, descriptive, or causal research.

STUDY QUESTIONS

1. What is the definition for each of the following two terms?
   a. Research
   b. Sport management research
2. What is the role of research for sport business?
3. What is the role of research for the academic field of sport management?
4. What is the value of research for students in sport management?
5. What are the three characteristics of sport management research?
6. What are the differences between the two philosophical approaches to sport management research?
7. What are the differences between applied sport management research and basic sport management research?
8. What are the differences among the three types of sport management research: exploratory research, descriptive research, and causal research?

References

Baumgartner, T. A., Strong, C. H., & Hensley, L. D. (2002). *Conducting and reading research in health and human performance* (3rd ed.). New York: McGraw-Hill.

Creswell, J. W. (1994). *Research design, qualitative and quantitative approaches*. London: Sage Publications.

Creswell, J. W. (1998). *Qualitative inquiry and research design: Choosing among five traditions*. Thousand Oaks: Sage Publications.

Creswell, J. W. (2005). *Educational research, planning, conducting, evaluating, quantitative and qualitative research* (2nd ed.). Upper Sadle River, NJ: Pearson Merrill/Prentice Hall.

Gay, L. (1992). *Educational research* (4th ed.). New York: Macmillan.

Guba, E. (1990). *The paradigm dialogue*. Newbury Park, CA: Sage Publications.

Guba, E. G., & Lincoln, Y. S. (1994). Competing paradigms in qualitative research. In N. K. Denzin & Y. S. Lincoln (Eds.), *Handbook of Qualitative Research* (pp. 105–117). Thousand Oaks, CA: Sage Publications.

Inglis, S. (1992). Focus groups as a useful qualitative methodology in sport management. *Journal of Sport Management, 6*, 173–178.

Isaac, S. (1964). *Careers and opportunities in sports*. New York: E. P. Dutton & Co.

Iso-Ahola, S. E. (1986). A theory of substitutability of leisure behavior. *Leisure Sciences, 8*(4), 367–389.

Kerlinger, F. N., & Lee, H. B. (2000). *Foundations of behavioral research* (4th ed.). Fort Worth, TX: Harcourt College Publishers.

Leininger, M. (1994). Evaluation criteria and critique of qualitative research studies. In J. M. Morse (Ed.), *Critical issues in qualitiative research methods* (pp. 95–115). Thousand Oaks, CA: Sage Publications.

Lincoln, Y. S., & Guba, E. G. (2000). Paradigmatic controversies, contradictions and emerging confluences. In N. K. Denzin & Y. S. Lincoln (Eds.), *Handbook of qualitative research* (2nd ed., pp. 163–188). Thousand Oaks, CA: Sage Publications.

McMillan, J. H., & Schumacher, S. (2006). *Research in education: Evidence-based inquiry* (6th ed.). Boston, MA: Pearson.

Morse, J. M. (Ed.) (1994). *Critical issues in qualitative research methods*. Thousand Oaks, CA: Sage Publications.

Olafson, G. A. (1990). Research design in sport management: What is missing, what's needed? *Journal of Sport Management, 2*, 103–120.

Paton, G. (1987). Sport management and research—What progress has been made? *Journal of Sport Management, 1*, 25–31.

Patton, M. Q. (1990). *Qualitative evaluation and research methods* (2nd ed.). Newbury Park, CA: Sage Publications.

Pitts, B., & Stotlar, D. (2007). *Fundamentals of sport marketing* (3rd ed.). Morgantown, WV: Fitness Information Technology.

Pederson, P., & Pitts, B. (2001). Investigating the body of knowledge in sport management: A content analysis of the *Sport Marketing Quarterly. Chronicle of Physical Education in Higher Education, 12*(3), 8–9, 22–23.

Quarterman, J., Jackson, E. N., Kim, K., Yoo, E., Koo, G.Y.,

Prugger, B., & Han, K. (2006). Statistical data analysis techniques employed in the *Journal of Sport Management* January 1987 to October 2004. *International Journal of Sport Management, 7*(1), 13–30.

Quarterman, J., Pitts, B. G., Jackson, E. N., Kim, K., & Kim, J. (2005). Statistical data analysis techniques employed in the *Sport Marketing Quarterly:* January 1992 to October 2004. *Sport Marketing Quarterly, 14* (4), 227–238.

Riddick, C., DeSchriver, M., & Weissinger, A. (1984). A methodological review of research in *Journal of Leisure Research* from 1978 to 1982. *Journal of Leisure Research, 16*, 311–321.

Stainback, W. & Stainback, S. (1984). A rationale for the merger of special and regular education. *Exceptional Children, 51*, 102–111.

Van-Doren, C. S., Holland, S. M., & Crompton, J. L. (1984). Publishing in the primary leisure journals: Insight into the structure and boundaries of our research. *Leisure Sciences, 6*, 239–256.

Zeigler, E. F. (1087). Sport management: past, present, future. *Journal of Sport Management, 1*(1), 4–24.

Zhang, J. J., Pease, D. G., Hui, S. C., & Michaud, T. J. (1995). Variables affecting the spectator decision to attend NBA games. *Sport Marketing Quarterly, 4* (4), 29–39.

CHAPTER 2
THE RESEARCH PROCESS IN SPORT MANAGEMENT

OBJECTIVES FOR COMPLETING THIS CHAPTER ARE THAT STUDENTS WILL BE ABLE TO:

Understand the decision making continuum and the variables affecting the confidence of a decision.

Identify the steps in the process of sport management research.

Explain the details of each of the steps in the process of sport management research.

Compare and contrast qualitative and quantitative research methods in sport management.

Identify the common types of research designs or methods used in sport management research.

LIKE THEIR COUNTERPARTS IN other business settings, sport managers often make decisions based on information provided by the sport management researcher. To provide accurate information, it is important for the sport management researcher to follow the scientific model of research to derive the needed information. No matter how simple or complicated the issue that needs to be studied, the scientific model of research is always involved. This process includes a number of important steps.

The purpose of this chapter is to introduce students to the steps of the research process. To accomplish this goal, this chapter will explain the decision making continuum and the variables affecting a sport manager's confidence in making a decision. A detailed discussion on each of the steps in the process of sport management research and some common types of research designs or methods used in sport management research will follow.

This chapter will explain the research process from inception to completion.

DECISION MAKING AND RELATED VARIABLES

Decision making is formally defined as the process of resolving a problem or selecting from alternative opportunities. The decision maker must understand the nature and elements of the problem, determine how much information is readily available to help make a decision, determine what additional information is needed, and decide on the best method for collecting any needed information.

Every sports business problem or decision making situation can be categorized along a continuum of confidence. Figure 2-1 illustrates the continuum.

This continuum offers a look at the effects of the decision (Daft, 1990; Schermehrhorn, Hunt, & Osborn, 1991). In other words, how confident can the decision maker be with any decision? For example, is it possible for an individual to make a statement and be completely confident that the statement is correct? The answer is yes. If the individual is able to substantiate the statement with evidence that the statement is true and correct, then that individual can say that they are 100% confident, or that the statement is true with 100% certainty.

Certainty versus Uncertainty

Complete certainty can only exist when the decision maker has the best and most correct information possible to validate the decision. When there is information from research that was conducted in which the findings of the study reveal specific conclusions, the decision maker can make a decision with a high level of certainty. For example, the sport marketing director at a collegiate athletic program wants to know the demographics of its women's basketball season ticket holders. The director knows exactly what information is needed and how to obtain it. The director can determine if the information already exists. If not, then research must be conducted to get the information. Based on the research results, the director now has the information and can state with certainty the demographics of the season ticket holders.

Uncertainty exists when the decision maker has an idea about the concept of the problem or opportunity, but lacks specific information about it; or lacks information about alternatives. In this situation, decisions will be made with uncertainty. In other words, the decision maker will be guessing about the outcome of the decision. This kind of decision making can lead to disaster. A decision made with uncertainty has the potential to be wrong.

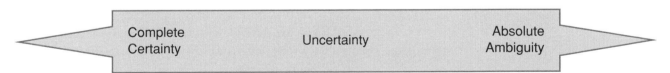

FIGURE 2-1. Decision Maker's Continuum of Confidence

Ambiguity

Ambiguity is a situation in which the problem to be solved in unclear. The cause of the problem is unknown or indistinguishable. Therefore, the problematic situation leads to vague descriptions, unclear objectives, and ambiguous solutions. All sports management professionals face ambiguous situations. For example, a sporting goods manufacturer will inevitably face a great deal of ambiguity when it decides to expand into a foreign market where the rules of doing business, the financial system and business relation issues are unclear, and business strategies that have been proven to be successful in the North America may no longer be applicable. It is under this situation that research becomes more desirable and advantageous. Typically, in these situations, the manufacturer making an expansion decision needs to take the time and money to conduct appropriate research that will move the situation from ambiguous toward certainty.

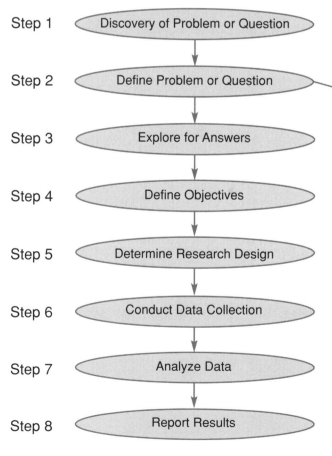
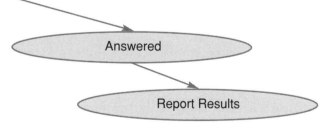

FIGURE 2-2. The Research Process

THE RESEARCH PROCESS IN SPORT MANAGEMENT

Sport management research actually begins when a problem or question arises. For instance, a sport marketing director is confronted with a situation where about 25% of the football season ticket holders did not renew their season tickets for next season. A process involving specific stages and steps for determining how to find a solution or an answer to the question (i.e., what caused the decrease in season ticket renewal) should begin. There is no one exact process to be followed in sport management research. However, there are specific stages or steps that should be consulted and followed closely so that a higher level of certainty can be reached. With a higher level of certainty, the sport management professionals can have a higher level of confidence that the information obtained from the research is valid.

There is no absolute adherence necessary in the research process. Some variation of the process can occur. Some steps can be started out of sequence, some can be omitted, and even some steps can be carried out simultaneously. This is acceptable as long as the integrity of the research is not compromised so that results are valid. Figure 2-2 illustrates a typical research process. Each time someone at the business needs to conduct research to attempt to gain information to help solve a problem or to answer a question, that individual should attempt to address the research process and follow the steps.

Step 1: Identify the Problem or Question

The first step is to discover the problem or question. The word *problem* typically suggests that something is wrong. This isn't always the case in sport management research. Problem might mean that someone in the company needs information in order to make a decision.

Let us use an example to illustrate this situation. As the Internet has been adopted by more individuals, innovations have been made utilizing this technology for a myriad of purposes. One such purpose is relationship building or social networking. Social networking has enabled Internet users to forge online relationships with individuals based on a variety of factors such as place of residence, school attended and occupation. Internet social networking has grown so quickly that many organizations do not fully understand the phenomenon. Without a solid grasp of the nuances of this phenomenon, organizations are unable to leverage the technology within their respective business model. Alltel, a cellular phone provider, wants to launch a college athletics themed social networking site, FanU to take advantage of the emergence of the social networking phenomenon. To fully understand the phenomenon, its management needs to conduct research to seek answers to a number of such questions as: Why do people use social networking sites? What features on social networking sites do people use the most? What features on social networking sites do people use the least? What features are missing from social networking sites that people would like to use? What social networking sites do people use the most?

On the other hand, a problem might be that the decision-maker has discovered something wrong—a problem—and needs information in order to correct or determine a solution to the problem. Why didn't people attend the games? Why was the sponsorship renewal rate low? Why didn't the team's website attract a high volume of traffic last quarter? These are a few common scenarios that require sport managers to find out the reasons and take action.

A question might arise from a simply wondering how, or why, or where, or what is or is not going on. An owner at a fitness center might wonder why clients are leaving clothing and keys lying around the workout areas. This could be triggered with a simple observation. When the owner asks the manager why this is happening, the manager may or may not have an answer. If the manager has no answer, then this is a question for investigation. The question formally becomes "Why are fitness center members putting clothing and keys and other items on the floor and equipment while they are working out?" It may seem innocuous. However, items lying around are a health and legal risk hazard. They create the potential for accidental injury, and they pose a health risk because they are laden with bacteria that can be left on the surfaces they touch. Additionally, from a purely aesthetic perspective, they make the club appear cluttered and disorganized—definitely not the image that the owner wants for the fitness center.

The owner might request the manager to take some time to "look into" this situation and then offer solutions. At this point, the manager will need to approach the situation in a formal manner. This is the point at which the manager will determine a more formally defined problem or question.

Step 2: Define the Problem or Question

Once an individual in the company determines that a problem needs a solution, or a question needs answered, then that individual can begin to formally define the problem or question. Simply stating that there is a problem is not enough. One must describe the problem with specificity. Otherwise, research cannot be conducted that will bring about solutions. Not all problems or questions are researchable; some may not require a formal research process. So, one must begin by determining if the problem or question is researchable.

In addition, a question might be in a form that is too simple for formal investigation. In the earlier example about the fitness center, the original question might appear to be simple enough. But it needs formulation and refinement so that the manager can look for answers that will bring about real solutions. For instance, if the manager studies the question and learns that the reason personal items are left lying about the center is because the center has no locker room facilities for personal item storage, then the search for decisions and solutions to this situation can be done with an educated purpose.

In one example, the athletic administrators of Central University realize that tickets to the men's basketball games are not selling, while tickets to the women's basketball games are always a sellout. They want men's basketball to sell out its tickets too.

Therefore, this is a problem that needs a solution.

In another example, the Acme Sporting Goods Company, a company that manufacturers golf clubs, determines that two of their six models isn't selling as well as the others. The executives of the company want all models to sell equally or they may need to terminate some models. In order to decide about how to sell the models, they will have to determine *why* the models aren't selling as well as the others.

In the golf clubs example, the models that aren't selling as well as the others may or may not be a problem. It is up to the executives to decide if this is a problem. It could be considered a problem if the sales totals for the two models are below the cost to manufacture, thus creating a situation in which there is loss instead of profit. The executives will need to decide if this is acceptable or not. If not, then it is considered a problem. The *question* then is developed out of the situation: why aren't the two models selling? Based on this question, research can now be conducted to try to answer the specific question. The results of the research will then be used to create a solution to the problem.

Step 3: Explore for Answers

Once the problem or question has been defined, the sport management researcher can begin to search for answers. There is the potential that the answers might already exist in available information. For example, if the question is, "What is the going price for high-end tennis rackets?" this information can be found easily by conducting a web search. In that instance, the question is answered and the results can be reported. In another example, if the question is, "What are tennis participation rates for a specific year?" it is also possible to find this information in a number of places. Most likely, a research company or a tennis organization has this information. You can access it and the question is answered. This existing information is usually called *secondary data*. This means that the information came from someone besides you who conducted the research and produced the information.

The *primary data* are information created or collected by the researcher. That is, the researcher has conducted the research personally—or oversaw the process—and the information was developed by the primary source.

Step 4: Define Research Objectives

After identifying the problem or the question, the sport management researcher needs to develop a formal statement of the problem and the research objectives. The objectives will establish exactly what should be researched. This will help identify what type of information is needed and provide a framework for the research project.

Too many researchers overlook this very important step. Yet, this is the critical step that delineates what is to be accomplished. Otherwise, the project has no direction and worse, it is likely that wrong or inappropriate information will be gathered. The danger of this is that using wrong information to will lead to inappropriate decisions that will most likely be unsuccessful.

Such a question as "Why aren't current university students attending the women's and men's basketball games?" is a typical research question. The objective then might be stated as "The objective of this research is to determine why current university students do not attend the women's and men's basketball games." A research objective is a precise statement indicating the problem and what should be researched (what needs to be accomplished in a further research) (Zikmund, 2000). Both the research question and objective are exchangeable. Either the question or the objective can be used to state the problem.

The research question or objective should be one that can be measured or tested. For example, with the objective of the project to find out why university students aren't attending basketball games, this can be measured. In the simplest form, the sport management researcher would survey the current students and ask them why they don't attend the games. This one question would provide a simple answer to the problem. Once the objective has been developed, the next step is to determine the best research design.

Step 5: Determine the Research Design

After the research objective has been determined, the research design can be developed. A research design is the master plan that identifies the research methods and procedures for the development of the study, collection of the data, and analysis of the data. The objectives of the study are used as the basis around which the design will be built. This will ensure that the information to be collected is appropriate.

The sport management researcher must build into the design the sources of information, the research methodology, sampling methods, project schedule, and costs. Particularly, this step is a good place to determine what the research will cost and check the budget to see if there is enough funding to carry out the chosen design. If the money is available, then the project can be carried out as planned. If the money is not available, then the researcher must decide on a less costly design that will provide the best information possible to answer the research question without hurting the integrity of the research.

The research design begins with choosing the type, or method, of research to use. Regardless of the research design chosen, the sport management researcher often begins with a search of existing studies on the topic. This is called a *review of the literature*. A *literature review* is a search of published studies in journals and books that have already been conducted on the same or similar topic. It is done to determine the legitimacy of the research. Specifically, the purpose of reviewing literature is two-fold: (a) to find out what other people have found concerning a particular topic, and (b) to determine clues and suggestions on how to proceed with setting up the investigation and data gathering. More specifically, the review of literature may provide the team with a framework and clues for its questionnaire design. If previous studies can be found, then it must be determined if the studies and the findings answer the research question or provide solutions for the research problem. If not, then another approach is needed.

The sport management researcher may also use some exploratory research to better understand the issue at hand. One of the frequently used exploratory techniques is a pilot study. A *pilot study* is a precursor to the regular study. Often, a pilot study is a much smaller trial run of the regular study. Sometimes, the findings of a pilot study offer enough information to solve the research problem, answer the research question, or meet the research objectives. In this case, no further research need be conducted at the moment. For example, to understand sport sponsorship in China, Geng, Burton and Blackmore (2002) designed a questionnaire to gather information from representatives of all major Chinese sport organizations and a large number of commercial corporations that have purchased sport sponsorship. Before putting the questionnaire in use, they conducted a pilot study to test the language and format of the instrument within the Chinese community in central Utah, using 40 university graduates working in various business corporations in the area.

QUALITATIVE RESEARCH METHODS IN SPORT MANAGEMENT

Case Study. Case study is a qualitative method commonly used in the exploratory stage of a research project (see Chapter 4 for more information about the use of case study as a research method in sport management). According to Creswell (1994), case study "explores a single entity or phenomenon ('the case') bounded by time and activity (a program, event, process, institution, or social group) and collects detailed information by using a variety of data collection procedures during a sustained period of time" (p. 12).

In recent years, case studies have been employed more than other qualitative designs in sport management research. While using case study, the sport management researcher conducts an in-depth investigation of an individual subject (situation, instance, or issue) for the purpose of gaining a comprehensive understanding into the subject being investigated. Long, Thibault, and Wolfe (2004) examined the influence over a sponsorship decision in a Canadian university athletic department. The authors used a single case study of an athletic department from a Canadian university to address three research questions: (a) What are the differentiating attributes of those who are perceived to have influenced the exclusive sponsorship decision? (b) What methods of influence are used by head coaches and senior administrators to influence this decision? and (c) To what extent do policies and procedures in the athletic department influence the process? The study involved semistructured interviews with coaches and administrators, participant observation, and document analysis. Burden and Li (2005) performed a case study to reveal both advantages and disadvantages of outsourcing as well as the circumstantial factors affecting athletic administrators' outsourcing decisions. The study closely reviewed the outsourcing cases of three institutions, The Air Force Academy, Stanford University and the University of Virginia, to identify their respective motives and circumstantial factors related to outsourcing.

Interviews. An interview refers to having a trained person asked prescribed questions of a respondent and then record the responses on a standard form. It is a conversation with a purpose. Interviews are method of collecting data in which an interviewer obtains responses from a subject in a face-to-face encounter or through a telephone call. There are three types of interviews: (a) unstructured, (b) structured, and (c) semistructured (Merriam, 1988; Kvale, 1996). When using unstructured interviews, interviewers are given a great deal of freedom in asking different questions of the study respondents. When using structured interviews, the interviewer asks the same key questions, in the same order and in the same manner, of all the respondents of the study. When using semi-structured interviews, the interviewer ask a certain number of key questions; however, probes are allowed. There are additional prompting questions that encourage the respondent to further elaborate on the topic.

The interview should not be undertaken without an organized and strategically planned set of interview questions. The questions should be designed to acquire specific information from the participant; otherwise, the information is invalid. Chapter 5 includes an indepth review of interviews as a research method in sport management.

Focus Group. As a qualitative method, focus groups are increasingly popular in sport management research (see Chapter 6 for more discussion on this method). The focus group is a method of gathering a specifically chosen group of targeted individuals that represent a good sample of the population. Similar to interview, a focus group session is guided by specific questions to elicit appropriate information from the consumer. Sometimes, a focus group can be used to sample or experiment with a product. In most instances, the focus group is used to gain insight into the thoughts and perceptions of consumers about the company, the product, advertising activities, facilities, event management, or any other factor about which the company needs consumer feedback." For example, a sport marketing agency wants to know what consumers think about a potential advertising campaign for the Paralympics. The researcher gathers a target group of consumers for a three hour focus group session. In the session, the researcher will show the elements of the advertising campaign and lead a discussion of the thoughts and reactions of the group. Based on the feedback of the group, the researcher may now take this information into consideration before moving forward with the campaign.

Observation. Observation refers to a personal witnessing of an ongoing activity. It involves recording a participant's behavior, interactions among a group of subjects, various events and field notes (Marshall & Rossman, 1995). Observation may be participatory or nonparticipatory. With participant observation, a qualitative researcher becomes involved in the actual activity of being studied. Non participatory involvement means that the researcher does not participate in the activity while obtaining data. The indoor soccer facility manager can watch consumers as they come and go and record their patterns of traffic when inside the arena for use in consideration of remodeling. The golf course pro can observe how many players use the practice range facility prior to playing a round of golf to determine if the practice facility is feasible. An athletic director at a university can observe fans at a softball game to determine their apparent comfort in the stands and their appreciation of the food and drink offered for sale at the concession stand. With these observations, the professional can make *educated* decisions critical to the business. Otherwise, the professional would just be guessing—a practice that can lead to failure. The following is an actual example in which the sport management researchers use observation to accomplish their research objectives.

Bennett and Hardin (2002) investigated management behaviors of an elite intercollegiate baseball coach. The authors used a combination of three different data collection procedures for this study including: participant observation, interviews and documentary analysis. For this study, the purpose of observation was to analyze the managerial behaviors and leadership strategies utilized by an elite intercollegiate baseball coach, the interactions between and among the coaches and players, and their casual conversations with the coach. The coach was observed at each practice and other places during the baseball season. According to the authors the observation of the coach allowed for a more intense analysis of the purposes of this particular study (p. 203). More information about observation as a qualitative research method can be found in Chapter 7.

QUANTITATIVE RESEARCH METHODS IN SPORT MANAGEMENT

Secondary Data. As mentioned previously, *secondary data* are data collected in an earlier study or research project. They may be found in a number of places. For example, this information may be found in organizations that specialize in research, such as marketing research agencies. This type of information can be found with associations of a particular topic. For instance, the *Bicycle Industry Retailer* is a trade publication published to provide market information to the bicycle manufacturer and retailer. Annually, the publication will publish an article about the study of that year of trends in bicycling sales. The bicycle retailer can use this information to guide decisions about what kind of bicycles are selling and which ones are failing.

Secondary data is readily available from a number of sources, and is much less costly than conducting your own research project. However, secondary data might not be current or may not meet the exact objectives or needs of the research project. Nevertheless, secondary data has been beneficial to many researchers. Secondary data can also be used as an exploratory tool or a method of descriptive research. Detailed discussion on the use of secondary data as a research method in sport management research can be found in Chapter 8 of this book.

Surveys. The most common method of sport management research is the survey. A *survey* is a research method used to collect information from a sample of people through the use of a questionnaire (Wiseman, 1999). The survey, if properly designed, collects information in direct response to the research questions. The survey can be conducted in person, by email, regular mail, the Internet, or by phone. The survey technique relies on the honesty and correct memory of the study participant. This is both a strength and a weakness of this technique. The strength benefit comes when the consumer (study participant) can rely on correct memory and will be honest. The weakness of survey technique is caused by questionable memory recall, guessing at answers, and a dishonest study participant. Nevertheless, the survey is a heavily used and relatively reliable research method for gathering information. Chapter 9 provides an indepth description of how to implement a research project in sport management with the use of surveys as a research design. Chapter 13 and 14 explains the intricacies of designing a questionnaire used to measure people's attitudes.

Experiment. If the purpose of the study is to establish basic cause-and-effect relationships in a situation, an experiment is a good way to accomplish that goal. An experiment is one type of research design in which conditions or procedures are arranged so as to test a hypothesis about a cause-and-effect relationship between two events or variables (Fraenkel & Wallen, 2000). The use of experimentation allows for setting up a test and determining the effects of that test. For instance, in an experiment, a sports marketing director can test whether specific promotional give-aways at a sports event increase attendance. The director can schedule different give-aways at a set number of events and survey the attendees about which give-away had a positive effect on whether they attended the event.

In an experiment, the researcher controls certain conditions so that the effects of each can be determined. In another example of an experiment, a manufacturing company for a sports product, let's say golf clubs, can experiment with different promotional techniques to determine which one gets the attention of the golfer. In this example, the manufacturer can set up three different promotional techniques at three different retail outlets in order to judge which technique increased the attention of the golf consumer. In another experiment, the golf club manufacturer has a laboratory in which different materials and designs for golf clubs perform at preset standards. Usually the standards are rigorous. Any club design or material that fails the standards will not be put into production.

In a different experiment, the researcher can use a technique called market testing (also called test marketing). In this method, the researcher will have groups of consumers use product mock-ups for a period of time and report their experiences with the product. The company may then bring the product to market, make modifications and test again, or determine that the product failed. Detailed discussion on the use of experiments in sport management research can be found in Chapter 10.

If the research will involve humans, then it must be determined *who* will be involved in the research. In other words, a sampling method must be chosen to select participants for the study. A *sample* is a representative group of the whole population. The *population* is the entire group of people targeted, or, under consideration. It is typically not possible to use an entire population in a study—depending on the size of the population. For instance, a sports facility manager wants to know what attendees at a sports event think about the aspects of the facility. If the facility seats and the event attract a sellout crowd of the 75,000 seat facility, the population for that study is the 75,000 attendees. It would be practically impossible to survey all 75,000 individuals. Instead, it is much more practical to survey a representative sample—a smaller group—of that population. When the population under investigation is small enough and the researcher wants to study the entire group, then the investigation is commonly referred to as a census. Chapter 15 of this book gives specific methods for selecting a proper sample.

Step 6: Conduct Data Collection

Once the research method has been chosen, then the date collection procedure can be carried out. Certainly, the research method chosen will determine some of the procedures of data collection. Survey method will require data to be collected in the technique selected for that method. For example, if it was determined that telephone surveys will be conducted, then the specifics of the collection procedure can be planned and performed.

During the research design determination stage, procedures for the physical collection of data should be mapped out. That is, if the research design calls for telephone surveys, it should also be predetermined how the caller will record the information. Once it is recorded, procedures for preparing the data for analysis should be established and followed. For example, while conducting surveys at a sports event, there should be a procedure for storing the surveys for later data analysis. The researcher who collects surveys from 1,500 attendees at a sports event should have a procedure for handling and storing those surveys until the data analysis procedure begins

Step 7: Analyze the Data

After the data has been collected, it must be converted into a format that can be analyzed according to the research design selected, and can be used to develop solutions to the problem, or answer the research questions. It is typical that a research design will stipulate exactly *how* data will be analyzed before it is collected. The analysis technique will affect the design and collection of the data. The sports arena manager who wants to know what attendees think about the facility might have incorporated an answer system that asks the participant to rank their answers. This is usually called a rank order scale. When asked what the attendee thinks about the food offered at the facility, the research may offer a category scale set of answers from which the attendee will choose one. The answers offered will range from 1 to 5, with 1 meaning *poor*, and 5 meaning *excellent*. The study participant must choose only one answer. The researcher will then analyze the data using a chosen statistical analysis from simple to complex.

The analysis selected must be one that offers information that can be examined and from which conclusions can be made. If the sports facility manager finds that all answers to the food question averaged 4.5, then the manager can be assured that the attendees think the food offerings are quite good. If, however, the manager finds that the average was 1.5, then the researcher must give serious thought to and consider further research on why attendees rank the food choices at the facility so poorly. Four chapters of this book (17, 18, 19 and 20) are devoted to the description of statistical procedures that are commonly used in sport management research.

Step 8: Report the Results

Once the analysis stage is concluded, recommendations and conclusions have been drawn, then the researcher must put the results together in a format that can be used for the reason the study was con-

ducted. Most sports business research is applied research so that a business decision can be made. The researcher must consider one last question: "What does this mean and how can it be used (applied)?" The sports facility manager found that attendees at the facility thought the food choices were poor. But can the manager answer *why* they think the food choices are poor? Was there a follow-up question on the survey to determine this? If so, what were those results? Let's say that question was asked and the results showed that attendees think that the choice of just an old hot dog and a watered down soda is too limited. Now, the facility manager has information that is usable. The facility management can make decisions about adding more selections to the food concessions.

The report should begin with outlining and describing the original purpose of the research project, especially restating the research problem or question. The report should be organized similar to the steps of the research process. There should be much discussion of the findings of the research, conclusions drawn based on the findings, and recommendations on the practical application of the findings. (See Chapter 21 for more information about how to report research findings.)

THE RESEARCH PROPOSAL

Once the sport management researcher identifies an issue to investigate, the first step is to develop a research proposal that outlines detailed procedures in terms of how the in-depth study will be executed. A research proposal is "a written statement of the research design that includes a statement explaining the purpose of the study and a detailed, systematic outline of a particular research methodology" (Zikmund, 2000, p. 95). Specifically, it is a master plan specifying the methods and procedures for collecting and analyzing the needed information.

A research proposal in sport management typically includes a number of sections such as introduction, methodology, research budget and schedule, and appendices. The introduction explains why the research will be undertaken and what it aims to discover. In other words, the introduction acquaints a reader with the background of the problem through reviewing previous research. The specific hypothesis, or research questions or objectives, and a discussion of the importance of the study should also be included in the introduction. Basically, such items as background of the problem, review of previous research, hypotheses or research questions or research objectives, and significance of the study are suggested to be included in this section.

Who, what, where, when, and how are the five questions that need to be addressed in the methodology. It should provide a detailed description about subjects, research design, instrumentation, procedures used in data collection, and statistical analysis. The subjects' section contains a description of the population of interest. The size of the sample to be used in the study is mentioned. Furthermore, characteristics of the sample will also be listed and described. Anything related to the methods to be used in data collection will be included in the instrument section. Specifically, such questions as how the survey instrument will be developed—where the questions will come from; how the questionnaire will be validated; how many sections will be included in the instrument; and what the samples of the questions will look like.

The procedures' section includes what will be done to collect the needed data. The description of the data collection procedures includes how the sample will be identified (who is the target population, what sampling frame will be used, and how they will be selected), when and where the survey instruments will be given to the subjects, and how the instruments will be collected. The description of the statistical methods that will be utilized in analyzing the collected data is given in this section. Briefly, what kind of computer software will be applied in data analysis. If secondary data will also be collected, describe it briefly here.

The research budget and schedule section contains information about the cost analysis of the proposed activities (costs for stamps, stationary, printing, envelopes, manpower, etc.) and proposed activities and target dates of completion. Figure 2-3 shows an example of an abridged research proposal in sport management.

RESEARCH PROPOSAL

Identification, Selling, and Activation of Non-traditional Sponsorships in Sport

Introduction

As the amount of sponsorships spending continues to grow in sports, teams and agencies are continually searching for "the next best sponsorship." Identification, selling, and activation of non-traditional sponsorships have thus become focal points of their marketing efforts.

Sponsorship is one of the fastest growing forms of marketing in the United States. IEG predicted that in 2007 the amount spent on sponsorships would reach $14.3 billion. A traditional, or typical, sponsor spends $1.90 on activation for every $1 it pays properties to be associated with them, which is also a record high amount (IEG Sponsorship.com, 2007a). Much of the traditional sponsorship activation is due to the increasing return on investment, which also implies that retention rates may be increasing. In addition, IEG believes there is an "emergence of new funding sources and the continued expansion of what is defined as 'sponsorship'" will help the growth of sponsorships in the United States (Nardone & See, 2007). All of this is promising news for the emergence and, potentially, the study of non-traditional sponsorships in the United States.

Traditional sponsorships always relate back to the same categories and those corporations that are willing to pay out a large sum of money to place their logo on or inside an arena, advertise, do promotions, and are economically sustainable. Some of the common categories and industries that pay out the most and are viewed as traditional sponsors are: airlines, automotive/car, bank/financial, clothing, and telecommunications (IEG Sponsorship.com, 2007b). Over the past decade, sponsorships have transformed and progressed, moving from alternative advertising as a way of obtaining media exposure to more of an emphasis and focus on image enhancement and awareness and increasing sales (Crompton, 2004). Considerable research has also been done on why companies choose to sponsor, noting that sponsorship should be used more as an integrated marketing method and not simply just advertising (IEG Sponsorship.com, 2007c).

In comparison, non-traditional sponsorships are beginning to be recognized as those organizations that are outside of market trends and do not attract a

FIGURE 2-3. Example of an Abridged Research Proposal in Sport Management

lot of attention. It is the actual revenue potential that is not realized by the sport organizations, such as professional and minor league sports leagues (IEG Sponsorship.com, 2007d). Non-traditional sponsors are up and coming, and the sports industry has only seen a glimpse of what is likely to develop from non-traditional sponsors. Researchers and sports analysts suggest that the potential to attract non-traditional sports advertisers with non-traditional sports content will continually increase, especially with the increasing attention in sports entertainment and online sites (Migala, 2003).

Currently, there has not been a significant amount of research conducted on non-traditional sponsors within sports. At this point, most of the literature published on non-traditional sponsorships has been opinion-based. *SportsBusiness Journal* is a fore-front publisher on activity within non-traditional categories of sponsorship (Lefton, 2005). Generally speaking, most of the activity of non-traditional sponsorships is happening among professional teams (Migala, 2006). The purpose of this study is to gain better understanding of the best practices of identifying, selling, and activating non-traditional sponsorships in major and minor league sports. Specifically, four objectives are established for this study:

- To understand how sport marketing professionals classify their sponsors
- To understand trends in non-traditional sponsorship categories
- To determine the driving factors of non-traditional sponsors
- To understand how sport marketing professionals prospect, sell, and activate non-traditional sponsorships

The study will provide sport marketing executives with first-hand knowledge about how to generate additional revenue among the segment of non-traditional categories and sponsors among their various properties.

Methodology

Subjects
The population of interest includes marketing professionals who currently hold positions within the National Football League, National Basketball Association, National Hockey Association, and Minor League Baseball. The size of the sample is expected to be over 100 individuals. Each individual holds the position of manager, assistant director, or director within the organization.

Instrumentation
Survey will be the method to gather the necessary information. A questionnaire will be developed by the research team of this project. The research team will validate the questionnaire with a panel of experts in sport sponsorship to make sure that all areas of interest are covered in the questionnaire. Prior to administering the questionnaire, the research team will conduct a pilot study with 3–5 current or former sport marketing professionals to test the content validity of the instrument.

When the pilot study has been completed, the research team will revise the survey instrument, if necessary, and develop an electronic version of the questionnaire on SurveyMonkey.com. The questionnaire will have three sections: overview, prospecting and selling non-traditional sponsorships, and team demographics. These sections will help create valuable insight on retention rates, drivers of non-traditional sponsorships, and motivational factors affecting sponsorships.

Data Collection Procedures
The research team will conduct the survey between January [year] and March [year] by sending an email to the identified sport marketing professionals. The email will invite each of them to participate in the study by filling out the online survey. The email will include a link to the survey instrument posted on SurveyMonkey.com, a confidentiality clause, and contact information if the participant has questions or concerns for the research team. The research team will send out additional rounds of emails as follow-ups to remind and encourage the identified sport marketing professionals to complete the online questionnaire. It is the research team's hope that a response rate of 40%–50% will be achieved. When the respondents have completed the survey, their answers will be extracted from SurveyMonkey.com into a Microsoft Excel spreadsheet.

Methods of Data Analysis
The research team will use a number of statistical procedures to analyze the data and accomplish the purpose of this study. First, descriptive statistics will be calculated to present the basic characteristics of the data. Second, multivariate statistical procedures, such as MANOVA and regression analysis, will be applied in data analysis.

References

Crompton, J. L. (2004). Conceptualization and alternate operationalizations of the measurement of sponsorship effectiveness in sport. *Leisure Studies, 23*(3), 267–281.

IEG Sponsorship.com. (2007a). IEG's guide to why companies spon-

FIGURE 2-3. Example of an Abridged Research Proposal in Sport Management (*continued*)

sor. Retrieved October 29, 2007, from http://www.sponsorship.com/Resources/What-Companies-Sponsor.aspx.

IEG Sponsorship.com. (2007b). IEG performance research study highlights what sponsors want. Retrieved October 29, 2007, from http://www.sponsorship.com/Resources/IEG-Performance-Research-Study-Highlights-What-Spo.aspx.

IEG Sponsorship.com. (2007c). Sponsorship spending. Retrieved October 29, 2007, from http://www.sponsorship.com/Resources/Sponsorship-Spending.aspx.

IEG Sponsorship.com. (2007d). Top US sponsors: Companies spending more than $15 Million. Retrieved October 29, 2007, from http://www.sponsorship.com/Resources/Top-U-S—Sponsors—Companies-Spending-More-than-$1.aspx.

Lefton, T. (2005, November 14). Dew films not "limited' to action sports. *SportsBusiness Journal, 9*. Retrieved October 31, 2007, from www.sportsbusinessjournal.com/index.cfm?fuseaction=article.printArticle&articleid=47887.

Migala, D. (2003, July 14). LPGA looks into players' lives for popular new web site section. *SportsBusiness Journal, 14*. Retrieved October 31, 2007, from www.sportsbusinessjournal.com/index.cfm?fuseaction=article.printArticle&articleid=31876.

Migala, D. (2006, July 5). To heck with tradition. *Migala Report*. Retrieved October 16, 2007 from http://migalareport.com/reports.cfm?report=jul06_story1.cfm&printer=1.

Nardone, J., & See, E. (2007). Measure sponsorships to drive sales. *Advertising Age, 78*(10), 20–21.

FIGURE 2-3. Example of an Abridged Research Proposal in Sport Management (*continued*)

SUMMARY

Decision making is formally defined as the process of resolving a problem or selecting from alternative opportunities. Information is a critical element of making decisions. Information derives from research.

Research begins with the recognition of a problem, or a question, that needs a solution or an answer. Findings of the research provide the information needed to develop solutions and answer questions.

Research proceeds in an eight step process, although strict adherence to the steps is not absolutely necessary and some variation can occur. Some steps can begin out of sequence, and some can be carried out simultaneously. This is acceptable as long as the integrity of the research is not compromised.

A research design is selected based on which design is best to appropriately study the problem. The most commonly used and basic types of research in sports business include exploratory, experimental, survey, interview, observation, and focus groups.

STUDY QUESTIONS

1. What is the so-called "decision making continuum" and what are the variables affecting the confidence of a decision?
2. What are the steps in the process of sport management research?
3. Among all the steps in the research process, which step is considered the most critical one?
4. What are the differences between qualitative and quantitative research methods in sport management?
5. What are the common types of research designs or methods used in sport management research?

LEARNING ACTIVITIES

1. Review carefully the following situations and identify the most appropriate research design for each.
   a. The athletic department of XYZ University wants to identify the demographic characteristics of its men's and women's basketball season ticket holders.
   b. The marketing director of a major league baseball team wishes to know if in fact sales promotion increases attendance.
2. Identify an issue or a topic that is significant enough in sport management to warrant an in-depth examination of it, and then develop a research proposal that outlines detailed procedures in terms of how the in-depth study will be executed.

References

Bennett, G., & Hardin, B. (2002). Management behaviors of an elite intercollegiate baseball coach. *International Journal of Sport Management*, *3*(3), 199–214.

Burden, W., & Li, M. (2005). Circumstantial factors and institutions' outsourcing decisions on marketing operations. *Sport Marketing Quarterly*, *14* (2), 125–131.

Creswell, J. W. (1994). *Research design: Qualitative & quantitative approaches*. Thousand Oaks, CA: Sage Publications.

Daft, R. (1990). *Management*. Fort Worth, TX: Dryden Press.

Fraenkel, J. R., & Wallen, N. E. (2000). *How to design and evaluate research in education* (4th ed.). Boston, MA: McGraw Hill.

Geng, L., Burton, R., & Blackmore, C. (2002). Sport sponsorship in China: Transition and evolution. *Sport Marketing Quarterly*, *11*(1), 20–32.

Kvale, S. (1996). *Interviews: An introduction to qualitative research interviewing*. Thousand Oaks, CA: Sage Publications.

Long, J., Thibault, L., & Wolfe, R. (2004). A case study of influence over a sponsorship decision in a Canadian University Athletic Department. *Journal of Sport Management*, *18*, 132–157.

Marshall, C., & Rossman, G. B., (1995). *Designing qualitative research* (2nd ed.). Thousand Oaks, CA: Sage Publications.

Merriam, S. B. (1988). *Case study research in education: A qualitative approach*. San Francisco: Jossey Bass.

Schermehrhorn, J. R., Hunt, J. G., & Osborn, R. N. (1991). *Managing organizational behavior*. New York, NY: John Wiley & Sons.

Wiseman, D. C. (1999). *Research strategies for education*. Belmont, CA: Wadsworth Publishing Company.

Zikmund, W. G. (2000). *Business research methods* (6th ed.). Fort Worth, TX: Harcourt College Publishers.

CHAPTER 3
INTERPRETATION OF QUALITATIVE RESEARCH IN SPORT MANAGEMENT STUDIES

OBJECTIVES FOR COMPLETING THIS CHAPTER ARE THAT STUDENTS WILL BE ABLE TO:

Define qualitative research

Explain the differences between qualitative and quantitative research strategies

Understand the circumstances under which qualitative research is chosen in sport management research

Use critiquing criteria to evaluate the qualitative research report

Determine the benefits of combining quantitative and qualitative research methods

THE PURPOSE OF THIS CHAPTER is to provide an overview of qualitative research methods, techniques, and tools that can be used to assist the students in better appraising and interpreting sports management research.

The nature and scope of qualitative research will first be examined, followed by the discussion of the relationships between qualitative and quantitative research strategies as well as the philosophical differences between the two types of strategies. The merits of combining qualitative and quantitative research as a research strategy will also be reviewed. Examples from the sport management literature are provided throughout the chapter to aid at facilitating the students' understanding of the information presented.

QUALITATIVE RESEARCH DEFINED

The fundamental objective of qualitative research is to gain insight into and understand the meaning of a particular human experience. This may include human experiences as an individual, as a group, and as an organization. It is an in-depth, subjective analysis of the characteristics and significance of human experience. Unlike quantitative research, it is an interpretation of data based on the meaning that individuals give to their experiences rather than verification. It is used to explore little-known or ambiguous phenomenon.

Qualitative researchers generally state the purpose for their research clearly and explicitly before beginning their research project. In most qualitative studies, some guiding research questions are first developed in order for the researcher to focus the data collection and analysis phase of the research. However, it is anticipated that these questions may change during the course of the study (Lincoln & Guba, 1985). Qualitative research designs are thus more fluid, flexible, and responsive to data than most quantitative designs.

Qualitative research questions are also more open-ended and exploratory. The generic question qualitative researchers often ask is "What's going on here and why?" Qualitative researchers attempt to approach their data without a priori assumptions, working to make "the familiar strange," to see events in a new way before interpreting what they see. They conduct their explorations in natural contexts and focus on looking at events and actions in holistic, rather than a reductionistic manner.

Describing the nature of qualitative research is not an easy task because there are so many ways the concept has been defined by academic scholars. A content review of the definitions of qualitative research have been provided in a number of recent books and articles indicate that some authors view it as an interpretation of databased on the meaning of how individuals explain their experiences

Creswell (2003) has defined qualitative research as an approach "in which the inquirer often makes knowledge claims based primarily on postpositivist claims for developing knowledge (i.e. cause and effect thinking, reduction to specific variables and hypotheses and questions, use of measurement and observation, and the test of theories), employs strategies of inquiry such as experiments and surveys, and collects data on predetermined instruments that yield statistical data" (p. 18). Straus and Corbin (1990) define it as "any kind of research that produces findings not arrived by means of statistical procedures or other means of quantification" (p. 17). The authors have also maintained that the key contributions of qualitative research can be used to:

1. assist scholars in bettering understanding phenomenon about which little is known;
2. gain new and different viewpoints on phenomena for which much is already known; and
3. gather in-depth information about that which may be hard to understand quantitatively.

In trying to condense these extended definitions to a useful description, the following comprehensive definition is offered: Qualitative research method is a scientific, purposeful, systematic, and rigorous subjective method of collecting, analyzing, and interpreting data about some characteristic of individual(s), group(s), organization(s), concepts, and/or theories in order to gain new knowledge or add to the existing knowledge base of the field of sport organization management studies. Qualitative researchers tend to use inductive analysis of data to generate critical themes out of the data (Patton, 1990). Boghan and Biklen (1991) generally define inductive qualitative data analysis as working with data, organizing it, breaking it into manageable units, synthesizing it, searching for patterns, discovering what is important and what is to be learned, and deciding what to tell others.

The key contribution of qualitative research is heuristic in nature, that is, its usefulness lies in its ability to explore new knowledge or add to existing knowledge for enhancement of theory or clinical practices in organizations of the sport industry. The study conducted by Lachowetz, McDonald, Sutton, and Hedrick (2003) is one example illustrating the use of qualitative research in sport management. They conducted in-depth interviews with the corporate sales managers for selected NBA teams to provide further insight regarding the factors that lead to high corporate sponsor retention. The collected data was analyzed using the inductive analysis method. As one of the well-recognized methods of coding qualitative data, inductive methodology allows categories to emerge both during and after analyzing the data. Results of the inductive analysis yielded three primary themes: added value, relationship building/developing and customer education. According, to the managers, these three areas were most responsible for their franchise retaining corporate purchasers over the three-season period of 1998–1999 to 2000–2001.

QUALITATIVE RESEARCH VERSUS QUANTITATIVE RESEARCH

Qualitative research is one of two major research strategies for investigating diverse phenomena. Its counterpart is quantitative research. Qualitative and quantitative are two distinctive and complementary approaches to research. Each has its own functions and characteristic activities. These approaches originate from different philosophical perspectives and use different methods for data collection and analysis. Qualitative research is rooted in the fields of anthropology, sociology, and philosophy.

Quantitative research is rooted in the fields of psychology, economics, and management. The differences between the two approaches are based on the extent to which the analysis can be done by converting observations into numbers or using narrative text to describe human experiences. It is best to think of the qualitative-quantitative distinction as dualistic in nature. Qualitative research is a method of research designed for discovery rather than verification. Thus, this type of research is used to explore little-known or ambiguous phenomena. Quantitative research uses numbers to measure variables. As such, it is a method to verify if there are differences or relationships about phenomena. Quantitative research uses numbers to measure variables. Qualitative research is in-depth, subjective analysis of the characteristics and significance of human experience. Table 3-1 depicts the philosophical differences between quantitative and qualitative research modes of inquiry.

The Choice of a Qualitative Research Approach

Qualitative researchers prefer natural or real-world settings. They do not attempt to control variables, manipulate procedures, create research or comparison groups, or isolate a particular phenomenon. Rather, qualitative researchers immerse themselves in a naturally occurring setting to observe and understand it.

As mentioned earlier, qualitative and quantitative are two distinct and complementary approaches to research for the development of an empirical knowledge base in the field of sport management. The issue is not whether one type of research is better than the other. Each has its own functions and characteristic activities. Quantitative designs usually begin with a hypothesis, which, through measurement, generates data (usually expressed in numbers) and by deduction allows a conclusion to be drawn. In contrast, qualitative design begins with the intention of observing, describing, understanding, or interpreting experiences from the perspective of those experiencing it. Qualitative research is useful in the early stages of knowledge development.

It is suggested that a qualitative research design is chosen under the following circumstances:

TABLE 3-1
The Philosophical Differences between Quantitative and Qualitative Research Mode of Inquiry

Factor	Quantitative	Qualitative
Paradigm	• Positivist • Reality is singular, objective	• Naturalistic • Reality is subjective
Relationship	• Researcher is independent of what is being researched	• Researcher interacts with what is being researched
	• Researcher does not influence the findings • Primarily rooted in psychology and sociology	• The interaction between the researcher and "researchee" creates the findings • Primarily rooted in history, philosophy, and social anthropology
Interpretation of data	• Researcher writes in a formal style using quantitative terminology	• Researcher writes in a literary, informal style, using qualitative terminology
Research findings	• Deductive reasoning (logic) through inferences from numerical data • Researchers have specific questions in mind and are usually more concerned with outcomes or products • Attempts to prove or disprove a hypothesis	• Inductive reasoning (logic) through creativity and critical thinking • Researchers use natural settings as sites of study and are usually more concerned about meaning and understanding of phenomena • Attempts to generate a hypothesis
Subjects	• Known as participants or respondents	• Known as informants
Data collected	• Primarily numerical values	• Primarily narrative descriptions
Data collection techniques	• Passive interaction through questionnaire and/or experimental design	• Active interaction with sample population • (Observation by active participation)

Data analysis	• Interpretive through statistical data analysis
	  ■ Descriptive
	  ■ Inferential (parametric and non-parametric)
		• Interpretive through themes
		
		• Constant comparative procedures
		• Descriptive (rankings frequencies and percentages)

Sample population	• Large sample size relative to concepts on phenomena to be investigated	• Small sample size relative to phenomenon to be investigated
Data collection	• Survey (non-experimental)	• Observation and interview
Research variables	• Small number • Before/after treatment (experimental)	• Large number
Sample population	• Random sampling	• Purposive sampling
Instrument tools	• Questionnaires, scales, equipment, etc.	• Tape recorder, transcriber, computer

■ A valid and reliable instrumentation is not available or readily developed.

■ There is a need to personalize the evaluation process (i.e., meet with various individuals face-to-face to elicit their perceptions, experiences, and feelings).

■ A single, in-depth case study approach is appropriate.

■ Sport management personnel are interested in detailed descriptive information.

■ There is a need for information that cannot be tapped by quantification.

■ Decision-making personnel need subjective information about the strengths and weaknesses of a program.

■ An inductive approach is desired.

■ No preconceived notions about an idea, concept, theory, issue, opinion, attitude, or program have been proposed.

The Choice of a Quantitative Research Approach

A quantitative research design is often chosen under the following circumstances:

- A standardized instrument is available that is reliable and valid.
- Use of a standardized instrument is easily administered, cost-effective, and safe.
- Comparisons of the findings are to be made at various points in time.
- The evaluation question asks, "How much?"

DATA COLLECTION TECHNIQUES OF QUALITATIVE RESEARCH

Data collection for qualitative research typically is extensive and is in the form of words rather than numbers. The primary concern is with observation and opinion as they are collected from a subject's environment. Quantitative research designs usually begin with a hypothesis, which through measurement, generates data (usually expressed in an amount account) and by deduction allows for conclusions to be drawn. In contrast, qualitative research design begins with the intention of observing, describing, understanding, or interpreting experiences from the perspective of those experiencing an event. As mentioned in Chapter 2, the most common data collection techniques of qualitative research are case studies, interviews, focus groups, and observation. Each of these four qualitative research techniques will be discussed in detail in the following four chapters.

TRUSTWORTHINESS OF QUALITATIVE RESEARCH RIGOR

Four criteria used to measure the rigor of qualitative research include: creditability, transferability (fittingness), dependability, and confirmability (Guba & Lincoln, 1989; Miles & Huberman, 1984; Lincoln & Guba, 1985). According to the aforementioned authors, in qualitative research trustworthiness is analogous to the psychometric measurements of validity and reliability and quantitative research. Credibility of qualitative research is analogous to the validity of quantitative research. Transferability of qual-

itative research is analogous to generalizability of quantitative research. Dependability of qualitative research is analogous to reliability of quantitative research. Confirmability of qualitative research is analogous to objectivity of quantitative research (For a summary of the criteria see also Table 3-2).

COMBINING QUALITATIVE AND QUANTITATIVE RESEARCH

One relative advantage of qualitative research is that it can be a source of rich descriptions and explanations of lived experiences. Although information gained from purely qualitative research may be useful, combining qualitative and quantitative approaches can help the researcher benefit from the relative advantages of each method (Teddlie & Tashakkori, 2003). Accordingly, researchers recognize that mixed method research—combining qualitative and quantitative methods—can lead to stronger inferences and enhance overall knowledge of the research issues (Rohm, Milne, & McDonald, 2006)

There are two ways of combining qualitative and quantitative research simultaneously: qualitative plus quantitative and quantitative plus qualitative. Such procedures are also called mixed method designs. When qualitative methods initiate the inquiry and are then followed by quantitative techniques, the problem implies an exploratory design. When data are collected sequentially-quantitative first, qualitative second-the quantitative phase provides general results that are then explained with qualitative data. When data are collected sequentially, an explanatory design is implied (McMillan & Schumacher, 2006).

For qualitative plus quantitative, there is a qualitative foundation and quantitative methods are used to provide complementary information. This is a mixed method design. For a quantitative plus qualitative method, there is a quantitative foundation and qualitative methods are used to provide the complementary information (Creswell, 2002; McMillan & Schumacher, 2006).

Following are examples of recent mixed studies in sport management research using a qualitative plus quantitative method. Martin (1990) identified and analyzed "mentoring and networking among se-

TABLE 3-2
A Comparison of Accuracy and Precision in Qualitative and Quantitative Research

Quantitative concept	Equivalent in qualitative research
Validity Addresses the question: Are we measuring what we think should be measured?	**Credibility** Addresses the questions: How accurately are the particular parameters of the study (who, where, when) described? How well has the researcher interpreted the collected data? Is ensured by reviewing the researcher's conclusions to be sure they are correct. Other techniques that support credibility: ■ prolonged engagement ■ triangulation ■ peer debriefing ■ member checking ■ data saturation
Reliability Addresses the question: Are there consistency and stability of the scores of the measurement scale(s) that is being utilized?	**Dependability** Addresses trustworthiness in qualitative research met and is accomplished through securing credibility of the findings
Generalizability Addresses the question: Should the results of a study be applied to groups other than the one studied?	**Transferability (Generalizability)** Addresses the ability to generalize the findings of a study to the population at large (Lincoln & Guba, 1985)
Objectivity Addresses the question: Is the result of the research applicable outside the research situation	**Confirmability** Addresses the question: Did the researcher conduct the investigation in a rigorous manner so as to guarantee the trustworthiness of the findings? Refers to an assessment of the overall quality of the findings of a study (for instance, through use of an expert reviewer of by verifying the interpretations with the participants of the original study).

Sources:
Dempsey, P.A., & Dempsey, A. D. (2000). *Using nursing research: Process, critical evaluation, and utilization* (5th ed.). Baltimore, MD: Lippincott, Williams, & Wilkins.
Lincoln, Y. S., & Guba, E. G. (1985). *Naturalistic inquiry.* Beverly Hills, CA: Sage Publications.

lected male and female administrators employed by National Collegiate Athletic Association (NCAA) institutions." In his study, a mail questionnaire was followed with a semi-structured interview for approximately 30 minutes at one of the institutions or by telephone. Young (1990) identified and analyzed mentoring and networking among selected male and female administrators employed by National Collegiate Athletic Association (NCAA) institutions. She used frequencies, contingency tables, chi-square statistics besides semistructured interview.

In the Martin (1990) and Young (1990) examples, data were collected sequentially through a mail questionnaire and follow-up interview. In this example, quantitative data were collected first then qualitative data were collected second. When data are collected sequentially in this manner, an explanatory design is implied (McMillan & Schumacher, 2006).

FUTURE DIRECTIONS AND PUBLICATIONS OF QUALITATIVE RESEARCH IN THE FIELD OF SPORT MANAGEMENT AND SPORT MARKETING

During recent years, there has been a heightened interest in qualitative research as recorded by an increasing numbers of reports of qualitative research in sport management and sport marketing peer reviewed journals (Quarterman, Pitts, Jackson, Han,

Haung & Ahn, 2007, unpublished work). This has been illustrated by an increasing number of reports of qualitative research investigations in sport management journals. A review of three journals: *Journal of Sport Management, International Journal of Sport Management, and Sport Marketing Quarterly* indicates that since 1987 (or the journal's first issue date if prior to 1987) to 2004 that these types of reports have more than tripled (see Table 3-3 and Figure 3-1 for details). It must be noted that this figure does not conclusively reflect the total amount of qualitative research conducted in sport management. It is merely offered as an example of an upward trend in qualitative research in sport management publication outlets. The upward trend implies

that researchers have come to recognize the value of qualitative research in sport management studies.

Many fields have affirmed the value and impact that qualitative inquiry can have on professional practice. In fact, many journals have committed to publishing qualitative research projects. Examples relative to sport management and sport marketing include: *Journal of Sport Management* (1987), *European Sport Management Quarterly* (1994), *The Sport Journal* (1995), *Sport Management Review* (1998), *International Sport Journal* (started 1999—ended 2004), *International Journal of Sport Management* (2000), *The SMART-Journal* (2005), *Sport Management Education Journal* (2007), *Sport Marketing Quarterly* (1992), *Cyber Journal of Sport Marketing*

TABLE 3-3
Percentage of Qualitative Research Articles among All Articles Published in Three Sport Management-Related Journals

Type of article	Operational Definition	JSM 1987–2006		IJSM 2000–2006		SMQ* 1992–2006		Row Total	
		NO	%	NO	%	NO	%	NO	%
Quantitative research articles	Articles in which the writer(s) presented an essay in form of research of a significant idea, concept, theory, issue, opinion, attitude, or program that was primarily represented by an amount or count.	186	53.45%	106	70.67%	174	62.37%	466	59.97%
Qualitative research articles	Articles in which the writer(s) presented research in form of data of a significant idea, concept, theory, issue, opinion, attitude, or program that was primarily represented by words and phrases.	34	9.77%	14	9.33%	17	6.09%	65	8.37%
Mixed research articles	Articles in which the writer(s) presented research that employed both quantitative and qualitative values.	11	3.16%	5	3.33%	8	2.87%	24	3.09%
Conceptual articles	Articles in which the writer(s) presented an essay in the form of a critical analysis of some significant idea, concept, theory, issue, opinion, or program without employing data analysis.	117	33.62%	25	16.67%	80	28.67%	222	28.57%
Column Total		348	100	150	100	279	100	777	100%

Source: Quarterman, J., Pitts, B., Jackson, N., Han, K., Haung, J., & Ahn, T. (2007). Statistical data analysis techniques employed in the *Journal of Sport Management, Sport Marketing Quarterly, & International Journal of Management:* 1987 to 2006. Unpublished manuscript.

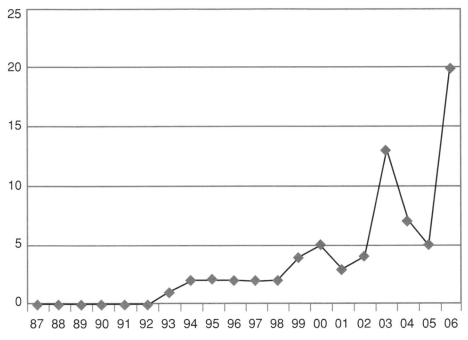

FIGURE 3-1. Trends in qualitative research in *JSM, SMQ,* and *IJSM*: 1987 to 2006

(started January 1997—ended July 2000), *International Journal of Sport Marketing and Sponsorship* (2005), *and International Journal of Sport Management and Marketing* (2006).

Arguments about whether quantitative and qualitative research has more merit have raged for years and have produced a number of debates and propositions. Sport management research must recognize that these two research approaches answer different types of questions and both can facilitate an understanding of the field of sport management. In many instances, a study can use both quantitative and qualitative methods in a mixed-methods approach.

Qualitative research has come to be recognized as a separate field with its own growing body of literature providing guidance on various aspects of the conduct of qualitative research. A number of doctoral programs in sport management now recommend their students take a course in qualitative research.

SUMMARY

Qualitative research has been recognized as an important strategy for inquiry in the field of sport man-

agement. It is highly valued as a strategy for articulating the meaning of human experience in sport industry organizations. While the tradition of qualitative research in the field is relatively short, an increasing number of qualitative investigations are expanding our understanding of the human experience in the relatively new and emerging field of sport management.

Qualitative research is a scientific, purposeful, systematic and rigorous subjective method of collecting, analyzing, and interpreting data about some characteristic of individual(s), group(s), organization(s), concepts, and/or theories in order to gain new knowledge or add to the existing knowledge base of the field of sport management. It is social science-based, designed for discovery rather than verification. The fundamental objective of qualitative research is to gain insight into and understand the meaning and interpretation of a particular human experience. Data collection for qualitative research typically is extensive and is in the form of words rather than numbers.

There are four criteria by which rigor is measured in qualitative research, including: creditability, fittingness, auditability, and confirmability.

Case studies, interviews, focus groups, and observation are qualitative research methods that are commonly used by sport management researchers.

Both qualitative and quantitative research methods are viable means of inquiry in sport management research. When the answer to a research question or hypothesis requires accuracy, quantitative methods are preferred. However, when the answer to a research question or hypothesis involves capturing complexity in a situation or understanding meaning, qualitative methods are preferred.

References

Bogdan, R.C., & Biklen, S. K. (1991). *Qualitative research for education: An introduction to theory and methods.* Boston, MA: Allyn and Bacon.

Creswell, J. W. (2002). *Educational research: Planning, conducting, and evaluating quantitative and qualitative research.* Upper Saddle River, NJ: Merrill/ Prentice Hall.

Creswell, J. W. (2003). *Research design: Qualitative, quantitative, and mixed methods approaches* (2nd ed.). Thousand Oaks, CA: Sage Publications, Inc.

Guba, E. G., & Lincoln, Y. S. (1989). *Fourth generation evaluation.* Newbury Park, CA: Sage.

Lachowetz, T., McDonald, M., Sutton, W. A., & Hedrick, D. G. (2003). Corporate sales activities and the retention of sponsors in the National Basketball Association (NBA). *Sport Marketing Quarterly, 12*(1), 18–26.

Lincoln, Y. S., & Guba, E. G. (1985). *Naturalistic inquiry.* Beverly Hills: Sage Publications, Inc.

Martin, C. L. (1990). The employee/customer interface: An empirical investigation of employee behaviors and customer perceptions. *Journal of Sport Management, 4*(1), 1–20.

McMillan, J. H., & Schumacher, S. (2006). *Research in education: Evidence-based inquiry* (6th ed.). Boston, MA: Pearson.

Miles, M., & Huberman, A. (1984). *Qualitative data analysis.* Beverly Hills, CA: Sage Publications, Inc.

Patton, M. Q. (1990). *Qualitative evaluation and research methods* (2nd ed.). Newbury Park, CA: Sage Publications, Inc.

Quarterman, J., Pitts, B. G., Jackson, E. N., Han, K., Haung, J., & Ahn, T. (2007). Statistical data analysis techniques employed in the *Journal of Sport Management, Sport Marketing Quarterly, & International Journal of Management: 1987 to 2006.* Unpublished manuscript.

Quarterman, J., Pitts, B. G., Jackson, E. N., Kim, K., & Kim, J. (2005). Statistical data analysis techniques employed in the *Sport Marketing Quarterly:* January 1982 to October 2004. *Sport Marketing Quarterly, 14*(1), 158–167.

Rohm, A. J., Milne, G. R., & McDonald, M. A. (2006). A mixed-method approach for developing market segmentation typologies in the sports industry. *Sports Marketing Quarterly, 15,* 29–30.

Strauss, A., & Corbin, J. (1990). *Basics of qualitative research: Grounded theory procedures and techniques.* Newbury Park, CA: Sage Publications, Inc.

Teddlie, C., & Tashakkori, A. (2003). Major issues and controversies in the used of mixed methods in the social and behavioral sciences. In A. Tashakkori & C. Teddie (Eds.), *Handbook of mixed methods in the social & behavioral research.* Thousand Oaks, CA: Sage Publications, Inc.

Young, D. (1990). Mentoring and networking: Perceptions by athletic administrators. *Journal of Sport Management, 4*(1), 71–79.

CHAPTER 4
CASE STUDY RESEARCH IN SPORT MANAGEMENT

OBJECTIVES FOR COMPLETING THIS CHAPTER ARE THAT STUDENTS WILL BE ABLE TO:

Identify and discuss the similarities and differences of the various definitions

Describe the basic types of case studies

Identify and discuss the five steps in designing a case study

Explain the standards useful for evaluating the quality of case study data collection

Understand the concept of triangulation

Identify at least four types of triangulation/crystallization

Identify and discuss fully several strengths, as well as some limitations, of case study research

Identify basic strategies useful for analyzing case studies

THE USE OF CASE STUDY as a research design is challenging because the sport management researcher is often called upon to handle a variety of evidence derived from diverse data collection points and techniques. Sport management students or researchers with limited social-science training—in fields such as anthropology, political science, psychology, sociology, or philosophy—may be unfamiliar with just what constitutes a case study. This unfamiliarity can make case study research intimidating. Other researchers may view case study research as hierarchically inferior to other forms of research, with case studies seen as exploratory step-children to surveys and histories, or distant and impoverished cousins of causal inquiries (experiments). Such a view relegates case studies to a position as a preliminary research strategy not sufficiently rigorous to describe or test propositions.

However, social-science research, by definition, occurs within a social context. Conducting such research in a social setting involves investigating individuals, groups and organizations, and social and political phenomena. Therefore, from an interpretive perspective, a qualitative researcher's understanding of such phenomena depends on uncovering the "how" and "why" of the constructed social reality and how social interaction occurs within this reality. Case study research, as will be detailed in this chapter, fosters such understanding by focusing on contemporary events and not requiring control of behavioral events. However, case study research still has sufficient rigor for a researcher to answer how and why research questions.

The issues associated with case study research reflect the social world's complexity. To better understand the complexity of case study research, it is helpful to first discuss its historical origins. This context allows a better understanding of just what a case study is and what constitutes a research case study. Against this backdrop, the remainder of this chapter will present more practical information regarding (a) various types of case studies, (b) design-ing case studies, (c) conducting case studies, (d) analyzing case study evidence, and (e) reporting case studies.

CASE STUDY AS A RESEARCH DESIGN: HISTORICAL CONTEXT

In order to better understand the research case study, it is helpful to briefly discuss its historical roots in sociology and anthropology. Hamel, Dufour, and Fortin (1993) identified Malinowski's World War I era participant observation fieldwork, conducted in Melanesia in the Trobiand Islands, as one of the earliest examples of modern anthropology and one of the earliest examples of a research case study. In the United States, early 20th century sociological inquiry was influenced by case studies developed by scholars associated with what was known as the "Chicago School" (Hamel et al., 1993). These naturalistic field studies focused on urban communities, where rural immigrants had begun to settle. Robert Park, reacting to what he termed "armchair sociology" challenged his students to investigate urban problems such as poverty, delinquency, and deviance by getting close to their subjects—getting their hands dirty (Gubrium & Holstein, 1997). As part of their research sociology, students at the University of Chicago were encouraged to go beyond a reliance on official documents and come into personal contact with subjects and experience the poverty and deviance (Hamel).

The Chicago School dominated American sociological research and the case study was the preeminent sociological research method. Other methods, including statistical surveys, were not seen to be in conflict or competition with case studies, but rather complementary or exclusive. However, during the time period of 1927–1935 the relevance of case study research was questioned by statisticians, including several positivist sociologists from Columbia University (Hamel, et al., 1993). Giddings, Ogburn and Stouffer criticized case studies as lacking the ability to validate a theoretical idea, being incapable of demonstration, proof, or verification (Bryant, 1985).

This criticism of case study methodology reflected the rise of a new "scientific" or statistically-based approach to sociological inquiry that called for a theoretical (deductive) basis for explaining social issues. Such a deductive process designed to test a theory incorporated technical statistical (quantitative) procedures that controlled or held in check any subjective attitudes or feelings (bias) that might arise in the researcher. Such methodology required no direct contact between the researcher and the object of study. With this increasing requirement that sociological research must involve "rigorous" and controlled experiments, the case study method became to be viewed by many researchers as trivial or, at best, a secondary/exploratory methodology (Gubrium & Holstein, 1997; Hamel et al., 1993).

CASE STUDY DEFINED

In attempting to define what constitutes a case study, Hamel et al. (1993) posed two basic questions: "Is the case study a method? Or is it an approach?" (p. 1). Yin (2003b) clearly delineated case study research as one of several ways of doing social science research and referred to it as a qualitative research strategy distinct from other social science research methods (i.e. experiments, surveys, histories, and archival analysis). Confusion surrounding case study research also results from lumping case studies into a discussion of ethnographies or participant-observations and so reducing case study research to just another data collection technique utilized in conducting "fieldwork." Stake (2003) posited an inclusive criterion for what constitutes case study research by not defining it as a specific methodology, but rather asserting that a case study is defined by the object of study's uniqueness and specificity. Amis (2005) was not as inclusive in his discussion of what constitutes case study research, but did discuss the merit of case study research that goes beyond simply focusing on a single case and analyzing data at various levels, including societal, governmental, organizational, subunit and individual.

One widely cited definition of a case study was developed in 1990 by the United States General Accounting Office. "A case study is a method for learning about a complex instance, based upon a comprehensive understanding of that instance obtained by extensive description and analysis of that instance taken as a whole and in its context" (U.S. General Accounting Office, 1990, p. 14).

This definition assists in framing a discussion of case study research because it highlights the contextual complexity in which case study research occurs and the need for researchers to consider not only particular actors or groups of actors, but also the interactions between these actors. This definition also suggests the multi-perspective nature of case study research.

Researchers have consistently viewed case study research as a method or strategy that utilizes an inductive approach in which the definition of the subject of investigation is not a matter of conjecture or happenstance. The subject's definition emerges or asserts itself during the course of investigation. By establishing increasingly close ties the investigator is able to break down the personal experiences of the actors thus uncovering or allowing the social reality to emerge. This allows the addressing of two questions:

1. How does the individual, group, organization or society generate/reflect the problem or phenomenon being investigated?
2. Why has this problem or phenomenon been deemed such by the individual, group, organization, or society?

Eisenhardt (1989) defined a case study as "a research strategy which focuses on understanding the dynamics present within single settings" (p. 534). Stake (2003) defined a case as a "specific one," while allowing that a case may be simple or complex. Yin (2003a, 2003b) also utilized the scope of a case study in his definition, but also noted the desire to investigate the case's contextual conditions as a central definitional element. Yin (2003b) recognized the importance of allowing uncontrolled contextual "variables" and phenomenon to remain entangled. "A case study is an empirical inquiry that investigates a contemporary phenomenon within its real-life context, especially when the boundaries between phenomenon and context are not clearly evident" (p. 13). Because of its real-life, non-experimental setting, case study's data collection and data analysis strategies are important in delineating it from other forms of inquiry. While scholars may not all agree whether case study research is a method or a research design (Mertens, 2005), there is seeming consensus among researchers that case study inquiry occurs in situations where there are many more variables of interest than data points. As a result it relies on multiple sources of evidence, with data needing to converge in a triangulating fashion, and as another result benefits from the prior development of theoretical propositions to guide data collection and analysis (p. 14).

Figure 4-1 is a case study involving a single tragic car accident. It illustrates many of the elements regarding what constitutes a case study discussed above. The specific case illustrates the dynamic

---

The National Football League and Its "Culture of Intoxication": A Negligent Marketing Analysis of *Verni v. Lanzaro* (Southall & Sharp, 2006)

On October 24, 1999 the parking lots at Giants Stadium, which opened four hours before kickoff, witnessed a Sunday game-day ritual played out at professional football stadiums across the United States: "pregame and post-game tailgate parties at which persons consume alcoholic beverages" (Sixth amended complaint and jury demand, *Verni v. Lanzaro*, 2003, p. 7). As the afternoon turned to early evening, the New York Giants had easily beaten the New Orleans Saints 31–3, to run their record to 4–3 on the season (NFL 1999 Season Archives, n.d.). Celebratory Giants fans, among them 30-year-old Daniel R. Lanzaro of Cresskill, New Jersey, poured out of Giants Stadium to begin their journey home or to continue their celebrations at one of the local bars, such as Shakers or The Gallery, in the borough of Hasbrouck Heights in Bergen County (Sixth amended complaint).

Returning home from a family outing to pick up pumpkins for Halloween, Ronald Verni, accompanied by his wife Fazila and their two-year-old daughter Antonia, passed through Hasbrouck Heights, about five minutes from Giants Stadium, via Terrace Avenue (Crusade against DWI, 2002; Cable News Network, 2003). After purchasing and consuming at least 14 beers and an undisclosed amount of marijuana (Sixth amended complaint, 2003) while participating in pregame tailgating and viewing the day's game at Giants Stadium, Lanzaro lost control of his 1994 Ford pickup, hit one vehicle, and then collided, head-on, with the Verni family's 1999 Toyota (Coffey, 2005).

The results of the accident were horrific. Antonia, who was resuscitated by Hasbrouck Heights emergency medical technicians, suffered a broken neck and spent the next 11 months in the hospital and in rehabilitation. The accident left the child "a quadriplegic in need of round-the-clock care.[1] Her mother went into a coma, needed reconstructive surgery on her face and had a rod inserted into her leg" (Coffey, 2005, para. 6). Antonia's father, Ronald, was unhurt in the accident.

According to a newspaper report of the accident, Hasbrouck Heights police officer Corey Lange found Lanzaro and a passenger sitting on the curb near the accident site. Both Lanzaro and the passenger had trouble standing up. When asked how much he had been drinking, Lanzaro replied, "Too much" (Gaudiano, 2002, para. 2). A security guard at the hospital reported finding a marijuana "joint" in Lanzaro's pocket (Gaudiano). Lange later said that Lanzaro admitted to drinking before and during the game, and also to smoking some "pot" (Gaudiano). According to police, Lanzaro's blood alcohol level was "0.266, $2^1/_2$ times the legal limit of 0.10" (Gaudiano, para. 2). In August 2003, Lanzaro pled guilty to vehicular assault and was sentenced to five years in Riverfront State Prison (Coffey, 2005).

In all likelihood, this tragic occurrence would have remained just another tragedy in just another newspaper, on just another weekend, soon forgotten by the general public, if the Vernis had simply chosen to sue Mr. Lanzaro. However, the Vernis chose to include several other parties in their complaint, including the New Jersey Sports and Exposition Authority, the New York Giants, Giants Stadium, Aramark, two local bars [Shakers, The Gallery], the National Football League (NFL), and NFL commissioner Paul Tagliabue (Sixth amended complaint, *Verni v. Lanzaro*, 2003, p. 1).[2] Suddenly, this tragic accident became much more than an isolated incident. It evolved into a lawsuit with major implications for arena/stadium concessions management policies and procedures.

---

1. It should be noted that Antonia Verni (age 2) was wearing a seatbelt, but was not in a car seat at the time of the accident (Dvorchak, 2005).

2. Since Lanzaro's insurance policy had a $200,000.00 liability limit, the list of defendants was consistent with a complaint based on allegations that the Giants and the NFL had the authority and ability to exercise control over Aramark as the concessionaire at Giants Stadium.

FIGURE 4-1. Case Study Example 1

nature of case research and how a single incident can illuminate a much larger societal issue.

CASE STUDY AS A RESEARCH DESIGN IN SPORT MANAGEMENT

The sports industry is a goal-oriented and results-driven enterprise. From the field or court to the front office, success is measured by wins and losses, play-off successes, gate receipts, attendance, and sponsorship packages. Most sport managers are concerned with the practical applicability of research. Because case study research utilizes inductive, open-ended strategies, it offers practical results for sport managers. One of the advantages of case study research is that both the results and theories generated are experientially credible, yet understandable to sport managers. In addition, one goal of case study research—to improve existing practices—appeals to sport managers looking to improve their organization's "bottom line." Case study research allows collaborative research in which participants and researchers are able to jointly analyze contexts, processes, and meanings. In some instances case studies can be the basis for developing surveys that can assess the generalizability of a case study's results. Secondary analysis and utilization of other research methodologies also may allow researchers to reach broader conclusions than can be formulated by the isolated use of case study research strategies.

In addition to the above reasons, utilizing case study research—or any qualitative methodology—can accomplish several additional purposes for the sport-management researcher. A case study can help both the researcher and participants understand the meanings developed to describe the events, situations, and actions studied. Such understandings can be beneficial to an organization's understanding of itself. Participants' perspectives on events and situations are part of the reality the researcher hopes to understand. In addition, since case study research typically involves a unique situation and not large samples and aggregations of data from many samples, the researcher is able to concentrate on the contextual uniqueness of a particular case and fully explore it. This concentration of focus allows managers to concentrate on their own organization and learn

from a relatively removed and more objective analysis of their own situation.

BUILDING THEORY FROM CASE STUDY RESEARCH

Various qualitative research strategies or methods have often been criticized for being "unscientific," since they do not allow for manipulation of variables in explanatory or causal inquiries (Shavelson & Townes, 2002). In addition, some researchers recognize the appropriateness of various qualitative research techniques, but only for specific types of research (i.e., case studies mainly for an exploratory purpose, and surveys and histories for seeking descriptive information). If case studies are only a viable preliminary research methodology, it has been said they cannot be used to describe or test theoretical propositions. This attitude may lead to the question, "If a case study is a specific 'One,' how can case study research help us either test or build a generalizable theories?" In the following section we will first ask the preliminary question: "What constitutes a theory?" We will then discuss the role of theory in designing and conducting case studies and how case study research can be utilized to build or develop theories.

What Is a Theory?

In the context of case study research, the term "theory" encompasses more than the common medical definition of a working probability-based hypothesis based on experimental evidence or factual or conceptual analysis (Merriam-Webster's Medical Desk Dictionary, 2002). Any discussion meant to define theory has difficulties. Merton (1967) recognized this difficulty:

> Like so many words that are bandied about, the word theory threatens to become meaningless. Because its referents are so diverse —including everything from minor working hypotheses, through comprehensive but vague and unordered speculations, to axiomatic systems of thought—use of the word often obscures rather than creates understanding (p. 39).

Sutton and Staw (1995) and Kaplan (1998) agreed with Merton (1967) that theories encompass answers to queries of why, and involve not just connections among phenomena, but are stories about why acts, events, structure, and thoughts occur. Building theory is a process. As such, it is full of contradictions and internal conflicts. In addition, while theory may often emphasize the nature of causal relationships and allows for identification of what comes first as well as the timing of such events, in case study research it also involves the design of research steps in according to some relationship to extant literature, policy issues, or substantive sources (Yin, 2003a).

Types of Theories

In addition to understanding what is a theory and the elements of theory-building, a researcher should develop an awareness of the various types of relevant theories. Through the process of reviewing the literature and questioning what is to be studied, why it is important to study it, and what the researcher hopes to learn from a study, a researcher can more fully explore pertinent theories and choose that type is most relevant to a study. Available theories can be categorized in accordance with units of analysis. Yin (2003a) was one of the first case study theorists to explicitly detail theory types and developed four theory types: *individual*, *group*, *organizational*, and *societal*. An individual theory is related to individual development; individual personality, perception, and learning; and individual interpersonal relationships. Group theories are concerned with explaining family, informal group, team, and interpersonal networks. Organizational theories explain bureaucracies, and organizational structures, performance. Societal theories predict societal relationships such as international behavior, market functions, and emerging technologies.

Theory Building

In order to build theory from case study research it may be helpful to discuss some elements that are necessary for theory building. Whetten (1989) delineated four essential elements as the "building blocks" of theory development. The first one is found by determining what factors (i.e. constructs, variables)

should be included in the explanation (theory). This judgment should be guided by evaluating the comprehensiveness and parsimony of the proposed theory, but keeping in mind it is preferable to err on the side of including too many variables rather than too few. The second element involves determining how the included factors are connected. This pattern delineation explicitly involves causality and seeks to preliminarily connect relationships among and between variables. Thirdly, a theorist justifies the selection of variables and the proposed causal relationships by providing a logical rationale that involves providing sound views of human nature or organizational/societal processes. Finally, limitations on the propositions generated by the theoretical model should be identified by answering questions of "who, where, and when." This type of mental exercise seeks to test the generalizability and contextual limits of a theory's core propositions.

In addition to identifying several theory building blocks, it is also helpful for researchers to eliminate from consideration research elements that should not be confused with theory building. Sutton and Staw (1995) outlined several such items that are critical to a research project, but are not theory. The initial element that is not theory includes "references." Referring to theory developed in previous research is a critical component in developing a context for considering a theory, but simply listing previous theories does not involve the third building block of theory building—explaining the casual logic contained in the listed theories. In addition, while organizational/social theory is based on data, data only describe observable patterns. Data does not explain "why" empirical patterns were observed. Data are also not predictive; they cannot explain what patterns are expected to be observed in the future. Data should not be confused with the inspired inferences. Just as data are important parts of theory, but are not the theory itself, so too variables and constructs are important to building theory, but do not alone constitute theory. Theory, according to Weick (1989), must explain why variables or constructs exist and how they are connected. Finally, hypotheses are also not theory. While they can serve as connections between theory and data, they do not contain logical arguments detailing why empirical relationships are predicted to occur. Hypotheses detail "what" is expected to occur, not "why" it is expected.

As can be seen from this brief discussion, building theories is not confined to quantitative research. Several social scientists, including Glaser and Strauss (1967) and Strauss and Corbin (1990) have defended qualitative research's ability to build "grounded theories" that can explain collected data. According to grounded theory, researchers can generate grounded theories from unanticipated contextual influences identified by either researcher or participants. Many grounded theorists adopted a positivist paradigm that assumed an objective, external reality in which the researcher allows for the existence of subjective realities among subjects, while the researcher adopts the role of an objective neutral observer who is able to "discover" data, develop analytic interpretations of data, and utilize these interpretations to focus further data collection (Charmaz, 2003). In addition to focusing data collection, developed theoretical frameworks allow for further refinement of theoretical analysis.

This *positivist* paradigm has been questioned by grounded theorists who have adopted a *constructivist* view that assumes multiple subjective social realities "created" by researcher and research subjects (Schwandt, 2000). This constructivist approach to grounded theory articulated by Charmaz (2003) is not rigid or prescriptive, furthers interpretive understanding, and can be adopted without adhering to the strictures of positivism. This reformulation of grounded theory is much more in alignment with Yin's (2003b) contention that a preliminary theory related to the topic of study should be constructed prior to conducting data collection. Yin's discussion of preliminary theoretical development reflects, in many ways, Eisenhardt's (1989) contention that *a priori* specification of constructs (i.e. conflict, power) can help shape the initial design of theory-building research because such specificity permits more accurate measurement of constructs if and when they emerge during data collection. If the constructs prove critically important, the emergent theory possesses an increased empirical grounding based on the utilization of triangulated data collection methods.

From this perspective, preliminary theory development (specification of constructs) is a research-design component, regardless of whether the ultimate goal of the research is to develop or test theory. The development of preliminary constructs places the case study in its appropriate context within the extant research literature. This type of theory development assists the researcher in more clearly articulating and addressing the study's questions, propositions, and unit(s) of analysis. By defining the unit of analysis (What is the actual case?), the researcher can more easily screen and select potential candidates. This screening also may suggest possible relevant variables and data to be collected as part of the case study. In addition, the theoretical framework which emerges from the specified constructs forms the basis for development of a logical method for linking developed propositions to collected data and interpreting the study's findings. (Note: These research design steps will be discussed more fully in the section, "Designing a Case Study.")

Figure 4-2 is an example illustrating the use of a theoretical construct to place a case study involving the Women's United Soccer Association in its appropriate context. The theories utilized assisted in clearly articulating the studies questions and propositions. In addition, several variables and important data that needed to be collected as part of the case study emerged from the theoretical frameworks. The theories also greatly assisted in the process of interpreting the study's findings.

TYPES OF CASE STUDIES

Building from various theorists' (Eisenhardt, 1989; Stake, 2003; Yin, 2003b) case study definitions and utilizing our understanding of case study methodologies, we can develop a case study matrix that describes cases by unit of analysis, purpose, and focus. This typology of case studies includes cases involving single or multiple units of analysis; cases with exploratory, descriptive, or explanatory purposes; and cases with either an intrinsic, instrumental, or collective focus.

The first type of case we can discuss is a single case. In addition, researchers also utilize case study research to study multiple cases. In defining case

Build It and They Will Come? The Women's United Soccer Association: Who Built It, Who Came, and Why It Failed (Southall, Nagel, & LeGrande, 2005)

Founded in 2001, the Women's United Soccer Association (WUSA) basked in the reflected glory of the unprecedented media coverage (11.4 Nielsen rating for final) and attendance (90,000 at the Rose Bowl for the Women's World Cup Finals) that accompanied the United States national team's 1999 World Cup shootout victory over China (Women's United Soccer Association, 2000a). The league was hailed as an historic culmination of several trends in women's sports in the United States: (a) Title IX's nearly 30-year influence on the culture and opportunities for women in collegiate sport, (b) the resulting, but specific, development of National Collegiate Athletic Association (NCAA) women's soccer's, and (c) the 20-plus-year boom in soccer participation among America's youth.

For any sport league to be successful it must generate sufficient revenue to cover operating expenses. There are several revenue sources that can support a league (e.g., ticket sales, broadcast rights, sponsorship, and merchandise). All of these revenue sources depend upon a sound marketing strategy for success. Although many components of a league contribute to its success or failure, this paper will primarily focus on the inability of the WUSA to either identify and communicate to fans, broadcast partners, or sponsors a single coherent marketing strategy, or to convince these stakeholders to adequately support the league.

Marketing Theories

Exchange Theory
In any successful business transaction all parties must feel there has been an exchange of value that satisfies the participants (Howard & Crompton, 2004). The desired outcomes are achieved only when the parties are willing to act in the best interest of all stakeholders or participants (Blalock & Wilken, 1979). Exchange theory is based upon three principles: *rationality, marginal utility,* and *fairness* (McCarville & Copeland, 1994). Rationality in marketing or sponsorship agreements focuses on the elucidation of the goals of all parties involved and the achievement of these stated goals. Blau (1967) and Homans (1974) contended that rationality was a response to presented agreement stimuli. A past favor-

able outcome for participants increases the likelihood of future agreements (McCarville & Copeland, 1994). Conversely, if a previous agreement has not fulfilled participants' expectations, the likelihood of any future agreement being finalized is diminished.

Marginal utility encapsulates the ability to obtain rewards and the value assigned to such rewards (McCarville & Copeland, 1994). Homans (1974) noted the existence of an inverse relationship between the ease and availability of compensation and its perceived value. Initial goals achieved during an initial contract period are not likely to be highly valued during subsequent negotiations. As a result, offering organizations must continually upgrade the available benefits included in their advertising or sponsorship packages. If the benefits remain constant, the law of "diminishing returns" often occurs. As a result, corporate partners may become dissatisfied with the status quo and demand new, more valued, benefits as part of any new agreement.

The fairness principle of exchange theory involves the perceived equitable distribution of rewards (McCarville & Copeland, 1994). Organizations entering into agreements seek specific and identifiable benefits (Kuzma, Shanklin, & McCally, 1993; Stotlar, 2001). If these benefits can be met through other more cost-effective means, the participating organization will be unlikely to agree to the initial agreement or renew an existing one. To ensure that corporate partners are receiving fair and equitable treatment, long-term contracts should have official (or unofficial) renegotiation clauses that allow both parties to propose altering the agreement's terms if the financial climate has changed since the agreement's inception (McCarville & Copeland, 1994).

Cause Marketing
Cause-related marketing (CRM) is most often defined as the public association of a for-profit company with a nonprofit organization, and is intended to promote the company's product or service and to raise money for the nonprofit (Polonsky & Macdonald, 2000). Pringle and Thompson (2001) described CRM as a strategic positioning and marketing tool that links a company or brand to a relevant social cause or issue, for mutual benefit. An example of a cause-related marketing campaign was American Express's 1983 involvement in the restoration of the Statue of Liberty. Cause-related marketing is not *social marketing*, which is the use by nonprofit and public organizations of marketing techniques in an attempt to impact societal

(Continued on next page)

FIGURE 4-2. Case Study Example 2

(Continued from previous page)

behavior (e.g., stop smoking, don't pollute, don't use drugs, don't drive drunk). Cause-related marketing attempts to link an organization's product(s) directly to a social cause through the implementation of a strategic marketing plan (Pringle & Thompson, 2001). Generally, an organization prefers to support "causes" that are of interest to its target market. Although there may be a philanthropic motive to cause-related marketing, the efforts of a cause-related marketing campaign tend to produce relatively short-term, product-related outcomes (LeClair & Ferrell, 2000).

Strategic Philanthropy

Strategic philanthropy evolved from nonprofit organizations recognizing the need for a new "giving" paradigm that combined elements of *benevolent philanthropy* (corporate giving and related activities not purposely aligned with the strategic goals and resources of the corporation) with a more synergistic use of an organization's core competencies and resources to address key stakeholders' interests and to achieve both organizational and social benefits (LeClair & Ferrell, 2000). It involves a company's long-term investment in a "cause" that provides societal benefits while also enhancing the company's reputation (Stotlar, 2001). Such strategic philanthropy may involve the participating organization's endurance of short-term business losses for the good of the cause and for the fulfillment of the organization's social responsibilities and long-term gain. As a result, strategic philanthropy requires support from a corporation's top management and shareholders, and coordination of corporate giving and employee volunteer programs with the overall corporate mission.

This redefinition of philanthropy recognizes that although businesses should be good corporate citizens, they must not forget their fundamental obligation to their shareholders and employees, and to the company's profit-and-loss statement. As Carroll (1979, 1991) noted, there are four components to the corporate responsibility model: economic, legal, ethical, and discretionary responsibilities. As a result of this need to synthesize organizational and societal needs, neither traditional benevolent philanthropy, nor strictly "business" objectives have primacy; both work in concert to benefit the other. However, it is often difficult for the various stakeholders in this process to discern where one element ends and another begins.

FIGURE 4-2. Case Study Example 2 (*continued*)

study research, Eisenhardt (1989) described it as an examination of the dynamics present within a single setting, while Stake (2003) defined a case as a "specific One," while allowing that a case may be simple or complex. A single case study is appropriate when the chosen case represents a critical instance that allows for testing a well-formulated theory. In addition, selecting a single case may be beneficial if it is either an extreme or unique case that may rarely occur, if it is a typical case that provides a representative example that is commonplace, or if it will reveal a situation or context that has not previously been explored. Although a single case may be unique, it may also reoccur over time, so a single case study may become a longitudinal case. In this situation, a researcher revisits the same case at various periods in time. This allows for the evaluation of a theory that posits how certain conditions change over time.

An often-leveled criticism of case study research is a lack of generalization. Evidence from multiple cases is often seen as providing more data to support a theory. It is important to think of multiple cases as analogous to multiple experiments, not as multiple respondents to a survey or multiple subjects within a single experiment. Using this concept, a researcher should use multiple cases to replicate findings from an initial case study by conducting several case studies. In some of these replicating cases, the researcher may attempt to duplicate the exact conditions of the original "experiment/case study." Such cases will be deemed *literal replications* that will predict results similar to the initial case. In other cases (*theoretical replications*), altered conditions will be considered and contrasting, but predictable, results will be theorized (Yin, 2003b). As can be seen, investigation of multiple case studies should be based on rich theoretical frameworks that can guide analysis of conditions in which a particular phenomenon will or will not occur.

Case studies can also be categorized by their purposes. The initial purpose of a given case study may be to explore a particular organization or situation in order to later develop hypotheses and propositions to be used in developing a theoretical framework to guide further research—a new case study.

By its very nature an *exploratory case study* involves fieldwork and data collection that is out in front of theoretical development. Such a case study is often viewed as a "pilot study," which is useful in designing a distinct case study. If an exploratory case study is not viewed in this manner, a researcher may mistakenly utilize the collected data in the later case study. Since the exploratory study or phase did not involve research questions, hypotheses, or even data collection methods, once it is completed, it should be considered complete and utilized as a resource or reference.

A *descriptive case study* utilizes a descriptive theory that delineates the scope and depth of the case being described. A descriptive case study does not simply involve random data collection, nor does it occur prior to the development of a descriptive theory. A descriptive case study must have a design (based on a descriptive theory) that allows for an examination (description) of the similarities and differences between previously developed theoretical patterns. A descriptive case study requires the development of "idealized" rival scenarios representing best-case alternatives. These best-case scenarios should be developed and reviewed by experts with no stake in the data collection. Data collection protocols can then be developed from these scenarios. It is important to remember that unanticipated findings are not precluded by the developed scenarios; such scenarios provide structure for the data collection.

A third case study purpose is to be explanatory in nature. An *explanatory case study* explains how events happen and so is much more aligned with an experimental approach. Explanatory case studies most often utilize either *factor theory* (utilizing correlation) or a causally linked explanatory theory to explain the case. Both types of explanatory case studies involve the identification of various independent variables. Some explanatory case studies simply discuss the degree of correlation between the independent variables and the dependent variable. Other explanatory case studies go further and posit a causal relationship between the variables. Because explanatory case studies propose a relationship between variables, correlation analysis, factor analysis, regression analysis, and analysis of variance are often utilized to account for interactions among independent variables. For many case study theorists, an explanatory case study's strength is dependent on the strength of the underlying theories (Yin, 2003b).

In addition to classifying case studies by their purpose, they may also be categorized by their focus. If a case study's focus is to better understand a particular case, without seeking to make any generalizations about other cases, the case study is termed an *intrinsic case study*. If, on the other hand, the focus of the case is to provide insight into a general issue or develop—or redevelop—a generalization drawn from the individual case, or a series of cases, the case study is an *instrumental case study*. With this focus, a particular case is of secondary interest. What is important is the developed generalization. Finally, a *collective case study* is actually multiple instrumental cases combined to allow for development of theories that can explain a large number of cases and/or generalizations (Stake, 2003).

DESIGNING A CASE STUDY

Now that we have discussed what a case study is, what a case study can do, how we can build theory utilizing a case study, and various types of case studies, we are ready to begin designing a case study. Fundamentally, designing a case study is no different from designing any research project. Research involves asking questions and searching for answers to those questions. Before you begin the process of designing a case study, you should already have asked other preliminary questions such as:

- Why do I want to do a case study on a certain topic?
- Should I do an experiment, survey, or archival search instead?
- Am I interested in conducting a specific type of case study? (See above discussion of types of case studies.)
- Who has conducted research on my topic of interest?

Based on these questions, a preliminary review of the literature can be conducted. Such a review should not be seen as just a step that has to be completed—a box to be checked off on the way to getting the real research started. A literature review should also not be seen as an end in itself. It is not just a search for answers—a catalogue of what is known about a topic—but a method for sharpening the questions to be asked about a topic. Look for what is missing. A thorough literature review should raise as many questions as it answers. After this initial questioning has occurred, the following guidelines will help you design a case study research project.

The first step in the design process is to develop specific research questions. Case study research questions guide the search for "how" and "why" answers. Because case studies are preferred in examining contemporary events in situations in which the examined behaviors cannot be manipulated, the questions developed should recognize case study's research limitations. For example, in developing a research question, you should ask yourself if there are any aspects of the question that cannot be answered by utilizing case study methodologies. In addition, if you can answer the developed research questions by successfully conducting a case study, how would you justify the significance of your findings to a reviewer? Will you have uncovered something significant, rare, or impressive? As can be seen, this initial questioning process should add precision to the proposed study. Research questions should have clarity and focus.

After research questions have been formulated, the next design step is identifying the study's purpose or identifying its propositions. An exploratory case study may not have specified propositions; nevertheless, the study should still have a purpose. Identifying and formulating propositions forces you to state and describe the theoretical underpinnings that will guide your exploration for relevant evidence. If the case study is exploratory and there are no theoretical underpinnings, you still need to describe the criteria by which you will deem the study a success. Propositions, therefore, should describe the theoretical framework(s), rationale, or direction of your research. At the very least, initial assumptions should be outlined. If there is an important theoretical issue to be examined, it should be detailed.

The third step in case study design is to specify the unit of analysis, or more specifically defining just

what constitutes your "case." Is the case an individual, several individuals, a decision or a series of decisions, programs, organizational change, or an implementation process? The research questions or propositions formulated are useful in guiding your selection of your case's unit of analysis. If you have accurately delineated your research questions, this will help in determining your unit of analysis. If you encounter difficulty in determining the unit of analysis, then perhaps your research questions are too vague or too numerous. By clearly defining your case, you can continue to clarify your unit of analysis and distinguish those persons or organizations to be included as part of the immediate topic of the case study. This focusing process demonstrates that the process of designing a case study is not necessarily a clear-cut linear process, but rather one that may involve revisiting previously listed steps.

After you have clearly developed your research questions and determined the appropriate unit of analysis, the next step is to establish how you are going to logically link the propositions to the data collected. By having an idea of how the evidence is to be analyzed, you can more easily prioritize your analytic strategy by defining and testing rival explanations. By being aware of rival explanations prior to data collection you can attempt to collect evidence about other possible influences. This logical consideration of alternative patterns and the investigation of possible alternative explanations is a crucial part of the research design process. It allows you to pretest your research questions and decrease the likelihood you are only looking for data to support your original hypothesis. Patton (1990) describes this logical linkage process decreasing a researcher's susceptibility to "stacking the deck" by pursuing other influences or logical explanations.

The final step in case study research design is to clearly articulate the criteria that will be utilized in interpreting the study's findings. What criteria will be used in comparing the rival propositions developed and determining which proposition best matches or explains the collected data. As will be detailed in the next section, this process of evaluating a case study's findings involves all of the previously discussed steps. As Yin (2003b) details, it is important for you, as a researcher, to develop these criteria a priori, since both your research design and findings will be subject to scrutiny by others. If you have not taken the time to evaluate your study's efficacy and develop tactics to answer the logical tests used to evaluate it, you put at risk the trustworthiness of your study's findings.

EVALUATING CASE STUDY RESEARCH DESIGNS

In designing a case study research study, the researcher should consider some basic questions about how the case's design will be evaluated. By asking these questions a priori, the result should be a better study. So, what are some of these basic questions?

1. What are the logical tests appropriately utilized to judge the quality of a case study's design and data collection?
2. What are some case study tactics I can utilize to pass these tests?
3. When do I need to perform these tactics?

Researchers or readers more familiar with quantitative research are familiar with the basic logical tests utilized to evaluate a research study's design and methodology: *reliability* and *validity*. However, one of the issues in qualitative research, of which case study research is a part, is the confusion caused by attempting to impose positivist or postpositivist definitions of reliability and validity onto research studies that have adopted constructivist ontology. As a result, many qualitative researchers (Guba & Lincoln, 1989; Mertens, 2005) have proposed replacing quantitative standards, such as reliability and validity, with more alternative qualitative referents. With this in mind, in our discussion of standards for evaluating the quality of case study data collection, we will utilize alternative concepts: *dependability* (in lieu of reliability) and *credibility* (instead of validity).

Dependability

Since change is a constant in an interpretive paradigm, it makes little sense to demand stability over time, but it is still critical to minimize errors and biases in a case study. Another researcher should be able to repeat an earlier case study by following doc-

umented procedures. To address this need for operational dependability through documentation, Mertens (2005) suggested the performance of dependability audits by members of the community of interpreters to "attest to the quality and appropriateness of the inquiry process" (p. 351). Yin (2003b) offered more specific tactics to overcome external reviewers' suspicions about a case study's dependability, including the development and use of a *case study protocol* and a *case study database*.

Yin's (2003b) proposed case study protocol should have the following components:

- An overview of the project, including objectives, issues, and relevant readings.
- Field procedures (credentials, case study site access, sources of information, and procedural guidelines).
- Specific case study questions to guide data collection, "table shells" for specific data arrays, and potential information sources for answering each questions. (A table shell is a table outline in which the rows and columns are clearly defined, but no actual data has been entered.)
- Case study report guide: Outline data format, use and presentation of documents, and reference material (p. 69).

Because any case study report should contain enough data to allow readers to draw their own conclusions about the case study, the development of a case study database is an important element to increase the study's dependability. The four database elements described by Yin (2003b) include:

1. Case study notes from investigator's interviews, observations, or document analysis.
2. Relevant case study documents arranged in primary and secondary files with annotated bibliographies to assist in easy retrieval for later inspection.
3. Tabular materials, including any surveys, observational counts, archival data, or other quantitative data.
4. Narratives and open-ended answers to questions in the case study protocol. These answers

should be answered by referring to relevant evidence (i.e. interviews, documents, observations, or archival evidence) (pp. 102–104).

Credibility

A discussion of a case study's credibility involves attempting to answer questions regarding the correspondence of the social constructs of case study subjects to the manner portrayed in a case study. In other words, are the researcher's inferences that a particular event resulted from some earlier situation as accurate as possible if the previous event was not observed. Prolonged engagement and persistent observation are other tactics that can increase a study's credibility. In addition, peer debriefing and discussions, and *triangulation* or *crystallization* of data sources, investigators, theories, and methods greatly enhance credibility. The use of multiple sources of evidence (e.g. field observations with diaries, numerous and extensive interviews, public records, personal files, and news articles) by multiple investigators may be a challenging proposition, but such triangulation/crystallization is invaluable in representing a case study's depth and establishing a study's credibility. (Note: Triangulation and crystallization are discussed in the next section, "Conducting Case Studies—Collecting the Evidence.")

The third example of case study is shown in Figure 4-3. It highlights complex legal, political, and public policy issues and utilized triangulation/crystallization, peer debriefing and discussions, and the use of multiple sources of evidence. The case study's depth and use of multiple data sources, investigators, legal theories, and methodologies greatly enhanced its credibility.

CONDUCTING CASE STUDIES

Now that we have discussed the tests used to determine a study's quality, it is important to address practical considerations and suggestions for actually conducting a case study. As with any project, proper preparation (including investigator skill assessment and improvement, and case study protocol development) is crucial. Part of our preparation process is making arrangements for conducting the study. Finally, guided by our discussions regarding

---

University of Minnesota v. Haskins: The University of Minnesota Men's Basketball Academic Fraud Scandal (Southall, Nagel, Batista, & Reese, 2003)

Analysis of Haskins' Employment Agreement with the University of Minnesota

Haskins and the University entered into a written contract effective July 1, 1992, for a term of 10 years. The contract was in full force and effect at the time the scandal arose. According to the terms of the agreement, Haskins was to "diligently and conscientiously devote his full time, attention and best efforts" to being head coach at the University of Minnesota. The agreement also required him to comply with the "laws, policies, rules and regulations" of the University, as well as the "constitution, bylaws, and rules and regulations" of the NCAA and Big Ten Conference. Further, he agreed to "attempt to have all assistant men's basketball coaches and any other University employees for whom Haskins is administratively responsible comply with" the same laws, policies, rules, and regulations (*University of Minnesota v. Haskins*, 2000).

The compensation terms of the contract included a base salary and provisions for annual raises, to be recommended by the athletic director and approved by the University president. The annual raises would "equal or exceed" the prior year's base salary, plus "the University's average percentage increase in the salaries of its tenured faculty." Further, Haskins was eligible for competition and administrative performance bonuses, media compensation (guaranteed to be at least $85,000 per year), and normal University benefits. Finally, Haskins was allowed to accept commercial endorsements, including operating a summer basketball camp (*University of Minnesota v. Haskins*, 2000, section 1.4).

In addition to the compensation provisions, the contract also contained extensive provisions for termination of the contract prior to the expiration of its primary term, including termination both for *just cause* and *without cause*. The contractual conditions allowing termination for just cause included the following:

- A major violation of a NCAA or Big Ten rule involving Haskins,
- A major violation of such a rule by an assistant coach with knowledge,
- Two separate major violations of such a rule by an assistant coach that Haskins "should have known about,"
- Commission and conviction of a felony by Haskins,

FIGURE 4-3. Case Study Example 3

- Substantial failure to perform the duties included in the contract, and
- A subsequent secondary rules violation by Haskins, after the NCAA or Big Ten had warned the University that Haskins' conduct evidenced a lack of institutional control, based on his commission of multiple prior rules violations (*University of Minnesota v. Haskins*, 2000).

Included in the for-just-cause termination section (Section 2.2 Deferred Compensation) was a detailed description of deferred compensation in the event that Haskins (1) was terminated by the University with or without cause, (2) died, or (3) became disabled. If the University chose to terminate Haskins' employment for just cause, Haskins would have been owed deferred compensation of $348,722.00 (prior to 7/1/1999) or $423,021.00 (after 7/1/1999).

The University also had the right to terminate Haskins' employment without cause by giving Haskins 90 days' notice of the termination. In the event that the University terminated him without cause, the University was required to pay Haskins his base salary, deferred compensation, media compensation, and University benefits for the remaining years left on the contract (*University of Minnesota v. Haskins*, 2000).

Legal Options and Remedies Available to the Board of Regents of the University of Minnesota

Faced with newspaper/web site headlines such as "Academic Scandal Makes Haskins' Philosophy a Fraud" (Ledbetter, 1999) and calls by local and national sports editors/columnists for Haskins' firing or resignation, the Board of Regents was in a precarious legal position. At this point, there was no legally sufficient evidence to support a just-cause termination under any of the contractual provisions for early termination. If the University relied entirely on media accounts, rumors, and hearsay to terminate Haskins for just cause, and did so without reliable proof, Haskins might file a breach of contract suit against the University. Further, from a practical standpoint, failure to prove the required conditions for a just-cause termination would leave the University open to negative publicity, including the dampening effect on the hiring of a new coach, together with possible charges of racism.

On the other hand, if the University decided to terminate Haskins without cause, then it would be liable for the balance of the agreed compensation for the remaining years of the contract. Moreover, the University faced the same potential negative publicity. The University was between the proverbial rock and hard place; either apparent legal option was perilous.

June 24–25, 1999: Haskins Is Bought Out

Apparently recognizing their tenuous position, the Board of Regents approached Haskins, seeking a mutual face-saving resolution to the dilemma. Rather than terminating Haskins through either alternative, the Board of Regents negotiated a settlement with Haskins, and he stepped down from his coaching duties on June 30, 1999 ("U chooses words carefully," 1999; "U of M reaches," 1999). The University "for the good of the program . . . [and] to restore public confidence" announced that a new men's basketball coach would be hired ("Mark G. Yudof statement," 1999, para. 2). Under the terms of the negotiated settlement, Haskins agreed to resign, in return for a lump-sum payment of $1,500,537.00 from the University. He also retained his faculty retirement plan and optional 403(b) retirement plan, received various transition services and expenses as needed for his departure, and received four (4) tickets to all University of Minnesota Men's home basketball and Big 10 Men's basketball tournament games (*University of Minnesota v. Haskins*, 2000).

In addition, the University and the Board of Regents agreed to the following: (a) release of all claims against Haskins in a non-admission of fault disclaimer, (b) issuance of public statement(s) thanking Haskins for his years of service, and (c) assurances that any statements regarding Haskins' resignation simply reflect the University's desire to *go in a different direction*, not an admission of any wrongdoing on Haskins' part ("Official Public Statement," 1999). University administrators, bound by the Agreement and Release clauses, were not permitted to publicly proclaim that Haskins was fired. As a result, President Mark Yudof's public statements could not raise the possibility of Haskin's direct involvement in the scandal. Interestingly, President Yudof not only refrained from making any derogatory statements about Haskins' possible culpability in the scandal, but proclaimed:

> He (Haskins) and his teams have provided many moments of entertainment and value for the university community and the citizens of the state of Minnesota. . . . The university is grateful for the 13 years of service Coach Haskins has provided and we wish him a future of success and good health ("Mark G. Yudof statement," 1999, para 3).

In a further show of institutional support and recognition of Haskins' "parental influence upon his athletes," University of Minnesota Board of Regents member William Hogan noted, "Coach Haskins' and Yevette Haskins' contributions to the community and church in general will long be remembered as the family approach that tried so hard to provide a sense of love and discipline to the players, and at the same time build their spiritual lives" ("William E. Hogan statement," 1999, para. 2).

FIGURE 4-3. Case Study Example 3 (*continued*)

dependability and credibility, it is important to outline and follow specified, but flexible, data collection procedures.

Preparing for Data Collection

Any researcher serious about conducting quality case study research should possess certain skills. Unfortunately, the requisite skills are not easily attainable, and no set method for their development is possible. In addition, it is difficult to assess a researcher's skill level, since there are no "objective" tests for case study researchers to pass before they can conduct case studies. However, a "good" case study researcher needs to possess and constantly work to improve certain skills. One of the most important skills is the ability to ask good questions and interpret the answers to questions asked. Consequently, it is critical that case study researchers be attentive and open-minded listeners and do not allow their own theories, ideologies, or preconceptions to limit what is "heard." Such an open-minded attitude must leave room for contradictory evidence. In addition, because each situation is unique, an adaptable and flexible researcher can turn a threatening situation into an opportunity for great data collection. Because reducing events and information to manageable proportions is critically necessary in case study research, an investigator should have an authoritative grasp of the issues being examined. If a researcher recognizes that he or she does not possess these skills, they can be developed. But, before skills can be developed or enhanced, an honest assessment of one's capabilities must take place.

Before any case study is undertaken, whether by a single investigator or an investigative team, a preparatory period must be completed. This training phase includes time for background reading on the case's subject matter, dialogue regarding the theoretical issues that affected the study's design, and delineation of the study's data-collection methods and tactics. Yin (2003b) contended that before any data collection takes place, it is critical that everyone involved in the study knows why the study is being conducted, what sort of evidence is being sought, what will constitute supportive or contradic-

tory evidence. Quite often this training can be accomplished by conducting a training seminar over an extended time-period. Such an immersion in a case study allows each team member to greatly increase their expertise and allows team members who may not have participated in the initial question-defining or research-design phases to become familiar with the proposed research project. Such training may also uncover problems with the case study plan or the research team's abilities, reveal incompatibilities among team members, or expose unrealistic deadlines or expectations. However, such negative possibilities can most often be overcome by confronting them early in a project. In addition, training may also uncover positive rapport among team members that suggests team pairings during data collection and allow for the development of investigation-team norms for data collection. Above all, such preparation will insure that the next steps of making arrangements for the study and actual data collection are more easily accomplished.

Arrangements for the Study

The designation of teams arises out of the preparatory phase discussed above. After these teams have been selected based upon the strengths/weaknesses, abilities, and skills determined during the preparatory phase, it is important that all team members have a solid understanding of the study's purpose. One way to determine each member's level of understanding is to have each person draft a brief summary of the project that can serve as a possible overview section for the eventual case study report. Having each team member compose an overview prior to data collection serves to perform another check on the team's understanding of the project.

The eventual official study overview that emerges from these member-drafts should be part of an introductory packet sent to all prospective individuals or organizations that may be eventually be a case subject. This introductory packet should include a formal introductory letter that serves to introduce a team member, briefly describe the nature of the study, and solicits participation and/or support for the proposed case study.

Case Selection and Conducting a Pilot Study

Case study research is a scientific endeavor. The research's purpose is to gain an understanding of the chosen situation or phenomena. For this reason, the specific case or cases chosen are expected to be representative of a population of cases. Due to the nature of case study research and its small sample sizes, random sampling is not warranted. Instead, purposive sampling is the chosen methodology, with built-in variety and intensive study the objectives of our research. You may choose to study an extreme or unique case, or you may have several possible cases from which to choose. In this situation you should develop a formal case screening procedure, based upon an examination of documents or asking knowledgeable sources about possible cases. Cases may be selected based upon the site's willingness to participate and the richness of the available evidence.

In some instances a pilot case study may be conducted to provide an opportunity to refine collection plans. The pilot study may be a convenient site, either because of geographic proximity or because the site has an abundance of documents or data. The pilot study is not a pretest, but is formative in nature; it allows the researcher to develop relevant questions and refine the research design. The pilot study will be much broader and will not be nearly as focused as the actual case study. However, a pilot study allows insight into conceptual and methodological issues, as well as the issues being studied.

Collecting the Evidence

Although everything that has preceded the actual collection of evidence is crucial to a successful case, no design will guarantee success. The case study data collection process is a complex one. This complexity requires that a researcher possesses flexibility and versatility, but there is also a need for methodological consistency and formalized procedures to insure dependability and credibility during data collection.

In order to collect case study evidence, it is important that a researcher be aware of the basic sources of such evidence. Although the richness and variety of evidence is a characteristic of case study research, there are several easily identified sources of evidence (Yin, 2003b). These sources include:

1. Documents: letters, memos, agendas, minutes of meetings, proposals, formal studies, newspapers, mass-media articles, Internet blogs, etc.
2. Archival records: service records, organizational records, maps and charts, databases, survey data, and personal records.
3. Interviews: open-ended, but guided, conversations with key individuals.
4. Direct observation: formal to casual data collection opportunities during site visits.
5. Participant observation: evidence collected by researcher while he or she fulfills a designated real-life, on-site role.
6. Physical or cultural artifacts: tools, instruments, works of art, computer printouts, or technological device.

Principles of Case Study Data Collection

In order to make the most effective use of the data collected from the identified evidence sources, and to increase the data's dependability and credibility there are a few basic principles that should be followed. These principles are applicable to other qualitative research methods, but our discussion will focus on their applicability to case study research. The data-collection principles include:

■ Using multiple sources of evidence (i.e. triangulation or crystallization),
■ Creation of a case study database, and
■ Maintenance of a "chain-of-evidence," which allows for a confirmability audit.

(Denzin, 1989; Janesick; 2000; Mertens, 2005; Yin, 2003b)

Triangulation/Crystallization

By its very nature, one of the strengths of case study research is the opportunity to access and uncover a wide variety of evidence sources. If multiple sources of evidence are not utilized in developing a case, the effectiveness of the case is often dramatically diminished. Because each investigator should also be viewed as a source of evidence, the use of investigative teams is also desirable. The concepts of triangulation and the more recently developed crystallization offer a methodological rationale for multiple sources of evidence. Denzin (1978, 1989) identified four types of triangulation:

1. Data triangulation: utilizing a variety of data sources,
2. Investigator triangulation: using several different researchers,
3. Theory triangulation: employing multiple perspectives to interpret a single set of data, and
4. Methodological triangulation: drawing upon a variety of methods to investigate a problem.

Richardson (2000) agreed with the need for a multiplicity of data sources and investigative perspectives, but she proposed that the triangle, "a rigid, fixed, two-dimensional object," (p. 934) inadequately imagines a fixed point or object to be investigated and triangulated. Richardson contended that there are many more than "three" sides to every story. A crystal grows, changes, and alters, but is not an amorphous entity. It is a prism "that reflects externalities and refract within themselves. . . . What we see depends upon our angle of repose. . . . [W]e have moved from plane geometry to light theory, where light can be *both* waves *and* particles" (p. 934) at the same time and for two different observers.

Both triangulation and crystallization deconstruct the notion of validity and within the postmodernist/constructivist paradigm proposes a complex, varied, and thorough data-collection process. However, within this paradigm, our understanding of the case, though deep, will still be partial. Although we will know more, we will doubt what we have learned. In addition, we will recognize there is much more to be learned.

Case Study Database

In drafting a case study report, the researcher presents a synopsis of the collected data, analyses of the data, and conclusions drawn from the analyses. In contrast to experimental or survey research, it is quite common and acceptable for the case study researcher to perform data collection and data analysis at the same time. It is possible for the researcher to present the "collected data" as part of a developed narrative in the case report. However, in order to allow readers to draw their own conclusions based upon an inspection of the collected data, a researcher should develop a distinct case study database. Developing and maintaining a formal, presentable database allows other investigators, theoretically, to review the collected evidence directly and not be limited to the case report.

Yin (2003b) outlined the four minimum components of a case study database: field notes, documents, tables, and narratives. Field notes may include interviews, observations, or content/document analysis. They may be handwritten, typed, or audio/video tapes. Retaining all documents collected during a case study may be problematic, but with modern electronic storage capabilities it is much more practical today. If it is determined that some documents will not be retained, an annotated bibliography of all documents should be created. Any tabular material collected on-site or created by the research team that was not included in the case study report should be organized and retained for later use. Finally, narratives, both questions and answers, should be considered part of the formal case study database and retained. By developing and maintaining such a database, the study's credibility, as well as the ability to conduct future projects, will be greatly enhanced.

Chain of Evidence

Maintaining a chain of evidence increases a case study's informational dependability by allowing an observer (i.e., the reader of the case study) to follow the entire research process, from the development of research questions to case study conclusions. The concept is analogous to the care of evidence during a police investigation. Detectives and other forensic personnel collect evidence, and it is placed under police "control" in an evidence room until being produced at trial. In other words, the case study report must contain the same evidence collected during the investigation. In addition, the report must contain sufficient citation to the specific elements of the developed case study database (i.e., documents, interviews, etc.). Moving back through the chain of evidence, if the database should ever be examined by an external "auditor," it should contain the actual evidence. Finally, the database should also contain a description of the time and location of data collection; and this should be consistent with what is reported in the case report. If a consistent chain of evidence is maintained, an external reviewer will be able to ascertain and follow the entire case study process, and see the connection between procedures and collection of evidence.

CASE STUDY ANALYSIS

After case study evidence has been gathered, it is important for a case study researcher to be able to analyze the collected data. Yin (2003b) outlines three basic and general strategies (listed from most to least preferable) for analyzing case studies: (a) relying on general propositions, (b) using rival explanations to develop an alternative framework from the one initially developed, and (c) developing a descriptive framework for organizing the data. During the initial phase of designing the case study, theoretical propositions—reflecting the study's research questions, review of literature, and newly developed hypotheses—were developed. These propositions guided data collection and, therefore, should be used to prioritize the analytic strategies. Theoretical propositions help the researcher determine which data to focus upon and which to ignore. The strategy of using rival explanations utilizes rival hypotheses that might have been included in original theoretical propositions. Developing rival explanations should have been part of the case study deign process and rival explanations should have been vigorously pursued during data collection and utilized again in the analysis stage. (Remember, we previously noted that data collection and analysis may often occur simultaneously in case study research.) A final analysis strategy is to develop a case description that can be used to organize the case study. Such a descriptive approach may help identify the causal links to be analyzed. Utilizing one or all of these analytic strategies helps guide the case study's analysis and help define and prioritize what to analyze and why to analyze it.

After a strategy (or combination of strategies) has been chosen by which a case will be analyzed,

there are several analytic techniques that case study researchers have developed. These techniques are not simply statistical techniques that can be performed on data; they are introspective processes that will take time and practice to master. Once mastered, however, they can be used to perform powerful analyses resulting in relevant and forceful case studies.

Campbell (1975) and Yin (2003b) proposed the use of time-series or other pattern matching logics to compare an empirically based pattern with a predicted pattern or series of patterns. The time series pattern can be simple, involving only one dependent and one independent variable, or it can be more complex, with two different patterns of events having been hypothesized and compared to the collected evidence. Other pattern matching techniques may utilize rival explanations involving patterns of mutually exclusive independent variables. In other words, if one explanation is valid, the other ones cannot be.

A specific type of pattern matching proposed by Yin (2003b) is *explanation building*. The goal of this technique is to build an explanation of the case by stipulating a presumed set of causal links and a resulting series of iterations. These iterations include:

- Making an initial theoretical statement or initial proposition about policy or social behavior
- Comparing the findings of *an initial case* against a statement or proposition
- Revising the statement or proposition
- Comparing the details of the case against the revision
- Comparing the revision to the facts of a *second*, *third*, *or more cases*
- Repeating the process as many times as needed (pp. 121–122).

Another technique that is often identified as a type of time-series analysis is compiling a chronology of events. Such a compilation of events is not simply a descriptive technique. Arraying events in a chronological fashion can be used to investigate presumed causal events. The purpose of this technique is to compare the empirical chronology with that predicted by a proposed theory. A chronology can be utilized in analysis, if the explanatory theory has specified one or more of the following conditions:

- Some events must always occur before other events, with the reverse *sequence* being impossible.
- Some events must always be followed by other events, on a *contingency* basis.
- Some events can only follow other events after a prespecified *interval of time*.
- Certain time periods in a case study may be marked by classes of events that differ substantially from those of other time periods

(Yin, 2003b, p. 126).

Case analysis is the most difficult and complex phase in case study research. Analysis techniques cannot be robotically performed; they require practice and are fraught with challenges. If a researcher can begin by designing and conducting simple cases, more complex cases can be tackled as more experience and insight is gained.

PRESENTING A CASE STUDY

Presenting a case's results is the most critical phase of case study research. Results must be organized so not only is the underlying theory is either confirmed or rejected, but the reader is able to find answers to questions of concern. Fundamentally a case study presents a series of answers to such questions. Questions may be organized thematically or chronologically, and may reflect the interests and concerns of various parties, as well as the researcher.

A case study's organization should allow for inclusion of important contextual and explanatory information and descriptions of the organization(s) and/or individual(s). Since presenting results in a mechanical fashion may preclude in-depth descriptions and a more fluid and creative reporting structure, a researcher must balance the ease of writing a case following a template with the need to provide a richer analysis. In addition, a researcher who does not believe in the expressed dichotomy between qualitative and quantitative research can utilize both types of data in presenting the case study.

The case study examples in this chapter demonstrate various methods of organizing the presentation of a case study. However, while each example's presentation protocol may vary, it is important to note the consistency within each case. Such consistency should extend to the use of parallel procedures and methods within each case study, especially a multi-case study with multiple investigators, and is critical to the design and conduct of a case study. The protocol should be readily apparent in the study's presentation.

In writing or presenting a case study's results, the researcher should refer to the study's protocol, which itemizes or details questions or issues that should have been addressed by the case study investigator(s) and the procedures that were followed throughout the field investigations. As the researcher's role changes from investigator to author/ presenter, the researcher can obtain data to illustrate the protocol's questions from a variety of sources: documents, direct observations, interviews, etc. As a result, the topics or questions in a well-designed protocol can serve as an outline for the case study report.

Stylistically, determining how to present a case study may involve asking several questions. Stake (2003) suggested several questions to be asked before developing a case study report:

- Should the report be a "story"? How much of a story should it be?
- Is it effective, relevant to compare this case with others?
- Should readers be left to draw their own generalizations, or should they be formalized in the presentation?
- How much description of organization(s) or individual(s) should be included in the report?
- How personal or anonymous should the report be?

As Stake (2003) noted, "Single or few cases are poor representation of a population of cases and questionable grounds for advancing grand generalization" (p. 156). However, he also correctly pointed out, "The purpose of a case report is not to represent the world, but to represent the case" (p. 156). Therefore, in presenting a case, the researcher should put forth a best effort to present a cogent and particularized experience for readers.

Evaluating the Quality of Case Study Reports

Although various researchers and theorists may vary in their preferences for utilizing case study research, there are some basic guidelines that can be utilized for evaluating the efficacy of a case study report. Whether the case study method is the only research design utilized, or if it is part of a multi-method research approach, there are certain areas that can be reviewed. These include the report's design, the data collection, the database management and analysis techniques, the reporting itself, and the level of impartiality and generalizability (Datta, 1997).

Many of the guidelines for evaluating a case study have already been covered in sections in this chapter (e.g., "Evaluating Case Study Research Designs," "Principles of Case Study Data Collection"). However, it is a great idea to develop a checklist that contains several questions for each area as a guide for evaluating other researchers' case study reports, as well as a tool for self-evaluation of one's own ongoing research.

Based upon several sources (Datta, 1997; Janesick 2000; Stake, 2003; and Yin, 2003b), some possible questions for such a checklist might include:

- Are the evaluation questions clearly and explicitly stated?
- How was the case selected? Is the basis for this selection presented?
- Are the data collection methods discussed fully?
- Are the data sources clearly and completely described?
- If the data collection methods appropriate for the case and its purpose?
- If there are multiple investigators, are they all properly trained, and is such training clearly delineated?
- Were there any differences in evaluators' interpretations? If so, were these differences resolved?
- Adequate information is provided to allow the reader to judge the generalizability of the conclusions.
- Does the report discuss the limitations of the study?

Concerns with Case Study Research

Because a case is, by definition, a particular instance, expressed concerns associated with the case study method involve not only the degree to which a particular case can be used to make generalizations about existence, but also the extent to which case study research exposes both researchers and those researched to more risk than other research methodologies. The elements of a particular case that make it a distinct occurrence must be balanced against the case's ability to allow generalizations to be drawn from it. Many academic researchers (Denzin, 1989; Stake, 2003; Yin 2003b) have noted concerns that case study research may be more appropriate as an exploratory means to lay the groundwork for studies that offer more generalizability. Because many case study researchers are intrinsically interested in the subject(s) of the study, it is critical that what is important about the case within its own "world" can be effectively translated or communicated to others.

Case study researchers face difficult decisions throughout the research process. They must decide how much and for how long a complex case should be studied. The case must be sufficiently described so that readers can experience and understand the situation and draw their own conclusions; however, not everything about a case can or must be studied. It is possible for a researcher to become either too focused on uncovering everything about the case being studied and lose sight of possible generalizable elements, or too committed to generalizing or theorizing that the researcher's attention is drawn away from the case's uniqueness.

Summary

This balancing act is part of what makes case study research so challenging. The various contexts in which the researcher may be placed and the varieties of evidence derived from diverse data collection points and techniques with which the researcher may be forced to grapple make case study research unique. In addition, since many sport-management researchers or students have limited social-science training, and are therefore unfamiliar with just what constitutes a case study, they are sometimes intimidated and reluctant to utilize the methodology in their research. In addition, while other researchers may not be timid about utilizing case study methods, they may view it as simply exploratory and subservient to other forms of inquiry.

It is important to remember that investigating individuals, groups or organizations, as well as other social and political phenomena, occurs within a social context. In order to understand such entities it is necessary to uncover not only "what" constitutes them, but also "how" and "why" such social interaction occurs within these socially constructed realities. As has been detailed in this chapter, case study research encourages our understanding of how and why this takes place.

In addition, case study research has the ability to serve an important refining or tempering role. Although a generalizable theory may be more easily realized through utilizing another research methodology, case studies have the ability to reveal the limitations of such generalizability by highlighting the need for further theoretical refinement and/or additional in-depth, specific investigation. Perhaps case studies serve their highest purpose as reflections of the human experience and their ability to speak for and to those whose "personal" cases may have gotten lost in a statistical shuffle. While not discounting the usefulness of a test for significance, it is also imperative to remember that such a test is "intended to assess the evidence provided for data against a null hypothesis H_0 in favor of an alternative hypothesis H_a" (Moore & McCabe, 1989, p. 478). Significance, in a statistical sense, does not mean "important." It is up to each of us individually, and all of us collectively, to determine the importance of our research.

STUDY QUESTIONS

1. There were several definitions of a case study offered in this chapter. List the similarities and differences of the various definitions.
2. Can you describe each of the following types of case studies?
   - Exploratory
   - Descriptive
   - Explanatory
   - Intrinsic
   - Instrumental
   - Collective
3. What are the five steps in designing a case study? Explain
4. What are the two standards useful for evaluating the quality of case study data collection? How do these two concepts differ from the logical tests (reliability and validity) utilized to evaluate quantitative research?
5. Why is the concept of triangulation/crystallization so crucial to a case's research effectiveness? Identify at least four types of triangulation/crystallization.
6. What are several of the strengths, as well as some of the limitations, of case study research?
7. What are three basic strategies useful for analyzing case studies? Which strategy do you find preferable? Why?

References

Bryant, P. (1985). *Positivism in social theory and research.* London: Macmillan.

Campbell, D. T. (1975). Degrees of freedom and case studies. *Comparative Political Studies, 8,* 178–193.

Charmaz, K. (2003). Grounded theory: Objectivist and constructivist methods. In N. K. Denzin & Y. S. Lincoln (Eds.), *Strategies of qualitative inquiry* (2nd ed., pp. 249–291). Thousand Oaks, CA: Sage Publications.

Datta, L. (1997). Multimethod evaluations: Using case studies together with other methods. In E. Chelimsky & W. R. Shadish (Eds.), *Evaluation for the 21st century: A handbook* (pp. 344–359). Thousand Oaks, CA: Sage Publications.

Denzin, N. K. (1978). *The research act: A theoretical introduction to sociological methods.* New York, NY: McGraw-Hill.

Denzin, N. K. (1989). *Interpretive interactionism.* Newbury Park, CA: Sage Publications.

Eisenhardt, K. M. (1989). Building theories from case study research. *Academy of Management Review, 14*(4), 532–550.

Glaser, B. G., & Strauss, A. L. (1967). *The discovery of grounded theory: Strategies for qualitative research.* Chicago: Aldine.

Guba, E. G., & Lincoln, Y. S. (1989). *Fourth generation evaluation.* Newbury Park, CA: Sage Publications.

Gubrium, J. F., & Holstein, J. A. (1997). *The new language of qualitative method.* New York: Oxford Press.

Hamel, J., Dufour, S., & Fortin, D. (1993). *Case study methods.* Qualitative research methods series: Vol. 32. Newbury Park, CA: Sage Publications.

Janesick, V. J. (2000). The choreography of qualitative research design: Minuets, improvisations, and crystallization. In N. K. Denzin & Y. S. Lincoln (Eds.), *Handbook of qualitative tesearch* (2nd ed., pp. 379–399). Thousand Oaks, CA: Sage Publications.

Kaplan, A. (1998). *The conduct of inquiry: Methodology for behavioral science.* New York: Oxford University Press.

Merriam-Webster's medical desk dictionary (rev. ed.). (2002). Springfield, MA: Merriam-Webster, Incorporated

Mertens, D. M. (2005). *Research and evaluation in education and psychology: Integrating diversity with quantitative, qualitative, and mixed methods* (2nd ed.). Thousand Oaks, CA: Sage Publications.

Merton, R. K. (1967). *On theoretical sociology.* New York: Free Press.

Moore, D. S., & McCabe, G. P. (1989). *Introduction to the practice of statistics.* New York: W. H. Freeman and Company.

Patton, M. Q. (1990). *Qualitative evaluation and research methods* (2nd ed.). Newbury Park, CA: Sage Publications.

Richardson, L. (2000). Writing: A method of inquiry. In N. K. Denzin & Y. S. Lincoln (Eds.), *Handbook of qualitative research* (2nd ed., pp. 923–948). Thousand Oaks, CA: Sage Publications.

Schwandt, T. A. (2000). Three epistemological stances for qualitative inquiry: Interpretivism, hermeneutics, and social constructivism. In N. K. Denzin & Y. S. Lincoln (Eds.), *Handbook of qualitative research* (2nd ed., pp. 189–214). Thousand Oaks, CA: Sage Publications.

Shavelson, R., & Townes, L. (2002). *Scientific research in education.* Washington, D.C.: National Academies Press.

Southall, R. M., Nagel, M. S., Batista, P. J., & Reese, J. T. (2003). The Board of Regents of the University of Minnesota v. Haskins: The University of Minnesota men's basketball academic fraud scandal: A case study. *Journal of Legal Aspects of Sport, 13*(2), 121–144.

Southall, R. M., Nagel, M. S., & LeGrande, D. (2005). Build it and they will come? The Women's United Soccer Association: A collision of exchange theory and strategic philanthropy. *Sport Marketing Quarterly, 14*(2), 158–167.

Southall, R. M., & Sharp, L. A. (2006). The National Football League and its "culture of intoxication": A negligent marketing analysis of Verni v. Lanzaro. *Journal of Legal Aspects of Sport, 16*(1), 101–127.

Stake, R. E. (2003). Case studies. In N. K. Denzin & Y. S. Lincoln (Eds.), *Strategies of qualitative inquiry* (2nd ed., pp. 134–164). Thousand Oaks, CA: Sage Publications.

Strauss, A. L., & Corbin, J. (1990). *Basics of qualitative research: Grounded theory procedures and techniques.* Newbury Park, CA: Sage Publications.

Sutton, R. I., & Staw, B. W. (1995). What theory is not. *Administrative Science Quarterly, 40*, 371–384.

U.S. General Accounting Office (GAO). (1990, November). *Case study evaluations.* Transfer Paper 10.1.9. Retrieved January 4, 2007 from http://archive.gao.gov/f0202/143145.pdf

Weick, K. E. (1989). Theory construction as disciplined imagination. *Academy of Management Review, 14*(4), 516–531.

Yin, R. K. (2003a). *Applications of case study research* (2nd ed.). Applied social research methods series: Vol. 34. Thousand Oaks, CA: Sage Publications.

Yin, R. K. (2003b). *Case study research: Design and methods* (3rd ed.). Applied social research methods series: Vol. 5. Thousand Oaks, CA: Sage Publications.

CHAPTER 5
THE INTERVIEW

OBJECTIVES FOR COMPLETING THIS
CHAPTER ARE THAT STUDENTS WILL
BE ABLE TO:

Understand the research objectives of interviews
as a qualitative technique

Appreciate the factors affecting the use of
interviews in problem solving

Understand the differences in types and formats
of interviews

Identify an appropriate setting to conduct
interviews based on the research objectives

Understand the roles of interviewers

Understand how to train interviewers

Follow the proper procedure to
conduct interviews

Appreciate the advantages and disadvantages
of interviews

A S ONE OF THE QUALITATIVE research designs, interviews frequently have been used by sport management researchers to provide in-depth information about a particular research issue or question through gathering the needed information from a small number of participants. For example, Goslin (1996) used interviews to validate the selected contents and instructional design generated from a survey for training sport managers in South Africa.

The purpose of this chapter is to introduce how sport management professionals can use interviews as a valuable technique in solving their research problems. Specifically, a number of issues related to the use of the interview technique, such as the objectives of interviews and the types and formats of interviews will first be discussed. In the latter part of the chapter, other aspects of the interview technique, including the place to conduct interviews, the roles of interviewers, the training of interviewers, and the procedure to conduct interviews will also be reviewed. The advantages and disadvantages of interviews will be assessed in the last part of the chapter.

The Nature of the Interview as a Qualitative Research Technique

The interview is a qualitative research method that involves a planned question and answer discussion session with an individual to collect information. It can be a challenging method, but it is a rewarding form of measurement. The interview is a common method of collecting research data in sport management. It is a traditional form of collecting information in market research. It is used less often in academic research in sport business, but could be used more often.

The interview can be conducted using the in-person method or conducted by telephone. The in-person interview is used more frequently because it has a number of advantages over the telephone method. In a personal interview, the interviewer can gain a better understanding of the interviewee be-cause the interviewer can watch for body language, voice inflection, changes in eye contact, and other observations that can only be made with an in-person interview.

Conducting an interview might seem an easy task. How hard can it be? Just ask some questions and record the responses, right? Wrong! Interviewing for research purposes is not so simple. The purpose of the interview, the questions posed, the discussion encouraged, and even the interaction of the interviewer with the interviewee can affect the quality of information collected (Berstell & Nitterhouse, 2001). It is also important that interviewers be trained to recognize their own biases so that recording responses can be done without bias.

Additionally, it must be understood that the interview is also a form of survey research (Kahan, 1990), which means it can be used as a quantitative research tool. A set of questions about a particular topic is developed in order to collect information from subjects. A survey is developed in a specific manner, and so is the questionnaire that will guide the interview. Detailed discussion on personal interviews as a survey technique will be provided in Chapter 9.

Objectives of the Interview

The primary objective of the interview is to get unrestricted comments and opinions of the subject's thoughts or why they behave a certain way. This information will help the sport management researcher get an in-depth understanding of these opinions and behaviors and the underlying reasons for them. For instance, Wagstaff, Hanton, & Cardiff (2007) interviewed 10 athletes for the sake of determining how individuals actually cope with organizational strains or stressors and their responses to them. The results of the interviews allowed the researchers to build a model of the athletes' stress story using a diagnostic approach.

It is very important to compile information and identify common themes among the opinions and behaviors. These themes will help the researcher understand consumer thought and behavior that can be used in decision-making about products, the company, pricing, and more.

Factors Affecting the Use of Interviews

The sport management researcher must decide when it is best to use the interview method as compared to using any other method. The interview is a versatile method, but it requires careful planning, preparation, and execution. The interview method provides an opportunity for the researcher and the subject to interact and to carry on a conversation; whereas survey or other research methods are primarily one-way communication from the subject to the sport management researcher. Using the interview method is best when in-depth discussion and information are needed. The interview is most appropriate in research when certain situations, as depicted in Figure 5-1, are to be considered.

> - When the research issues are not clear
> - When issues, opinions, attitudes, and motivations need in-depth exploration
> - When processes and other data need to be described in detail
> - When detailed explanation is needed
> - When detailed understanding is needed
> - When product testing is needed
> - When personal reaction is needed
> - When respondents are scattered and not available for group research
> - When a subject's story needs to be followed from beginning to end
> - When extensive comment and discussion is needed from the subjects
> - When the topic is sensitive
>
> Source: Hague, Hague, & Morgan (2004)

FIGURE 5-1. When to Use Interview Method

Interviewing is usually a question-and-answer session involving a planned set of questions designed to elicit information from the respondent. Another factor to consider is what kind of information is desired—qualitative or quantitative. If the research project is planned to gather opinion, insights, attitude, perception, values, and other such exploratory information, the interview questions and the session can be loosely structured and flexible enough to provide freedom to explore the topics without limitation. However, if the sport management researcher wants to measure and quantify the to-be-collected information, the interview should be structured with a formal and restrictive set of questions designed to gather quantitative data.

Figure 5-2 provides an illustration of the continuum of different types of interviews. According to the continuum, if the research project need is to explore a topic through discussion and discourse, then the interview questionnaire is prepared with the flexibility for conversation and discussion of that topic. On the other hand, if the research project need is for information to measure something, then the interview questionnaire is prepared with specific questions to elicit measurable responses.

Types and Formats of Interviews: In-Person, Telephone, Online

There are three primary types of interviews: in-person, telephone, and online. Additionally, there are different formats of interviews that can be structured and conducted. These include open-ended, fill-in-the-blank, binary choice, scaled-response, and unscaled-response interview format. Some of the formats are mainly for collecting qualitative information; others are for a quantitative purpose. The sport management researcher must determine what type and what format will be used. This decision will affect the type of information the respondent will provide as well as the possible alternative responses. Depending on the type of information de-

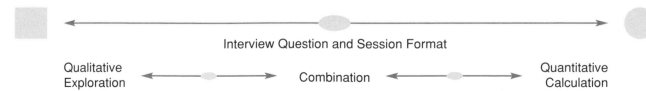

FIGURE 5-2. The Continuum of Qualitative-Quantitative Interview Method

sired, the interview format will generally have a combination of all of these formats.

Open-ended question format. An open-ended question is one in which the respondent is asked to make a response with no limitations or restrictions on the response. This allows for a spontaneous, unstructured response. However, the question should be tightly focused to elicit the kind of information that the sport management researcher needs. After the researcher has asked the question, that individual should be ready to record the response as accurately as possible. Sometimes, an audio recording of the interview is used so that the researcher can focus on the question and answer instead of having to be burdened with writing every response. The audio recording allows the researcher to record responses at a later date. Figure 5-3 provides a sample open-ended question interview questionnaire.

Fill-in-the-blank question format. This question format offers a relatively restrictive method for question and answer. A fill-in-the-blank question offers a sentence with one or more blank spaces that the respondents need to "fill-in" with their answers. This format is good for obtaining information needs of short-answer or simple-answer responses. For instance, the purpose of the question might be to get the respondents' information about attending sports events at a facility. The sentence would be: "I have attended {how many} sports events at this arena, and they included {list of events}." In the middle or at the end of each question, if it appears as though interviewees may be having trouble remembering what they have done, the interviewer may use probes or prompts—ways of getting respondents to recall experiences and other information. In the previous fill-in-the-blank question, if the interviewee begins to answer with

---

Interview Questionnaire for Atlanta Arena

"Hello, my name is _____. I am conducting a survey for the new Atlanta Arena on how the Arena can better serve your interests as a sports fan. As you know, the Atlanta Arena is being built right now; it will be brand new and is a privately owned facility that can stage a variety of sports events. We want to know what kinds of facility amenities you would like so that we can incorporate them into the facility. And we want to know what sports you like and would like to see in the Arena.

So, let me ask you some questions. Feel free to take as long as you want to answer them.

Question 1.

To start, did you know that the Atlanta Arena is being built?
  Yes ____ No ____

Do you know where it is being built? Yes ____ No ____
  Where? _____

Do you like the area where it's being built? Yes ____ No ____
  Why/why not? _____

_____

_____

How did you find out about it? _____

Do you like this idea? Yes ____ No ____ Why? Or why not?

_____

_____

Question 2.

What do you know about the plans (what facilities are being included) for the Arena? _____

_____

_____

Do you think these are okay? Yes ____ No ____ Why/why not?

_____

_____

Is there something in the plans that you would like to see?
  Yes ____ No ____
  Explain. _____

_____

_____

FIGURE 5-3. Sample of Personal Interview Questionnaire

"Well, now, let me see if I can remember that. I think I remember that I went to a basketball game, but I'm not sure if that was this year or last year." Then the interviewer may prompt with triggers such as, "Okay. Do you remember what teams were playing? Was it a pro game or a college game? Was it a tournament? Or was it just a regular season game? Was it men or women?" When the interviewee begins to recall with these prompts and offers more information, the interviewer can continue to prompt until it appears as though the respondent has finally opened the box of memories of those events and can offer more detailed information.

Binary question format. Binary means that there is only one of two possible answers. For example, the question would be obtaining a response of either yes or no, or true or false. This type of response provides clear-cut information of a brief answer nature. A sport organization might be collecting information about its experiences with staff. It could be looking for specific information related to staff training. For example, the Atlanta Arena has provided a full-day workshop for staff who work on event nights at the arena. The facility has trained the staff in specific behaviors desired so as to provide a welcoming atmosphere for every person who attends the event. Part of the training included requiring staff to make eye contact and greet each person who enters the Arena for an event with a "Hello" and "How are you this evening?" In addition, the facility wants the staff to then ask individuals if they need any help with directions or in finding their seat in the Arena. The facility also wants to know that the training of the concessions staff has worked. The concessions staff was trained to smile and make eye contact with every person at the counter; and in addition to say, "Thank you," and "Have a nice evening tonight," to each customer.

To measure the training, the interview questionnaire would include questions such as the following, all of which are yes-no questions.

- Did Arena staff greet you at the door with a hello? Yes or no.

- Did Arena staff smile and ask if you needed help? Yes or no.
- Did Arena staff answer any questions you had? Yes or no.
- Did you find the information to be helpful? Yes or no.
- Correct? Yes or no.
- Did concessions staff greet you with a smile and a hello? Yes or no.
- Did they say, "Thank you," after you completed your order?" Yes or no.

Although at first glance this might seem simple, it is designed to obtain information to answer specific research questions that the facility has. With the information from the interview, the company can determine if its training is working, or if it needs to reconsider what to do.

Scaled-response question format. This format consists of a question for which a list of alternative responses that increase or decrease in intensity in an ordered format. Often, these types of questions are called *ranking* questions because the question asks the respondent to *rank* something. Figure 5-4 shows how the scaled-response question responses are reported. This response contained a scale of 1 to 5. In this example, the interviewer would ask: "On a scale of 1 to 5, with 1 being 'least influence' and 5 being 'highest influence,' how would you respond to the following features about a graduate program in athletic training. The first item is 'identified points of distinctiveness' of the program. Does this have little influence or high influence for your decision to attend this program? Remember to answer with a number from 1 to 5" (Seegmiller, 2006).

An often-measured area of research for companies in the business of sports entertainment, such as professional sports, is consumer behavior. Specifically, these companies are in the business of selling sports as a spectator product—hence, spectator sports. Figure 5-5 provides an example of the questionnaire in scaled-response format often used to evaluate the factors that affect an individual's attendance at a sports event. The market researcher can then use this information to provide feedback to the com-

Table	Measures of Central Tendency in Rank Order by Mean		
Item #	Contributor	Mean	≠± SD
11	Adequate numbers of qualified faculty	3.86	0.39
9	Program director's strong academic orientation and interest in student professional preparation	3.75	0.46
4	Goals and objectives related to enhancing students' critical thinking skills	3.72	0.51
12	Adequate numbers of qualified athletic training staff and other allied health personnel	3.70	0.51
3	Goals and objectives related to increasing students' depth and breadth of understanding	3.64	0.58
13	Faculty and staff familiarity with program goals and objectives	3.61	0.56
17	Clinical experiences	3.61	0.60
21	Ongoing program evaluation	3.59	0.58
22	Analysis of evaluation results with periodic program revision	3.59	0.56
6	Adequate administrative support	3.58	0.59
5	Providing students with advanced knowledge and skills to prepare them for leadership roles	3.52	0.61
20	System of evaluating student performance	3.46	0.59
7	Day-to-day oversight of program operation, coordination, supervision, and evaluation by the program director	3.45	0.61
1	Identified points of distinctiveness	3.43	0.53
19	Facilities and equipment	3.43	0.58
2	Long-term and short-term goals and objectives	3.39	0.62
18	Admission criteria of NATABOC certification and an earned baccalaureate degree	3.37	0.70
14	Courses leading to a research experience	3.27	0.70
8	Program director's NATABOC certification and 3 years of teaching and research experience	3.26	0.77
15	Research experiences designed to expand the body of knowledge in athletic training	3.25	0.68
10	Program director's ongoing involvement in athletic training research and other scholarly work	3.20	0.73
16	Sufficient time and opportunity for research	3.16	0.75

FIGURE 5.4. Example of Reported Interview Questions Using Scaled-Response Format

Source: Seegmiller, J. G. (2006). Perceptions of quality for graduate athletic training education. *Journal of Athletic Training, 41*(4), 415–421.

pany. The company will then use the information to make any needed changes to the product—in this case, the facility, concessions, or event.

Unscaled-response question format. In this format, the respondent is asked to choose one or more options from a list. For example, the interviewer will ask: "Which of the following would you be willing to pay for a ticket to the Paralympic Games Opening Ceremonies: $50.00; $100.00; $150.00; $200.00; or other?" In this format, the interviewer needs to include a possible answer of "other" so that the respondent doesn't feel forced to select one of the provided answers. If the interviewee answers "other," the interviewer should then ask what "other" would be. In this situation, the respondent can then feel comfortable to respond with the following example:

Factors That Influence Tournament Attendance—Interview Questionnaire

1. Think about the many factors that influenced your decision to attend this event and please share your thoughts with me on a scale of **1 as No Influence, to 5 as Strong Influence**, or **NA** (or Not Applicable).

   Which of the following factors influenced your decision to attend the NCAA Women's Final Four Tournament? Please tell me what you think best reflects your opinion on a scale of **1 (No Influence)** to **5 (Strong Influence)**, or **NA (Not Applicable)**.

   (As the interviewee answers each question, circle that response on the sheet.)

1. Entertainment value of the games	1	2	3	4	5	NA
2. A chance to attend a championship tournament	1	2	3	4	5	NA
3. Availability of ticket(s) to purchase	1	2	3	4	5	NA
4. Price of ticket(s)	1	2	3	4	5	NA
5. Promotion of the event/media advertising (TV, radio, newspaper, Internet, etc.)	1	2	3	4	5	NA
6. Support of the teams playing in the tournament	1	2	3	4	5	NA
7. Dates games are scheduled	1	2	3	4	5	NA
8. Days of the week games are scheduled	1	2	3	4	5	NA
9. Tournament location/the City of Atlanta as a destination for this event	1	2	3	4	5	NA
10. Other activities taking place in the City	1	2	3	4	5	NA
11. The Georgia Dome as a venue	1	2	3	4	5	NA

2. The Georgia Dome as a facility for this event.

   What do you think about the Georgia Dome as a facility for this event? As I ask you about a particular item, rate it on a scale of

   1 as Poor, to 5 as Excellent., or **N/A (Not Applicable)**.

   (As the interviewee answers each question, circle that response on the sheet.)

• Facility location	1	2	3	4	5	N/A
• Directional signage	1	2	3	4	5	N/A
• Professionalism/courtesy of staff	1	2	3	4	5	N/A
• Food quality	1	2	3	4	5	N/A
• Food and beverage service	1	2	3	4	5	N/A
• Seating comfort	1	2	3	4	5	N/A
• Sound	1	2	3	4	5	N/A
• Content and clarity of video/message display boards	1	2	3	4	5	N/A
• Stadium temperature	1	2	3	4	5	N/A
• Housekeeping/building services	1	2	3	4	5	N/A
• Facility security	1	2	3	4	5	N/A
• Parking	1	2	3	4	5	N/A

FIGURE 5.5. An Example of the Interview Questionnaire in Scaled-Response Format

"Well, I really think about $75.00 would be about right." With this, the interviewer can prompt with the follow-up, open-ended question, "Why do you think that amount is about right for this event?" This prompt will encourage the interviewee to explain the perspective about that amount being about the price for this particular event. This follow-up question will provide a look inside the thinking of the respondent. In this particular example, the interviewee now has the opportunity to explain why this amount is how the ticket ought to be priced.

WHERE TO CONDUCT INTERVIEWS

The interview may be conducted in a number of settings. The most common settings are a residence, the street, the mall, a venue, and at an office designated for the interview research.

Residence. Using the interviewee's residence as a place to conduct the interview has advantages and disadvantages. The interviewee will most likely be more comfortable because of the familiar surroundings. This setting encourages the interviewee to open up for discussion and to share thoughts and ideas that might not be as forthcoming in an unfamiliar setting. However, typical residence activities can be a distraction, such as the phone ringing, kids playing, people coming in and out curious about the visitor, and a need to make the interviewer comfortable. Another disadvantage is the travel involved for the sport management researcher, who must determine the address and location of the interviewee's residence, then hope that typical travel setbacks don't happen, such as car trouble, heavy traffic, or other complications that could make the interviewer late or even miss the appointment altogether.

Street. Conducting interviews on "the street" also has a set of advantages and disadvantages. One of the advantages is that it is a good method for getting the opinion of the "person-on-the-street." This is often seen on television news or human-interest programs in which the purpose of the research is to gauge opinions or gain insight from the average person. The street interview, however, has its disadvantages. One disadvantage is that there is no control for sampling. The sport management researcher is left to get interviews from whoever is willing to stop and take the time to be interviewed.

Mall. There are times that the purpose of research and the sample needed will be people in a mall setting. For instance, the sporting goods retailer with a store location in a mall might want to measure shoppers' reactions to mall signage. The researcher will organize to intercept individuals in the mall and ask them to be interviewed. This is typically called the "mall intercept" method and is also used in survey research. The "mall intercept" principle is commonly applied in a sport economic impact study when the sport management researchers are strategically located in various locations of a sports venue to intercept spectators randomly to conduct interviews. For example, Bernthal and Regan (2004) conducted an economic impact study of a NASCAR racetrack on a rural community and its surrounding region. More than 1,000 spectators were intercepted and interviewed at a numerous locations throughout the racetrack. Additional discussion on the "mall intercept" interview method can also be found in Chapter 9, "Survey Research."

Venue. In the sport industry, there are a number of different types of sports venues at which research may take place. There are sports arenas, recreation areas, fitness facilities, gyms, sports clubs, golf courses, stadiums, tracks, trails, parks, complexes, and centers, to name just a few! Often, the purpose of the research project calls for the study to be conducted on site—that is, at the site of the event or business. Often, sport management professionals need to know what consumers think about their facility, business, or event. In that case, the research will need to be conducted on site.

Office for interviews. Interviews may take place at an office especially set up and designed for the interview project. This might be temporary based on the length of the project, or, if space is available, it could be permanent. For example, to determine the effectiveness of the LG Electronics' on-site sponsorships, Choi, Stotlar and Park (2006) conducted interviews at a temporary office set up at a sport facility used for the LG Action Sports Championships.

THE INTERVIEWER'S ROLE

The interviewer's role is complex and multifaceted. There is an *art* to the science of conducting interviews. Many of the basic skills needed to conduct interviews can be taught, but some of the characteristics needed are mostly innate. An individual is either comfortable conducting interviews with complete strangers, or not, although over time the interviewer can gain confidence and eventually the comfort level desired for conducting interviews. Figure 5-6 illustrates some of the skills of the interviewer.

Engaging people in conversation is an art. The most successful interviewer will be the person who has the ability to put interviewees immediately at ease and to coax them into opening up and sharing their thoughts and ideas. If interviewees don't feel comfortable with the interviewer, information will not be forthcoming. So, the interviewer's first responsibility is to make interviewees feel comfortable at the interview setting.

- The interviewer must be able to communicate clearly and effectively and at a level that the respondent can understand.
- The interviewer must be able to motivate the interviewees to do a good job. Explaining the research is a good beginning, but the interviewer needs to be able to convince the interviewees to want to participate fully and be forthcoming with responses.
- The interviewer must be motivated enough about the purpose of the research and the interview process that this is evident to the interviewee. After all, if the researcher isn't excited about the interview, why should the respondent be?
- It is a must that the interviewee be able to clarify any questions, confusion, or concerns on the part of the interviewee. This means that the interviewer must understand the research and all of its aspects so as to be able to answer any questions with confidence.
- The interviewer needs to be able to conduct a good interview. Each interview will have a life of its own, because each interviewee is a different person with a different personality and set of characteristics. The successful interviewer will be able to assess this quickly and make adjustments in style and method so as to get the most out of the interviewee.
- The interviewer's biases will have a negative influence on research if the researcher is not able to identify them, keep them in check, and keep them from seeping into the research project. Everyone has biases. The difference

The Interviewer . . .
- Is knowledgeable about the topic.
- Can explain the purpose of the interview.
- Can structure the interview process.
- Keeps the interviewee interested.
- Can communicate clearly and comfortably.
- Is tolerant of, sensitive to, and patient with provocative or unconventional opinions.
- Can control the course of the interview.
- Is unbiased in recording the responses of the interviewee.
- Can retain the information from the interviewee.
- Can interpret what the interviewee is attempting to say.
- Can engage personally with the interviewee.
- Can remain neutral.
- Is adept at transitioning between topics.
- Shows appreciation for the interviewee's time and effort.

FIGURE 5-6. Skills Needed for the Interviewer: The interviewer becomes successfully effective when the following skills are accomplished.

is when people know how to work around them and not allow them to prejudice their work or their research.

- The interviewer should always be confident. Respondents will feel easier about opening up if they believe that the interviewer knows the job.
- The interviewer must understand that difficulties will arise at some point. The interviewer should be prepared to notice these and to work around them or through them.
- The interviewer should keep the interest level up, be vigilant about the energy level of the respondents, and make moves that will lower the chances of their losing interest (Hague, Hague, & Morgan, 2004).
- The interviewer should close the session with an honest showing of thanks and appreciation for the time, work, and energy that the interviewee has shared for the project's purposes. The interviewer should be sure to comment on the amount of time the interviewee has taken for this and is truly thankful for it. The interviewer can also show appreciation by giving interviewees a surprise gift.

Interviewees are expecting only the offered incentive in exchange for their time and effort, and an additional surprise gift can let them know that the interviewer appreciates their "going the extra mile."

Training the Interviewer

Considering the characteristics and skills needed by the interviewer as outlined in the previous section, the interviewer can be offered training that will train the beginning interviewer and, secondarily, enhance the skills of the intermediate or advanced interviewer. The training can be in the form of workshops or seminars for those individuals who will be interviewers. Additionally, training can be offered through local organizations, and the potential interviewers can attend their training workshops. Either way, an individual who will become an interviewer will need some training. The following are some of the major topics that should be covered in training.

- *What is the research project?* The interviewer should be well versed in the details of the research project for which the interviews will be conducted. It is important that the interviewer understand the purposes of the research in order to ensure a more successful interview.
- *What is interview method?* The interviewer needs to learn about the interview method chosen to gather the needed information.
- *What is sampling?* The process of sampling is important. Interviewers need to understand this process so that they can relate to the interviewees during the process.
- *What is interviewer bias?* Interviewers need to know the many different possible ways that they can inadvertently, or even blatantly, bias the results. They must understand why it is important that they not bias the study. They must know that it is not appropriate to slightly slant the recorded responses so as to bias the results.
- *How does the interviewer conduct an interview?* Interviewers need to know the procedures of conducting an interview, from beginning to end.

- *How does the interviewer communicate with the interviewees?* A very important skill of the interviewer is to know how to communicate effectively with the interviewees. Some basic skills specific to interviewing should be offered in the training.
- *How does the interviewer record interviewee responses during the interview?* The interviewer needs to know the different possible methods for recording responses during the interview and should be skilled in these methods. Training should include practice interviewing and practice in the use of the different methods of recording responses.
- *How does the interviewer analyze responses?* If it will be expected that the interviewers will be analyzing the responses, then they must be taught how to do this. Refer to other sections of this chapter and book on analyzing qualitative data.

CONDUCTING THE INTERVIEW

When all preparations have been made, it is time to conduct the interviews. This section gives a summary of the process for conducting an interview.

- *Arrival and Preparation.* Do not be late to arrive at an interview. In fact, it is important that you arrive early and prepare the room and any materials for the arrival of the interviewee. Have everything ready to go. Have drinks and snacks on hand to offer to the interviewee. Be courteous and thoughtful. Thank the interviewee for taking the time for such important research.
- *Opening Remarks.* Once settled in, begin the session with prepared remarks. This opening should include such topics as the purpose of the research, confidentiality, feeling comfortable, directions to the restrooms, instructions about timing, and an overview of what to expect in the session.
- *The Interview.* Work your way through the interview questions. Use prompts and probes where needed. Allow the respondent time to answer questions completely. Ask every question—don't skip. Don't finish sentences; allow

the respondent to finish. Remember to ask the interviewee to elaborate where necessary. Record responses according to the interview protocol for that study.

- *Conclude the Interview.* When you have completed the interview portion of the session, thank the respondent. Don't be hasty. Allow a comfortable amount of time for closure.
- *Post-Interview Notes.* Just after the interview is completed, there should be time planned for going through your notes and making more notes, filling in where you left blanks, and completing sentences where you stopped. Do this until you are satisfied that your notes are complete.

ADVANTAGES OF THE INTERVIEW METHOD

There are some advantages in conducting interviews. In a personal interview, the interviewer gains a better understanding of the subjects' responses. The well-trained interviewer can use the face-to-face time to observe the subjects' body language and can engage them in delving deeper into explanations. This gets farther into the subjects' thinking as compared to other research methods.

In a personal interview, the subject has more time to respond to the questions and can ask for clarification when needed. Time is taken to be sure respondents understand the purpose of the research, the meaning of the questions, and what they need to think about when responding.

The interview also provides a slightly greater level of legitimacy than some other research methods. The interviewee gets to see the researcher, has the opportunity to ask questions, and will often open up for discussion more easily than through a written survey method. This way, it is easier for the respondent to explain why a question was given a certain answer.

DISADVANTAGES OF THE INTERVIEW METHOD

Increased Cost. Cost is a major disadvantage for interview method. Personal interviews are nearly always more expensive than other methods.

Whereas phone interviews can run up quite a phone bill, they are usually less costly than the personal interview.

Increased Time. Whereas a paper survey can be completed in minutes, a personal interview can take up to three hours of time. Additionally, the amount of time needed for the researcher/interviewer is greatly increased per respondent. In a paper survey, hundreds of respondents can be surveyed in a small amount of time; an interview process will result in a very low number of respondents in a large amount of time.

Decreased Sample Size. When a research method per respondent can take between one to three hours, the number of subjects will most likely be decreased, resulting in a lower sample size.

Increased Organization Time. Organizing an interview takes time. The respondents must be recruited, they must be enticed, and the interviews must be scheduled around their calendars.

Geographic Limitations. The personal interview has geographic limitations. That is, the researcher is limited to those respondents who are local, unless the company is willing to pay for travel of either the interviewer or the subject. If interview research is needed by the sports company's headquarters in Miami, for instance, and the customers or respondents for the interview are in Seattle, then the company will need to cover the expenses of the researcher's travel to Seattle, or for the interviewees' travel to Miami.

SUMMARY

In this chapter, fundamentals for interview as a research method are presented. The interview is a qualitative research method that involves a planned question-and-answer discussion session with an individual to collect information. The interview can be conducted using the in-person method or can be conducted by telephone. The personal interview is used more often because it has a number of advantages over the telephone method. In a personal interview, the interviewer can gain a better understanding of the interviewee because the interviewer can watch for body language, voice inflection, changes in eye contact, and other observations that can only be made with a personal interview.

There are three primary types of interviews: personal, telephone, and online. Additionally, there are different formats of interviews that can be structured and conducted. These include open-ended, fill-in-the-blank, binary choice, scaled-response, and unscaled-response interview format.

The interview may be conducted in a number of settings. The most common settings are the residence, the street, the mall, a venue, and at an office designated for the interview research.

The interviewer's role is complex and multifaceted. There is an *art* to the science of conducting interviews. Many of the basic skills needed to conduct interviews can be taught, but some of the characteristics needed are mostly innate. Considering the characteristics and skills needed by the interviewer as outlined in the previous section, interviewers can be offered training based on their level of experience with the technique.

STUDY QUESTIONS

1. What is the purpose of the interview as a research method? How does it differ from other qualitative or quantitative research methods?
2. Why is setting objectives important for interview research?
3. What are the different formats of interviews? Describe each one.
4. What are the different places where interviews might take place?
5. What does an interviewer do in order to conduct a successful interview?
6. What are the major topics that need to be covered in an interviewer training?
7. What are the advantages and disadvantages of the interview method?

LEARNING ACTIVITIES

Assume that you want to conduct a study to determine whether a new professional football league will be well received by the sport consumers. You have decided to use the interview as research design to gather information. Prepare a list of questions.

References

Bernthal, J. M., & Regan, T. (2004). The economic impact of a NASCAR racetrack on a rural community and region. *Sport Marketing Quarterly, 13*, 26–34.

Berstell, G., & Nitterhouse, D. (2001). Asking all the right questions. *Marketing Research, 13*(3), 14–20.

Choi, J.A., Stotlar, D.K. & Park, S. R. (2006). Visual ethnography of on-site sport sponsorship activation: LG action sports championship. *Sport Marketing Quarterly, 15*(2), 71–79.

Goslin, A. (1996). Human resource management as a fundamental aspect of a sport development strategy in South African communities. *Journal of Sport Management, 10*, 207–217.

Hague, P., Hague, N., & Morgan, C.A. (2004). *Market research in practice: A guide to the basics*. London: Kogan Page Ltd.

Kahan, H. (1990). One-on-ones should sparkle like the gems they are. *Marketing News, 24*(18), 8–9.

Seegmiller, J. G. (2006). Perceptions of quality for graduate athletic training education. *Journal of Athletic Training, 41*(4), 415–421.

Wagstaff, C., Hanton, S., & Cardiff, D. (2007). Coping with stressors encountered in sport organizations. *Journal of Sport and Exercise Psychology* (supplement), *29*, S210–S211.

CHAPTER 6
FOCUS GROUP RESEARCH

OBJECTIVES FOR COMPLETING THIS
CHAPTER ARE THAT STUDENTS WILL
BE ABLE TO:

Understand what focus group research is and
what its objectives are

Differentiate various types of focus
group research

Understand how to select and recruit focus
group participants

Identify the common places where focus groups
are conducted

Appreciate the important roles that a focus
group moderator plays

Follow the process to conduct a focus group

Appreciate the advantages and disadvantages
of the focus group method

FOCUS GROUP RESEARCH has been used by sport management researchers to solve their research problems for many years. The *Journal of Sport Management* published the first article explaining the use of focus groups as a useful qualitative methodology in sport management in 1992. In the article, Inglis (1992) argued that focus groups are particularly suited to research and practice in sport management and reviewed the features of qualitative methodology and merits of focus groups. Since then, many sport management research projects have adopted this methodology.

This chapter will open with a discussion of the nature of focus group research and the objectives of this type of qualitative research methodology. The common types of focus group research, the issues in the selection and recruitment of focus group participants, the common places where focus group research is conducted, and the important roles that a focus group moderator plays will also be discussed. The focal point of this chapter is the process of how to conduct a focus group. In the last section of the chapter, the advantages and disadvantages of the focus group method will be reviewed.

THE NATURE OF FOCUS GROUPS AS A QUALITATIVE RESEARCH TECHNIQUE IN SPORT MANAGEMENT

The focus group is a research method used to collect information through a structured question-and-discussion activity with a targeted group of individuals. The individuals are recruited, based on the commonality of their experience, by the researcher to discuss a topic. It is called a "focus" group because the researcher, in the role of moderator, presents a topic for a focused discussion and keeps the group's individuals focused on the discussion of that particular topic.

The focus group method is used when a research topic can't be explored as well as other methods allow. The focus group method is flexible, whereas other research methods are much more formalized. Other methods are limited in what information they can collect and don't allow for as much in-depth discussion and exploration of a topic. Therefore, the focus group method is used when the researcher needs unstructured, unlimited, and spontaneous discussion about a topic. Additionally, the focus group information is qualitative data that is "rich in words and descriptions, rather than numbers" (Hague, Hague, & Morgan, 2004, p. 49).

The researcher uses a structured method but allows for flexibility as the discussion progresses. Typically, the size of a focus group ranges from 5 to 10 people, although it may be larger. The group needs to be small enough to allow each person the opportunity to share thoughts, reactions, experiences, perceptions, and opinions. Larger groups can inhibit input from every individual because shyer ones will talk less, allowing the group discussion to be controlled by the more outspoken individuals in the group. The disadvantage in this is that the researcher doesn't get the interaction and diversity of opinion and experience.

An example of the use of focus groups as main research design in sport management research is the study that was conducted by Taylor, Marcy, Hoye, & Guskelly (2006). Using psychological contract theory to explore the set of expectations and obligations that community sport club volunteers regard as part of their volunteering experience, the researchers conducted 16 focus groups with 98 community sports club administrators about the methods used to manage volunteers and the organizational expectations of the volunteers. The participants consisted of board or committee members including presidents, secretaries, and registrars as well as one paid employee with responsibility for managing club rugby.

Objectives of Focus Group Research

There are three main objectives of focus group research:

- To generate ideas
- To provide in-depth qualitative information about the focus group participants
- To discover the participants' needs, attitudes, characteristics, and perceptions about issues of interest to a sport organization

To "generate ideas" means that the focus group will be used to discover and develop new ideas about the products, the service, and many other aspects of a sport organization. For instance, to determine what consumers think about the Georgia Dome as a sports facility, the sport management researcher used focus group research to discover that consumers like the seating arrangements of the Dome, but that sound in the Dome was thought to be too loud, and it warbled, echoed, and reverberated too much for it to be enjoyed ultimately. The consumers revealed that in today's world of digitally mastered sound, the sound in the Dome doesn't measure up. Some of the individuals in the group said that the sound was distracting from the event, so much that for certain events, the consumers said they would not attend additional similar events in the future. With this new information and feedback from its consumers, the Georgia Dome now has information that can be used to make changes to a certain element of its product.

To "provide in-depth qualitative information" about the consumer means that the sport management researcher will collect a deeper set of quality information about the focus group participants than would be possible with other research methods. Often, after some research has been conducted, the researcher is left asking more questions based on the data collected. However, with these methods, the data set is final. That is, the researcher must attempt to interpret the data without further input of explanation from the consumer. In focus group research, the researcher has the opportunity to question the participants directly and to ask them to explain the meaning behind their responses.

To discover the needs, attitudes, perceptions, and likes of the participants means that the researcher can collect information directly from those people who participated in the focus group about what they like or dislike, what they think works or doesn't work, or how they perceive a product or the service provided, or the image or reputation of a sport organization.

Types of Focus Groups

Focus group method is adopted based on the purpose of the research. A focus group session can have the purpose of discussing a television commercial, obtaining feedback on testing, determining reaction to and perception of a product idea, brainstorming about the modification of a product to meet consumer needs, or seeking suggestions from the employees of a sport organization for reform. This can lead to different types of sessions, as follows.

Stand-alone method. In this method, the data and information collected from the focus groups are the singular set of data for the research. No other type of research is conducted to supplement the focus group research. Thus, the sport management researcher must be careful that this research method will provide all that is needed.

Survey supplement. In this method, the data collected from the focus groups are supplementary to another research method, such as a survey. This combination of research methods provides the opportunity for further information that can enhance and contribute to the overall conclusions and recommendations.

Multiple-method design. Here, the focus group research is one of several methods of research being used to study a topic. This will add even more depth and breadth of information to contribute to the conclusions and recommendations. A good example of this approach is the study conducted by Funk, Ridinger, and Moorman (2003). They used focus groups comprising women's basketball season ticket holders to clarify the conceptual framework of the Sport Interest Inventory (SII) and to identify if any contextual motives related to basketball exist that have not been found in the literature.

Online focus group methods. With the use of the Internet continuing to increase, its use in research methodologies is also increasing. Conducting a focus group in an online environment has become a reality. Various *blogs* or *chat rooms* have been used to obtain information. The biggest advantage of the online focus group method is that it seeks information from the participants who are not physically located in the same place. For example, in a study that examined the consequences of work-family conflict with 41 mothers who are Division I head coaches,

Bruening and Dixon (2007) used asynchronous online focus groups in data collection. They believe that the online focus groups not only have similar properties to the traditional in-person focus groups (i.e., in-depth discussion and the ability to build off of each other's discussion), but also allow sport management researchers to gather a group of participants who could not otherwise meet.

Such method, however, does come with a specific set of limitations. The participants are limited to their skills of expressing their opinions through writing. Additionally, the moderator is limited in observing the participants and thus is limited in the use of effective group dynamics.

Another online method is the *video conference,* or *streaming media,* focus group. This can limit who can participate to those who have the equipment needed for video conferencing or streaming media. On the other hand, this method can be used to connect a company representative in one area of the country to a moderator and focus group meeting in another area of the country.

Selecting Focus Group Participants

The participants in a focus group are selected specifically for their similar characteristics based on what the research is exploring. Other relevant attributes may play a part in the selection process if the topic warrants. For instance, a city's sports council is considering whether to bring a WNBA franchise to the city. The type of participant needed for open discussion about the feasibility and potential popularity and support for this product should come from individuals who are sports fans. These individuals might be found as local season ticket holders of other professional or college sports in the area—especially basketball fans. The focus of the discussion would be to determine if there would be enough interest for the product to start with an initial supporting fan base, and build ticket sales and fan support from there.

The participants in the group should have similar demographics or other characteristics because they may well be strangers who are meeting for the first time and will be expected to openly share their ideas. The more they have in common, the more they will feel comfortable with each other and thus sharing their thoughts.

Recruiting Focus Group Participants

Focus group participants should be recruited based on the purpose and focus of the research. The researcher will first determine where such individuals can be found. For instance, using the example above, to find basketball fans who could give feedback on the aspects of bringing a WNBA franchise to a city, the sport management researcher could ask local professional and college basketball organizations for their season ticket holder list. Other groups who might be interested in a WNBA franchise would be high school basketball players and fans. Additionally, because there is crossover interest in watching different sports, fans of any other local professional sports teams could be considered for selection.

Incentives should be a serious consideration. The researcher will be asking an individual to give up one or two hours of their time. Thus, offering an enticement for the person to show up is common practice. Some incentives typically used include a gift, dinner, free products, gift certificate, and monetary compensation. Using an incentive doesn't ensure that the participant will show up, but it can help in sealing the deal. In fact, "no-shows" are a problem that must be included into the plan of the research. One way to overcome the problem is to overrecruit potential participants. Another method is to use a backup list of individuals who have promised to be substitutes. A confirmation call is made as a way to find out whether or not an individual can make it to the session. If something has come up, then the list of backups will be consulted and someone from that list will be called and invited to join the group.

The Number of Groups or Sessions

There are no rules about how many focus groups to get or how many sessions to hold. One focus group might give information that the sport management researcher deems reliable and useful; another similar group might turn out to be a flop. Multiple groups can be planned if different market groups are sought.

To acquire information that will increase the researcher's confidence level, the best plan is to have three or four focus group sessions. However, the higher the number of groups, the more difficult it is to draw conclusions from and analyze the information.

A Place to Stage the Focus Group Session

Staging the session is important. For the traditional, face-to-face focus group sessions, the researcher must plan to conduct the session in a setting that is clean, bright, warm, and welcoming. This will help the group members feel comfortable and thus help in getting them to open up for discussion. It is the researcher's job to create an atmosphere in which the focus group participants can feel secure, intimate, and comfortable about expressing their opinions openly in this type of setting.

Traditionally, focus group sessions can take place in a variety of settings: a hotel meeting room, a conference room, a convention area, or an exhibition room. There are no rules about what kind of setting is required. It should be a venue that is of good quality, convenient, accessible, and one in which the focus group participants are taken good care of upon arrival. The ideal setting is a dedicated focus group facility. This can be a cluster of rooms dedicated specifically for the purpose of the focus group gatherings and sessions. It can also be comprised of only one room. Most focus group rooms are set up similarly to a conference or board room with a large table and comfortable chairs around it. Some are configured with a set of chairs facing a screen where film can be shown for feedback. In the cluster setting, there may be one room dedicated as a reception area, another room set up board meeting style, another room as a viewing room, and another room set up as a break room with kitchen and resting areas.

The Focus Group Moderator

The person who will run the focus group session is the moderator. The opening remarks by the focus group moderator are important because they will set the stage and tone for the session.

Focus group moderators need to be influential individuals as the effectiveness of a focus group session depends to a great extent upon the ability of the moderator to keep the session on track Accordingly, the moderator must be skilled in observation and interpersonal communication, as well as group dynamics, in order to manage a productive focus group session. The moderator must understand exactly what information is needed in this research project and the purpose and objectives of the research in order to be successful at leading discussion and phrasing questions so as to get the individuals to effectively participate. Figures 6-1 and Figure 6-2 present moderator suggestions for enhancing a positive experience for the group.

The Focus Group Process

As with any research method, there is a general process to be followed when conducting focus group research. Figure 6.3 offers an illustration of a process in setting up a focus group.

Develop proposal. The first step in the process of developing a focus group research proposal is to develop a precise and specific purpose statement and research objectives. Based on the purpose statement and research objectives, the sport management researcher can develop the right questions to collect the needed information through the focus group and identify the right group of participants.

Develop a research time. The sport management researcher must have a clear sense of the length of executing each of the tasks involved in the focus group research. For example, how long will it take to identify the participants, develop and test the focus group questions, invite and follow up with the participants, etc. The following are timelines suggested by Simon (1999) for a number of preparatory activities for a focus group session:

- Write the purpose statement: 6–8 weeks prior
- Identify the participants: 6–8 weeks prior
- Select a moderator: 4–5 weeks prior
- Develop the questions and write a script: 4–5 weeks prior
- Write and send out invitations to the participants: 3–4 weeks prior

- To steer the discussion through a range of topics relevant to the research question
- To be a catalyst to encourage responses from the participants
- To encourage those who are quiet to participate in the discussion, and to limit those who are outspoken to keep them from monopolizing the conversation
- To provide audio or visual materials if needed for the discussion
- To keep the discussion on track
- To manage the group dynamics
- To steer the discovery of information by guiding the participants with questions of why, how, and what
- To show appreciation for the interviewee's time and effort

FIGURE 6-1. The Focus Group Moderator's Role

- Follow up the invitations with phone calls: 2 weeks prior
- Place a reminder call to the participants: 2 days prior

Develop participant guidelines and process. As part of the proposal process, characteristics of focus group participants will be considered and clearly defined. What are the characteristics of individuals needed for these discussions? Where will these people be found? What incentives will be available to entice participants? How will the participants be approached and asked to participate?

Develop moderator's discussion guide. Formulate the questions and topic areas that the moderator will need to cover during the focus group.

How do you make your groups great every time?	Be prepared. Be energized. Be nice but firm. Make sure everything about the experience is comfortable.
How do you build rapport quickly?	Make meaningful eye contact during each person's introduction. Learn and remember names. Let them create their own name cards. Welcome folks as they come into the room and use small talk.
How do you bring a drifting group back into focus?	Tell them that topic is for another group or time and that they need to focus on the topic for this group and time. Make a note and tell them that they will come back to this topic if there is time. Suggest that they can talk about it on their own after the focus group is over.
How do you get them to talk about deeper things than top-of-the-mind answers?	Play naïve or dumb and ask them to help you understand by explaining. Use probes such as "Tell us more about that," or "Can you go deeper on that?" Ask for specifics such as "Tell me about the last time that you . . ." Pair them up and give them 10 minutes for each pair to come up with a solution or suggestion.
What about management of the "back room" where your clients are observing?	Orient clients with a 10-minute overview of focus groups, research objectives, and what to expect. Check with the clients during breaks, written exercises, and so on to make sure things are going well. Have an associate or colleague there to work with the clients. If you don't have an associate for the back room, ask the client to select one person to be the point person to communicate with you.

FIGURE 6-2. "Tricks of the Trade" for the Focus Group Moderator

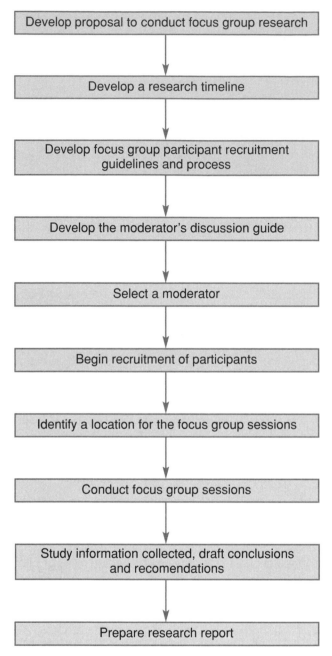

```
┌─────────────────────────────────────────────┐
│ Develop proposal to conduct focus group research │
└─────────────────────────────────────────────┘
                       ↓
┌─────────────────────────────────────────────┐
│          Develop a research timeline          │
└─────────────────────────────────────────────┘
                       ↓
┌─────────────────────────────────────────────┐
│  Develop focus group participant recruitment  │
│             guidelines and process             │
└─────────────────────────────────────────────┘
                       ↓
┌─────────────────────────────────────────────┐
│    Develop the moderator's discussion guide   │
└─────────────────────────────────────────────┘
                       ↓
┌─────────────────────────────────────────────┐
│             Select a moderator                │
└─────────────────────────────────────────────┘
                       ↓
┌─────────────────────────────────────────────┐
│         Begin recruitment of participants     │
└─────────────────────────────────────────────┘
                       ↓
┌─────────────────────────────────────────────┐
│ Identify a location for the focus group sessions │
└─────────────────────────────────────────────┘
                       ↓
┌─────────────────────────────────────────────┐
│          Conduct focus group sessions         │
└─────────────────────────────────────────────┘
                       ↓
┌─────────────────────────────────────────────┐
│ Study information collected, draft conclusions │
│              and recomendations                │
└─────────────────────────────────────────────┘
                       ↓
┌─────────────────────────────────────────────┐
│          Prepare research report              │
└─────────────────────────────────────────────┘
```

FIGURE 6-3. Focus Group Organization Process

These should be questions specifically developed to guide the discussions toward the needed information. Since a focus group session usually lasts one to two hours, the moderator may only have time to ask and probe four to five in-depth questions. The focus group questions should be open-ended to invite thorough discussion. The moderator needs to proceed from the general to the specific.

The moderator could develop a discussion guide or script. The guide begins with an introductory section that describes the nature of a focus group to the participants. Then it outlines and describes the topics to be covered. The third part of the guide is to thank the participants, provide them with the moderator's contact information should they have additional comments or input, and explain how the information collected will be used. The reasons for using a discussion guide are several-fold. First, it helps to ensure that all sessions will be conducted in a similar manner so that the results will be reliable. Secondly, the discussion guide will help the moderator focus on the tasks (Simon, 1999).

Select the moderator. As mentioned above, the success of a focus group session depends greatly on the moderator. Thus, the selection of skilled and experienced moderator is one of the steps in focus group research whose importance should not be overlooked. The moderator could be the researcher himself or herself or a professional who specializes in focus group moderation.

Begin participant recruitment. After the focus group participant recruitment process has been started, it needs to be conducted until enough participants have agreed to participate. The researcher should be sure that enough information has been given to the participants about the activity, where to meet, what time to meet, what to bring and not bring, and any other information they will need before attending the group session. To ensure that an adequate number of people will participate in the focus group session, the researcher must follow up with the invited participants by phone calls or emails to remind them of the scheduled focus group session.

Identify a location to conduct the session. As discussed previously, a focus group session could be conducted in a number of different locations. Regardless of the chosen location, the sport management researcher should keep in mind that the number one criterion in location selection is that it be a setting where participants will feel comfortable to provide their opinions. Simon

(1999) suggests that the following questions be asked while choosing a location for the focus group session (pp. 5–6):

- What message does the setting send? (Is it corporate, upscale, cozy, informal, sterile, inviting?)
- Does the setting encourage conversation?
- How will the setting affect the information gathered? Will the setting bias the information offered?
- Can it comfortably accommodate nine to fifteen people? (six to twelve participants plus the moderators), so that all can view one another?
- Is it easily accessible? (Consider access by people with disabilities, safety, transportation, parking, etc.)

Conduct focus group. After everything has been planned and coordinated, it is now time to conduct the focus group session(s). The researcher must prepare beforehand with the venue and other logistical needs for the sessions. Having a welcome area for the participants as they arrive provides them with a good first impression and helps make them more comfortable.

Analyze data. After the sessions have been conducted, it is time to study the data collected. As with most qualitative research, great care must be given to this process so that researcher bias can be kept to a minimum. The researcher needs to formulate conclusions based on the information and develop recommendations based on the conclusions.

Prepare report. Preparing a final report is the last step of the process. In this stage, the researcher can put together the full report of the focus group research.

ADVANTAGES AND DISADVANTAGES OF THE FOCUS GROUP METHOD OF RESEARCH

Every method of research has advantages and disadvantages. The focus group method is quick, inexpensive, and relatively easy to conduct. It can obtain rich data in participants' own words and developing deeper insights, and the focus group session allows participants to build on one another's responses and come up with ideas they might not have thought of in one-on-one interviews. Focus group research also has disadvantages, limitations, and shortcomings similar to those of other forms of qualitative research. As a specific disadvantage, focus group research *must* have a competent and experienced moderator. Without a skilled moderator, the session will be ineffective and the results will be questionable. Secondly, focus group participants are chosen for their similarity of characteristics. This is a limitation because such a homogeneous group may not be representative of the whole population. Thirdly, a few dominant focus group members can skew a session.

A FOCUS GROUP CASE IN SPORT MANAGEMENT

Rehman and Frisby (2000) conducted a study to examine the work experience of women consultants in the fitness and sport industry to test the two competing theories on self-employment for women. The liberation theory believes that self-employment gives women a sense of self-fulfillment, autonomy, and control; substantial financial rewards; and increased flexibility in balancing work and family demands. The marginality theory, on the other hand, insists that "self employment is a low paying, unstable form of home-based work that combines incompatible work and domestic roles while marginalizing women's work in the economy" (Rehman & Frisby 2000, p. 41). The two researchers specifically raised five research questions in order to address the proposed research goal (p. 43):

- Do the reasons for entering careers as fitness and sport consultants reflect the liberation or marginality perspectives?
- Is the nature of work performed described as being liberating or marginalizing?
- Is it possible for women to balance work and their personal lives or are these largely incompatible?
- Does the stage of business development influence whether the women describe their work experiences as liberating or marginalizing?

■ How do the women's definitions of business success and reasons for career exit reflect the liberation or marginality perspectives?

A list of 38 full-time women fitness and sport consultants was generated in a large metropolitan area in western Canada. From the list, 13 women were identified as subjects of the study with a set of criteria (women who currently or previously owned and operated a fitness or sport consultant business as their primary source of income; diversity in marital status and family situation; and women who operated different types of consulting businesses). The identified subjects were contacted requesting their consent to participate in the study. All agreed to participate.

Semi-structured interviews were first conducted with the subjects. The results of the interviews were transcribed and transferred into a qualitative data analysis program (i.e., the Qualitative Solutions and Research Nonnumerical Unstructured Data, Indexing, Searching and Theorizing, or Q.S.R. NUD.IST) for data analysis. Five main themes and a number of sub-themes were created through the data analysis process.

To ensure the sub-themes extracted from the analysis process adequately represented the experienced of the women fitness and sport consultants, the researchers subsequently conducted two additional focus group sessions to validate the results. All the sub-themes were confirmed.

SUMMARY

Focus groups are usually comprised of 5 to 10 participants who are recruited specifically to participate in a discussion session led by a skilled moderator with a specific agenda. The moderator guides the group so that opinions, ideas, or reactions are effectively received from the participants. The findings of focus group research provide in-depth understanding of the consumer's opinions, ideas, or reactions to a specific topic.

A small number of sessions are usually held in to ensure that all the topics and questions are covered. Typically, the number of sessions is three to four.

The most important element of focus group research is the moderator. This person must be skilled and competent at guiding a discussion and in using questions and other activities to prompt participants to express their thoughts openly and comfortably.

STUDY QUESTIONS

1. What is focus group research? What are its objectives?
2. What are the different types of focus group research?
3. How are focus group participants selected and recruited?
4. Where are the common places to conduct focus groups?
5. What are the important roles that a focus group moderator plays?
6. What is the process to conduct focus groups?
7. What are the advantages and disadvantages of the focus group method?

LEARNING ACTIVITIES

1. Develop a hypothetical situation in which focus group research would be the ideal research method for studying this situation.
2. For activity 1 above, develop the focus group topics and questions that need answering for the focus group session.
3. Using the class as a sample, create a focus group method and conduct the session. Report the results in class.

References

Bruening, J. E., & Dixon, M. A. (2007). Work-family conflict in coaching II: Managing role conflict. *Journal of Sport Management, 21*(4), 471–496.

Funk, D. C., Ridinger, L. L., & Moorman, A. M. (2003). Understanding consumer support: Extending the Sport Interest Inventory (SII) to examine individual differences among women's professional sport consumers. *Sport Management Review, 6*(1), 1–31.

Hague, P., Hague, N., & Morgan, C. (2004). *Market research in practice: A guide to the basics*. London: Kogan Page Ltd.

Inglis, S. (1992). Focus groups as a useful qualitative methodology in sport management. *Journal of Sport Management, 6*(3), 173–178.

Rehman, L., & Frisby, W. (2000). Is self-employment liberating or marginalizing? The case of women consultants in the fitness and sport industry. *Journal of Sport Management, 14*(1), 41–62.

Simon, J. S. (1999). *How to conduct a focus group*. St. Paul, MN: Amherst H. Wilder Foundation.

Taylor, T., Marcy, S., Hoye, R., & Guskelly, G. (2006). Using psychological contract theory to explore issues in effective volunteer management. *European Sport Management Quarterly, 6*(2), 123–147.

CHAPTER 7
OBSERVATION RESEARCH

OBJECTIVES FOR COMPLETING THIS
CHAPTER ARE THAT STUDENTS WILL
BE ABLE TO:

Explain under what circumstances a sport
management researcher should use observation
as a research design to collect data.

Elaborate on the advantages and disadvantages
of observation as a research method.

Compare and contrast the six types of commonly
used observation methods in sport management.

Explain the sequential steps used to design
an observational study.

As mentioned in Chapter 3, observation is an essential form of qualitative research designs used by sport management researchers in acquiring information. In recent years, participant observation has been a common tool in many qualitative studies (Bennett & Hardin, 2002; Chalip & Scott, 2005; Fairley, 2003; Shaw, 2006). With any qualitative technique (e.g., case study, interviews, and focus groups) the use of observation as an instrument in data collection requires the researcher to have a clear understanding of certain skills. This chapter will discuss observation as a qualitative research method in five topics: the nature of observation, objectives of observation, types of observation, factors affecting the use of observation, and how to design and conduct an observation study.

The Nature of Observation

The observation design is used in solving certain research questions for which it is the most appropriate technique (Gay & Diebl, 1992). Observation, as a research design, refers to "the unobtrusive watching of behavioral patterns of people in certain situations to obtain information about the phenomenon of interest" (Johnson & Christensen, 2000, p. 147).

Characteristics of Observation as a Research Data Collection Technique

According to Black and Champion (1976), observation as a research data collection technique should have a number of basic characteristics as opposed to any casual, spontaneous observation in which the observer does not intend to obtain information. Those characteristics include:

1. It captures the natural social context in which a person's behavior occurs.
2. It grasps the significant events and/or occurrences that affect social relations of the participants.
3. It determines what constitutes reality from the standpoint of the world view, philosophy, or outlook of the observed.
4. It identifies regularities and recurrences in social life by comparing and contrasting data

obtained in one study with that obtained in studies of other natural settings (p. 330).

Clearly, those characteristics imply that to collect research-worthy data, the observer must follow a well-designed, systematic process to execute the observation technique.

Advantages and Disadvantages

Like any data collection method, observation also has its advantages and disadvantages. One obvious advantage is that it can be used to collect data in non-descriptive studies (Gay & Diebl, 1992). For example, the management of a sporting goods store decided to use a courtesy training program to improve the quality of customer services. Before the training program, employees were observed to determine the level of courtesy they demonstrated. After the training program, the level of courtesy exhibited by the employees was again observed. The management could then compare the results of the two observations.

It is a common belief that there is always some incongruence between attitudes and behavior (Johnson, & Christensen, 2000). In other words, the data collection from other research designs, no matter whether they are qualitative (e.g., interviews and focus groups) or quantitative in nature (e.g., survey and experiment), may reflect only a portion of the true feelings and perceptions of those people from whom the data were collected. As such, the other advantage of observation is that it gives the researcher the opportunity to record in real time the behavior of the research participants, instead of relying on the self-report of their preferences and intended behavior. In other words, observation records the actual behavior of research participants, not what they say they said or did, or not what they say they will do. The results of observation can then be used to compare the statements made by the research participants to check for the validity of their responses. This is important especially when dealing with behavior that might be subject to certain social pressure (e.g., people are less tolerant than they deem themselves to be) or conditioned responses (e.g., people say they value nutrition but will pick foods they know to be fatty or sweet), the observation technique

TABLE 7-1
Comparison of Observation and Survey Research Designs

	Observation	Surveys
What is learned?	Actions	Intentions
What is the dimension of focus?	Behavioral	Attitudinal
Is there interaction with participants?	None or limited	Some
How is its reliability?	High	Uncertain

can provide greater insights than the survey technique in this regard.

The third advantage of observation is that it does not rely on the memory or willingness of the research participants to gather data. Table 7-1 is a comparison of behavioral and attitudinal research designs that may reveal the intended differences between observation and survey.

As shown in Table 7-1, observation is particularly appropriate for action research and can be used to obtain information concerning behavior. Since the observer, in most cases, is not in direct contact with the research participants while collecting data, the researcher can collect data related to social processes or problematic issues without the awareness of the participants. As such, the data collected are more reliable.

Observation is not without shortcomings. First of all, observation does not help the researcher understand what is happening within a research participant. For instance, what are their motivation and attitudes (emotions and perceptions) toward an issue. Particularly, it does not provide the researcher with any insights into what the research participant may be thinking or what might motivate a given behavior or comment. This type of information can be obtained only through a survey that asks the research participant directly or indirectly. To overcome this disadvantage, the researcher must understand that observation can obtain behavioral cues only to answer the question of "what," not "why." So, if the objective of the research is to seek information about "what" and "why," a second stage needs to be added to the research after the conclusion of observation to acquire data in the attitudinal dimension,

such as beliefs, feelings, and motives (Seymour, 1988). For example, a study that is designed to understand the kind of behaviors (e.g., shouting at the players of the visiting team, charging onto the field, climbing up and shaking down the goal post, etc.) that are typically demonstrated by students during a football game involving a rival institution and why they behave that way, the researcher should apply a two-stage research design that involves both observation and interviews. A study conducted by Shaw (2006) also demonstrated the importance of using the two-stage model in sport management research. However, observation and interviews were used in an intertwined matter. In that study, designed to analyze social processes within a sport management context, observation was utilized to clarify the data collected during interviews. The information collected through observation also enabled the researcher in developing the context and depth of interview questions as the study progressed.

The second disadvantage is that observation requires the researcher have well developed observational skills in order to collect valid data. The researcher must know what to observe as the behavioral outcome could occur quickly. Also, as the data collected from observation are what the researcher observes, selective perception is a potential problem. Unskilled observers tend to observe behaviors that are related to their background and experience, and omit the important behavior cues and details that seem to be irrelevant to them, consequently presenting bias to the data. Training and the use of multiple observers are suggested approaches to limit the impact of this problem on the validity of the data acquired through the use of observation.

During observation, the researcher tends to believe that what is being observed is representative of the behaviors that are also demonstrated by a larger population of which the individuals or groups under investigation are a part (Seymour, 1988). As a matter of fact, there is a high tendency that the individuals or groups whom the researcher is observing may be unrepresentative. The behaviors they demonstrated may be "isolated incidents" (Seymour, 1988, p. 70). This is another disadvantage of the observation technique. In other words, the generalizability of the results obtained from an observational study could be low due to the issues involving sampling. To reduce the sampling error, the researcher should carefully examine the situation and circumstances when and where observation will take place to ensure that the subjects to be observed can reveal the general characteristics of the overall population. For example, in the case about observing student behaviors in a home football game involving a rival institution, the researcher should randomly select a number of institutions as settings of observation.

Reactivity is another disadvantage of observation (Seymour, 1988). In most of the cases involving observation as a research technique, the presence of an observer may change the behavior of the group being observed, and accordingly reduce the reliability of the observation outcome when the research participants know they are the objects of observation. As Seymour (1988) put it, "observation influenced behavior" (p. 70). Also, in a participant observation, the researcher may lose objectivity as a result of being a participant. The results of observation then may be biased because of the researcher's interactions with the research participants. To control this particular disadvantage, the researcher should determine if participant observation or unobtrusive measurement is required based on the objectives of the research.

Other disadvantages of observation also include (a) the observer has little or no control over the situation or environment where observation takes place; and (b) the observation research design has limited effectiveness for large and/or heterogeneous groups (Gay & Diehl, 1992; Ghauri, Gronhaug, & Kristainslound, 1995; McDaniel & Gates, 1991; Wrenn,

Stevens, & Loudon, 2002). Costs and time are other reasons observation is less preferred by researchers than other designs. It usually not only costs more money than survey, but also requires the researcher to devote more time conducting observation than other research approaches (Johnson & Kristensen, 2000).

OBJECTIVES OF OBSERVATION

Observation, as a research design, is used to achieve three basic objectives (Black & Champion, 1976). These are: (a) to capture human behavior in real time as it occurs and give the researcher the opportunity to view the demonstrated behavior in process, (b) to "provide more graphic description of social life than can be acquired in other ways" (p. 332), and (c) to explore a situation to provide the researcher some exploratory information.

Capturing Human Behavior in Real Time

As mentioned previously, observation allows the researcher to record information on how research participants actually behave. As such, observation as a type of research design may be used specifically to address the dynamic nature of behavior (Black & Champion, 1976). For example, Bechtol (2002) passively observed five selected athletic directors in their natural environment in order to capture the managerial behaviors, roles, and activities of Division I athletic directors. The study found that most of their verbal contacts took place in their offices. Traveling and conducting and participating in scheduled meetings took up most of their out-of-office time. They spent approximately one-quarter of their time handling managerial activities in after-business hours and weekend hours. The observed athletic directors used their executive assistants only in a few managerial tasks.

Providing Visual Description

In managing a sport event that sells alcohol, event managers often encounter situations caused by intoxicated fans. A study that aims at developing effective measures to deal with the impaired spectators could use observation as a technique in data collection. The data collected through the use of observation should give the event managers with such information as:

- What do intoxicated fans commonly do to cause trouble?
- When should they be confronted by event security staff?
- What are their reactions if confronted?

Providing Exploratory Information

Observation can be used as a means of exploration to understand a specific issue. The information obtained from the exploration may then provide the researcher with some sense of direction for research. For example, Fairley (2003) conducted a study using both participant observation and interviews as methods of data collection to provide exploratory information about why fans travel to follow professional sport teams in Australia. The participant observation was intended to observe reactions of those fans who traveled to follow their beloved teams. The interviews following the observation revealed the motives of why the fans did what they did.

CONDITIONS FOR USING OBSERVATIONS

Certain conditions or elements must be presented before observation can be used as a valid means of data collection in sport management. As such, the sport management researcher must be aware of those prerequisites prior to attempting to use the observation technique. First, the wanted information or data must be accessible to observation. In other words, the behavior must be an observable act. As mentioned previously, the objective of observation is to obtain information about behavior (i.e., what people do and how they do it). If the purpose of a study is to seek information about what people think and believe and why they think and believe that way, observation is not an appropriate research technique for the objective.

Second, the behavior to be observed must be repetitive, frequent, or predictable. The condition requires that the behavior be an act that has a certain level of consistency (e.g., an intoxicated fan usually acts in a certain manner) and is demonstrated a number of times during the observation for the researcher to record. Predictability implies that the act will occur under certain circumstances. In that way,

the researcher can anticipate and be ready to record when the behavior of interest may occur. Third, the behavior is demonstrated in a relatively short duration. Otherwise, it would be extremely costly to study.

According to Black and Champion (1976), a number of other factors may also affect the selection of observation as an appropriate method of data collection. These factors include the problem itself, the researcher's skills and characteristics, and the characteristics of the subjects to be observed.

Problem Itself

In some situations or social settings, observation may be a better research design option to choose. "Observation is especially suited to what might be called 'micro-social' as opposed to 'macro-social' questions" (Black & Champion, 1976, p. 336). Micro-social questions are specific and immediate to the life experiences of the subjects of interest, whereas macro-social questions are raised to address more global issues. For example, it may not be effective to study issues related to sport gambling through other forms of research design, such as surveys.

Researcher's Skills and Characteristics

It is believed that the validity and usefulness of the information obtained from observation depend heavily on the skill levels of the observer. It is especially true in participant observation, as the technique has a stringent requirement on the observer. That is, the observer's act of recording the information may interfere with his or her participation; the participation also may impede the results of observation.

Characteristics of the Subjects

The characteristics of the subjects are also another factor dictating whether or not observation is the appropriate method to use in data collection. "The possibility of using the techniques of observation increases as the ability of the observed to control their privacy decreases" (Black & Champion, 1976, p. 339). The ability of the subjects to control their privacy is related to several such factors as occupation, economic and political positions, sub-cultural factors, and normative standards (Black & Champion, 1976).

TYPES OF OBSERVATION

There are commonly six different ways of classifying observation methods by researchers (Black and Champion, 1976; Gay & Diebl, 1992; Johnson & Christensen, 2000): (1) participant and nonparticipant observation, (2) obtrusive and unobtrusive (or physical trace) observation, (3) observation in natural or contrived settings, (4) disguised and nondisguised observation, (5) structured and unstructured observation, and (6) direct and indirect observation.

Participant and Nonparticipant Observation

Depending on whether or not the researcher is part of the natural setting in which observation takes place, the observation technique can be classified as participant or nonparticipant observation.

One of the most fundamental distinctions that differentiate observational strategies concerns the degree to which the observer adopts an active role and becomes an integral part of the phenomenon being studied. The task of observation can be pursued along a participation continuum. On one extreme, the observer remains detached, separated from the activities being studied. . . . An alternative to this kind of description is to become a part of activities being investigated. (Seymour, 1988, p. 58)

The participation continuum of observation is depicted in Figure 7-1. In the following section, a detailed description is provided to each of the observation methods. In addition, the strengths and weaknesses of each method will also be examined.

Participant observation. A researcher who wants to study fan behavior and violence and thus becomes a spectator in a sporting event is an example of the participant observation. Participant observation requires the researcher to actively engage in the setting (e.g., to truly be part of the rowdy fans, the researcher has to demonstrate a similar level of boisterous behavior) and that individual's behavior becomes an integral part of the fan behavior. The rationale for using the participant observation technique is simple. That is, in some situations, participant observation is a better technique to use to obtain quality data, as it can provide the researcher with a better perspective on the issue being studied. To understand the dynamics of conflicts among youth sport clubs in a swimming league, Chalip and Scott (2005) utilized a number of qualitative research methods, including participant observation, in their study. One author served as a consultant to the league. The other helped with the establishment of a club and served on the executive board of the league. As active participants in the league operations, they were able to obtain first-hand information about the dynamics in decision making. This example demonstrates the other use of participant observation in sport management research.

The biggest strength of this type of observation is that the researcher not only observes what occurs but also feels as a participant involved in the situation. The observer's sharing of "feelings, thoughts, intentions and meanings" with the true subjects of the study is called "intersubjectivity" (Seymour, 1988, p. 58). Seymour maintains that "intersubjectivity" gives the researcher the opportunity to make better inferences on the data collected through observation. Making better inferences is always a challenge to researchers using the observation technique. Being a part of the situation, the researcher is more able to make sense of the data than a bystander does. Being a part of the situation, the researcher is also more

FIGURE 7-1. The Participation Continuum of Observation

Source: Johnson, B. & Christensen, L. (2000). *Educational research: Quantitative and qualitative approaches.* Boston. MA: Allyn & Bacon.

sensitive to "situational variables which may be important to understanding the situation under investigation" (Seymour, 1988, p. 59). The main disadvantage of participant observation is that there may be some role confusion occurring to the researcher, subsequently affecting the keenness of observation and taking for granted some of the behaviors under observation.

Nonparticipant observation. In a nonparticipant observation, the researcher does not get involved in the situation to be observed or interact with the research participants as required in participant observation. Instead, the researcher observes the behavior of the subjects of an observational study in a natural setting as a bystander. The subjects are usually not aware of being observed. It is believed that if the setting in which observation takes place is not natural, the behavior then demonstrated by the subjects of their studies may not be the behavior that would occur in a natural setting (Gay & Diebl, 1992). So the major advantage of nonparticipant observation, due to its unobstructive design, is that the behaviors are recorded in a natural setting; there is limited reactivity (i.e., people being observed are not aware thay they are being observed, so they do not intentionally alter their behavirors" (Johnson & Christensen, 2000).

Obtrusive and Unobtrusive Observation

Based on whether or not the subjects being studied can detect the presence of the observer or the devices used in observation (e.g., hidden microphones or cameras used to observe behavior), observation can be referred to as either obtrusive observation or unobtrusive observation. In an obtrusive observation, the subjects to be observed are made aware of the presence of the observer or the observational devices stationed in the setting in which the observation is conducted. Participant observation, when the observer does not intentionally disguise himself or herself, is an example of obtrusive observation. In a study conducted to obtain an understanding of the complexity of the body and physicality in women's rugby, Chase (2006) adopted the method of obtrusive participant observation in collecting informa-

tion. The researcher not only attended team meetings, but also stayed with players on the teams involved in the study. The researcher also sometimes traveled with a team to an out-of-state tournament.

Unobtrusive observation, also referred to as ethnographic observation, occurs when the researcher wants to observe people doing things in an environment that has not been intentionally altered. People perform their daily routines without noticing the existence of an observer. Nonparticipant observation is in fact a great example of this type of observation. To avoid alerting the subjects so that they will exhibit their behaviors freely and naturally, researchers usually focus their attention on physical traces that people leave behind. For example, to observe the drinking behavior and determine alcohol consumption of college football fans, the researcher can use garbage audits to accomplish the goal.

Observation in Natural or Contrived Settings

Observation can be classified as observation in natural settings or contrived settings. Observation in natural settings occurs when the behavior of interest is observed unobtrusively when and where it naturally occurs. The observer does not alter the setting in which observation will take place. The people being observed are not aware that they are under observation (MaDaniel & Gates, 1991). To verify the validity and reliability of the Youth Sport Behavioral Assessment System (YSBAS), an instrument designed to assess the behaviors of parents and coaches at youth sport games, Apache (2006) and colleagues attended 284 youth sport games in various sport leagues and involving several sports to observe and record comments made by coaches and parents during regularly scheduled games (natural settings). On the other hand, observation in contrived setting refers to the kind of observation in which the situation is recreated or manipulated by the researcher to speed up the appearance of the behavior of interest. The researcher performs an observation in contrived settings like executing an experiment. The researcher first alters the environment in advance for the sake of observing the intended behavior demonstrated by the subjects so as to determine the causal relationship between the treatment (i.e., alteration to the environment) and the behavior. For example, a sporting goods company selected a number of its chain stores to carry out an experiment to determine if the ways in which athletic shoes are displayed and arranged would affect consumers' purchasing decisions. Observation would take place to examine the actual behaviors exhibited (e.g., body language such as facial expressions) and the sales records. By contriving and manipulating the situation, the management of the company would be able to use the exhibited behaviors by consumers to make a managerial decision in a timely manner.

Disguised and Non-disguised Observation

One of the decisions that the researcher must make once observation is chosen as a research design is to decide whether or not the observer should disguise the observation. In disguised observation, the researcher intentionally keeps the purpose of the study and the role of the observer secret from the subjects so that the subjects being observed are not aware that they are being studied. In other words, researchers in disguised observation typically pretend to be someone else (e.g., just another fan in the tailgates before the football games, to watch the alcohol consumption behaviors) as opposed to letting subjects know that they are researchers. Neal (2005) conducted a study to reveal what motivates gamblers to sustain their gambling behaviors. The disguised observation method was used to gather data. The researchers regularly visited a number of gambling places over a year. Accordingly, they were viewed by the frequent gamblers as members of their group. Such acceptance facilitated the researchers' observation and data collection as the gamblers were more willing to share their thoughts.

Structured and Unstructured Observation

Structured observation refers to the kind of observation in which guidelines or checklists are used to record the exhibited behavior of interest. It is typically used when the researcher already has prior knowledge of the behavior of interest. Then the researcher can design a detailed reporting sheet or checklist to register the data. For example, Bechtol

(2002) collected data with a chronological record form and a record system for verbal contacts that were made beforehand to examine the managerial roles and activities of selected NCAA Division I athletic directors. Researchers sometimes also refer to structured observation as systematic observation.

On the other hand, in an unstructured observation, the observer does not have a preconceived objective or hypothesis in the observation. Instead, the observer is open-minded to observe what happens as it actually occurs. This type of observation is usually used in the exploratory stage of a research project (Seymour, 1988). Structured observation can be evaluated and reported as any other numerical/statistical data.

Direct and Indirect Observation

Depending on whether the behavior is being observed as it occurs or after the fact, observational methods are classified as direct or indirect observation. Most observational methods used by sport management researchers are direct observation, as the observers record the behavior of interest in real time. While using direct observation, the observer uses recording devices to record the behavior of interest first and analyzes the obtained information.

DESIGNING AND CONDUCTING AN OBSERVATIONAL STUDY

To conduct a study that employs observation as a research design, the researcher should use a research process that not only follows the essential steps required by scientific research, but also reflects the nature of observation. Specifically, the process of an observation study consists of a number of sequential steps: defining the problems and variables involved in the observational study, selecting an observation method, training observers, conducting and recording observation, and interpreting the results of observation (Gay & Diehl, 1992).

Definition of Observational Problems and Variables

Like any other research design in sport management research, defining problems and variables is always an essential step, as it helps the researcher narrow down the focus of the observational study to a few variables. Subjects who are under observation usually demonstrate a variety of behaviors, and it is difficult to record every behavior they exhibit during the observation. So the researcher should base the objectives of the observational study on identifying a small number of variables.

Selecting an Observation Method

The selection of an observation method is probably the most essential step in designing an observational study, as it provides the researcher with information that will help answer several specific questions related to the methodology of an observational study. These questions include:

- Where is the observation taking place?
- From whom is information being obtained?
- What types of data are being collected?
- How are data being collected?

Where is the observation taking place? To answer the question of where the observation is taking place, the researcher must first have a clear understanding of the behavior to be observed, particularly where it most likely occurs. Does it happen at a meeting, on the playing field, or at the spectator stand? The researcher also must decide how many places the behavior of interest could be observed. As mentioned in the section on the disadvantages of observation, representativeness is an issue that should be carefully

dealt with in order to increase the generalizability of the study. As such, to reduce the sampling error, the researcher needs to identify a number of points of observation.

From whom is information being obtained? While finalizing the methodology for the observational study, the researcher should determine who the subjects of the study would be (from whom the behavior of interest could be observed). The subject determination also affects the choice of sampling technique, ultimately impacting the validity of the study.

What types of information or data are being collected? Basically, the question of what to observe dictates the types of information or data to be collected. If the behavior of interest is concerned with the purchasing intention of a certain type of golf clubs, then information should be collected about the number of questions asked about the product, the number of clubs purchased, and so on.

How is the information or data being collected? This question basically asks what specific method of observation will be used in data collection. As Table 7-2 shows, the researcher has to contemplate a number of questions before selecting the correct observation method. Different methods may require different ways of data collection. One of the issues that the researcher must de-

TABLE 7-2 Basic Decisions for Observation Studies	
Natural versus Contrived Observation	To what extent will the situation to be observed be "set up" rather than occurring without intervention from the researcher?
Open versus Disguised Observation	To what extent will the respondents be aware that they are being observed?
Structured versus Unstructured Observation	To what extent will the observer be told which aspects of the overall situation to observe?
Direct versus Indirect Observation	Will the observations be made on the behavior of interest or on the results of that behavior?
Human versus Mechanical Observation	Will the observations be made by humans, by machines, or by some combination?

cide while selecting a specific kind of observation method is: to what extent will the situation to be observed be manipulated or altered so as to increase the occurrence of the behavior of interest, or is intervention from the researcher to the situation not required? If the situation calls for the researcher's intervention, then it is logical to choose the type of observation that is appropriate to use in a contrived setting.

Training Observers

To increase the reliability of an observational study, researchers should attend training workshops on observation techniques to improve their observational skills if they are not proficient in the use of observational techniques. On the other hand, if other observers are used, the researcher must make sure that the observers also participate in a training program to improve their knowledge and skills in observation. It is always a great idea to conduct a number of observation practice sessions in which the observers will have the opportunity to observe and record the behavior of interest in a setting or situation similar to the one in the actual study (Gay & Deibl, 1992). One of the critical methodological elements in using observation as a research design is to have at least two observers involved in the same observational tasks. The results of their recorded observations can be used to assess the reliability of the study. This is another justification for having involved observers participate in the training program. One aspect of the training program would be to make sure the observers develop the same level of understanding of the specific behaviors to be observed, what constitutes the behaviors of interest, and how behaviors are coded. It is commonly agreed that in order for an observational study to have reliability, a score of 80% inter-observer agreement must be achieved (Gay & Deibl, 1992, p. 268).

Conducting and Recording Observation

The next logical step in executing the observational study is to conduct the observation to collect the data. Because the behavior the researcher wants to record usually exhibits in a short period of time, to efficiently record and collect the information of interest, the researcher needs to employ a recoding or coding system that is simple and easy to use (Gay & Diebl, 1992; Seymour, 1988). "Most observation studies facilitate recording by using an agreed-upon code or set of symbols, and a recording instrument (Gay & Diebl, 1992, p. 264). There are a variety of types of recording forms. Some can be used like a checklist, and some serve as a rating scale. For example, the study that examined the managerial roles and activities of selected NCAA Division I athletic directors conducted by Bechtol (2002) collected data with a chronological record form and a record system.

Interpreting the Results of Observation

After the behavior of interest has been recorded, the information obtained will be analyzed to determine if the behavior displayed by the subjects demonstrates a certain pattern. After such determination, the researcher should then attempt to make sense of the observed behavior with a theory or interpretation.

ETHNOGRAPHY AND OBSERVATION

Sport management researchers often combine participant observation and other data collection methods such as interviews in a natural setting to obtain a comprehensive view of a particular situation. Such an approach in gathering information, with the use of participant observation in conjunction with other research methods, is generally referred to as ethnography (Gay & Diebl, 1992). In a study designed to gain an understanding of how political rivalries, policy coalitions, and conflicts emerge in an amateur sport league, Chalip and Scott (2005) adopted an ethnographical approach in data collection. They frequently attended the league's executive meetings to observe the group dynamic among the executives of the organization, interviewed the league's executives, and examined the league's records including minutes and reports. It is the authors' belief that the ethnographical approach is the most appropriate in obtaining the kind of information to answer their research questions.

Several advantages of ethnography are commonly recognized by scholars. One of the advantages is that it can provide the researcher with "a much more comprehensive perspective than do other forms" of data collection (Fraenkel & Wallen, 2000, p. 546). The method allows the researcher to gain insight into a particular situation that is not possible to get with the use of other research method is another advantage of ethnography. The major limitation of ethnographical approach is similar to that of observation. That is, the findings obtained from ethnography usually lack generaliability.

USING ETHNOGRAPHY RESEARCH TECHNIQUES IN SPORT MANAGEMENT: A CASE ANALYSIS

To determine the effectiveness of the LG Electronics' on-site sponsorships, Choi, Stotlar and Park (2006) utilized a visual ethnographic inquiry method to investigate what an average spectator at a sporting event visually records in a two-hour span in order. They purposefully selected 17 adult spectators (18 years or older) who were in attendance at the LG Action Sports Championships in Pomona, Georgia, between September 10 and 12, 2004. The participants were approached and agreed to voluntary participation. Information about their right to volunteer and the procedure of the study were clearly explained to the participants.

Each participant was provided with a digital camera phone with instructions to take pictures throughout the two-hour duration. A one-on-one interview was conducted with each participant when that individual returned the camera to the researchers. The participant was asked first to show all the pictures that this individual had taken to the researcher. During this process, the researcher asked the participant questions, such as the motives and reasons behind taking each picture. The researcher also asked questions related to LG's on-site activities, other off-site brand activities, and the overall experience. Other types of information, such as brand loyalty, cell-phone experience, and general thoughts on LG, were also obtained in the interview.

Based on repetition and relevance to the purpose of the study, the researchers broke down the collected data into several categories or themes. They compared the pictures that the spectators took and the activities that the sponsor (LG) used to activate its sponsorship at the venue to determine whether or not the sponsors had achieved their intended purpose.

SUMMARY

As one type of qualitative research design, observation has been used periodically by sport management researchers in solving their research problems. This chapter discussed several common topics related to observation, such as the nature of observation, objectives of observation, types of observation, factors affecting the use of observation, and how to design and conduct an observation study.

Observation can be the most appropriate technique for achieving a certain type of research objectives. A well-designed observational study should comprise a number of basic characteristics, such as (a) capturing the natural social context in which a person's behavior occurs; (b) grasping the significant events and/or occurrences that affect social relations of the participants; (c) determining what constitutes reality from the standpoint of the world view, philosophy, or outlook of the observed; and (d) identifying regularities and recurrences in social life by comparing and contrasting data obtained in one study with those obtained in studies of other natural settings.

Observation has its advantages and disadvantages. The advantages include: (a) it can be used to collect data in non-descriptive studies; (b) it records in real time the behavior of the research participants, instead of relying on the self-report of their preferences and intended behavior; and (c) it does not rely on the memory or willingness of the research participants to gather data. The shortcomings of observation are: (a) it does not indicate what is happening within a research participant; (b) it may not produce valid data due to the use of unskillful observers, (c) sampling errors could affect the generalizability of the study; and (d) reactivity is a problem.

There are three basic objectives of observational studies: (a) to observe human behavior in real time, (b) to allow more detailed description of what is going on, and (c) to provide exploratory information.

Observation can be used effectively under three conditions. First, the behavior of interest must be an observable act. Second, the behavior to be observed must be repetitive, frequent, or predictable. Third, the behavior is demonstrated in a relatively short duration. In addition, a number of factors need to be considered while deciding if observation is appropriate to use. These factors include: (a) the problem itself, (b) the researcher's skills and characteristics, and (c) the characteristics of the subjects to be observed.

In general, observation methods can be classified into six types: participant and nonparticipant observation, obtrusive and unobtrusive (or physical trace) observation, observation in natural or contrived settings, disguised and non-disguised observation, structured and unstructured observation, and direct and indirect observation.

The process of designing and conducting an observational study usually consists of five steps: (1) defining the problems and variables, (2) selecting an observation method, (3) training observers, (4) conducting and recording observation, and (5) interpreting the results of observation.

STUDY QUESTIONS

1. Explain under what circumstances a sport management researcher may use observation as a research design to collect data.
2. Elaborate on the advantages and disadvantages of observation as a research method.
3. Compare and contrast the six types of commonly used observation methods in sport management.
4. Explain the sequential steps used to design an observational study.

LEARNING ACTIVITIES

1. Using observation as the method of data collection, design a study to determine the types of customers who are most likely to enter a sporting store in a shopping mall when they are walking by the store.
   a. What is your sampling method?
   b. What type of information will you collect from the customers?
2. Outline a study using observation as a research design for each of the following situations:
   a. A sports drink manufacturer wishes to determine how sports participants use its products while playing sports.
   b. A sport management researcher wants to know how many female athletes have been featured on the cover of *Sports Illustrated* in the past five years.
3. Watch ESPN SportsCenter for one week. Observe how much time the anchors spend on professional sports, college sports, and other amateur sports.

References

Appache, R. R. (2006). The behavioral assessment of parents and coaches at youth sports: Validity and reliability. *The Physical Educator, 63*(3), 126–133.

Bechtol, D. L. (2002).Structured observation description of the managerial roles and activities of selected NCAA Division I athletic directors. *International Journal of Sport Management, 3*(1), 11–33.

Bennett, G., & Hardin, B. (2002). Management behaviors of an elite intercollegiate baseball coach. *International Journal of Sport Management, 3*(3), 199–214.

Black, J. A., & Champion, D. J. (1976). *Methods and Issues in Social Research.* New York, NY: John Wiley & Sons, Inc.

Chalip, L., & Scott, E. P. (2005). Centrifugal social forces in a youth sport league. *Sport Management Review, 8*, 43–67.

Chase, L. F. (2006). (Un)disciplined bodies: A foucauldian analysis of women's rugby. *Sociology of Sport Journal, 23*(3), 229–247.

Choi, J. A., Stotlar, D. K., & Park, S. R. (2006). Visual ethnography of on-site sport sponsorship activation: LG action sports championship. *Sport Marketing Quarterly, 15*, 71–79.

Fairley, S. (2003). In search of relieved social experience: Group-based nostalgia sport tourism. *Journal of Sport Management, 17*(3), 284–304.

Fraenkel, J. R., & Wallen, N. E. (2000). *How to design and evaluate research in education* (4th ed.). Boston, MA: McGraw Hill.

Gay, L. R., & Diebl, P. L. (1992). *Research methods for business and management*. New York: Macmillan Publishing Company.

Ghauri, P. N., Gronhaug, K., & Kristianslund, I. (1995). *Research methods in business studies: A practical guide*. New York: Prentice Hall.

Johnson, B., & Christensen, L. (2000). *Educational research: Quantitative and qualitative approaches*. Boston, MA: Allyn and Bacon.

McDaniel, C., & Gates, R. (1991). *Contemporary marketing research*. St. Paul, MN: West Publishing Company.

Neal, M. (2005). "I lose, but that's not the point": Situated economic and social rationalities in horserace gambling. *Leisure Studies, 24*(3), 291–310.

Seymour, D. T. (1988). *Marketing research: Qualitative methods for the marketing professional*. Chicago: Probus Publishing Company.

Shaw, S. (2006). Scratching the back of "Mr X": Analyzing gendered social processes in sport organizations. *Journal of Sport Management, 20*, 510–534.

Wrenn, B., Stevens, R., & Loudon, D. (2002). *Marketing research: Text and cases*. Binghamton, NY: Best Business Books.

CHAPTER 8
SECONDARY DATA

OBJECTIVES FOR COMPLETING THIS
CHAPTER ARE THAT STUDENTS WILL
BE ABLE TO:

Understand the nature of secondary data as a
quantative technique in sport management
research

Understand the different ways that sport
management researchers can use secondary
data to serve their research needs

Understand the common sources of secondary
data for sport management research

Appreciate the advantages and disadvantages
of secondary data

Follow the steps in the process of secondary data
research to conduct a research project

A S MENTIONED IN CHAPTER 2, data can be described as either primary or secondary. Most of the research conducted in sport management involves the collection of new data, or the primary data, to solve a particular problem. Nevertheless, sport management researchers sometimes may turn their attention to secondary data to help solve their research problems. This is confirmed by Li and Lawrence (2007) in their study that examines the use of secondary data in sport management. The authors reviewed the articles published in the *Journal of Sport Management* since 1992 and in *Sport Marketing Quarterly* since 2003. The results of their reviews indicate that about 10% of the 250 articles reviewed used the secondary data design.

This chapter provides an overview of secondary data as a quantative research design in sport management. The nature of this type of research design and the common ways that sport management researchers and professionals use it to facilitate their decision making will first be reviewed. Other topics, such as the sources of secondary data for sport management research and the advantages and disadvantages of secondary data, will also be discussed. The process of secondary data research will be looked at in the last part of the chapter.

THE NATURE OF SECONDARY DATA IN SPORT MANAGEMENT RESEARCH

Secondary data refer to the type of data that have previously been gathered and that might be relevant to the problem at hand (McDaniel & Gates, 1991). That means that, while using the secondary data design, the sport management researchers do not have to collect their own data. Instead, they can use data that already exist in the public domain to test their hypotheses or solve their problems. Secondary data may exist in many forms, including census reports, a public opinion poll, or a survey of attitudes to a particular social issue. For example, if the focus of a research project is sport participation, the sport management researcher can examine data released in the Statistical Abstract of the United States, reports

from the Sporting Goods Manufacturers Association (SGMA), and the National Sporting Goods Association (NSGA), etc. Of course, the regularly gathered information on a variety of variables, such as sales, costs, and customer satisfaction by an organization can also be used to track the trend on those variables.

Secondary data can be used to meet a number of research needs: to answer a research question, to clarify and understand a situation, to provide exploratory information, to help make a decision, to verify findings of primary research, and to build a statistical model (Blankenship, Breen & Dutka, 1998; Wrenn, Stevens & Loudon, 2002; Zikmund, 2000).

To answer a research question. One of the most common uses of secondary data in sport management research is to answer a research question or approve a hypothesis. "The first tenet of data gathering among researchers is to exhaust all sources of secondary data before engaging in a search for primary data" (Wrenn et al., 2002). In fact, many research questions can simply be answered with the analysis of the data collected from a secondary source. For example, to understand whether or not winning has a significant impact on alumni giving, Stinson and Howard (2004) examined the secondary data on donors making gifts of $1,000 or more between 1994 and 2002 to the Annual Giving Program at the University of Oregon. They found "in almost every year, alumni giving to athletics has increased with an associated increase in success by high profile intercollegiate athletic teams" (p. 136).

In a study conducted to approve the seven proposed hypotheses concerning personnel replacement rates in sport organizations, Theberge and Loy (1976) used secondary data included in the *Baseball Encyclopedia* published in 1969 for the 16 teams of the American and National Baseball Leagues during the period 1951–1960 to empirically test the hypotheses. Gladden and Milne (1999) also used secondary data on Major League Baseball, the National Basketball Association, and the National Hockey League to help sport managers understand the contribution of brand equity and winning to merchandise sales in the professional sport setting. The examples mentioned here imply that secondary data are the most appropriate data to solve a research question of this kind, which requires information in multiple years.

The results of the study conducted by Li and Lawrence (2006) examining the use of secondary data as a research design in sport management confirm that researchers often use secondary data to either answer a research question or approve a hypothesis (e.g., Ahlstrom, Si, & Kennelly, 1999; McDonald & Rascher, 2000; Orders & Chelladurai, 1994; Stinson & Howard, 2004; Zygmont & Leadley, 2005).

To clarify and understand a situation. The second common use of secondary data is fact finding (Zikmund, 2000). For example, to verify the validity of such a statement, "Soccer is greatly gaining popularity in the United States," the researcher could approach the research problem with the help of secondary data. Basically, the researcher can examine data obtained from a variety of secondary data sources including the Statistical Abstract of the United States to determine whether or not the numbers of soccer participants over the years have demonstrated an upward trend, whether or not the sales of soccer related equipment have been getting stronger, and if the numbers of soccer clubs at all levels have increased. Turco (2004) conducted an analysis of secondary data from a number of selected sports halls of fame in responding to a concern raised about whether or not the glory days of sports halls as celebratory sport tourism attractions have passed. The secondary data research confirmed that a decline in tourist visitations occurred to the sports halls of fame under investigation.

To provide exploratory information. Sport management researchers also utilize secondary data to provide exploratory information to a large-scale research project that requires the collection of primary data. As a matter of fact, many studies that collect primary data involve the use of secondary data to provide exploratory information

to clarify the situation or help form hypotheses for the primary data research. To examine the issues of cultural diversity in women's sport, Taylor (2003) first used secondary data to generate exploratory information about the participation rates in sport and physical activities among women from minority ethnic backgrounds and Anglo-Australian women to verify that the former group of women had a lower participation rate. To further confirm the findings from the secondary data research, the researcher conducted a survey to investigate the issue with a specific sport—netball. The empirical data confirmed that the levels of female participation from culturally diverse backgrounds in netball were significantly below those of Anglo-Australian females.

This case exemplifies the substantial role that secondary data play in the exploratory phase of the research when the task at hand is to define the research problem and to generate hypotheses. The assembly and analysis of secondary data almost invariably improve the researcher's understanding of the marketing problem, the various lines of inquiry that could or should be followed, and the alternative courses of action that might be pursued.

To help make a decision. A secondary data research project can be executed to give a firm that wants to make a long-term investment in a particular product line useful exploratory data to make a decision. Assume that a national chain fitness company (e.g., Gold's Gym) wants to know whether or not Lancaster, Ohio, is a good location for one of its franchises. To facilitate the decision, the research team of the company carefully examined the census data of the city on population and trend of growth, income profiles, etc. The examination of the data collected from secondary sources indicates the market size of that particular location may not be large enough to successfully sustain a Gold's Gym franchise. This example illustrates the use of secondary data to help sports firms make an informed decision in terms of expansion or relocation.

To verify and complement the findings of primary research. Secondary data research not only can help the researcher verify findings that are obtained from a completed primary research project, but also can provide context for interpretation of primary research. For example, the sport council of a city wanted to convince the owners of a professional sports league that the city was an ideal location for future expansion. To demonstrate the degree of fan support and enthusiasm, the council first conducted a survey of local residents. The results indicated a strong fan support of this initiative. The council then compiled a report using the attendance records of a minor league franchise in the same sport for the last ten years to confirm the findings of the survey research.

To build a statistical model. In the previous study conducted to examine the use of secondary data in sport management research, Li and Lawrence (2007) found that 12 out of the 25 identified studies using secondary data (48%) were designed to build a statistical model that has the ability (a) to specify and make prediction about relationships between variables, or (b) to approve a conceptual model (e.g., Agthe & Billings, 2000; Boronico & Newbert, 1999; DeSchriver & Stotlar, 1996; Maxcy & Mondello, 2006; Todd, Crook, & Barilla, 2005; Yokum, Gonzalez, & Badgett, 2006). For example, Hadley and Gustafson (1991) used secondary data to establish a single-equation model of baseball salaries. The study found that variables such as years of Major League service and eligibility for arbitration had a great impact on players' salaries in Major League Baseball.

The following is an example demonstrating the conceptual process used in building a statistical model that has the ability to specify and make prediction about relationships among variables. A researcher established an empirical model/equation for explaining National Football League (NFL) franchise operating income with the use of available secondary data. Nine variables were included in the consideration, and they were believed to have a direct impact of the operating income of an NFL franchise. The following formula shows such a statistical (multiple regression) model and the nine variables included in the model:

NFL operating income = $f(X_1, X_2, X_3, X_4, X_5, X_6, X_7, X_8, X_9)$

Where

X_1 = Median Family Income
X_2 = The Average Cost of Living
X_3 = The Average Unemployment Rate
X_4 = The Total Population of the Metropolitan Area
X_5 = Usability of the Public Transportation
X_6 = % of 65 or older Population in the Metro Area
X_7 = The Franchise's Win/Loss % in a Given Year
X_8 = The Minimum Face Price on a Single-game Ticket to A Regular Season Game
X_9 = The Capacity of the Stadium/Dome

All the data required for the establishment of such a statistical model can be obtained from secondary data sources. The multiple regression analysis yields some interesting results.

NFL operating income = $-0.59 + 4.31X_1 - 0.076X_2 - 0.22 X_3 + 5.66 X_4 + 6.37X_5 + 6.78X_6 + 9.88X_7 - 1.21X_8 + 0.45X_9$

The results show that an NFL franchise's win/loss percentage in a given year is the biggest predictor of the operating income of the franchise under investigation, followed by the percentage of 65 or older population in the metropolitan area, the usability of the public transportation system, the total population of the metropolitan area, etc. The average cost of living in a particular metropolitan area is the weakest predictor and has an inverse relationship with the franchise operating income.

SOURCES OF SECONDARY DATA

In general, secondary data are available at two levels, the internal and the external. The internal level data are the information originating within a particular firm or organization. The NCAA annual

TABLE 8-1
Example of the NCAA EADA Report Released by the NCAA

Institution	Classification	Male	Female	Total	A4	A5	A6	A7
Alabama A & M University	NCAA Division I-AA	2187	2435	4622	1727412	1141431		2868843
University of Alabama at Birmingham	NCAA Division I-A	4441	6843	11284	2944657	1709816		4654473
University of Alabama in Huntsville	NCAA Division II (without football)	1976	1907	3883	676855	539253		1216108
Alabama State University	NCAA Division I-AA	1598	2360	3958	1003671	681966		1685637
The University of Alabama	NCAA Division I-A	7421	8410	15831	3317599	2697787		6015386
Central Alabama Community College	NJCAA Division I	435	758	1193	128700	108900		237600
Auburn University-Montgomery	NAIA Division I	448	1204	1652	440040	303254		743294
Auburn University Main Campus	NCAA Division I-A	9746	9150	18896	3674886	2615544		6290430
Birmingham Southern College	NCAA Division I-AAA	614	797	1411	1109150	1457679		2566829
Chattahoochee Valley Community College	NJCAA Division I	349	708	1057	90400	88000		178400
Concordia College	Other (USCAA)	343	498	841	0	0		0
Enterprise-Ozark Community College	NJCAA Division I	626	428	1054	190124	147037		337161
James H. Faulkner State Community College	NJCAA Division I	808	1258	2066	311993	292720		604713
Faulkner University	NAIA Division I	644	866	1510	483407	304681		788088
Gadsden State Community College	Other Some NJCAA Div. I & II	1319	1645	2964	192593	232657		425250
George C. Wallace Community College-Dothan	NJCAA Division I	781	1144	1925	119024	106483		225507
George C. Wallace State Community College-Hanceville	NJCAA Division I	1161	1853	3014	318425	200108		518533
George C. Wallace State Community College-Selma	NJCAA Division I	340	857	1197	111026	35804		146830
Huntingdon College	NCAA Division III (with football)	371	362	733	0	0		0
Jacksonville State University	NCAA Division I-AA	2459	3255	5714	1296901	1006119		2303020
Jefferson Davis Community College	NJCAA Division I	284	733	1017	167375	126683		294058
Jefferson State Community College	NCAA Division II	1162	1628	2790	113509	104518		218027
Lawson State Community College-Birmingham Campus	NJCAA Division I	565	1169	1734	263648	159482		423130
University of West Alabama	NCAA Division II (with football)	752	987	1739	474853	255935	58248	789036
Lurleen B. Wallace Community College	NJCAA Division I	536	908	1444	178465	161398		339863
Marion Military Institute	Other	USCAA	230	26	256	92268		92268
Miles College	NCAA Division II (with football)	733	890	1623	353724	126093		479817
University of Montevallo	NCAA Division II (without football)	748	1589	2337	318004	353414		671418
Northwest Shoals Community College-Muscle Shoals	NJCAA Division I	1861	2921	4782	214882	260473		475355
University of North Alabama	UNA Box 5001 NCAA Division II (with football)	1955	2489	4444	755791	397993		1153784
Alabama Southern Community College	NJCAA Division I	338	524	862	108246	92483		200729
Bishop State Community College	NJCAA Division I	813	1566	2379	138801	136802		275603
Samford University	NCAA Division I-AA	1032	1859	2891	2033470	1427007		3460477
Shelton State Community College	NJCAA Division I	1419	1643	3062	157363	213315		370678
Snead State Community College	NJCAA Division II	464	630	1094	134096	148556		282652
University of South Alabama	NCAA Division I-AAA	3067	4501	7568	818434	1047937		1866371

expense report is an example of the secondary information compiled by a sport organization but available for the public use. The secondary information obtained from outside sources is referred to as the external level secondary data.

Internal Records of and Data Released by a Public Organization

Table 8-1 shows a section of the NCAA EADA report released by the NCAA that discloses financial information about member institutions. Sport management researchers who are interested in issues in intercollegiate athletic administration may find the data useful as a number of statistical procedures can be applied to analyze the financial data. The Institute for Diversity and Ethics in Sport at the University of Central Florida periodically releases information related to gender and race in amateur, collegiate, and professional sports. The released information is a good source of secondary data for researchers who have a research focus on gender and race in the sport industry. In other words, the data can be re-analyzed to achieve a particular objective of a secondary data research project. For example, in 2003, the Center released "Classroom Counts," a study on the impact of Division I-A football realignment on conference graduation rates (Institute for Diversity and Ethics in Sport, 2003). Description statistics were used in data analysis. To further understand the issues surrounding conference realignment and its effect on graduation rates, more sophisticated statistical analyses could be applied to analyze the obtained data, which may include, but are not limited to, a two-way ANOVA to determine the interaction between realignment and the race of student-athletes.

Internal Data Released by a Private Trade Organization

Industry associations often publish data on size and characteristics of their industry. As mentioned earlier, the SGMA periodically releases information about the trends of the sporting goods industry and sport participation. The *Superstudy of Sports Participation*, published annually by American Sports Data, Inc., serves as a useful secondary source for people who are interested in determining a trend of sports participation in the United States. Table 8-2 contains information about the participation patterns of Americans in water-based recreational sport activities (American Sports Data, Inc., 2003). As shown in Table 8-2, Americans' participation in water-related recreational sports soared over the 13-year period from 1990 to 2003. Particularly, there was a roughly 78% increase in the number of people who sailed and almost a 23% hike in the number of enthusiasts who scuba-dived. During the same period, consumer participation in both boardsailing/windsurfing and water skiing decreased.

TABLE 8-2
Trends of Participation in Water-based Recreational Sport in the United States (in thousands): 1990–2003

	1990	1993	1998	1999	2000	2001	2002	2003
Boardsailing/Windsurfing	1,025	835	1,075	624	655	537	496	779
Sailing	5,981	3,918	5,902	5,327	10,835	10,593	9,806	10,648
Scuba Diving	2,615	2,306	3,448	3,095	2,901	2,744	3,328	3,215
Snorkeling	n/a	n/a	10,575	10,694	10,526	9,788	9,865	10,179
Surfing	1,224	n/a	1,395	1,736	2,180	1,601	1,879	2,087
Wakeboarding	n/a	n/a	2,253	2,707	3,581	3,097	3,142	3,356
Water Skiing	19,314	16,626	10,161	9,961	10,335	8,301	8,204	8,425

Source: American Sports Data, Inc. (2003). The superstudy of sports participation (Volume III): Outdoors Activities. Hartsdale, NY: Author.

Internal Data from a Private Firm

All sport businesses record their daily operations in a number of ways, such as the orders received and delivered, the sales invoices, and the cost records of producing, storing, transporting, and marketing each of its products or services. Some of the secondary data studies that sport managers of those businesses can conduct using the information include the determination of the most profitable products and customers, and the tracking of sales trends in their existing customer groups.

Data from Previous Surveys

Data from previous surveys are sold as printed reports or raw data by survey research firms. A good example of such firms is Scarborough Research. Scarborough Research specializes in marketing research focusing on shopping patterns, lifestyles, and media habits of consumers locally, regionally, and nationally. Scarborough Research has data sets on 75 local market studies in the United States, which examine consumers' retail shopping behaviors, lifestyle characteristics, in-depth consumer demographics, and media usage patterns. Interested businesses can purchase a secondary data set from Scarborough Research so as to obtain a better understanding of consumers in a particular local market (Scarborough Research, 2005). Let's assume that the sponsorship sales staff of the Columbus Blue Jackets wants to present a sponsorship proposal to a local corporation. To prepare the proposal, the sales staff purchased a specific marketing data set for the Columbus metropolitan area. They analyze the data set and include the results of their analysis in the sponsorship proposal, which includes a section on shopping patterns, lifestyles, and media habits of consumers in that market.

Previously Published Research

The data from previously published research projects are reported in a summary form, but the original data may be available from the authors upon request. It is important that the researcher communicate with the authors of the original data to see if the latter is willing to share the information and under what conditions the data could be reused.

Publications Released by Government Agencies

The most common external sources of the secondary data are those publications released by a variety of government agencies. The following is a list of government agencies from which researchers in sport management can obtain the secondary information:

- U.S. Bureau of Economic Analysis, Survey of Current Business—http://www.bea.doc.gov
- U.S. Bureau of Labor Statistics—http://www.stats.bls.gov, good data source and excellent links
- U.S. Census Bureau—http://www.census.gov
- U.S. Economic Census—http://www.census.gov/econ/census02/
- U.S. Government Materials—http://www.fedstats.gov
- U.S. Office of Trade and Economic Development—http://www.ita.doc.gov/tradestats
- U.S. Statistical Data International and National Stat-USA—http://www.stat-usa.gov/, excellent links and information
- U.S. White House Economic Briefing Room—http://www.whitehouse.gov/fsbr/esbr.html

In addition to the secondary data released by government agencies, online databases can also be external sources for secondary data researchers. For example, sport marketing researchers may find SecondaryData.com a useful source.

ADVANTAGES OF SECONDARY DATA

Secondary data have several advantages. They include saving time and money, better research design, and availability.

Saving Time and Money

The most obvious advantage of secondary data is its readiness to use, as the name of this type of data implies: they were obtained by others but are available and accessible (Zikmund, 2000). Thus, the researcher does not have to go through the process as required in primary data collection, which usually involves the design of a questionnaire or data collection instrument, verification of its validity and reliability, the collection of data through field work, etc. The completion of those steps takes time and resources. When compared to the cost in executing a research project, the secondary data research is substantially lower than the primary data research. The cost typically associated with secondary data is to acquire the published source. There is no design cost (Wrenn, Stevens, & Loudon, 2002). The time commitment required of a researcher to complete a research project that uses secondary data starts only after the data have been extracted from a source.

Better Research Design

As mentioned previously, the NCAA releases annually the expense report that includes financial records of most of its affiliated institutions. Researchers who are interested in a project that investigates the financial strengths of each of the three NCAA Divisions may find the report extremely useful as it is very difficult, if not impossible, for any individual researcher to collect such primary data through a survey. The response rate is usually quite high due to the sponsorship of the NCAA in this type of research.

Availability

There is some information that is only available in the secondary data form (Wrenn, Stevens & Loudon, 2002). For example, the internal level data originated within a particular sport firm or organization, such as personnel and financial related data can only exist and be accessed in the secondary data format. Also, as mentioned previously, secondary data research sometimes is the only research design appropriate and available to analyze longitudinal data.

LIMITATIONS OF SECONDARY DATA

Although the great benefits that secondary data can provide sport management researchers should be recognized, their shortcomings should also be acknowledged and discussed so that the sport management researchers can try to avoid those disadvantages while designing their secondary data research and be cautious in their application of secondary data. The limitations of secondary data are found in the following four areas:

Differences in Definitions

The researcher who decides to use the secondary data research design should carefully examine the definitions that have been used in generating the secondary data before attempting to use the data, as those definitions could be different from what the researcher has in mind. Assume that a researcher is interested in using secondary data to make comparisons of the sport participation rates between residents of America and residents of China. The concept of "regular participation" was used in the secondary data sets published respectively by the government agencies in these two nations. What is the definition of "regular participation" in sport? Does it mean three times a week and thirty minutes each time? Without obtaining a clear understanding of the definitions used in generating the data, it is methodologically inappropriate to pursue a study that will analyze the data comparatively.

Lack of Availability

Sometimes, even through it would be better to use the secondary data design to solve the research problem at hand, the researcher has no choice but to collect primary data to deal with the problem, due to the unavailability of secondary data (McDaniel & Gates, 1991). If ESPN wants to know how college students react to a new anchor for the *Sports Center* program, it must conduct a survey to obtain primary data to evaluate their reactions, as no secondary data have been generated yet.

Lack of Accuracy

It has always been a concern that some secondary data could suffer from a lack of accuracy. It is quite possibile that inaccuracies have occurred during the original collection of the data. For example, the data might have been collected from an unreliable source. It is possible that the inaccuracies in measurement were estimated by the original researcher. Nevertheless, these inaccuracies were sometimes not made available for the researcher who wants to reuse the data. To avoid using inaccurate secondary data, a number of guidelines have been suggested for the researcher to follow before attempting to adopt data from a secondary source (McDaniel & Gates, 1991, pp. 124–125; Wrenn, Stevens & Loudon, 2002, p. 65). Detailed discussion of those guidelines will be provided in the section "Process of Secondary Data Research."

Age of Secondary Data

The data produced could be out-of-date at the time when the researcher wants to make use of the statistics. For example, the U.S. Census Bureau conducts the Economic Census every five years. The 2002 Economic Census showed that the number of professional sports establishments (i.e., teams and franchises) was 388. The number would likely be much higher in 2006.

PROCESS OF SECONDARY DATA RESEARCH

To properly execute a secondary data research project, a sport management researcher should follow a four-step process. The steps involved are: (a) defining the data needed, (b) locating the data, (c) evaluating the data, and (d) verifying the data. Figure 8-1 depicts the process of secondary research.

Defining the Data Needed

The sport management researcher who wants to use the secondary data design should always start with the definition of the problem, followed by the deter-

mination of the type of information or data that are required to solve the problem. For instance, if the problem at hand is to obtain an understanding of the trend of usage of water sports facilities by American consumers, the nature of the problem dictates the application of historical data collected by various federal and local government agencies. Obviously, the analysis of those historical or secondary data will help the researcher outline the trend.

Locating the Data

As mentioned previously, one of the issues in the secondary data research is the availability of the data. So, once the type of secondary data needed for the research has been decided, the researcher then needs to investigate where the data are located. As discussed in the prior section on the sources of secondary data, they can be found through either online databases (e.g., the U.S. Census) or printed indices, such as the American Statistics Index or the Statistical Reference Index, that are available at most libraries.

Evaluating the Data

After a secondary data source has been located, the researcher must evaluate the source to determine its validity, reliability, relevance, appropriateness, and accuracy. The evaluation also indicates whether or not the data are relevant to the research problem

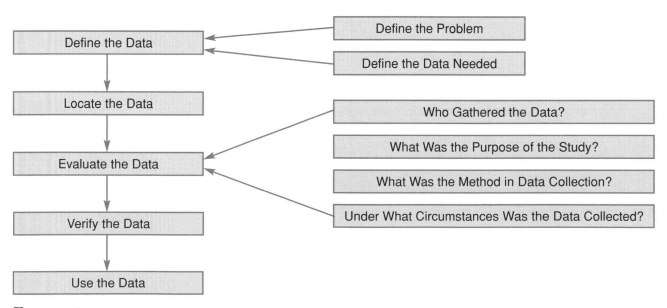

FIGURE 8-1. Process of Secondary Data Research

and situation at hand. The following are a number of questions to which the researcher should seek answers while evaluating the located secondary data.

Who gathered the data? The first legitimate question that the researcher who wants to use available data must ask is: Where did the secondary data come from? In other words, who was the individual or organization responsible for collecting the data, and was the individual or organization reputable and creditable? "The source of the secondary data is the key to its accuracy" (McDaniel & Gates, 1991, p. 124).

What was the purpose of the study? It is always an issue in secondary data research that the data compiled for another research project with different objectives may not completely fit the problem at hand (Ghauri, Gronhaug, Kristianslund, 1995). Understanding the reason the data was collected in the first place provides the researcher with clues about the quality of the data. For example, the researcher should be cautious while reviewing the secondary data compiled by a municipal sports commission on the attendance and consequent economic impact of a sports event on the local community, as the data could have been manipulated to serve some political purpose.

What was the methodology or research design used in data collection? Scrutiny should focus on such areas as the conceptual model used, the variables and their operational definitions, the measures employed, the sampling design used and the sample obtained, the data collection methods, and response rate obtained. Any flaw in the research design used in collecting the data will introduce inaccuracy to the data, consequently making the data unusable.

Under what circumstance was the information collected? The intent of this question is twofold. First, the researcher must understand that the data collected for another research project may not fit with or be relevant to the research problem at hand. It is important for the researcher to examine carefully the secondary data to deter-

mine if the unit of measurement is the same and the sampling frame is relatively similar. Second, the researcher must understand the circumstances in terms of what, when, and how the information was obtained.

After the evaluation is completed, the researcher still has to decide whether or not the obtained secondary data are sufficient to address the research problem. If not, the secondary data research must to be supplemented with primary data.

Gathering and Verifying the Data

If the result of the evaluation shows that the secondary data source appears to be valid, reliable, and accurate, the researcher should then secure a copy of the data. Before attempting to use the data set, the researcher should verify whether or not the data obtained are the right ones.

A CASE IN SPORT MANAGEMENT RESEARCH USING SECONDARY DATA

Gladden and Milne (1999) used secondary data as a research design to gain a better understanding of brand equity as a tool for guiding strategic marketing decisions in the sport industry. Specifically, the authors wanted to expand the conceptual understanding of brand equity and compare the importance of brand equity and winning in the realization of a marketplace outcome in the professional sport setting.

Secondary data were gathered from a variety of sources that provide comprehensive information on Major League Baseball, the National Basketball Association, and the National Hockey League.

A number of logistic regression analyses were conducted. The results revealed that both brand equity and winning significantly contributed to the attainment of merchandise sales. However, the impact of brand equity and winning differed by league.

SUMMARY

Secondary data research is one of the research designs commonly employed by sport management researchers for several purposes: (a) to answer a research question, (b) to clarify and understand a situation, (c) to provide exploratory information, (d) to help make a decision, (e) to verify findings of primary research, and (f) to build a statistical model.

Sport management researchers can access secondary data from two levels: internal and external. The internal level of secondary data includes the internal records of and data released by a public organization, the data released by a private trade organization, the data from previous surveys, and the previously published research. On the other hand, the external level secondary data primarily come from those publications released by a variety of government agencies.

There are some advantages and disadvantages of secondary data. Saving time and money, better research design, and availability are recognized advantages of secondary data. The commonly mentioned disadvantages of secondary data include differences in definitions, the lack of availability, the lack of accuracy, and the age of secondary data. To conduct a secondary data research project, it is suggested that the researcher follow a four-step model: defining the data needed, locating the data, evaluating the data, and verifying the data.

STUDY QUESTIONS

1. Give a summary description of the nature of secondary data as a quantitative technique in sport management research.
2. How many different ways can sport management researchers use secondary data to serve their research needs?
3. What are the common sources of secondary data for sport management research?
4. What are the advantages and disadvantages of secondary data?
5. What are the steps in the process of secondary data research?

LEARNING ACTIVITIES

1. The NBA wants to expand its development league, NBDL. Your consulting firm was just contracted to provide the NBA with recommendations in terms of which cities meet the expansion criteria. Based on the Census data, what city is most qualified for an expansion NBDL team?
2. The national headquarters of a sporting goods retailer wants to expand its market coverage into two Ohio cities by August 1 of the current year. The company's management knows from its past experience that a city must have a population of at least 100,000 people to support a store and that the bulk of its sales is to people between the ages of 27 and 32. Recommend two cities in Ohio, based on information available in the *Sales and Marketing Management's Survey of Buying Power*.

References

Agthe, D. E., & Billings, R. B. (2000). The role of football profits in meeting Title IX gender equity regulations and policy. *Journal of Sport Management, 14*(1), 28–40.

Ahlstrom, D., Si, S., & Kennelly, J. (1999). Free-agent performance in Major League Baseball: Do teams get what they expect? *Journal of Sport Management, 13*(3), 181–196.

American Sports Data, Inc. (2003). *The superstudy of sports participation (Volume III): Outdoors activities.* Hartsdale, NY: Author.

Blankenship, A. B., Breen, G. E., & Dutka, A. (1998). *State of the art marketing research.* Lincolnwood, IL: NTC Books.

Boronico, J. S., & Newbert, S. L. (1999). Play-calling strategy in American football: A game-theoretic stochastic dynamic programming approach. *Journal of Sport Management, 13*(2), 103–113.

DeSchriver, T. D., & Stotlar, D. K. (1996). An economic analysis of cartel behavior within the NCAA. *Journal of Sport Management, 10*(4), 388–400.

Ghauri, P. N., Gronhaug, K., & Kristianslund, I. (1995). *Research methods in business studies: A practical guide.* New York: Prentice Hall.

Gladden, J. M., & Milne, G. R. (1999). Examining the importance of brand equity in professional sport. *Sport Marketing Quarterly, 8*(1), 21–29.

Hadley, L., & Gustafson, E. (1991). Major league baseball salaries: The impacts of arbitration and free agency. *Journal of Sport Management, 5*(2), 111–127.

Institute for Diversity and Ethics in Sport. (2003). News Release: Conference graduation rates shift with realignment. Retrieved October 22, 2006, from http://www.bus.ucf.edu/sport/cgi-bin/site/sitew.cgi?page=/ides/index.htx.

Li, M., & Lawrence, H. (2007, June 1). *Use of secondary data in sport management research.* Paper presented at the 2007 NASSM Annual Conference in Fort Lauderdale, FL.

Maxcy, J., & Mondello, M. J. (2006). The impact of free agency on competitive balance in North American professional team sports leagues. *Journal of Sport Management, 20*(3), 345–264.

McDaniel, C., & Gates, R. (1991). *Contemporary marketing research.* St. Paul, MN: West Publishing Company.

McDonald, M., & Rascher, D. (2000). Does bat day make cents? The effect of promotions on the demand for Major League Baseball. *Journal of Sport Management, 4*(1), 8–27.

Orders, S. A., & Chelladurai, P. (1994). The effectiveness of Sport Canada's Athlete Assistance Program. *Journal of Sport Management, 8*(2), 140–152.

Scarborough Research. (2005). About Scarborough. Retrieved October 14, 2006, from http://www.scarborough.com/about.php

Stinson, J., & Howard, D. R. (2004). Scoreboards vs. mortarboards: Major donor behavior and intercollegiate athletics. *Sport Marketing Quarterly, 13*(2), 129–140.

Taylor, T. (2003). Issues of cultural diversity in women's sport. *Journal of the International Council for Health, Physical Education & Recreation, 39*(3), 27–33.

Theberge, N., & Loy, J. (1976). Replacement process in sport organizations: The case of professional baseball. *International Review of Sport Sociology, 11*(2), 73–93.

Todd, S. Y., Crook, T. R., & Barilla, A. G. (2005). Hierarchical linear modeling of multilevel data. *Journal of Sport Management, 19*(4), 387–403.

Turco, D. M. (2004). Glory days: Halls of fame as celebratory sport tourism attractions. *Journal of Sport Tourism, 9*(2), 195–197.

Wrenn, B., Stevens, R., & Loudon, D. (2002). *Marketing research: Text and cases.* Binghamton, NY: Best Business Books.

Yokum, J. T., Gonzalez, J. J., & Badgett, T. (2006). Forecasting the long-term viability of an enterprise: The case of a Minor League Baseball franchise. *Journal of Sport Management, 20*(2), 248–259.

Zikmund, W. G. (2000). *Business research methods* (6th ed.). Fort Worth, TX: Harcourt College Publishers.

Zygmont, Z. X. & Leadley, J. C. (2005). When is the honeymoon over? Major League Baseball attendance 1970–2000. *Journal of Sport Management, 19*(3), 278–299.

CHAPTER 9
SURVEY RESEARCH

OBJECTIVES FOR COMPLETING THIS CHAPTER ARE THAT STUDENTS WILL BE ABLE TO:

Describe different types of survey research techniques

Understand the process for conducting survey research

Understand various types of survey research and the advantages and disadvantages of each

Understand the types of errors that may incur from the use of survey as a method of data collection

Determine the most appropriate survey research technique with given research circumstances

As DISCUSSED IN CHAPTER 2, survey research, often simply called "survey," is a carefully prescribed measurement procedure that involves gathering information from a sample of respondents through a questionnaire. It is one of the most frequently used methods in sport management research (Quarterman, 2006). The purpose of this chapter is to expose students to survey research so that they can employ this particular research method proficiently. Specifically, a number of topics related to survey research will be discussed. These topics include the types of survey research techniques, their advantages and disadvantages, the types of errors that may incur from the use of survey as a method of data collection, and the selection of a survey research technique.

THE NATURE OF SURVEY RESEARCH: AN INTRODUCTION

Surveys are everywhere. They sit on the restaurant table requesting our feedback on service. They are in our hotel room, asking about the facilities. They reach us by mail, asking what we think about the product we just bought. They fall out of our magazines. They are thrust on us as we enter a mall or store requesting feedback on our experiences. They pop up on our computers as we surf the web wanting to know what we think about a website. How many times have you actually completed one of these? More importantly, were you completing it to offer praises about a service? Or, were you angered by the lack of service and wanted to voice your dissatisfaction? If you answered yes to the last question, you are an average customer—you typically don't think about service until you are negatively affected by it.

Surveys are very useful as a marketing practice. If conducted correctly, the sports company can gather good information that can be used in many decision-making processes in the business.

Survey research is the most commonly used type of research in sports marketing. It is one of the most common types of quantitative social, consumer behavior, and business research. The survey is a ques-

tionnaire (a written instrument) designed to collect data. The broad area of survey research encompasses a number of measurement procedures that involve asking questions of respondents (Trochim, 2006). With surveys, it is possible to collect information from a small or large sample of a larger population in person, by telephone, by mail, and by Internet. This "sample" is usually just a small percentage of the population being studied (The chapter on sampling offers details about establishing a sample of a population).

Survey research is one of the most important areas of measurement in applied sport business research. Surveys are used widely in sport business management. A sports business might want to know what its consumers think about its products, its customer service quality, or its promotional activities. The survey is the preferred method for collecting these types of information because it involves asking participants about their thoughts, experiences, or beliefs.

Survey research is a methodology that encompasses a measurement procedure that involves asking questions of respondents. A "survey" can range from a short feedback survey to an intensive one-on-one, in-depth interview. The length of a survey can range from one question to a questionnaire with an abundance of questions in one or more of a variety of formats. The survey question can be formatted to seek a simple yes or no response, or to gather an array of responses in such variable formats as multiple choice, rank, rate, and fill-in-the-blank. Further, survey method is highly flexible, which is a major reason for its high usage rate. For example, a survey study can be conducted in a variety of facilities or locations; it can be done by phone, mail, Internet, or in person; and it can be organized in a number of ways.

Surveys are used for a wide variety of purposes, depending on the problem or question needing data for use in answers. Here are some examples: A running shoe company wants to know what runners think about its new model, so the company conducts a survey. The national sporting goods retail company wants to know what time of year consumers purchase more camping gear, so it uses a survey to collect information from many stores about sales and consumer needs. The WNBA wants to know if a particular city is a good fit for a new franchise, so it conducts surveys of several kinds to collect a variety of needed data. NASCAR's sponsors want to know if consumers know that they are sponsors, if consumers recognize them, and if consumers are more willing to purchase their products because they are sponsors; they conduct surveys to collect information to answer their questions.

Surveys provide an important source of information needed to discover new knowledge, enhance existing knowledge, and inform understanding. Surveys can reveal simple, basic information, such as income numbers, as well as complex sociological behavior, such as consumer expenditure patterns. This flexibility is the primary reason that survey methodology is used in so many different fields and industries.

Worldwide and Local Work to Improve Survey Methods

There are several organizations focused singularly on improving survey research. Many are further focused on public opinion research, such as the American Association for Public Opinion Research (AAPOR) and the World Association for Public Opinion Research (WAPOR). The World Association for Public Opinion Research states that they exist to "maintain high standards for the collection, analysis and dissemination of public opinion data" (World Association for Public Opinion Research, 2007).

The Council of American Survey Research Organizations (CASRO) is an organization that "advances the business of research through standards, guidelines, professional development, and self-regulation in the process and performance of survey research" (Council of American Survey Research Organizations, 2007). An important document created by CASRO is the *CASRO Code of Standards and Ethics for Survey Research*. In this, CASRO puts forth standards related to responsibilities to survey respondents, confidentiality, privacy, avoidance of harassment, and responsibilities for reporting results.

Other organizations with an emphasis on survey research in business and marketing include the Market Research Association (MRA), Council for Marketing and Opinion Research, European Society for Opinion and Marketing Research, Market Research Society, and the American Marketing Association. The mission of the MRA is to advance, protect and promote, "knowledge, standards, excellence, ethics, professional development and innovation, for the global market and opinion research profession" (Market Research Association, 2007). The American Marketing Association, an association for "individuals and organizations involved in the practice, teaching and study of marketing," (American Marketing Association, 2007) has a special interest group on sports marketing.

What Is a Survey?

The word "survey" is used to describe a research method of gathering information from people. The group of individuals (population) surveyed will be a portion (sample) of the population. Most often, the information includes typical demographics and a variety of psychographics. Survey can also measure knowledge, attitude, opinion, values, perception, behavior, intentions, personality, and positions on issues or topics.

In a genuine survey, a questionnaire is developed and the sample is selected through a scientific process. The questionnaire is developed such that the questions gather information appropriate and pertinent to the research questions. The survey administration process is standardized so that individuals in the sample are asked the same questions in the same way. The sample is chosen through a sampling methodology that ensures that each person in the population will have an equal chance of selection so that the sample is a true representation of the population. The information collected from the specific sample can then be inferred to the population with greater confidence. The discussion on how to design a questionnaire is provided in Chapter 14.

Figure 9-1 provides an example of a survey of sports fans at a sports event. This survey will be used at a SuperCross event and the results will be

Please help with some important research that will be used confidentially by the Georgia Dome. Thank you!!

I. Factors that Influence Your Attendance

Which of the following factors influenced your decision to attend this event? Please circle the number that best reflects your opinion on a scale of **1 (No Influence)** to **5 (Strong Influence)** or **NA (Not Applicable)**.

1. Price to attend the event
   1   2   3   4   5   NA
2. Media promotion/advertising of the event
   1   2   3   4   5   NA
3. A chance to see the sport itself
   1   2   3   4   5   NA
4. A chance to see star riders
   1   2   3   4   5   NA
5. A chance to see your favorite rider perform
   1   2   3   4   5   NA
6. Current AMA Super Cross standings
   1   2   3   4   5   NA
7. Current World Super Cross GP standings
   1   2   3   4   5   NA
8. Entertain client(s)
   1   2   3   4   5   NA
9. Entertain family
   1   2   3   4   5   NA
10. Other: (please specify) _____
   _____

II. Economic Factors

1. With whom did you attend this event (family only; partner only; alone; friends only; family, friends, and partner; business associate; other [please specify]?
   _____
2. How many are in your party (including yourself)? _____
3. If you stayed overnight, where did you stay (hotel, friends/relatives, camping, etc.) and how many nights did you stay?
   Where: _____ **# of nights:** _____
4. Where do you live?
   City _____ State _____ Postal Code _____
5. Please estimate (in even U.S. dollars) how much you spent during your stay for this event. Include the following items: food and beverages, ticket(s), nightclub/lounges/bars, retail shopping, event souvenirs, lodging expenses, private auto expenses, commercial transportation, as well as any other expenses. $ _____

III. The Georgia Dome

1. How many events do you attend each year at the Georgia Dome? _____

2. Are you an Atlanta Falcons season ticket holder?
   ❏ Yes ❏ No
3. What other types of events do you attend at the Georgia Dome? _____
4. What form of transportation did you use to get to the Georgia Dome (car, MARTA, taxi, other)? _____
5. Please rate the following facility services and amenities at the Georgia Dome on a scale of **1 (Poor)** to **5 (Excellent)**. **N/A = Not Applicable**. Please circle the number that best reflects your opinion.
   - Facility location   1 2 3 4 5 NA
   - Directional signage   1 2 3 4 5 NA
   - Professionalism/courtesy   1 2 3 4 5 NA
     of staff
   - Food quality   1 2 3 4 5 NA
   - Food variety   1 2 3 4 5 NA
   - Seating comfort   1 2 3 4 5 NA
   - Sound   1 2 3 4 5 NA
   - Content and clarity of video/s   1 2 3 4 5 NA
     message display board
   - Stadium temperature   1 2 3 4 5 NA
   - Cleanliness of the facility   1 2 3 4 5 NA
   - Access/traffic flow   1 2 3 4 5 NA
   - Facility security   1 2 3 4 5 NA
   - Parking   1 2 3 4 5 NA
   - Overall satisfaction with your   1 2 3 4 5 NA
     experience at the Georgia Dome
6. How can we improve your experience at the Georgia Dome? _____

IV. Atlanta

1. What more can be done to improve Atlanta city services/features/amenities?
2. How do you rate your overall satisfaction with the city of Atlanta on a scale of **1 (Extremely Dissatisfied)** to **5 (Extremely Satisfied)**? **N/A = Not Applicable**. Please circle the number that best reflects your opinion.
   1   2   3   4   5   N/A

V. Demographics

Gender: ❏ Male ❏ Female   Age: _____

Marital/Household Status: _____

❏ Single ❏ Married ❏ Living with Partner £ Divorced

Occupation/Title: _____

Annual Income: _____

Ethnicity: _____

Any additional comments? _____

FIGURE 9-1. Example of a Survey Instrument

used by the facility staff to improve the event. The results will also be shared with stakeholders, such as the hotel industry, transportation industry, restaurant industry, and sponsors of the event.

Survey research is sometimes thought of as an easy research method when compared to other more complicated methods. However, as with any research method, survey research can be simple or complicated, can be developed as low or high quality, and can provide results that will be regarded as questionable or credible. It is therefore incumbent on the researcher to adhere to the highest of quality in the development of the survey instrument, especially its validity and reliability, and the implementation procedures of the survey process.

TYPES OF SURVEY RESEARCH TECHNIQUES

As the above definition on survey research implies, a sport management researcher administers a questionnaire to a sample of respondents from a population while conducting a survey. The questionnaire may be a written document that can be completed by a respondent with a pen, or an electronic file that is filled out online by the surveyed individual, or an instrument to be filled out by the researcher during a face-to-face interview or a telephone interview. Survey research can be conducted in a number of different ways depending upon the research circumstances.

There are two broad categories of survey techniques: the interview and the self-administered survey (Blackenship, Breen, & Dutka, 1998; Wrenn, Stevens, & Loudon, 2002). In each type, questions are prepared and used. The difference is in how the questions are formatted and how the survey is conducted. Based on the degree of interaction between the researcher and the respondent, a survey technique can also be classified either as a direct or as an indirect survey technique. In the direct technique, the survey is conducted in person with the survey respondent. Some direct interviews include the door-to-door the mall intercept, and surveys administered to a group. These are conducted according to the sampling methodology selected for the particular study. In the indirect format, the researcher or the individual who collects data does not have direct contact with the respondent. The survey is conducted through such means as the telephone interview, the mail survey, the respondent self-selected survey, and the online survey.

The Interview as a Survey Technique

In an interview, the survey is conducted in a one-on-one or group session. An interviewer asks the questions on the questionnaire and records the responses either by writing the responses or by audio and/or videotaping the session for later recording.

There are advantages and disadvantages regarding the interview as a survey technique. One advantage is that the interview method gives the interviewer the ability to answer questions from the interviewee. When the interviewee either does not understand a question or needs further explanation on a particular issue, the presence of the interviewer makes it easy to resolve the situation (Robson, 2002). The sport management researcher has more control over the response rate in the personal interview than with self-administered survey techniques, as the researcher completes the survey instrument at the conclusion of the interview or obtains the completed questionnaires by the respondents at the personal interview. The personal interview technique also permits "greater flexibility" (Schwab, 1999, p. 54) as it allows the interviewer to probe for more details of a particular question by asking the interviewee to elaborate on that answer.

The drawbacks of the personal interviews technique include relative high cost, potential bias, methodological limitations, and the attitude of interviewee. Interviews are a time-consuming process. The longer the researcher is involved in the interview process, the more costly it becomes. As such, the apparent disadvantage of the personal interview technique is the cost as compared to self-administered survey forms. A number of measurement errors could result from the involvement of the interviewer or the interviewee. A measurement error "occurs when there is a variation between the information being sought (true value) and the information obtained by the measurement process" (McDaniel &

Gates, 1991, p. 211). Detailed discussion on various measurement errors derived from survey research can be found in a separate section of this chapter.

Chapter 5 is devoted to providing a general description of the interview technique as a whole, and this chapter will discuss each of the interviews/survey techniques in detail, including its advantages and disadvantages, and the circumstances for use. In addition, an example in the sport management research using the interviews/ survey technique will be reviewed.

The telephone interview technique. The telephone interview method "is usually employed (1) when the study design requires speedy collection of information from a large, geographically dispersed population what would be too costly to do in person; (2) when eligibility is difficult; (3) when the questionnaire is relatively short; or (4) when face-to-face contact is not necessary" (Wrenn, Stevens, & Loudon, 2002, p. 96). The telephone interview technique could be executed from the researcher's home or office or from a centrally located phone bank. The development of technology has considerably improved the quality of the telephone interview technique. The computer-assisted telephone interviewing system is now widely used in large-scale sport marketing research. Prior to the interview, the interviewer programs the questionnaire into the computer. During the interview, the interviewer then reads the question shown on the computer screen and records the interviewee's answer by touching one of the response choices provided on the computer screen.

The biggest challenge of the telephone interview method is that it is inconvenient for the interviewee to answer questions that are constructed with the open-ended format and have a lot of answer choices. As interviewees do not have a copy of the questionnaire, it can be difficult for them to remember all of the answer choices, and sometimes even the question itself. To overcome this problem, the sport management researcher must be take special care in constructing the survey questions to provide

fewer answer choices. Today, telephone interview is probably the least preferred method of all interview survey methods, as many households have negative feelings about telemarketers and often hang up the phone upon receiving the calls.

The personal interview technique. The personal interviews/survey is a survey technique in which the sport management researcher (the interviewer) uses a survey instrument to gather information from the respondent (the interviewee) in face-to-face contact. There are two types of personal interview techniques: door-to-door interviews and mall intercept interviews.

The door-to-door interview involves, as the name suggests, going from door-to-door in a specified area. For instance, if Fay's Fitness Forum, a local fitness center, wants to determine who lives in a particular neighborhood, whether or not they are members of a fitness center, and whether or not they would consider becoming a member of Fay's Fitness Forum, the methodology would involve canvassing that particular neighborhood. Researchers, armed with the survey, would go door-to-door throughout the neighborhood asking residents to complete a survey. With the data collected, the managers of Fay's would then have information to answer their questions.

The advantage to using the door-to-door format is that an entire area can be targeted and included in the study. However, some disadvantages are that this type of research is time-consuming and can cost more than other survey methods.

Although both types of personal interviews are commonly found in business research, the mall intercept interview method is much more prevalent in sport management research. The mall intercept interview, as the name implies, involves approaching persons as they are shopping in a mall. It is also used as the descriptor when the survey is conducted in any area where individuals or crowds are gathered or pass by.

Many sport management studies use the mall intercept interview technique in obtaining needed research data. For example, Erin, the owner of a sporting goods store in a mall, would like to know if the store window display is attracting consumers. Erin instructs researchers to conduct a survey using the mall intercept approach. Researchers are placed in the mall area around the store. As shoppers pass by, the researcher intercepts and asks if they would please complete a short survey about the store.

In another example, to determine the economic impact of a particular sports event, the researcher dispatches interview teams to various locations of the venue where the sports event takes place, such as spectator stands, concession areas, information booths, entrances, and exits. Event attendees are "intercepted" (basically approached) by members of the survey teams. To ensure sample representation, the interviewers must employ a systematic random procedure to identify and approach potential interviewees. Without employment of such procedure, the results of the interviews/survey could be skewed.

Self-administered Survey Technique

The self-administrative survey technique is one in which a survey instrument, that is, a questionnaire, is administered by the respondent instead of the interviewer. In a self-administered survey, the information is obtained with the traditional "paper-and-pencil" format. This format can be conducted by getting the survey to the study participants in such a way that the participants can complete the survey on their own. This can be done in person, through the mail, through electronic mail, or as an online survey. The study participant completes the survey and returns it. In the following section, these two types of survey methods will be reviewed in details. This technique has four variations: mail surveys, respondent self-selected surveyed, surveys administered to a group, and online surveys.

Mail surveys. The mail survey technique is also commonly referred to as "the mail survey." The researcher mails out a questionnaire via to the postal service to the intended respondent. Often, a return postage paid envelope accompa-

nies the survey instrument to the respondent. The respondent puts the completed questionnaire in the envelope and mails it back to the sender, that is, the researcher. The mail survey is considered "a relatively simple and straightforward approach to the study of attitude, values, beliefs and motives" (Robson, 2002, p. 233).

Lewis and Quarterman (2006) conducted a study to determine the relative importance of choice factors that were most important to students who decided to matriculate in the field of sport management for a master's degree. They mailed questionnaires to the program or department chairs of 12 randomly selected universities listed on the NASSM website during fall 2003. Of the 360 questionnaires sent, 194 were returned for a response rate of 54%.

There are a number of advantages of the mail survey. It is relatively inexpensive as compared to other types of survey methods. Because there is no one-on-one contact between the researcher and the respondent in the mail survey, the respondent tends to have a greater sense of anonymity and be more willing to provide sensitive information about certain topics. Also, the technique allows the respondent to work on the survey at that individual's leisure and give thoughtful response. In addition, the researcher can utilize this type of survey technique to distribute the questionnaire to a relatively large population.

One of the biggest drawbacks to the self-administered mail survey technique is its low response rate (Blankenship, Breen, & Dutka, 1998) and relatively high non-response error (Wrenn, Stevens, & Loudon, 2002). The researcher also has minimal control of the sample (i.e., its size and who will or will not respond to the survey). The literacy level and language ability of the respondents, to a certain extent, affect the accuracy of the information corrected. And, because there is no personal contact between the researcher and the respondent in the mail survey, no probing can occur.

Many studies have been done that focus mainly on how to improve the response rate of the mail survey. A number of techniques were found to be effective in encouraging the respondents to complete the survey instrument (Zikmund, 2000):

1. *Follow-ups.* A follow-up letter serving as a reminder is a useful tool in increasing the response rate. There are a number of possibilities why a questionnaire is not returned to the researcher. Perhaps the respondent misplaced the questionnaire or the return envelope, or the respondent put the questionnaire aside and forgot to complete it. Follow-up mailings help overcome these aforementioned problems. Typically, the researcher sends out a postcard one week after the initial mailing of

[Date]

Dear [name]:

On [date], we started a study designed to examine institutional factors affecting the outsourcing decision of athletic administrators regarding marketing operations in NCAA Division I athletic programs. Two hundred thirty-two athletic directors were identified and contacted accordingly. Two subsequent rounds of mailing yielded a return rate of 37%. Due to the limited size of the sample, we would like to have a higher percentage of returns.

As of today, we have not received your response. Your participation is extremely important to the success of our study. Your thoughts and expertise will help us gain a better understanding of the issue. We sincerely hope that you could participate in the study by completing the survey and returning it by [date]. If you have already returned the questionnaire sent to you before, please ignore this letter and the survey instrument attached.

As a principal investigator of the research, I would be most happy to answer any questions you might have. Please call me at (xxx) xxx-xxxx or send me an email to this address: [username@domain.edu.]

Thank you very much for your assistance.

Sincerely yours,

[Name and title]
[Program]

FIGURE 9-2. A Sample Follow-up Letter

the questionnaire to either thank the respondents who have returned the survey instrument or remind those who have not completed and returned the questionnaire. In about three weeks, if the response rate is still not satisfactory, the researcher should mail out a new questionnaire with a cover letter that not only contains the same content as the initial cover letter, but also informs the respondent that no questionnaire has been received. No further follow ups are necessary after this point. Figure 9-2 is a sample of the follow-up letter.

2. *Preliminary notification.* Prior to mailing out the initial survey instrument, the researcher may consider sending the respondent an email or a postcard to alert them that they will be receiving a questionnaire from the researcher. The preliminary notification should briefly mention the objective of the survey. However, it should not contain too much information to become burdensome to the prospective respondents. Kent and Turner (2002) conducted a study to determine the effectiveness of a number of pre-notification methods. They found that in general, "pre-notification of the survey recipients significantly increased response rates, with the group receiving email pre-notification having the highest response rate among three groups [i.e., the group receiving email, the group receiving formal letter, and the control group]" (p. 230).

3. *Incentives.* By offering a tangible reward (e.g., a poster with players' autographs), the researcher can induce more respondents to respond. "There is nothing inappropriate about paying respondents for providing information" (Fraenkel & Wallen, 2000, p. 445). Respondents often ask, "What do I get for completing your questionnaire?" To motivate the respondents to participate in the survey, relying solely on altruism is not enough. If it is an onsite survey, providing the participants with some incentive has been proven to be effective. If the information the researcher wants

to obtain is of interest to the respondents, providing them with a summary report is also an excellent motivator. For example, a study conducted by Li and Burden (2002) on the current status of outsourcing of marketing operations among NCAA Division I institutions offered the participants (directors of athletics in those institutions) the opportunity to receive a copy of the research summary. The response rate of the study was about 65 percent.

4. *Survey sponsorship*. If a professional organization endorses a study, such endorsement will help increase the response rate of a survey conducted of the membership of the organization, as the respondents may feel the completion of the questionnaire is a way of fulfilling their obligation to the organization. A study that is supported and endorsed by a famous sports figure also increases response.

5. *Cover letter*. A well-written cover letter gives respondents a good impression. It provides the researcher with an opportunity to persuade respondents to participate in the survey by completing the survey. The cover letter should include information about the researcher, reasons or purpose for the survey, importance or significance of the study in relation to the respondents, a request of or appeal to them to complete the questionnaire, assurance of confidentiality, information about when and how to return the questionnaire, and name and telephone number of the researcher the respondents can call if they have any questions. Figure 9-3 is an example of a cover letter that includes all of these elements.

Respondent self-selected surveys. Respondent self-selected surveys refer to the type of self-administered survey in which the questionnaire is intentionally left by the researcher in convenient places for potential respondent to pick up, complete and drop off in a provided "depository or by a pre-paid-postage return envelope" (Blankenship, Breen, & Dutka, 1998, p. 130).

Although respondent self-selected surveys can provide quick and useful information about a

[Date]

Dear [name]:

The outsourcing of marketing operations and rights has lately become a common practice in American college athletics. It is estimated that more than half of the NCAA Division I-A athletic programs have outsourced some or all of their marketing operations and rights to nationally prominent marketing companies, such as Host Communication, International Sports Properties, and Learfield Communications. Nevertheless, a large number of Division I athletic programs are still keeping their marketing operations in-house.

This study was designed specifically to examine such polarized development in collegiate marketing. Attention was particularly directed to these two issues: why have some athletic programs decided to outsource their marketing operations, while others have not? and what are the perceived benefits of outsourcing sport marketing operations? It is hoped that the study would help those athletic programs that are currently contemplating whether or not they should outsource their marketing operations make a more rational decision. Your participation will be vital to the success of the study. Your input will help us gain a better understanding of athletic administrators' perceptions toward the issue of outsourcing. *It would be greatly appreciated if you could complete the questionnaire and mail it back to us in the enclosed, postage-provided envelop by* [date].

You may be assured of complete confidentiality. No institution or participant will be individually named. The questionnaire has an identification number for mailing purposes only. With the help of the number, we can check your name off of the mailing list once your questionnaire is returned. The results of this study will be made available to any participant who requests a summary of results by writing "copy of results requested" on the back of the returning envelope. I would be most happy to answer any questions you might have. My phone number and post and email addresses are as follows:

[Name and title]
[Institution name]

[Mailing address]
[City and state, zip code]

[Phone]

[E-mail address]

Thank you for your assistance.

Sincerely yours,
[Name and title][Program]

FIGURE 9-3. A Sample Cover Letter/Informed Consent Letter

certain issue, researchers must be mindful that it has a number of disadvantages. The most obvious one is that the results may lack of generalization due to the high possibility of incurring sampling error in the data collection process. Because respondents are those individuals who self-select to provide feedback, the probability is high that only people who have a strong opinion about the issue, positively or negatively, will reply.

Surveys administered to a group. This method is favored by a researcher when the opportunity arises to administer the survey to the members of a particular target group in the same place (Fraenkel & Wallen, 2000). Many sport management studies whose subjects were students used this type of survey technique in the data collection process. The biggest advantage of this technique is that the researcher can distribute the survey instrument to all the potential respondents, answer any questions they may have, and collect the completed questionnaires. The process ensures a high response rate. To apply this technique, the researcher must have a full access to the target population, a condition that does not always exist in sport management research. In a study designed to identify those individuals who were ready to make a voluntary commitment to fitness, Granzin and Olsen (1989) collected research data in Salt Lake City, UT. A quota sample comprised 12 categories of respondents based on their age and gender characteristics. The proportion of respondents in each category matched their occurrence in the area's most recent census. To represent socioeconomic characteristics of the population, interviewers were assigned to all sections of the geographic area. The interviewers administered the survey to the participants and obtained the completed questionnaires at the end of the survey.

Online surveys. The online survey technique has become the most popular survey technique in recent years, thanks to the development and availability of online survey software and tools. The researcher can create a web-based questionnaire and then guide the respondents via email to complete the survey instrument online. Bennett, Drane, and Henson (2003) used the online survey to collect data in a study designed to examine students' perceptions about service learning. The students were asked to navigate to a questionnaire posted on the Internet using the hyperlink provided.

The online survey technique is the least expensive survey technique of all. Online survey software not only allows researchers to deliver questionnaires to potential respondents in any part of the world in seconds (Bartlett, 2005), but also substantially reduces the time and effort required to input the survey data, because the software allows researchers to download the data directly from the web. Online survey software provides researchers with the opportunity to present survey instruments to respondents in an enriched manner with the use of skip patterns, colors, pop-up instructions, and drop-down boxes.

While employing the online survey technique, the sport management researcher must be aware of a number of its disadvantages. The biggest methodological concern is its limitation in sample demographics. In other words, only those people who have computer and online access will have the opportunity to complete the survey. Also, it is possible that the people who respond to the survey may not be the intended target population if the survey is completely open to the public. The aforementioned two disadvantages may invite sampling error.

The response rate is another issue. To improve response rate while using a mail survey, the researcher can usually employ a coding technique and directly send reminders to those identified respondents who have not responded to encourage and solicit their participation. In the online survey, it is impossible to track those who have completed the survey. In addition, the technical aspect of constructing an online survey could be intimidating if the sport management researcher does not have the needed computer expertise. Additional discussion on how to design an online survey instrument can be founded in Chapter 14, Questionnaire Design.

The five techniques reviewed previously for enhancing the response rate of mail survey are also applicable for online survey.

FACTORS AFFECTING THE CHOICE OF PARTICULAR SURVEY METHODS

As mentioned previously, there are a number of survey methods that could be used by sport management researchers to derive answers to their research questions. What are the circumstances under which a particular type of survey technique will be chosen? In the following section, five factors that affect the choice of a particular survey method will be reviewed. These factors include population issues, sampling issues, content issues, bias issues, and administrative issues.

Population Issues

Population issues are concerned about the accessibility, the level of literacy, and the geographical location of the population of interest. A sampling frame, from which a sample will be drawn, is required for both interviews and mail surveys. However, a sampling frame is difficult or impossible to compile for some populations. For example, the researcher who is interested in determining how users of professional sports teams' social networking sites react to the design features of those sites does not have a sampling frame of the user population of those sites. As such, the self-administered online survey technique may be appropriate for obtaining the needed information. All survey techniques involve the use of a questionnaire. Completing the questionnaire requires the respondent to have a certain level of literacy in order to read and understand the questions. Even if a respondent can read to a certain degree, the questionnaire may still possibly contain some difficult or technical terms that will cause response error.

If the population of interest is dispersed over too broad a geographic range, it is not feasible to employ the door-to-door interview technique. On the other hand, phone interviews, mail surveys, and online surveys are good options to reach a nationwide sample.

Sampling Issues

Does the researcher have the basic demographic information about the sample, such as home addresses, phone numbers, or email addresses? Is the sampling frame of the population of interest up to date? How accessible is the sample? Who is the right respondent? How critical is a high response rate to the research project? These are some of the sampling issues that are important for a researcher to consider while choosing the survey techniques in data collection. Let us use the last two questions to illustrate the importance of sampling (McDaniel & Gates, 1991).

For example, a researcher is interested in finding out the number of hours American households spend on watching sports programming on TV. The most pressing issue that the researcher faces is whether or not the researcher wants to acquire information from a specific person in the family, as a "household" is not a respondent. If the head of the household is whom the researcher desires to survey, how is the head of the household defined? Is the researcher willing to let any member of the household complete the survey instrument? Similar problems arise when a group, agency, or organization is chosen as a sample unit. Should any member of the group, agency or organization be allowed to complete a study?

If a high response rate is crucial for the researcher to draw a valid conclusion, neither a mail nor an online survey is recommended, as low response rates are among the most difficult of problems in those two types of survey research. In this case, the door-to-door or mall-intercept interviews may become appealing to the researcher.

Content Issues

If the content of a question asked requires the respondent to consult that individual's records before giving the answer, the mail or online survey technique is more advantageous than the face-to-face or phone interview, as the former two types of survey research techniques give the respondents ample time to consult with their records. For example, to respond to a question asking the amount of funds spent on facility renovation in the last five years, an athletic administrator may have to review the budgetary records in order to get an accurate answer.

Bias Issues

As mentioned previously, the use of survey research will inevitably incur some biases. However, the biases may be less problematic with a certain types of survey techniques. For instance, on-site, mail, or online surveys are better techniques to ask questions that involve social desirability. It is believed that people always want to "look good" in the eyes of others. As such, the respondent does not want to say anything that would be embarrassing. For example, a study is designed to investigate the use of iPhones to view NBA games among college students. In it, a question asks respondents the frequency with which they download and watch NBA games on their iPhones. If a student who does not have an iPhone is asked that question in a face-to-face interview, that individual may not tell the interviewer the truth but a fabricated answer.

If the value of a particular research project depends heavily on the expertise of a respondent, a face-to-face interview is the preferable option, as the researcher has no idea of who actually completed the questionnaire in the mail surveys. For example, a study is designed to ask the commissioners of all the NCAA Division III conferences for their opinions and predictions in terms of the best way to reform the Division. It is likely that the surveyed commissioners may actually ask their subordinates to respond to the survey instead of responding themselves.

Administrative Issues

The administrative issues deal with a number of factors that the researcher must consider while implementing the survey research. These factors include costs, facilities, time, and so on. It is believed that cost is the major factor that many researchers have to contemplate when choosing which type of survey method for their studies. Face-to-face interviews are probably the most expensive survey research technique. On the other hand, online surveys may cost very little but are subject to other limitations. To conduct phone interviews requires well-equipped phone surveying facilities. If time is of essence, the researcher must decide which survey method can provide responses in a relatively short period of time. Under that circumstance, mail surveys are not rec-

ommended, as it takes time to send out the questionnaires and follow-ups, and researchers must wait for the respondents to return the survey instruments.

In short, a number of issues should be reviewed and considered by researchers before they choose a particular type of survey technique. It must be pointed out that making such a decision is not an easy task, as there is no one type of survey method that is clearly the best of all. Each survey technique has its advantages and disadvantages. It therefore requires the researcher to carefully review the research objectives so as to identify a method that is the most appropriate to help accomplish them.

TYPES OF ERRORS IN SURVEY RESEARCH

While using survey research as a tool of collecting needed data, the sport management researcher must be aware that three types of errors could be derived from such usage. These errors typically come from different aspects of the research process. The error that arises when the researcher is drawing a sample is called "sampling error." The other two types of errors, "nonresponse error" and "response error," occur mainly in the data collection process. In the following sections, each of these three types of errors will be reviewed in detail.

Sampling Errors

As mentioned previously, sampling errors occur in the process of sampling. When a sample does not well represent the population from which the sample was taken, a certain amount of error may come with the sample. To try to ensure that the sample is representative, the researcher often employs a particular type of random sampling procedure in the selection process. (Chapter 15 is devoted specifically to discuss various types of sampling procedures.) However, no matter how random the sampling procedure is, the result will inevitably bring some error with it. This type of error is commonly referred to as "random sampling error" (McDaniel & Gates, 1991, p. 209) as it is a byproduct of the random procedure. Researchers can reduce this type of sampling error by increasing the sample size.

The other type of sampling error is "systematic

sampling error" and is associated with either the sampling design or the execution of the sampling process (McDaniel & Gates, 1991). The most common type of systematic sampling error comes from the use of an inaccurate sampling frame, list of population elements, or database that contains the population elements from which a sample will be drawn. For example, a researcher wants to investigate the perceived importance of collaboration between sport management academicians and practitioners in the United States and Canada among sport management educators in these two countries. The researcher sent a questionnaire to each professional member included in the membership list of the North American Society for Sport Management (NASSM). The results could be biased in that there are sport management educators who are not affiliated with the organization.

No matter how accurate the sampling frame is, the results may still be biased if the execution of the sampling process is flawed. A typical mistake committed by those involved in the sampling process is to select the population elements subjectively. Here is an example to illustrate how such subjectivity occurs in survey research: A college sport management professor wants to determine the reactions and favorability of viewers toward the advertisements shown at the recent Super Bowl using a mall intercept interview/survey design to gather data. A number of graduate students are recruited to conduct the interviews in a local shopping mall. Several survey booths are set up, in the major entrances of the mall. Each booth is operated by one student. According to the sampling design, the interviewers are to approach every 20th person walking by the survey booth. The interviewer might subjectively decide to not intercept certain types of shoppers by making assumption that those shoppers do not look like the traditional football enthusiasts.

Nonresponse Error

Nonresponse error refers to the "error that results from a systematic difference between those do and do not respond to the measurement instrument" (McDaniel & Gates, 1991, p. 212). In conducting a research project using a survey instrument to gather data, the biggest challenge that the sport management researcher faces is how to ensure that the study will have a high response rate. It is very common to see the response rate in sport management research ranging between 30% and 50%. If the response rate of a study is about 40%, a fundamental question that the researcher must answer is: Systematically, how different were the responses from those people who completed the questionnaire and those 60% of people who chose not to fill out the questionnaire? In other words, would the results be altered if the response rate increased to 50%? In reality, it is very difficult, if not impossible, to receive a response rate of 100% in the studies employing the self-administered survey method. Nevertheless, the researcher should try to use all the techniques discussed previously to increase the response rate.

Response Error

This type of error occurs when respondents provide inaccurate information in their responses to the survey instrument, consciously and unconsciously. It is very possible for people to fabricate their answers when being asked to answer sensitive questions concerning their household income, their knowledge about certain things, or the level of their performance and/or ability. For example, when asked about their golf handicaps, most amateur golfers will either say they do not have one (basically do not know) or deliberately exaggerate their level to make themselves feel good or avoid embarrassment. One way to reduce this type of error is to draft the survey questions in such a way that they will not make respondents feel intimidated and threatened.

Response error also occurs when the respondent unintentionally gives an inaccurate answer to a question due to misunderstanding the question (the question could be too difficult for the respondent to understand). Let us use an example to illustrate when and how this type of error happens. When responding to the question, "What was your total family income from all sources last year?" a respondent may give the researcher an incorrect total figure because of carelessly failing to include certain amounts of income in that figure (Bradburn, Sudman & Wansink, 2004). Telescoping, "the respondent pushes events backward into a time period previous to the one being asked about" (Bradburn, Sudman & Wansink, 2004, p. 29), also creates response error.

DESIGNING SURVEY RESEARCH

With any research design there are specific steps that should be followed in order to improve the scientific quality of the study. Increasing the quality of the study increases the confidence level of the results. Accordingly, to conduct survey research, it is important for the researcher to understand the planning process. Chapter 14 details the process of designing a questionnaire to be used in the survey research.

A SURVEY RESEARCH CASE IN SPORT MANAGEMENT

McDaniel (2002) conducted a study to examine the implications of audience demographics, personal values, lifestyle, and interests to sport marketing and media in the context of the 1996 Summer Olympic Games. The author formed three hypotheses: (1) respondents' level of interest in the 1996 Olympic Games is an additive function of their demographics (gender, age, race, and education level), personal values (patriotism and religiosity), and lifestyle (average weekly consumption of televised sports); (2) respondents' values (patriotism and religiosity) and attitudes (toward advertising) will differ significantly based on their level of interest in the Olympic Games; and (3) the total hours respondents estimated they spent watching the Olympics telecast is an additive function of their demographics (gender, age, race, and education level), personal values (patriotism and religiosity), lifestyle (average weekly consumption of televised sports), and interest in the Games.

The author used the phone interview/survey technique to collect data. First of all, the phone numbers of the potential respondents were obtained through a survey marketing company, which employed a stratified random sampling technique to generate the sample. Trained callers, using a telephone research facility at a major U.S. university, initiated the calls prior to the 1996 Atlanta Olympic Games between June 12 and July 12. All the respondents who participated in the first round of phone calls were asked if they would consent to a follow-up call. Only those who had agreed to be part of the second round of phone calls were contacted again. The second round of calls, lasting about a month, started on August 5 after the closing ceremony. The study generated 330 completed interviews in the first round of phone calls, representing 39% of the 847 people called. Approximately 75% of the respondents, or 248 people, who completed the interviews in the first round of calls completed the interviews in the second round of calls. The figure accounted for 29% of the total.

The results of the study indicated the following:

Male respondents' levels of interest in the Olympic Games were significantly related to their patriotic values and lifestyle. Those most interested in this event reported significantly higher levels of patriotism and religiosity than those less interested; likewise, the high event interest group reported enjoying advertising at a significantly greater level than their low event interest counterparts. Demographics, lifestyle, and event interest levels significantly influenced total amount of exposure to the event telecasted. (McDaniel, 2002, p. 117).

SUMMARY

Survey research is one of the research methods that is used to gather information from respondents through the use of a questionnaire. There are three types of survey techniques: the telephone interviews/survey, personal interviews/survey, and self-administered survey. Each of these survey techniques has its own advantages and disadvantages.

The personal interviews/survey method involves face-to-face contact. Such contact happens when the interviewer asks the interviewee(s) questions and then records the response on the survey instrument. Based on the location where the interviews take place, the personal interviews/survey method has two versions: the door-to-door interviews /survey, and mall intercept interviews/survey.

Unlike the interview methods in which the interviewer records the information obtained from interviewee in the survey instrument, the self-administered survey requires the respondents to fill out the questionnaire without the presence of the interviewer, except the *survey administered to a group* technique. Mail survey was once the most popular survey method, but its popularity has been eclipsed by that of the online survey. Follow-ups, preliminary notification, survey sponsorship, incentives, and cover letter are five techniques that can be used to increase response rates.

The sport management researcher should be aware of the types of errors that may occur from the application of survey research. In general, three major types of errors are found in sport management research: the sampling error, the non-response error, and the response error.

Each survey technique has its own uniqueness in application. As such, the sport management researcher should carefully examine the factors that affect the selection of a particular survey method. These factors include population issues, sampling issues, survey question-related issues, content issues, bias issues, and administrative issues.

STUDY QUESTIONS

1. Describe the various types of survey research techniques.
2. What are the advantages and disadvantages of each type of survey research?
3. What are the techniques used to enhance the response rate of mail surveys?
4. What are the types of errors that may occur from the use of survey as a method of data collection?
5. What are the criteria that can be used to select the most appropriate survey research technique?

LEARNING ACTIVITIES

1. What type of survey method is most appropriate for each of the following scenarios? Give your justification.
   a. To understand the preferences of athletic directors of NCAA Division III institutions toward a number of proposals on how to restructure their Division
   b. To obtain the opinions of the student population of a particular university toward the proposal calling for increasing student fees to support the athletic department
   c. To determine the user satisfaction of an ice ring
   d. To find out the level of consumer awareness to a new type of running shoes just introduced to the market by Nike
   e. To examine the attitudes of local residents about raising taxes to pay for the construction of a football stadium for the professional football franchise currently residing in the community
2. Provide your critique to each of the following survey designs:
   a. To determine what features users feel are important in a social networking site, such as Facebook, the researchers invite the users of Facebook to complete a questionnaire that they posted on SurveyMonkey.Com.
   b. A sporting goods store wants to find out if the service provided to customers is satisfactory. The general manager places packets containing a questionnaire, cover letter, and stamped return envelope at a number of locations in the store. Customers can pick up a packet if they wish.
3. Design a study that involves the use of each of the following survey techniques:
   a. The mail survey
   b. The mall intercept interviews/survey
   c. The online survey

References

American Marketing Association. (2007). Mission statement. Retrieved from www.marketingpower.com.

Bartlett, K. R. (2005). Survey research in organizations. In R. A. Swanson & E. F. Holton III (Eds.), *Research in organizations*. San Francisco, CA: Berrett-Koehler Publishers, Inc.

Bennett, G., Drane, D., & Henson, R. (2003). Student experiences with service-learning in sport management. *Journal of Experiential Education, 26*(2), 61–69.

Blackenship, A. B., Breen, G. E., & Dutka, A. (1998). *State of the art marketing research* (2nd ed.). Lincolnwood, IL: NTC Business Books.

Council of American Survey Research Organizations. (2007). Mission statement. Retrieved from www.casro.org.

Fraenkel, J. R., & Wallen, N. E. (2000). *How to design and evaluate research in education* (4th ed.). Boston, MA: McGraw Hill.

Granzin, G. L., & Olsen, J. E. (1989). Identifying those ready to make a voluntary commitment to fitness. *Journal of Sport Management, 3*(2), 116–128.

Johnson, B., & Christensen, L. (2000). *Educational research: Quantitative and qualitative approaches*. Boston, MA: Allyn and Bacon.

Kent, A., & Turner, B. (2002). Increasing response rates among coaches: The role of pre-notification methods. *Journal of Sport Management, 16*(3), 230–238.

Lewis, B. A., & Quarterman, J. (2006). Why students return for a master's degree in sport management. *College Student Journal, 40*(4), 717–728.

Li, M., & Burden, W. (2002). Outsourcing Sport Marketing Operations by NCAA Division I Athletic Programs: An Exploratory Study. *Sport Marketing Quarterly, 11*(4), 227–232.

Marketing Research Association. (2007). Mission statement. Retrieved from www.mra-net.org/about/mission.cfm).

McDaniel, C., & Gates, R. (1991). *Contemporary marketing research*. St. Paul, MN: West Publishing Company.

McDaniel, S. R. (2002). An exploration of audience demographics, personal values, and lifestyle: Influences on viewing network coverage of the 1996 Summer Olympic Games. *Journal of Sport Management, 16*, 117–131.

Robson, C. (2002). *Real world research: A resource for social scientists and practitioners-researchers* (2nd ed.). Oxford, UK: Blackwell Publisher.

Schwab, D. P. (1999). *Research methods for organizational studies*. Mahwah, NJ: Lawrence Erlbaum Associates, Publishers.

Trochim, W. M. K. (2006). Survey research: Research methods knowledge base. Retrieved January 27, 2007, from http://www.socialresearchmethods.net/kb/survey.php.

Wrenn, B., Steven, R., & Loudon, D. (2002). *Marketing research: Text and cases*. New York, NY: Haworth Press

Zikmund, W. G. (2000). *Business research methods* (6th ed.). Fort Worth, TX: Harcourt College Publishers.

CHAPTER 10
EXPERIMENTAL RESEARCH

OBJECTIVES FOR COMPLETING THIS
CHAPTER ARE THAT STUDENTS WILL
BE ABLE TO:

Discuss the issues that a researcher must address
while designing an experimental study

Explain how the independent variable is
manipulated in an experiment

Define internal validity and explain each of the
factors that may threaten the internal validity
of an experiment

Define external validity and explain each of the
factors that may threaten the external validity
of an experiment

Elaborate on the differences between experiment
and other research designs, such as survey

Compare and contrast preexperimental designs,
true experimental designs, and quasi-
experimental designs

EXPERIMENTAL RESEARCH IS ONE of the popular research designs frequently adopted by researchers in business research, as it helps the researcher establish the cause-and-effect relationship between two variables. Researchers in general believed that experimental research is the most scientific method among all business research methods, including surveys, secondary data, observation, and all qualitative research techniques, as it allows the variable causing a particular effect to be isolated (Crawford, 1997). Nevertheless, the research method has not been given adequate attention by sport management researchers; only a small number of studies found in the sport management literature have employed this technique.

The purpose of this chapter is to provide a thorough discussion on experiment as a useful research technique. Specifically, the chapter will first review the nature of experimental research, followed by the discussion on the two basic types of validity in experimental research (i.e., internal validity and external validity) and the factors affecting them. The three types of true experimental designs will also be examined.

NATURE OF EXPERIMENTAL RESEARCH

As mentioned in Chapter 2, in an experiment, the sport management researcher tries to arrange the experimental conditions or procedures so that a hypothesis about a cause-and-effect relationship between two events or variables can be tested. For example, the owner of a golf pro-shop wanted to determine, in an experimental research project, whether the packaging style of used golf balls affected their sales. First, the store sold the balls in an open bin for a month. After recording the sales of balls this way, the store packed and sold the balls in a slate of three. The change yielded better sales figures. The owner then wondered, "Did the packaging cause this sales increase?"

In the example illustrated, experimental research is intended to find out what caused a particular thing to happen (i.e., increase in sales) through manipulating the causes (i.e., packaging). Specifically, it helps the researcher obtain information on whether or not the packaging (independent variable) affects the sales of used golf balls (dependent variable). From this case, we know that the independent variable is the variable that makes the effect happen (the cause) and the dependent variable is the effect that depends on the independent variable. The independent variable is also referred to as "the experimental variable, the cause, or the treatment" (Gay & Diebl, 1992, p. 382). The dependent variable, on the other hand, is also called "criterion variable, effect, or posttest" (Gay & Diebl, 1992, p. 382). Experimental research is the only type of research design that allows researchers to prove a cause-effect relationship, that is, to draw conclusions about causation.

EXPERIMENTATION: BASIC ISSUES

Figure 10-1 illustrates the conceptual model of how an experiment is used to uncover the cause-effect relationship between independent variable or cause (the packaging of golf balls) and the dependent variable or effect (sales of the used golf balls).

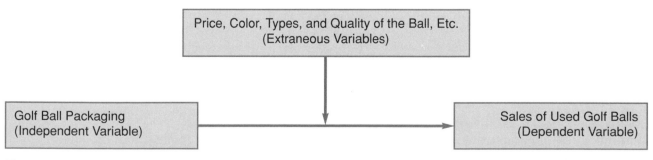

FIGURE 10-1. Conceptual Relationship among the Independent Variable, the Dependent Variable, and the Extraneous Variable

Before implementing experimental research, it is imperative to develop a plan or design that will address the following issues:

■ selecting subjects randomly from population
■ assigning subjects randomly to groups
■ assigning specific treatments or conditions of the experiment randomly to one or more groups
■ measuring the dependent variable (McDaniel & Gates, 1991).

To truly unveil the causal relationship, researchers commonly use several procedures. Such procedures include selecting subjects randomly from the population and assigning subjects randomly to the experimental group and the control group (Gay & Diebl, 1992). The experimental group is the one in an experiment that receives the specified treatment that is under investigation. The control group, on the other hand, refers to the group that is included in the experiment but not exposed to the experimental treatment. The use of the control group is to establish a baseline against which to measure the effect of the full treatment on the experimental group. In other words, the purpose of using a control group is to create equivalency among the groups involved in the experiment so that they are statistically equal to each other and no systematic difference exists among them, ultimately controlling the extraneous variables. Extraneous variables are referred to all the potential variables that are external to the experiment but may affect the results of the treatment on the subject, consequently interfering in the relationship between the independent variable and the dependent variable. Figure 14-1 also shows the influence of the extraneous variables on the cause-and-effect relationship between the packing of golf balls and the sales of used golf balls.

As Figure 14-1 shows, the cause-and-effect relationship between the packaging and sales may be compromised by other factors or the so-called extraneous variables, such as price, color, type, and quality of the balls. Specifically, under some circumstances, such as if the pro shop sells the packaged balls in a lower price per unit than that of those balls sold in the open bin, or the pro shop selects the balls with good quality and brands to be packaged (intentionally or not), the causal relationship between packaging and sales could not be clearly established. To truly discover the existence of the relationship between the independent variable and the dependent variable, the extraneous variables must be considered and controlled. To do that, the researcher must ensure that both groups come from the same population, and the subjects and the experimental treatment are randomly assigned to the groups. Random assignment of subjects to groups ensures that the differences between subjects in unsystematic (random) ways are distributed evenly so that there is no tendency to give an edge to any group. In that way, researchers can feel more secure about the results of their studies. Random assignment of experimental treatment refers to the random process to decide which group will receive the experimental treatment.

The main objective is for the randomization process to produce groups that are comparable in unknown as well as known factors that are likely to influence the outcome, apart from the actual treatment under study (Ghauri, Gronhaug, & Kristianslund, 1995). The existence of any systematic difference may weaken the outcome of the experiment and reduce the internal validity of the experiment.

The experimental treatment is the manipulation of the independent variable being investigated (Zikmund, 2000). The process to apply specific treatments or conditions of the experiment to the experimental group is called "manipulation." For example, a minor league baseball team wants to know whether promotional activities (independent variable) will increase game attendance. To test if such a relationship exists, the team first identifies 10 home games, the opponents of which all have similar win and loss records. Then, promotional activities are randomly implemented in five of those games. The implementation of promotional activities only to five games is the treatment applied in the experiment.

EXPERIMENTAL VALIDITY

Internal Validity Defined

The inside logic of an experiment is referred to as internal validity. Internal validity refers specifically to whether an experimental treatment/condition makes a difference or not, and whether there is sufficient evidence to support the claim. It basically asks the question: Does it seem reasonable to assume that the treatment has really produced the measured effect? In other words, the outcome of the experiment is the result of the experimental treatment, not something irrelevant to the experiment; otherwise, the experiment is not internally valid (Gay & Diebl, 1992).

Factors That Jeopardize Internal Validity

Campbell and Stanley (1972) identify eight basic factors that threaten the internal validity of an experiment. Their work has been widely cited. In the following section, each of the factors is explained with an example.

1. History—the specific external event (i.e., not part of the experiment) that occurs between the first and second measurement of the dependent variable that may affect the interpretation of the change to the variable. XYZ is a company that manufactures *Athrink*, a type of sport drinks that claims to have an exceptional effect in helping youths recover the lost minerals after an athletic activity, such as cross country running. The company has decided to introduce a new flavor. Before the introduction, it wants to determine whether or not it should use its traditional packing design or a new one that is more contemporary. The company chooses Columbus, Ohio, to test the product. In the first two months, it supplies all the stores with the new drink with traditional packaging. Then it replaces all the drinks with the new packaging design in the subsequent two months. Pricing and distribution will be identical in these stores during the experiment. The traditional packaging will act as the control in this experiment. The sales figures will be analyzed to ascertain if the new design led to the increase in sales after the four months of the experiment. In the third month of the experiment, a sponsorship agreement is entered into by the Ohio High School Athletic Association and XYZ. The agreement designates *Athrink* as the of-

ficial soft drink of the association's annual state cross country meet, which happens coincidentally during the third month of the XYZ's test market. The sponsorship agreement has overshadowed the effect of the new packaging design on sales.

2. Maturation—the physical and mental changes that may occur within the subjects over a period of time or the processes within subjects that occur as a function of the passage of time. The changes subsequently affect the subject's performance on the measure of the dependent variable. In the case discussed above about the test market on new packaging, if customers prefer *Athrink* over other brands of athletic drinks as a result of learning more about the new drink through the publicity surrounding the sponsorship agreement, the increased sales is more an effect of maturation than of the new packaging.

3. Testing—the improvement in the second test as a result of having taken the first test. The improvement in performance of the latter test can be attributed to the familiarity or memory of the test contents by the subjects. This particular threat happens only to experiments that require the subjects to take a pretest and a posttest that are identical. In a sport executive training program, for instance, the participants are given a short questionnaire that determines their levels of awareness and knowledge about basic facts of trends and shifts in consumer needs due to the changes in demographics in the United States. After a week of training, they are asked to complete the same questionnaire again. The sponsor of the training program uses the improvement in the executives' performance on the test to justify the effectiveness of the training program. The improvement contains a certain degree of familiarity by the executives to the questions in the questionnaire after already taking the pretest (Gay & Diebl, 1992).

4. Instrumentation—the lack of consistency or reliability in the measure of the dependent

variable as a result of changes occurring in the instrument, observers, or scorers. If the researcher decides to use two separate instruments (claimed to be substitutable to each other) to measure if improvement occurs in a pretest and posttest design to avoid the testing effect as discussed above, the researcher may encounter the instrumentation effect, another type of threat to the internal validity of the experiment (Zikmund, 2000). The instrumentation effect results from the non-equivalency or difference in the two instruments used. Such non-equivalency prevents the researcher from showing that the experimental treatment actually has the true effect on the dependent variable as indicated in the performance of the posttest. The instrumentation effect also presents when observers are used to evaluate the behavior of subjects in an experiment using the pretest and posttest design. The observers "may unconsciously tend to see and record what they know the researcher is hypothesizing" (Gay & Diebl, 1992, p. 389) or may become less interested or may improve their observation skills as time goes by. Consequently, the reliability of data collected by the observers from the pretest and posttest suffers.

5. Statistical regression—also known as regression to the mean. It occurs when the subjects are selected on the basis of their extreme scores. It is a common phenomenon that the subjects who perform the worst in the pretest would most likely improve their performance after the treatment applied to them. However, such improvement is not the outcome of the treatment, but the statistical regression instead. For example, after a test consisting of multiple-choice questions, a professor in a sport management class identifies all the students whose test scores are below the 15th percentile of the entire class. The professor immediately administers the test again to the identified students. Without any intervention (such as review sessions), the students' performance may be improved. These students

are chosen because they are expected to perform better (Gay & Diebl, 1992).

6. Selection of subjects—threat caused by the selection of comparison groups (i.e., the experimental group and the control group) that are different before the experiment even begins. The existing difference between the groups interferes with the interpretation of the difference in performance of the comparison groups in the posttest that could truly be caused by the experimental treatment. Randomization of group membership and randomization of assignment of treatment are methods that can reduce this threat.

7. Experimental mortality—threat caused by the loss of subjects, that is, the subjects voluntarily or involuntarily drop out of the experiment. The reduction in the number of subjects in the experimental group may cause the characteristics of subjects in the group to be different from those in the control group. The reduction in the number of subjects in the experimental group also may cause it to be less or non-representative of the population. In both cases, systematic errors will increase that blur the causal relationship between the independent variable (the experimental treatment) and the dependent variable. For example, an Internet-based introduction to sport management class started with 161 students, and only 95 of them completed the entire class. Those who stayed in the class to end may have been more motivated to learn and thus achieved higher performance.

8. Interaction with selection—threat originating from the selection of comparison groups and its interactions with other factors, such as history, maturation, testing, and so on. The interaction may then lead to confounding outcomes and the false interpretation that the treatment caused the effect.

External Validity Defined

External validity, on the other hand, refers to the proposed interpretation of the results of the study. It asks the question: With what other groups could we reasonably expect to get the same results if we used the same treatment? External validity implies the generalizability of the findings of an experiment or the degree to which the conclusions in an experiment could be repeated by other researchers in different settings at different times.

Factors That Jeopardize External Validity

There are a number of factors that threaten the external validity of an experiment or cause the researcher to the wrong generalization. Because an experiment in sport management research often involves people (fans) in a specific place (facility) and at a specific time (during the game or event), the generalizability of the results of the experiment to another context (for instance, another place, with slightly different people, at a slightly later time) could be affected by the three elements: people, place, and time. Different groups of fans in a different venue at a different time may alter the condition and thus alter the outcomes of the original experiment. The following are factors that may jeopardize external validity of experimental research in sport management.

1. Surrogate situations—threat exists when the experimental settings, the treatment applied, and the measurement units are different from those that would be found in the real setting (MaDaniel & Gates, 1992). The use of college students as experimental subjects potentially may jeopardize the external validity of any research. For example, a classroom is not a real sport marketplace when students are used by a faculty member in an experiment to determine which brand of sports drink the sport fans prefer. This threat to external validity is caused by the lack of population validity. The population validity is referred to as "the ability to generate to and across sub-populations in the target population (Johnson & Christensen, 2000, p. 216).

2. Selection-treatment interaction—threat caused by the non-randomization of experimental subjects. It will severely limit the generalizability of an experiment.

3. Reactive effects—threat caused by the subjects in the experiment who intentionally alter their performance as a result of being aware of an experiment. As such, it is difficult to generalize to other experimental settings.

4. Multiple treatment interference—threat occurs when multiple treatments are given to the same subjects. As a result, it is difficult to control for the effects of prior treatments. Both the reactive effects and multiple treatment interference are threats to the external validity, the ability to generalize the results across settings, of the experiment (Johnson & Christensen, 2000, p. 216).

There are several approaches to improve the external validity of an experiment. First, the researcher must ensure that the sampling used in the experiment is drawn randomly from a population so that it reflects the main characteristics of the population. Second, it is also important to keep the dropout rate low after the sample has been selected. Third, the researcher should conduct the experiment in a variety of settings with different people at different times. In that way, the ability to replicate the experiment is enhanced.

SELECTED EXPERIMENTAL DESIGNS

To make it easy to describe various types of experimental designs, symbols are often used to represent various procedures or acts taking place in an experiment.

X—Treatment
O—Observation or measurement
R—Random assignment

Specifically, "X" symbolizes the application of a treatment to the experimental group. "O" represents the observation or measurement given before and after the experiment. "R" signifies the randomization process applied to the assignment of treatment to the groups involving in the experiment.

Three types of designs are commonly seen in experimental research: preexperimental designs, true experimental designs, and quasi-experimental designs. The following section provides detailed descriptions for these three types of designs.

Three Preexperimental Designs

Three types of preexperimental designs are commonly used to illustrate threats to validity of an experiment in literature related to experimental research. The preexperimental designs do not select subjects and assign them randomly to groups. Two of the three common preexperimental designs do not have a control group. Because of these two features, the impact from extraneous variables on the results of the experiment is tremendous. Consequently, it is extremely difficult to establish a logical relationship between the independent variable and dependent variable. The three types of preexperimental designs are the one-shot case study, the one group pretest and posttest design, and the static group comparison.

The One-Shot Case Study

This design involves only a single group. The subjects in the group are introduced to a treatment or condition and then observed for changes that are attributed to the treatment. For example, a golf equipment manufacturer that produces a new driver has the players on the golf team of a university hit balls with the driver and then measure the distances they hit. This particular type of preexperimental design can be expressed as:

$$X \; O$$

where the symbol X represents exposure of the experimental group to the treatment of interest or the opportunity to hit balls with the new driver, and O refers to the measurement of the dependent variable or the distance hit with the new driver. In this type, treatment comes before measurement.

The most obvious problems with this design are:

1. There is a total lack of control. Also, it is of very little scientific value in terms of securing evidence to make comparisons, and recording differences or contrasts.
2. There is also a tendency to have the error of misplaced precision, in which the researcher engages in tedious collection of specific detail, careful observation, testing, and so on, and misinterprets this as obtaining good re-

search. A detailed data collection procedure does not necessarily equal a good design.
3. History, maturation, selection, mortality, and interaction of selection and the experimental variable are all threats to the internal validity of this design.

One-Group Pretest and Posttest Design

In this design, the subjects are given a pretest and then exposed to a treatment. After that, they are given a posttest. The difference between O_1 and O_2 is compared to determine whether or not the treatment has brought some change to the subjects. The symbolic expression of this design is as follows:

$$O_1 \; X \; O_2$$

Let us use an example to illustrate this type of preexperimental design. A researcher wants to assess the effects of a promotional campaign on consumer purchasing intention toward a sports drink. The researcher first uses a questionnaire to measure consumers' attitude toward and the consequent purchasing intention of the product. Then, the researcher launches a two-month long campaign to promote the drink. After the promotional campaign, the researcher uses the same questionnaire to measure any changes in consumers' attitudes and purchasing intention.

This type of design is better than the one-shot case study. Nevertheless, there still exist threats to the validity of this design:

1. Many events may have occurred apart from the treatment X to produce the differences in outcomes between O_1 and O_2. In other words, the change observed in O_2 may be caused by events outside the experiment rather than by the treatment. The longer the time lapse between O_1 and O_2, the more likely history becomes a threat. For example, the XYZ sporting goods company required its entire sales force to participate in a sales course that introduced several new sales techniques using the Internet. The sales performance in the six months prior to the course was first recorded. After the course, the sales performance in the

next six months was measured. The economic condition after the initial sales figures were calculated may have changed, accordingly affecting consumers' demand for the products of the company. That will make it difficult for the company to attribute to the course any change in sales in the second measure, taken after the course.

2. Between O_1 and O_2, the subjects may have grown older or internal states may have changed (e.g., getting more informed or more experienced) and therefore the differences obtained would be attributable to these changes as opposed to the treatment X. The sales representatives may be exposed to online technology through other channels after the initial observation on their sales performance has been taken. Consequently, the change observed in their performance in the second measure may be partially or completely attributed to their learning outside the course.

3. The effect of giving the pretest itself may influence the outcomes of the posttest. In the case of the sales course implemented by the XYZ sporting goods company, it is possible that the sales representatives know their performance after the course will be monitored so that they may work hard to increase their performance.

4. Experimental mortality could affect the interpretation of the results obtained in the posttest. The dropout of sales representatives between the first and second measures of sales performance creates disparity between the sales force before and after the sales course.

The Static Group Comparison

This is a two-group design in which the experimental group is exposed to the experimental treatment and the results are then tested; the control group is not exposed to the treatment but similarly tested in order to compare the effects of treatment. The difference between O_1 and O_2 represents the treatment

effect. This design is expressed symbolically in the following way:

$$X \: O_1$$
$$O_2$$

The major issue of this experimental design is that no pretest is used to establish a baseline to compare the performance of subjects in the experimental group before and after the treatment application. Because of that, this design inevitably inherits the following flaws:

1. The selection effect is one of the threats to the internal validity of this design—the subjects who participate in both the experimental and control groups may in fact have already been different prior to the treatment. So, the disparity among the two groups between the measures O_1 and O_2 may not be actually caused by the experimental treatment.

2. The differences between O_1 and O_2 may also be attributed to the dropout rate of subjects from one of the groups in the experiment, which would cause the groups to be unequal. This is the so-called experimental mortality effect. In the case discussed previously, the dropout of sales representatives between the two measures of sales performance creates disparity between the sales force before and after the sales course, potentially affecting the interpretation of the results obtained in the posttest.

3. The interaction of selection and maturation and interaction of selection and the experimental variable are also threats to the internal validity of this type of experimental design.

Three True Experimental Designs

To reduce the threats to both the internal and external validity of the experimental designs as discussed in the previous section, sport management researchers can seek help from the so called "true" experimental designs. In a true experimental design, they not only manipulate the independent variable as they do in the preexperimental designs, but also randomly assign subjects to either the experimental group or the control group. The random assignment of subjects to groups is the main characteristic of the true experimental designs. In general, there are three types of true experimental designs: the pretest-posttest control group design, the posttest-only control group design, and the Soloman four-group design. Detailed descriptions of each of these experimental designs are provided in the following section.

The Pretest-Posttest Control Group Design

This type of experimental design involves at least two groups of subjects. They are first randomly selected and then randomly assigned to either the experimental group or the control group. So, they are considered equivalent if not identical in the composition of subjects. Both groups are administered a pretest. Only the experimental group, however, receives the experimental treatment. In that way, subjects in both groups may be exposed to the same extraneous variables. The experimental treatment is applied only to the experimental group. After the application of treatment, a posttest is administered to both groups again. The difference between measures O_3 and O_4 can be interpreted as the contribution of extraneous variables. The effect of the experimental treatment X, therefore, can be obtained through the determination of the difference between (O_1-O_2) and (O_3-O_4). Symbolically, this design can be expressed as:

Experimental Group: R O_1 X O_2
Control Group: R O_3 O_4

This design controls for most of the threats to validity, such as history, maturation, instrumentation, etc., as described previously. Let us use an example to illustrate how this design controls for some of the threats. A sporting good manufacturer wants to measure the sales effect of a point of purchase display of a particular type of baseball glove. It randomly selects 20 retail stores to participate in the experiment, 10 of which are assigned the experimental group and 10 to the control group. Before the experiment, the participating stores' sales performances on the baseball glove are recorded. The manufacturer then places the point of purchase display in those stores selected in the experimental group for three months. After the point of purchase display has been in use in the experimental stores for three months, the manufacturer measures the sales of all stores selected in the experiment. Because of the use of randomization in assigning groups and treatment, the stores in the two groups involved in the experiment are equivalent. The maturation and testing are controlled because they are manifested equally in both experimental and control groups, as they are equivalent. The regression effect is controlled because both the experimental and control groups are randomly selected from the same extreme pool and randomly assigned to groups. If this occurs, both groups will regress similarly, regardless of treatment. The randomization procedure controls the selection effect.

There are, nevertheless, two threats that are still have some effect to the validity of this design: mortality and local history. During the three months the point of purchase display was used, one store in the experimental group was forced to close due to a tax problem and another store caught fire. The dropping out of the two stores may create disparity among the stores in the two groups, as the groups are composed of different subjects after the pretest. The lack of equivalency leads to selection bias, consequently affecting the interpretation of the results of the experiment. Unless the mortality rate is equal in both the experimental and control groups, it is impossible to indicate with certainty that mortality did not contribute to the experiment results.

Local history also affects the validity. During the experiment, a baseball tournament was held in the communities of three of the ten stores. The tournament inevitably leads to an increase in sales of baseball gloves. Because of the tournament, the change in sales between O_1 and O_2 couldn't absolutely be attributed to the application of the experimental treatment X, the point of purchase display.

The threats to external validity could not be completely eliminated either in this type of design. The effect of reactive arrangements (the point of purchase display and the subject's knowledge that the store is participating in an experiment) could have an impact on the experiment results.

The Posttest-Only Control Group Design

This design is similar to the *pretest-posttest control group design* except there is no pretest. This type of design is used when a pretest is not possible (Zikmund, 2000). Again, subjects are selected and assigned randomly to the two groups in the experiment. In that way, both the experimental and control groups are equivalent prior to applying the treatment to the experimental group. The equivalency not only forms a basis of comparison but also ensures that all extraneous variables have effects on both groups. After the experimental group is exposed to the experimental treatment, a test is administered to both the experimental and control group. By determining the difference between (O_1-O_2), the effect of the experimental treatment X can be extracted. The symbolic expression of this design is as follows:

Experimental Group:	R	X O_1
Control Group:	R	O_2

Similar to the *pretest-posttest control group design*, most of the threats to validity, such as testing and instrumentation, are controlled in this true experiment design. In addition, as a pretest is not administered to both groups, it can be assumed that both groups have experienced the same current events and same developmental processes, thus minimizing both the history and maturation effects. Because the subjects are selected and assigned into either the experimental or control group, they are considered approximately equivalent. Also, the selection effect is not a problem in this type of design.

The t-test is the simplest form of statistical tests for this design. However, other forms of statistical analysis (e.g., covariance analysis) can also be used as they increase the power of the significance test similarly to what is provided by a pretest.

The Soloman Four-Group Design

To eliminate the threats to validity of the previously mentioned two true experimental designs, the researcher can use the so-called Soloman four-group design. This design is in fact the combination of both the *pretest-posttest control group design* and the *posttest-only control group design*. To implement this type of experimental design, the researcher randomly selects and assigns subjects to four different groups: the experimental group with both the pretest and posttest, the experimental group without the pretest, the control group with both the pretest and posttest, and the control group without the pretest. By using experimental and control groups with and without a pretest, both the main effects of testing and the interaction of testing and the treatment are controlled. In addition, the impact of extraneous variables is also eliminated. The effect of X is replicated and isolated through several ways and comparisons, that is, (O_2-O_1)—(O_4-O_3), (O_5-O_5), and (O_2-O_4). Even through the Soloman design is considered the gold standard of experimental design, due to its impractical nature (the time, effort, and financial resource required), it is rarely used in business and sport management research. The symbolic expression of this design is shown as follows:

Experimental Group 1:	R	O_1 X O_2
Control Group 1:	R	O_3 O_4
Experimental Group 2:	R	X O_5
Control Group 2:	R	O_6

A good way to test the results is to rule out the pretest as a "treatment" and treat the posttest scores with a 2X2 analysis of variance design.

QUASI-EXPERIMENTAL DESIGNS

Because of the application of procedures commonly observed in both the preexperimental and true experimental designs to control and eliminate threats to the internal validity, such as the use of two groups in the experiment and the randomization in subject selection and assignment of treatment, the generalizability of experiments to other populations and settings is severely affected and compromised. To deal with the problem, *quasi-experimental designs*, also referred to as *compromise experimental designs*, are introduced, as they are usually more feasible in real-world settings.

In a quasi-experimental design, the randomization of selection of subjects or assignment of subjects to groups is not observed due to practical constraints. For example, in a study that involves the employees of an athletic department, it is not possible for the researcher to assign subjects into groups randomly. Instead, the researcher must use existing units within the department. Under this kind of special research circumstances, the researcher then must use a number of the so-called quasi-experimental designs that still have a certain level of control over the threats to the validity of an experiment. To ensure that an experiment has adequate validity, however, it is strongly recommended that the researcher use the true experimental design if feasible (Gay & Diebl, 1992).

A number of quasi-experimental designs have been commonly discussed in literature in business research (Gay & Diebl, 1992; McDaniel & Gates, 1991; Zikmund, 2000). They include the time-series design, multiple time series design, and nonequivalent control group design.

Time-Series Design

The time-series design is in fact the expansion of the one-group pretest and posttest design, one of the preexperimental designs. In this design, the subjects are repeatedly pretested and then exposed to a treatment. After that, they are again repeatedly posttested. The difference between O_1 and O_2 is compared to determine whether or not the treatment brings some change to the subjects. This design is especially appropriate for an experiment that requires repeated measurement that is "unobtrusive" and participants are that "not reactive" (McDaniel & Gates, 1991). The symbolic expression of this design is as follows.

$$O_1 \; O_2 \; O_3 \; X \; O_4 \; O_5 \; O_6$$

The time series design provides greater control over extraneous variables than the one-group pretest and posttest design, as the participants are tested repeatedly before and after the treatment. As discussed previously, history is a threat to the internal validity of an experiment using the one-group pretest and posttest design. This is because events occurring between O_1 and O_2 could affect the interpretation of treatment X on the dependent variable, as the change observed in O_1 may result from the events rather than the treatment. To illustrate how the time-series design can help minimize the history effect

but not completely eliminate it, let us use the example in which the XYZ sporting goods company requires its entire sales force to participate in a sales course that introduces several new Internet sales techniques. Before the course, the company records the performance of its sales force in the following manner: six months prior to the course, four months prior to the course, and two months prior to the course. It then measures the performance of its sales force with the same two-month interval after the course: two months after the course, four months after the course, and six months after the course. The repeated measures can detect any unexpected surge in sales performance. If the performance of the sales force is essentially the same in a number of measures prior to the course, and significantly improved in a consistent manner after the course as reflected in a number of measures, the company can be confident that the course is effective. The events that occur after the last pretest and before the first posttest potentially are still a problem that may confuse the company's understanding of the true effect of the course.

Multiple Time-Series Design

To improve the effectiveness of the time-series design, it is suggested that another group be added as a control group to the basic design. This design is called the multiple time-series design. The symbolical expression is as follows:

| Experimental Group: | $O_1 \; O_2 \; O_3 \; X \; O_4 \; O_5 \; O_6$ |
| Control Group: | $O_1 \; O_2 \; O_3 \; X \; O_4 \; O_5 \; O_6$ |

This variation of the time-series design helps control history and other threats to internal validity such as instrumentation. The key issue for this design is to select a control group that is closely equivalent to the experimental group in the characteristics of interest.

Nonequivalent Control Group Design

The third quasi-experimental design is the nonequivalent control group design, in which there are two groups of subjects involved in the experiment (i.e., the experimental group and the control group). Both groups receive a pretest before the treatment is applied to the experimental group. After that, a posttest is administered to both groups. This design is similar to one of the true experimental designs, the pretest-posttest control group design, except subjects are not randomly assigned to the two groups. So, the researcher cannot be sure that the two groups are equivalent in terms of their composition. As shown in the following symbolical expression, it can be noticed that the R is missing.

Experimental Group: O_1 X O_2
Control Group: O_3 O_4

The lack of randomization in group assignment presents problems to this design. Nevertheless, as mentioned previously, the quasi-experimental designs are options in research situations in which it is impossible to randomly assign subjects to groups. The use of a control group, even through it may be equivalent to the experimental group, still can help the researcher interpret the effect of treatment on the experimental results (O_2–O_4). The challenge to the researcher is to find a way to achieve equivalency of the two groups. The more similar they are, the more likely the threats to validity can be controlled effectively.

AN EXAMPLE OF EXPERIMENTAL RESEARCH IN SPORT MANAGEMENT

An experiment was conducted (McCarville, Flood, & Froats, 1998) to determine the effectiveness of several promotion activities on spectators' assessments of a sponsor. Specifically, they wanted to seek answers to the following research questions:

1. Will different message types offered in a sponsorship context alter spectators' impression of the sponsor being promoted?
2. Will different message types offered in a sponsorship context alter spectators' impression of the product being promoted? Specifically,
   a. Will different message types offered in a sponsorship context alter spectators' impression of the quality of the product being promoted?
   b. Will different message types offered in a sponsorship context alter spectators' likelihood of future purchase of that product?

The experimental design involves 163 undergraduate students who are randomly assigned into one of five groups, four of which are the experimental groups and the fifth is the control group. The four experimental groups are exposed to different sponsorship messages (treatments). The specific arrangement of each experimental group and the treatment it receives is as follows:

Experimental group I: Exposed to the sponsor's logo

Experimental group II: Received the sponsor's information

Experimental group III: Received the sponsor's discount coupons

Experimental group IV: Tried the product

The control group receives no relevant sponsor-related information or treatment.

During the experiment, the subjects were given the sponsor-related information while they were watching a slide show of a volleyball match in a large lecture theater setting with the presence of many other students. After the slide show, the subjects in all five groups were asked to complete a questionnaire that contained questions related to the efficiency, reliability, responsibility, worth of the business, and product quality.

This is a posttest-only control group design with more than one experimental group. No survey was administered to the students before the treatments and the slide show. The experimental design successfully eliminated most of the threats to its interval validity.

1. Both the history and maturation effects are controlled as the posttest (i.e., the survey administered to the subjects) was given immediately after the subjects finished viewing the slide show. No possible history events could occur that may have jeopardized the internal validity of the results. It is equally true that the time was too short to have any maturation effect on the outcome of the experiment.
2. The selection bias is also effectively controlled. It is accomplished through the use of

the randomization procedure in subject assignments into groups. Because of randomization, it can be assumed that the five groups are equivalently similar in demographic characteristics. The difference observed in the dependent variable can then be attributed to the treatments.

3. The effects of testing and instrumentation are effectively eliminated because only a posttest was used.

The only threat to the validity of the experiment is that it was not conducted during a live sport competition. Even though the subjects watched the slide show at a large lecture theater setting with the presence of many other students to simulate a true competition venue, their experience may be quite different while watching a live event at a sport facility. This might be the drawback of the research.

WHY ARE EXPERIMENTS NOT USED MORE OFTEN IN SPORT MANAGEMENT RESEARCH?

As mentioned in the beginning of this chapter, experimental research is one type of research design that can reveal a cause-and-effect relationship between two events or variables. As such, it should be a very powerful means for sport management research. However, a brief review of all the research published in the several leading sport management journals indicates that far less than 1% of all sport management research published in those journals can be described as experimental research. Why?

Three reasons experimental research is limited in business research were presented by McDaniel and Gates (1991, pp. 300–301). They are high costs of experiments, security issues, and implementation problems. The same reasons are also applicable to sport management research.

It is often the case that experimental research is more costly and time consuming than survey design. Experiments are also used as a primary means of test market. To implement the experiment, certain elements of the marketing plan may have to be disclosed. Consequently, competitors may learn about

the business actions of the company that wants to test the market, and accordingly come up with reactive strategies. Because of being afraid of losing their competitive edge, companies are very careful in using experimental research.

Researchers may encounter some problems in implementing an experiment, which include, but are not limited to, difficulty in gaining cooperation, subject contamination, difference between test markets and the total population, and lack of a group of people or geographic area as a control group (McDaniel & Gates, 1991, p. 300).

ETHICAL ISSUES IN EXPERIMENTAL RESEARCH

When the design of an experiment involves double-blind conditions in which subjects are not informed concerning thing to which they will be exposed, a certain level of deception is required, and informed consent can be difficult to establish. This deception can cause harm to subjects and violate their rights. The research code of conduct requires that the subjects be adequately informed of the experiment. In certain experiments, to avoid the interaction between selection and treatment, researchers often hide the purpose of the experiment from the subjects.

Debriefing can be used to mitigate this tendency. Debriefing is a process in which subjects are given the information about the experiment, such as its nature and purpose, after the experiment has been completed (Zikmund, 2000).

SUMMARY

Experimental research is one of the quantitative research designs in sport management. In an experiment, conditions or procedures are arranged so that the researcher can test a hypothesis about or determine if a cause-and-effect relationship exists between two events or variables.

A well-executed experimental research often involves elements such as random selection of subjects from population, random assignment of subjects to groups, random assignment of experimental treatment or treatments to groups involving in the experiment, and measurement of the dependent variable.

Two types of validity are often observed in experimental research: internal validity and external validity. The internal validity refers specifically to whether an experimental treatment or condition makes a difference or not, and whether there is sufficient evidence to support the claim. It is about the inside logic of an experiment. On the other hand, external validity is concerned about the generalizability of the findings of an experiment or the degree to which the conclusions in an experiment can be repeated by other researchers in different settings at different times.

To improve the internal validity of an experiment, it is important for the research to control threats that may jeopardize the interpretation of the causal relationship between the independent variable and dependent variable. These common threats include history, testing, instrumentation, maturation, mortality, selection, statistical regression, and interaction with selection. Four common threats to external validity in experimental research are surrogate situations, selection and treatment interaction, reactive effects, and multiple treatment interference.

Three types of preexperimental designs are commonly used to illustrate the threats to the validity of an experiment. There are the one-shot case study, the one group pretest and posttest design, and the static group comparison. Because of the lack of control over extraneous variables, it is very difficult to make causal inference between the independent variable and dependent variable.

The researcher can employ three true experimental designs to reduce and prevent the threats of extraneous variables from contaminating the internal validity of their experiment. The three true types of experiments include the pretest-posttest control group design, the posttest-only control group design, and the Soloman four-group design. True experimental designs can effectively control most of the threats that jeopardize the validity of an experiment.

If the random assignment of subjects to groups is impermissible in some research environments, the researcher can turn to the quasi-experimental designs (they are also called compromised experimental design) for help. The three commonly used quasi-experimental designs include the time-series design, the multiple-series design, and the nonequivalent control group design. To improve the validity of the type of experimental designs, the researcher should try to create similarity between the two groups involved in the experiment.

STUDY QUESTIONS

1. What are the issues that a researcher must address when designing an experimental study?
2. How is the independent variable manipulated in an experiment?
3. What is internal validity? Explain each of the factors that may threaten the internal validity of an experiment.
4. What is external validity? Explain each of the factors that may threaten the external validity of an experiment.
5. What are the differences between experiment and other research designs, such as survey?
6. Compare and contrast the preexperimental designs, true experimental designs, and quasi-experimental designs.

LEARNING ACTIVITIES

1. Design an experiment that uses one of the three good experimental designs to determine the effect of a sales workshop on the performance of the participants.

2. What type of experimental design will you recommend in each of the following situations? Be sure to explain the details of your design.

    a. A professional baseball team decides to use variable ticketing in formulating its ticket sales strategies. The management wants to determine the impact of the combination of price and type of game on ticket sales.

    b. A sporting goods store wants to know whether or not the presence of a professional player will attract shoppers to the store and increase its sales.

References

Campbell, D. T., & Stanley, J. C. (1972). *Experimental and quasi-experimental designs for research*. Chicago, IL: Rand McNally.

Crawford, I. M. (1997). *Marketing research and information systems* (Marketing and Agribusiness Texts—4). FAO, Rome: Agricultural Support Systems Division.

Gay, L. R., & Diebl, P. L. (1992). *Research methods for business and management*. New York: Macmillan Publishing Company.

Ghauri, P. N., Gronhaug, K., & Kristianslund, I. (1995). *Research methods in business studies: A practical guide*. New York: Prentice Hall.

Johnson, B., & Christensen, L. (2000). *Educational research: Quantitative and qualitative approaches*. Boston: Allyn and Bacon.

McCarville, R. E., Flood, C. M., & Froats, T. A. (1998). The effectiveness of selected promotions on spectators' assessments of a nonprofit sporting event sponsor. *Journal of Sport Management, 12*(1), 51–62.

McDaniel, C., & Gates, R. (1991). *Contemporary marketing research*. St. Paul, MN: West Publishing Company.

Zikmund, W. G. (2000). *Business research methods* (6th ed.). Fort Worth, TX: Harcourt College Publishers.

CHAPTER 11
ETHICS IN SPORT MANAGEMENT RESEARCH AND PUBLICATIONS

OBJECTIVES FOR COMPLETING THIS CHAPTER ARE THAT STUDENTS WILL BE ABLE TO:

Explain the differences between a utilitarianism view and a deontological view of ethical philosophy

Trace the major historical development of ethical codes and guidelines for conducting research

List and explain three general ethical principles for conducting research on human subjects.

Explain the major roles of the American Psychological Association (APA) in guiding ethics for research in sport management studies

Explain the major roles of institutional review boards in guiding ethics for research in sport management studies

Explain the major roles of the North American Society for Sport Management and the Sport Marketing Association in guiding ethics for research in sport management studies

Explain what is meant by informed consent

Identify the essential elements of an informed consent form

THE PURPOSE OF THIS CHAPTER is to provide the students with an understanding of the ethical considerations for the study of humans in sport management research. The philosophical paradigms and historical events that have influenced the development of research ethical practices of human subjects will be discussed first. Next are the ethical principles underlying the basic rights involved when dealing with the protection of human subjects and historical events influencing the development of research practices of human subjects, followed by the development of ethical codes of conduct for conducting research on human subjects.

In the latter part of the chapter, the guidelines and procedures for protecting human rights when conducting research are presented. The chapter concludes with a discussion of the nature and scope of the processes of informed consent and the institutional review boards (IRBs). Examples of the use of the aforementioned principles, guidelines, and procedures are summarized from selected articles in the sport management literature.

THE NATURE AND SCOPE OF ETHICS

What are ethics? Describing the nature of ethics is a difficult task because so many different perspectives on the field exist. More specifically, ethics is typically associated with morality, and both ethics and morality deal with matters of right and wrong. The term "ethics" also has been defined by a number of different authors and researchers. A few of such definitions are: "applying moral and ethical standards to the behavior of individuals" (Baron & Greenberg, 1990, p. 429), "study of moral values and moral behavior" (Nelson & Quick, 1994, p. 125) ,"study of moral issues and choices" (Kreitner & Kinicki, 1995, p. 99), "science that deals with principles of right and wrong, good and bad" (Sullivan & Decker, 1997, p. 416), and "moral principles or standards of conduct that generally govern the conduct of an individual" (Aaker, Kumar, & Day, 1998, p. 14). These definitions either are too general, for our purposes, or do not directly deal with the phenomenon of sport management.

Even though no generally accepted definition of the term "ethics" exists, behavioral and social sciences have agreed on at least five common features of ethics; they relate to principles of right and wrong, codes of ethics, and moral standards. Such common features can used to develop an operational and conceptual definition for sport management research ethics. For our purposes, sport management research ethics refers to a set of consensually accepted principles and standards of behavior for sport management researchers to follow when conducting research with human subjects. The principles and guidelines are grounded in philosophical principles and theories.

Philosophical Paradigms of Ethical Research

Given the aforesaid operational definition, the question is: How do we arrive at a comprehensive approach to use in making decisions of procedures for protecting human rights in sport management research? This question is almost always debated when philosophical paradigms are considered, because they are difficult to interpret for a relatively new field, such as sport management. A starting point to consider for protecting human rights in sport management research is the philosophical paradigms for interpreting ethical behaviors. This chapter will cover two predominant philosophies governing ethics: (1) teleology, or the utilitarianism view of J. Locke and J. S. Mill, and (2) the deontological view of I. Kant.

Teleologic ethical paradigms are used to determine what is wrong based on balancing an action's consequences. The most relevant teleological for guiding behavior in research is called utilitarian ethical philosophy. Utilitarian ethics is a balancing approach that implies that the good that comes of an action is weighed or balanced against the possible harm. A researcher who operates from this perspective would argue that costs should not be a problem, provided the research offers the greatest benefits for the research participants while at the same time producing the least physical harm for such participants.

Unlike teleological ethical theories, deontologic ethics are rule-based and give much weight to obeying principles and guidelines. When adhering to this mode of inquiry, sport management researchers must conduct their research on the basis of universal codes such as the Ethical Principles of Psychologists and Code of Conduct from the American Psychological Association (2003), which are commonly known as the APA Ethical Codes.

Historical Events Influencing the Development of Research Practices of Human Subjects

Since the 1930s, there has been a history of clearly unethical practices of research of human subjects; primarily in medical research. Two of the most infamous examples of unethical research were the Nuremberg Medical Studies and the Tuskegee Syphilis Study (Brandt, 1978). Although such practices were in medical research, they have influenced the formulation of guidelines in ethical decision making and ethical codes that give direction to the conduct of research in the psychological, sociological, political, historical, and political sciences, as well as in sport management.

- Nuremberg Medical Studies. During the 1940s, prisoners in German concentration camps were deliberately infected with bacteria by German physicians. There were numerous types of experiments conducted on the prisoners. Three of the experiments included: (1) freezing experiments (placing prisoners in ice water to determine how long it would take to lower body temperature to the point of death); (2) malaria experiments (exposing a prisoner to mosquitoes that carried malaria virus to determine what drugs were most effective for treatment of malaria); and (3) high altitude experiments (exposing a prisoner to high altitude to determine how much pain one could take before dying.
- Tuskegee Syphilis Study (Brandt 1978). Between 1932 and 1970, rural African-American males were used as subjects for a large-scale study of syphilis. The study was initiated in 1932 and conducted under the auspices of the US Public Health Services (Gamble, 1997). The purpose of study was to test the effective-

ness of mercury in treating syphilis. The participants were not made aware of the purpose of the study or the danger that it proposed for them. There were no attempts by the researchers or the government to explain the study to them. Participants were enticed with a variety of inducements such as physical examinations, free rides to clinics, meals, and a $50 stipend as a burial fee when they died. The participants were also enticed to assure the physicians that they did not receive treatment from other physicians. This study violated nearly all of the guidelines of ethics for research with humans, from needing to inform to protecting participants from physical harm. In addition, the study did not become public knowledge until 40 years after it was started. President Clinton made a formal public apology to the eight remaining survivors of this study in the late 1990s (Gamble, 1997).

These types of practices supported the need for guidelines for subjects to be sufficiently informed and to be allowed to volunteer for research studies. Such studies give rise to a need for ethical guidelines for the increase of human subjects in research for the current day academic enterprise. Many of the guidelines developed can be used to guide research practices in sport management.

The Development of Ethical Codes of Conduct for Research on Human Subjects

Since the 1940s, various codes for the proper and responsible conduct of human experimentation in medical research have been adopted by different organizations. The best known of these are the Nuremberg Code of 1947, the Helsinki Declaration of 1964 (revised in 1975), and the 1971 Guidelines (codified in Federal Regulations in 1974) issued by the U.S. Department of Health, Education, and Welfare.

The Nuremberg Codes. During the 1940s, the Nuremberg Codes were initiated because of the infamous Nuremberg medical studies that were conducted during the 1930s. The codes are recognized as the first international or world effort to establish codes of conduct for protecting human subjects when conducting research. The codes were embedded in both the philosophies of teleologic and deontologic ethical theories. (i.e., the balance of benefits outweighing risk, and adequate protection of subjects from risk or harm (Katz, 1972; Katz, 1996). Shown in Figure 11-1 are the Nuremberg Codes.

The Helsinki Declaration of 1964 (revised in 1975; World Medical Association, 2003). Extensions of the Nuremberg Codes, these codes were developed as principles for controlling unethical practices in the medical sciences.

The Belmont Report. The Tuskegee Syphilis Study and other nonconsensual experiments on human

---

The great weight of the evidence before us is to the effect that certain types of medical experiments on human beings, when kept within reasonably well-defined bounds, conform to the ethics of the medical profession generally. The protagonists of the practice of human experimentation justify their views on the basis that such experiments yield results for the good of society that are unprocurable by other methods or means of study. All agree, however, that certain basic principles must be observed in order to satisfy moral, ethical and legal concepts:

1. The voluntary consent of the human subject is absolutely essential.

    This means that the person involved should have legal capacity to give consent; should be so situated as to be able to exercise free power of choice, without the intervention of any element of force, fraud, deceit, duress, overreaching, or other ulterior form of constraint or coercion, and should have sufficient knowledge and comprehension of the elements of the subject matter involved as to enable him to make an understanding and enlightened decision. This latter element requires that before the acceptance of an affirmative decision by the experimental subject there should be made known to him the nature, duration, and purpose of the experiment; the method and means by which it is to be conducted; all inconveniences and hazards reasonably to be expected; and the effects upon his health or person which may possibly come from his participation in the experiment.

    The duty and responsibility for ascertaining the quality of the consent rests upon each individual who initiates, directs or engages in the experiment. It is a personal duty and responsibility which may not be delegated to another with impunity.

2. The experiment should be such as to yield fruitful results for the good of society, unprocurable by other methods or means of study, and not random or unnecessary in nature.

3. The experiment should be so designed and based on the results of animal experimentation and a knowledge of the natural history of the disease or other problems under study that the anticipated results will justify the performance of the experiment.

4. The experiment should be so conducted as to avoid all unnecessary physical and mental suffering and injury.

5. No experiment should be conducted where there is an a priori reason to believe that death or disabling injury will occur, except, perhaps, in those experiments where the experimental physicians also serve as subjects.

6. The degree of risk to be taken should never exceed that determined by the humanitarian importance of the problem to be solved by the experiment.

7. Proper preparations should be made and adequate facilities provided to protect the experimental subject against even remote possibilities of injury, disability, or death.

8. The experiment should be conducted only by scientifically qualified persons. The highest degree of skill and care should be required through all stages of the experiment of those who conduct or engage in the experiment.

9. During the course of the experiment the human subject should be at liberty to bring the experiment to an end if he has reached the physical or mental state where continuation of the experiment seems to him to be impossible.

10. During the course of the experiment the scientist in charge must be prepared to terminate the experiment at any stage if he has probable cause to believe, in the exercise of the good faith, superior skill, and careful judgment required of him that a continuation of the experiment is likely to result in injury, disability, or death to the experimental subject.

Source: Trials of War Criminals before the Nuremberg Military Tribunals under Control Council Law No 10, Vol. II. Nuremberg, Germany, October 1946–April 1949.

FIGURE 11-1. The Nuremberg Codes

subjects led Congress to establish the National Research Act, which established the National Commission for the Protection of Human Subjects of Biomedical and Behavioral Research. Out of this Commission the Belmont Report (National Institutes of Health, 2008) was formulated. The Belmont Report is recognized as the first effort to articulate ethical principles for conducting research in the U.S.

General ethical principles as opposed to ethical theories and international codes were found to be more inspirational in nature. Their intent is to guide and inspire researchers toward the very highest ethical ideals of the profession.

A REVIEW OF ETHICAL PRINCIPLES

Several ethical principles grew out of the Belmont Report, as well as from scholarly work in ethics. According to the Belmont Report, there are three general ethical principles underlying the protection of human subjects: respect for human dignity, beneficence, and justice. Beauchamp and Childress (2001) have also identified four major principles: autonomy, nonmaleficence, beneficence, and justice. Such principles can be currently recognized in sport management research. These can be used by sport management researchers in designing ethical guidelines for selecting subjects and acquiring written consents for proposed research investigations.

Autonomy. (Respect for People's Rights and Dignity). The principle of respect for people's rights and dignity requires researchers to treat research participants as autonomous individuals and to obtain their informed consent to participate in a research investigation (Hully & Cummings, 1988). This principle is embedded in utilitarian ethics and is articulated in the Belmont Report and the current APA Ethical Codes. It is composed of two ethical convictions: (1) assurance of the right to self-determination, and (2) assurance of the right to full disclosure. A research participant must be free to make independent decisions about participating in an investigation without the coercion of the researcher.

Beneficence. According to this principle, the researcher must balance the benefits and risks of the subjects participating in a research investigation. The benefits are to out weigh the related categories of risks including physical, psychological, social, and economic (Levine, 1981). The principle of generosity to ethical decisions in research is inherent in deontological and utilitarian ethics. It simply means that researchers must be generous to subjects who participate in their research. For example:

Nonmaleficence. According to this principle, sport management researchers must ensure that the research participants have the right to freedom from harm and exploitation during the research process. As with beneficence, this principle is inherent in deontological and utilitarian ethics.

Justice. The principle of justice is embedded in both deontological and teleological (utilitarianism) theories of ethics. According to this principle, researchers are obligated to provide assurance of the right to fair treatment and assurance of the right to privacy of subjects who participate in research investigations.

WAYS TO ENSURE THAT RESEARCH IS ETHICAL

Following the Guidelines of Professional Associations

In addition to the Belmont Report, professional associations have formulated and articulated ethical principles and guidelines for conducting research activities with human subjects. In the U.S., many professional associations in such disciplines as medicine, law, management, marketing, political science, and psychology have established their own codes of conduct in human subject research. Listed below are several examples of professional associations that exist for articulating standards of conduct in research on human subjects:

- The American Medical Association
- The American Marketing Association
- The American Sociological Association

- The American Society of Criminology
- The American Political Science Association
- American Statistical Association
- The American Historical Association
- The American Psychological Association

Since 1953, the American Psychological Association has published principles for research involving human subjects commonly known as the APA Ethical Codes. They are considered public statements of principles used to promote and maintain high standards of conduct guiding and inspiring researchers toward the very highest ethical ideals of a field or discipline. Codes for the conduct of social and behavioral research have adopted the format of the APA. The codes are inspirational in nature and available to guide the professional conduct of sport management researchers when ethical issues surface.

The American Psychological Association has published a set of ethical principles that govern psychologists' research. These principles are as follows:

- Using recognized standards of competence and ethics, psychologists plan research so as to minimize the possibility of misleading results. Any ethical problems are resolved before research is started. The welfare and confidentiality of all participants are to be protected.
- Psychologists are responsible for the dignity and welfare of participants. Psychologists are also responsible for all research they perform or that is performed by others under their supervision.
- Psychologists obey all state and federal laws and regulations as well as professional standards governing research.
- Except for anonymous surveys, naturalistic observations, and similar research, psychologists reach an agreement regarding the rights and responsibilities of both participants and researcher(s) before research is started.
- When consent is required, psychologists obtain a signed, informed consent before starting any research with a participant.
- Deception is used only if no better alternative is available. Under no condition is there decep-

tion about (negative) aspects that might influence a participant's willingness to participate.
- Other issues covered include sharing and utilizing data, offering inducements, minimizing evasiveness, and providing participants with information about the study.

These codes are illustrated in nearly all of the scholarly journals created for sport management studies. Also, both the North American Society for Sport Management and the Sport Marketing Association closely adhere to the APA Ethical Codes and the Belmont general ethical principles. Therefore, it is most pragmatic to address the APA Ethical Codes and procedures in sport management research. It is the responsibility of sport management researchers to carefully examine each of their investigations with all the conscience and candor that they can summon to assure that the rights of their subjects are protected. The aforementioned guidelines underscore the ethical principles for conducting research on human subjects in sport management.

Obtaining Institutional Review Board Approval

Federal regulations require that institutions (including all colleges and universities) must maintain an Institutional Review Boards (IRB) to oversee all research involving human subjects. Further, any institution involved in any research that receives significant federal funding or conducts drug or medical device research regulated by the Federal Drug Administration (FDA) must establish IRBs. The 2006 Code of Federal Regulations clearly described the activities under the review board's jurisdiction as follows: "any research, development, or related activities which depart from the application of those established and accepted methods necessary to meet the subject's needs or which increase the risk of daily life" (Federal Register, May 30, 1974). The following is information that should be provided by researchers who seek IRB approval:

- A statement that the study involves research, an explanation of the purposes of the research and the expected duration of the subject's participation, a description of the procedures to be followed, and identification of any procedures that are experimental;

■ A description of any reasonably foreseeable risks or discomforts to the subject;

■ A description of any benefits to the subject or to others that may reasonably be expected from the research;

■ A disclosure of appropriate alternative procedures or courses of treatment, if any, that might be advantageous to the subject;

■ A statement describing the extent, if any, to which confidentiality of records identifying the subject will be maintained;

■ For research involving more than minimal risk, an explanation as to whether any compensation and an explanation as to whether any medical treatments are available if injury occurs and, if so, what they consist of, or where further information may be obtained;

■ An explanation of whom to contact for answers to pertinent questions about the research and research subjects' rights, and whom to contact in the event of a research-related injury to the subject

■ A statement that participation is voluntary, refusal to participate will involve no penalty or loss of benefits to which the subject is otherwise entitled, and the subject may discontinue participation at any time without penalty or loss of benefits to which the subject is otherwise entitled.

The Institutional Review Board is also known as the Human Subjects Committee or Human Subjects Review Board. This committee is considered the hub for upholding research standards and principles established by the federal government and the professional associations. The duty of the IRB is to make certain that all research proposals meet the federal government (National Institutes of Health, 2008) and professional association requirements for ethical research.

An IRB is made up of scholars and researchers across a wide range of disciplines of an institution. At least one member of the IRB must be a member of the community who is not associated with the in-

stitution in any way. The IRB system is decentralized. Therefore, each local IBR can interpret and implement the federal and associations' procedures using its own forms and guidelines. Although the IRBs' criteria and procedures may vary slightly from one institution to another, the requirement on its membership is the same, which is that a minimum of five persons make up the board, the members must come from varied backgrounds, they must be adequately competent to review research, and they must be diverse enough to promote the welfare of human subjects.

The IRB system places much emphasis on carefully scrutinizing the process of informed consent to assure that the rights and welfare of subjects are protected. This group review also serves an important role in the protection of the rights and welfare of human research subjects. The board is responsible for ensuring that the procedures are not in any way harmful to the research participants and that the participants' privacy and anonymity are assured. An IRB can approve the proposed plan of study, require that it be modified, or disapprove the proposed plan.

The Institutional Review Board is the primary agency for soliciting informed consent under the APA Ethical Codes. According to the Codes, when obtaining informed consent as required in "standard 3.10, Informed consent," research investigators must inform the participants about the following:

■ the purpose of the research, expected duration, and procedures;

■ their rights to decline to participate and to withdraw from the research after participation has begun;

■ the foreseeable consequences of decline or withdrawing;

■ reasonably foreseeable factors that may be expected to influence their willingness to participate such as potential risks, discomfort, or adverse effects;

■ any prospective research benefits;

■ limits to confidentiality;

■ incentives for participation; and,

■ whom to contact for questions about the research and research participant's right.

It may not be necessary to cover all of the aforementioned standards in order to inform a potential research participant; however, it is important to include what is appropriate for the study being carried out (Fischman, 2000).

GUIDELINES AND PROCEDURES FOR PROTECTING HUMAN RIGHTS IN SPORT MANAGEMENT RESEARCH

Almost all of the current guidelines for sport management research fall under the purview of the Belmont Report, the APA Ethical Codes, and the Institutional Board Review of the institution for which the research is being conducted. The guidelines are written in a more objective manner than the codes and principles. The procedures for protecting human rights in sport management research usually fall into one or more of the following guidelines through the process of informed consent:

- assurance of protecting the study participant's rights of confidentiality,
- clearly debriefing the participants about the purpose of the study
- assurance of protecting the study participant's rights of anonymity,
- assurance of the study participant's rights to volunteer,
- assurance of protecting the study participants from harm,
- assurance of protecting the study participants' rights for self-determination,
- assurance of protecting the study participant's rights of full disclosure,
- assurance of protecting the study participant's rights to privacy, and
- assurance that the participants have the freedom to withdraw from a study at any time during the investigation.

The aforementioned guidelines underscore the ethical principles for conducting research on human subjects in the relatively new fields of sport management and sport marketing. The guidelines are illustrated in nearly all of the scholarly journals created for sport management studies. Also, the professional organization for sport management (the North

American Society for Sport Management, known as NASSM) as well as the one for sport marketing (the Sport Marketing Association, known as the SMA) for scholars and practitioners in sport marketing closely adhere to the APA Ethical Codes and the Belmont general ethical principles. Therefore, it is most pragmatic to address the APA ethical principles and procedures for sport management studies.

Assurance of Protecting Study Participants from Harm

This guideline implies that sport management researchers should take measures to ensure that research participants are protected from undue physical, emotional, legal, financial, or social harm. The risk of harm refers to how much a research participant is exposed to the possibility of injury when participating in a research investigation. For example, risks of injury in sport management research may involve emotional factors, such as exposure to stress or anxiety, or social factors, such loss of privacy and confidentiality.

Assurance of Protecting the Study Participant's Rights of Confidentiality

Anonymity and confidentiality are often confused. Confidentiality is usually maintained by use of code numbers. Confidentiality refers to the assurance given by the researcher not to reveal the identity of persons who provided research information (Ellis 1998, p. 278). This guideline implies that sport management researchers must not disclose data or information that should be kept private in order to prevent harm to a research participant. If such data or information must be revealed about a subject, it must not be made public or available to others without the subject's consent.

Assurance of Protecting the Study Participant's Rights of Self-Determination

This guideline is captured within the ethical principle of autonomy. It implies that sport management researchers must take measures to ensure that research participants feel free from constraints, coercion, or any undue influence during the research process. This guideline acknowledges that when the research participants, such as children or those in the prison system, lack the capacity for-self determination, it is the researcher's duty to protect such rights of the participants.

Assurance of Protecting the Study Participant's Rights of Full Disclosure

Full disclosure is considered a basic right of human subjects and it is one of the ways to protect the study participant's privacy. It can be done in a prestudy interview with each research participant prior the investigation. This guideline acknowledges that the researcher must fully describe the nature of a research study to a potential subject. It implies that the sport management researcher must take measures to ensure that the research participant is provided with information about what participating in the study will involve, and not with false or misleading information.

Debriefing the Participants about the Results of a Study

This guideline implies that the research participant has the right to a post-study interview with the researcher. During this session, it is the responsibility of the researcher to protect the study participant's rights to full disclosure (Johnson & Christensen, 2004, p. 110). Questions or misunderstandings of the subject's performance or responses are addressed. The following is an example of debriefing the participant's about the results of a study.

Frey, Czech, Kent, and Johnson (2006) explored female athletes' experiences and perceptions of male and female coaches. The researchers informed the participants that they had the right to participate in the study voluntarily and to terminate participation at any time.

Assurance of Protecting the Study Participant's Rights of Anonymity

As with full disclosure, anonymity is another way to guarantee privacy. This guideline requires the researcher not to link or identify a specific participant to the information reported in particular research investigation. The records cannot be linked to the participants' names. In this way, the identity of the participant is kept from everyone, including the researchers themselves in some studies. Butts' study (2006) demonstrates an example of how to protect the study participants' rights of anonymity. The study examined "the overall and specific sports gambling activity among athletes and non-athletes enrolled in a Southern, regional NCAA II university. Both student-athletes and non-athlete students completed the survey instrument in the presence of research assistants. Complete anonymity was guaranteed and names were not associated with the collected questionnaires. Permission to conduct the study was granted by the IRB at the University of West Georgia."

Assurance of Protecting the Study Participant's Rights to Volunteer

Frey, Czeck, Kent, and Johnson's study (2006) is a good illustration of the use of this principle in protecting the study participant's rights to volunteer. The participants were informed that their involvement was voluntary.

Assurance of Protecting the Study Participant's Rights of Privacy

According to this guideline, the researcher must keep the participants' responses or performances strictly confidential. For example the researcher must give each participant a code number and use it to label documents rather than use the person's name or institution.

Folkman (2000) has identified six threats to privacy that are of concern for researchers in sport management: (1) subpoenas (legal actions), (2) access by third parties to data, (3) use of new technologies, (4) data sharing, (5) mailed questionnaires, and (6) publication or presentation of data (pp. 52–56)

Assurance of Protecting the Study Participant's Rights of Withdrawal

Again, the study conducted by Frey et al. (2006) exemplifies how to protecting the study participant's rights of withdrawal. All participants were advised of the ability to terminate participation at any time.

Obtaining Informed Consent

Informed consent refers to a legal principle that requires researchers to obtain voluntary consent from the research participant. By law, the researcher must provide the research subjects with all the facts about the study before they participate. The information must be explained to each subject in a way that the subject clearly understands it. Informed consent is closely related to voluntary participation. It ensures that the potential subjects receive adequate information about the research study, are able to comprehend the information, and have the option to choose freely to participate or not participate in the study (Ellis, 1998).

Before subjects participate in a study, they should be presented with consent forms and asked to give their consent to participate. According to Fischman (2000), a consent form is a written document attesting to the fact that participants are informed about the study for which they are volunteering. Figure 11-2 is an example of a written consent form used in a sport management research project. The consent form includes information about the purpose of the study, a brief identification of the primary researcher, an explanation of the risks or harm of participating in the study, an estimation of the time it will take to complete the survey, confidentiality, and the voluntary nature of participation

---

Perceived Freedom and Leisure Satisfaction in Mothers with Preschool-Aged Children
Name of the Student
Department of Recreation and Sport Sciences
Ohio University

Federal and university regulations require signed consent for participation in research involving human subjects. After reading the statements below, please indicate your consent by signing this form.

You are invited to participate in a research study, which will explore the freedom and satisfaction in leisure of mothers with preschool-aged children. The study will provide information on perceptions of leisure dependent on involvement in social support groups for mothers of preschool-aged children. I am a graduate student at Ohio University, Department of Recreation and Sport Sciences, and this study will fulfill the thesis requirements of my master's program.

Approximately 80 mothers of Athens county area are participating in this study during Spring 2003. Your participation is voluntary. If you decide to participate, I will schedule a convenient date during which you will fill out a questionnaire with three parts: Demographics, Perceived Freedom in Leisure, and Leisure Satisfaction Measure. The questionnaire should take about ten to fifteen minutes.

Any information you provide through this study will remain confidential. Although your name appears on this consent form, it will not appear on the questionnaires. Your records will never be released in a way that your name could be associated with them. Your participation is entirely voluntary and your decision whether or not to participate will involve no penalty or loss of benefits to which you are otherwise entitled. If you decide to participate, you are free to discontinue participation at any time without penalty or loss of benefits to which you are otherwise entitled.

If you have questions about the research at any time, please contact [Name of the Investigator]. If you have any questions about your rights as a participant in a research project, feel free to contact [Name of the Director], Director of Research Compliance, Ohio University (740) 593-0664.

I certify that I have read and understand this consent form and agree to participate as a subject in the research described. I agree that all known risk to me has been explained to my satisfaction and I understand that no compensation is available from Ohio University and its employees for any inquiry resulting from my participation in this research. I certify that I am 18 years of age or older. My participation in this research is given voluntarily. I understand that I may discontinue participation at any time without penalty or loss of any benefits to which I may otherwise be entitled. I certify that I have been given a copy of this consent form to take with me.

Signature _____ Date _____

Printed name _____

FIGURE 11-2. An Example of a Written Consent Form

in the study. It is the responsibility of the researcher to guarantee that consent has been obtained before allowing a volunteer to participate in a study. Fischman (2000) has suggested that twelve components be included in a consent form. Researchers in sport management must make every effort to develop and implement a form that clearly communicates these components in order to properly inform those participating in a study.

- *An invitation to participate.* An invitation to participate makes it clear that the participant is volunteering for the role of research participant.
- *Purpose of the research.* The purpose includes the overall reason for the research, including research goals at the individual and group level when appropriate.
- *Selection bias.* A clear statement of the reasons why the participant is appropriate for the study has the added advantage of allowing prospective participants to exclude themselves if they do not believe that they meet the criteria for inclusion.
- *Study procedures.* The study procedures should be clearly described to prospective study participants.
- *Descriptions of risks and discomforts.* Volunteers are unable to make informed decisions about whether to participate in a research study if they are not adequately informed of possible risks and discomforts.
- *Description of benefits.* In general, benefits can be summarized under the general category of anticipated additions to a systematic body of knowledge.
- *Available alternatives.* The requirement to provide information about available alternatives is primarily for the therapeutic studies in which nonvalidated interventions are being studied.
- *Assurance of confidentiality.* It is impossible to guarantee absolute confidentiality; however, the extent and limits to that guarantee should be described as part of the informed process.

- *Financial considerations.* Any costs of participating in the research should be clearly described. Economic advantages can include money, merchandise vouchers, food, access to improved facilities, therapy, physical exams, and subsidized transportation.
- *Offer to answer questions.* It is important for participants to know whom to contact for answers to any questions they might have, any problems they encounter as participants, and any inquiry they might incur while participating.
- *Noncoercive disclaimer.* Participation in research should be voluntary, and a decision not to participate or to discontinue should not result in any penalty or loss of the benefits to the participants.
- *Incomplete disclosure.* Although the researcher should provide sufficient information for each potential participant to make an informed decision about whether to participate in a specific study, there are times when some information may be withheld. Although generally not the first choice of researchers, it is sometimes necessary to omit information in order to protect the validity of the data collected. To the extent possible, information necessary to make an informed decision should be presented and, if possible, a statement in the consent form that some information is being withheld is a reasonable approach to the issue (Fischman, 2000).

The American Psychological Association published a set of ethical guidelines that govern psychologists when obtaining informed consent to research. These guidelines are as follows:

- The purpose of the research, expected duration, and procedures
- The right to decline to participate and to withdraw from the research once participation has begun
- The foreseeable consequences of declining or withdrawing
- Reasonably foreseeable factors that may be

expected to influence their willingness to participate such as potential risks, discomfort, or adverse effects

■ Any prospective research benefits
■ Limits of confidentiality
■ Incentives for participation
■ Whom to contact for questions about the research and research participants' rights.

Researchers rarely cover all of the aforementioned components in an informed consent form. However, it is important for them to include those that are appropriate for the study being carried out.

There are two forms of informed consent: written informed consent and implied consent. When taking the written informed consent approach, the researcher basically requests all the research participants to give their consent to participate in writing before executing the study. Here is an example of the use of the written informed consent in sport management. Mahony and Moorman (1999) conducted a study to examine the "conditions impacting fans' preferences for watching their most disliked team and the favorite team" (p. 43). They used a two-stage model in data collection.

After receiving permission to collect data from the Human Subjects Committee at the University of Louisville, respondents signed an informed consent form before beginning the first stage of data collection. Each respondent was assigned a number that was placed at the top of the surveys for both stages of data collection. In order to assure confidentiality, the list of assigned numbers was kept separate from the surveys and was destroyed after all respondents completed the second stage of data collection" (p. 52).

Researchers rarely use written informed consent when they use self-administered questionnaires. Instead of the traditional written informed consent, they assume what is called implied consent. When using this type of consent, the researcher assumes that when a participant returns the questionnaire in its completed form, this action reflects voluntary response. More specifically, the return of the questionnaire in its completed form implies the consent to participate. Implied consent is not always warranted. For example, when conducting a study with a group of students in a class, the students may feel threatened that their final grade may be affected by not participating in a study.

AN EXAMPLE OF IRB APPROVAL IN SPORT MANAGEMENT STUDIES

Cianfrone and Zhang (2006) conducted a study to examine "the differential effectiveness of television commercials, athlete endorsements, venue signage, and combined promotions as assessed by Generation Y consumers" (p. 322). The following paragraph describes how the authors of the study obtained the IRB approval:

The institution's review board for the use of human subjects approved the study. The researchers contacted all 35 instructors who taught the general sport and fitness classes that enroll students from various academic departments and majors in the university. With the permission of the instructors, the researchers made an announcement in their classes recruit participants who were within the upper age bracket of Gen-Y consumers. Those who volunteered for this study were randomly assigned into one of the eight experimental conditions. . . . The study was conducted in a classroom setting. The participants in each group were informed that they were involved in a study that was related to action sports; however, the purpose of the study and the experimental conditions were not explained to them. After filling out an informed consent form, the study proceeded in the following sequence: (a) administration of background information questionnaire, (b) playing the videotape that was appropriate to the particular group, (c) administration of the unaided recall questionnaire, (d) administration of the aided recall questionnaire, and (e) administration of the recognition questionnaire. Each questionnaire was handed out when the previous round was completed. This process prevented subjects from obtaining information across the different sections of the survey." (p. 331)

SUMMARY

The purpose of this chapter was to provide a common understanding of ethics in sport management. Ethics is typically associated with morality, and both ethics and morality deal with matters of right and wrong. There are many definitions of the term "ethics." For the purpose of sport management research, ethics is referred to as a set of consensually accepted principles and standards of behavior for sport management researchers to follow when conducting research with human subjects.

The teleologic ethical paradigms and deontologic ethics are the two ethical theories that have been used in developing ethical principles and conduct codes in human subject research. The Nuremberg Codes, established on the basis of these two ethical theories, are recognized as the first international effort to establish codes of conduct for protecting human subjects when conducting research. The Belmont Report is recognized as the first effort to articulate ethical principles for conducting research in the U.S.

Four general ethical principles are relevant when conducting research on human subjects: respect for human dignity, beneficence, nonmaleficence, and justice. The principles of respect for people's rights and dignity require researchers to treat research participants as autonomous individuals and to obtain their informed consent to participate in a research investigation (Hully & Cummings 1988). To follow the principle of beneficence, the researcher must balance the benefits and risks of the subjects participating in a research investigation. According to the nonmaleficence principle, sport management researchers must ensure that the research participants have the right to freedom from harm and exploitation during the research process. The principle of justice states that researchers are obligated to provide assurance of the right to fair treatment and assurance of the right to privacy of subjects who participates in research investigations.

The procedures for protecting human rights in sport management research fall into one or more of such guidelines as confidentiality, debriefing, institutional approval, harm, self-determination, full disclosure, privacy, freedom to withdraw. There are two forms of informed consent: written informed consent and implied consent. The process of informed consent is to assure that the rights and welfare of subjects are protected.

Considered the hub for upholding research standards and principles established by the government and professional associations, Institutional Review Boards (IRBs) are made up of scholars and researchers across a wide range of disciplines of an institution.

STUDY QUESTIONS

1. What are the differences between a utilitarianism view and a deontological view of ethical philosophy?
2. Briefly describe the historical development of ethical codes and guidelines for conducting research.
3. What are the three general ethical principles for conducting research on human subjects?
4. What are the major roles of the American Psychological Association in guiding ethics for research in sport management studies?
5. What are the major roles of Institutional Review Boards in guiding ethics for research in sport management studies?
6. What are the major roles of the North American Society for Sport Management and the Sport Marketing Association in guiding ethics for research in sport management studies?
7. What is informed consent?
8. What are the essential elements of an informed consent form?

LEARNING ACTIVITIES

1. Review an article that was published during this year in one of the journals created specifically for sport management or sport marketing and document in writing how the process of informed consent was explained in the article.

2. Review an article that was published during this year in one of the journals created specifically for sport management or sport marketing and discuss how one or more of the general ethical principles was explained in the article.

3. Visit the website for your institution and two others. Compare and contrast the IRB policies and procedures for each of the institutions.

4. Review a research article that was published this year in one of the journals created specifically for sport management or sport marketing and answer the following questions:
   - Was the study approved by an IRB or other group or committee?
   - Is there evidence that informed consent was obtained from all subjects or their representatives? How was it obtained?
   - Were the subjects protected from physical or emotional harm?
   - Is the research study designed to maximize the benefit(s) to human subjects and minimize the risks?

5. Review a research article that was published this year in one of the journals created specifically for sport management or sport marketing and answer the following questions:
   - Were subjects coerced or unduly influenced to participate in this study?
   - Did they have the right to refuse to participate or withdraw without penalty?
   - Were vulnerable subjects used?
   - Were appropriate steps taken to safeguard subjects?
   - How have data been kept anonymous and/or confidential?

6. Draft an informed consent form to make sure that the essential elements are included.

References

Aaker, D. A., Kumar, V., & Day, G. S. (1998). *Marketing research* (6th ed.). New York: John Wiley & Sons, Inc.

American Psychological Association. (2003). Ethical Principles of Psychologists and Code of Conduct. Retrieved August 2, 2007, from http://www.apa.org/ethics/code2002.html.

Baron, R. A., & Greenberg, J. (1990). *Behavior in organizations: Understanding and managing the human side of work* (3rd ed.). Boston, MA: Allyn and Bacon.

Beauchamp, T., & Childress, J. (2001). *Principles of biomedical ethics* (5th ed.). New York: Oxford University Press.

Brandt, A. M. (1978). Racism and research. The case of the Tuskegee syphilis study. *Hastings Center Report, 8*(6), 21–29.

Butts, F. (2006 Fall). A study of gambling activity in an NCAA division II institution. *The Sport Journal 9*(4). Retrieved March 31, 2008, from http://www.thesportjournal.org/article/study-gambling-activity-ncaa-division-ii-institution

Cianfrone, B., & Zhang, J. (2006). Differential effects of television commercials, athlete endorsement and venue signage during a televised action sports event. *Journal of Sport Management, 20*(3), 322–344.

Ellis, L. (1998). *Research methods in the social sciences.* New York: McGraw-Hill, p. 278.

Fischman, M. W. (2000). Informed consent. In B. D. Sales & S. Folkman, (Eds.), *Ethics in research with human participants* (pp. 35–48). Washington, DC: American Psychological Association.

Folkman, S. (2000). Privacy and confidentially. In B. D. Sales & S. Folkman (Eds.). *Ethics in research with human participants* (pp. 49–58). Washington, DC: American Psychological Association.

Frey, M., Czech, D. R., Kent, R. G., & Johnson, M. (2006). An exploration of female athletes' experiences and perceptions of male and female coaches. *The Sport Journal*, (9)4. Retrieved March 31, 2008 from http://www.thesportjournal.org/article/exploration-female-athletes-experiences-and-perceptions-male-and-female-coaches.

Gamble, V. N. (1997). Under the shadows of Tuskegee: African Americans and health care. *American Journal of Public Health, 87*(1), 1773–1778.

Hully, B., & Cummings, S. R. (1988). *Designing clinical research: An epidemiological approach.* Baltimore, MD: Williams & Wilkins.

Johnson, B., & Christensen, L. (2004). *Educational research* (2nd ed.). Boston, MA: Pearson Education Inc., p. 110.

Katz, J. J. (1972). *Semantic theory.* New York, NY: Harper & Row.

Katz, J. J. (1996). The unfinished Chomskyan revolution. *Mind and Language, 11,* 270–294.

Mahony, D. F., & Moorman, A. M. (2000). The relationship between the attitude of professional sport fans and their intentions to watch televised games. *Sport Marketing Quarterly, 9*(3), 131–139.

National Commission for the Protection of Human Subjects of Biomedical and Behavioral Research (April 18, 1979). *The Belmont Report: Ethical principles and guidelines for the protection of human subjects of research.* Re-trieved September, 19, 2006, from http://ohsr.od.nih.gov/guidelines/belmont.html .

National Institutes of Health. (2008). The Belmont Report: Ethical principles and guidelines for the protection of human subjects of research. Retrieved March 31, 2008, from http://ohsr.od.nih.gov/guidelines/belmont.html.

Nelson, D. L., & Quick, J. C. (1994). *Organizational behavior: Foundations, realities, and challenges.* St. Paul, MN: West Publishing Company.

Public Health Services Report. (1973). Tuskegee Syphilis Study Ad Hoc Advisory Board. Washington, DC: U.S. Government Printing Office.

Sullivan, E. J., & Decker, P. J. (1997). *Effective leadership and management in nursing* (4th ed.). Menlo Park, CA: Addison Weisley Longman.

World Medical Association. (2003). Declaration of Helsinki. Retrieved March 31, 2008, from http://www.wma.net/e/policy/b3.htm.

CHAPTER 12
MEASUREMENT AND SCALING IN SPORT MANAGEMENT STUDIES

OBJECTIVES FOR COMPLETING THIS CHAPTER ARE THAT STUDENTS WILL BE ABLE TO:

Differentiate between the four levels of measurement

Recognize the levels of measurement used in articles of sport management studies

Define reliability

Compare and contrast the concepts of stability, equivalence, and internal consistency as they relate to reliability

Define validity

Compare and contrast content, criterion-related, and construct validity

Interpret the coefficient of correlation based on the standards reported in major research and statistical textbooks

Explain why validity and reliability are critical attributes in evaluating a quantitative research report

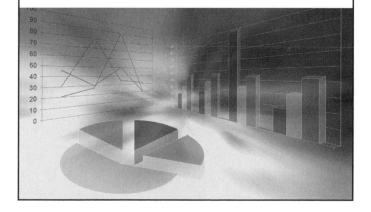

THE PURPOSE OF THIS CHAPTER is to provide students with an understanding of the concepts of measurement; the concepts of stability, equivalence, and internal consistency as related to reliability; and the concepts of face, content, criterion-related and construct as related to validity. These techniques are used in basic, applied, and evaluation research and can be used in experimental or non-experimental research (McMillan & Schumacher, 2006).

This chapter introduces the system for classifying the level of measurements. When using this system researchers are instructed to follow the procedures of one or a combination of four classifications of measurement commonly known as nominal, ordinal, interval and ratio scales. The nature and scope of reliability as a feature for measuring the consistency of the scales of research instruments used in sport management studies are then discussed. Seven procedures are captured within three approaches for measuring the reliability of quantitative measuring instruments. In the later part of the chapter, the nature and scope of validity as an element for measuring the accuracy of the scales of research instruments used in sport management studies are also reviewed. Several of the most common procedures are captured within three approaches for measuring the accuracy of quantitative measuring instrument in sport management research investigations. In addition, coefficient correlation is explained and illustrated to show how the degrees of consistency and accuracy are calculated for reliability and validity respectively.

CLASSICAL LEVELS OF MEASUREMENT

As with most principles and constructs used in research and statistics, research scholars seldom agree on how to define the term "measurement." A number of references demonstrate a variety of definitions: "the process of assigning numbers to variables" (Nieswiadomy, 2002, p. 191); "assigning numbers to characteristics according to specified rules to reflect the quantity of the characteristic that the test products possess" (Shao, 2002, p. 219); "the translation of observations into numbers" (DePoy & Gitlin, 1994, p. 195); and "a standardized process of assigning numbers or other symbols to certain characteristics of the objects of interest, according to some prespecified rules" (Aaker, Kumar, & Day, 1998, p. 274).

When choosing a proper measurement scale, it is important that the researcher be knowledgeable and fully understand the levels of measurements. There are typically four classical levels of measurement, known as nominal, ordinal, interval, and ratio levels. These dimensions have been adopted and commonly discussed in most of the conceptual research methods and statistics textbooks (DePoy & Gitlin, 1994; Gall, Gall, & Borg, 2003; McMillian & Schumacher, 2006; Neuman, 2003). Presented in Table 12-1 is a summary the primary qualities and example of each of the levels of measurements.

The Nominal Level of Measurement

The nominal level of measurement refers to data that can only be named, labeled, or categorized. Such data are mutually exclusive in nature, are exclusive of other data, and cannot be ranked in a meaningful order of magnitude. This level of measurement is considered the least sophisticated degree of quantification (Triola & Franklin, 1994, p. 8). The unique aspects of nominal variables are that they allow for the researcher to classify people, objects, or events into mutually exclusive categories that are based on the qualification of having a common characteristic (Aczel, 1995, p. 8). The categories must be distinct from each other (mutually exclusive categories) and include all of the possible ways of categorizing the data (exhaustive categories). "Mutually exclusive" means that each item classified (e.g., male or female, etc.) falls into one and only one category. "Collectively exhaustive" means that there is a complete set of categories (e.g., gender) available so that all items can be classified (Aczel, 1995). The NCAA football designations (i.e., Division I-A, Division I-AA, Divison I-AAA, Division II and Division III) are a good example of the nominal level of measurement.

TABLE 12-1

TABLE 12-1
Summary of the primary qualities and example of each of the levels of measurement

Level of measurement	Qualities	Example
Nominal (Categories)	• Data are given names or categories. • Names and categories are mutually exclusive (they have no relationship to each other). • Has the lowest degree of quantification.	• Gender (male or female) • Marital status • Racial differences • Employment settings (high school, college/university, clinic, industrial, professional) • Numbers of football jersey • Categories of sport products • A list of motives for measuring job satisfaction or organizational commitment
Ordinal (Category and Order)	• Data are given names and or categories. • Names and categories are not mutually exclusive; however, they are ordered (they have relationship to each other). • Distances between the categories are not equal and have no meaning beyond indicating a more-or-less relationship between each category.	• Years of work experience • A subject's responses on a scale (1 = always, 2 = frequently, 3 = sometimes, 4 = rarely, and 5 = never) • Ranking the categories of a sport product as "good," "better," "best" • Ranking the categories of a sport product as "1st", "2nd", "3rd", and "4th" • Ranking the standards for employment performance • Managerial levels (supervisor, middle management, upper management)
Interval (Category, Order, and Spacing of Equal Intervals)	• Data are given names and or categories. • Categories are not mutually exclusive; however, they are ordered (they have relationship to each other). • Distances between the categories are equal and have meaning beyond indicating a more-or-less relationship between each category. • No inherent starting point.	• Number of subjects responding for each of the categories on a 5-point Likert scale (1 = Strongly Agree, 2 = Agree, 3 = Neutral, 4 = Disagree, and 5 = Strongly Disagree) • Evaluation of a sport product in relative terms on a scale of 1 to 100 (100 as best and 1 as worst) • Spaces between the hash marks on a football field
Ratio (Category, Order, Spacing of Equal Intervals, and a Zero Point)	• Data are given names and or categories. • Categories are not mutually exclusive; however, they are ordered (they have relationship to each other). • Distances between the categories are equal and have meaning beyond indicating a more-or-less relationship between each category. • No inherent starting point. • Has the highest degree of quantification.	• Making an assessment of the numbers of study participants in specified age, height, weight, or salary ranges • Evaluation of a sport product in relative terms on a scale of 0 to 100 (100 as best and 0 as worst) • Making an assessment of sexual orientation using the Kinsey Scale (respondents use 0–1–2–3–4–5–6 rating, with 0 = exclusively heterosexual, 3 = equally heterosexual and homosexual, and 6 = exclusively homosexual, Gill et al., 2006)

The Ordinal Level of Measurement

Like nominal variables, ordinal level variables are identified by name, classified, or categorized but have an additional property of a logical or rank order of the variables or values. Data that can be rank-ordered as well as placed into categories are at the ordinal level of measurement. Although ordinal variables are arranged in order, the interval between the variables cannot be measured (Triola &

Franklin, 1994; Levine, Ramsey, & Brenson, 1995; Gall, Gall, & Borg, 2003). For instance, a review committee rank-ordered a series of program proposals as first, second, third place, and so on. The members of the committee may have felt that a proposal ranked in a higher order was better than the ones ranked in a lower position. However, they did not give a quantifiable distinction in terms of how much one is better than the other as the differences between intervals are not reflected in this level of measurement. So, the exact differences between the ranks cannot be specified with this type of data. The numbers that are obtained from this measurement process indicate the order rather than the exact quantity of the variables. The unique aspects of ordinal level variables are that they allow the researcher to classify as well as to rank people, objects, or events into mutually exclusive categories that are based on the qualification of having a common characteristic. (See summary in Table 12-1.) Ordinal level variables provide only for comparison of scores or categories in terms of smaller or larger, higher or lower, or best to worst. They do not permit comparisons in terms of how much larger, lower, or better. The ordinal level of measurement involves data that may be arranged in some order, but differences between values either cannot be determined or are meaningless (Triola & Franklin, 1994, p. 8). The measurement scale that sport managers commonly use to assess the quality of a sports event ("excellent," "good," "fair," and "poor") is an example of the ordinal level scale.

The Interval Level of Measurement

The interval level of measurement has ordered values and has the additional property of equal distances or intervals between scale values. The interval level of measurement identify, name, classify, or categorize as do nominal and ordinal scales and have ordered categories or values like ordinal scales with an additional property for determining specific distances between the order or ranks of the data (Triola & Franklin, 1994). Equal distances or intervals between scores or scale values are an important property of the internal level of measurement (Aczel, 1995).

The Ratio Level of Measurement

The ratio level of measurement has all the properties of nominal, ordinal, and interval level variables plus an absolute zero point. The absolute zero point means that a scale value or score of zero represents a complete absence of the characteristic being measured (Levine, Ramsey & Berenson, 1995, p.10). The ratio level of measurement is actually the interval scale modified to include the inherent zero starting point. For values at this level, differences and ratios are meaningful (Triola & Franklin, 1994, p. 9). The ratio scale is the strongest scale of measurement (Nieswiadomy, 2002). Common examples of ratio scales are height, weight, age, salary, and net worth. Because ratio scales have equal intervals between scales values like interval scales, all the arithmetic operations that can be performed on interval data can also be used with ratio data.

An example of a study in sport management research using the ratio scale is the one conducted by Gill, Morrow, Collins, Lucey, and Schultz (2006). In the study, Gill et al. assessed the attitudes of professional students toward racial/ethnic minorities, older adults, and persons with disabilities as well as toward gay men and lesbians. Using the evaluation thermometer, a single-item measure was used to assess the overall positive or negative evaluation toward a particular group. Respondents were asked to circle a number on the thermometer, with the positive end anchored by 100 (extreme favorable), the negative end anchored by 0 (extremely unfavorable), and the 50-degree mark (neither favorable nor unfavorable).

MEASUREMENT CRITERIA IN SPORT MANAGEMENT RESEARCH

The criteria for determining how accurate or consistent repeated measurements are to describe phenomena in sport management are known as reliability (consistency) and validity (accuracy). In a general way, reliability is the extent to which a measure obtains similar results on a repeated trial. Validity is the extent to which a situation as observed reflects the true situation or the degree to which data or results of a study are correct or true. Reliability and validity are viewed as two different aspects for measuring the credibility of measurement scales in sport management research. Both quantitative and qualitative researchers are concerned about establishing creditability in terms of reliability and validity during data collection.

Without validity and reliability, there would be no criteria for which the findings of a study could be judged as credible. The results or findings of a study are only as trustworthy as the accuracy and consistency of its measures. Inaccuracy and inconsistency in measurement will undercut a well-designed research project and call its findings into question. Effective quantitative and qualitative designs demand that measurement techniques be reliable and valid. Reliability and validity provide the faith and trust that researchers as well as research consumers have in the findings and consequently any conclusions that are made from the findings. Reliability and validity both are dynamic in nature because they are neither static components of an instrument, nor automatically generalizable; therefore, they should be recalculated each time an instrument is used (Waltz, Strickland, & Lenz, 1984). However, if an instrument is adjusted or is applied to a new target population, it is crucial that its validity and reliability be reexamined to ensure the new instrument assesses with the same degree of accuracy in that new target population. The construct validation and the reliability should be checked after a measure is adapted to a new linguistic context (Geisinger, 1992; Lin, Chen, & Chiu, 2005).

Major Dimensions of Instrument Reliability

Nature of Reliability

The "reliability" of an instrument refers to its level of being stable, being equivalent, and possessing internal consistency over time (Gall, Gall, & Borg, 2003). "Internal consistency" refers to the degree of cohesion among items that form a scale. Reliability has been conceptualized in several different dimensions. However, only three major categories (stability, equivalence, and internal consistency; McMillan & Schumacher, 2006, p. 185) will be reviewed (as shown in Figure 12-1). Reliability as stability is determined by giving the same test to the same individuals at two different times and is reported in two

procedures: test-retest and intra-rater reliability. Reliability is used interchangeably with terms such as "consistency," "precision," "agreement," and "reproducibility." An instrument is consistent (reliable) when it behaves the same way under different circumstances or when it yields similar results when different people use it.

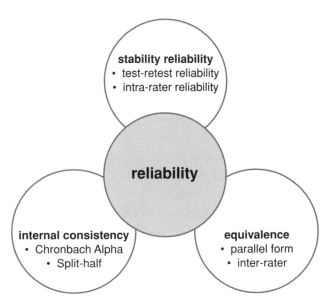

FIGURE 12-1. Major Dimensions of Instrument Reliability

Reliability as equivalence is determined by giving two equivalent forms of a test to the same individuals on two separate occasions. Reliability as equivalence is usually reported in two forms: the parallel form and inter-rater (also known as inter-rater agreement or interrcoder agreement). The third major category of reliability is internal consistency. It is determined by the extent to which all items on a research instrument measure the same variable. Internal consistency is usually reported as a Kuder-Richardson (KR20), Spearman-Brown split-half, odd-even coefficient, or Cronbach's alpha coefficient. Overall, reliability is concerned with instrument dependability (DePoy & Gitlin, 1994; Gall, Gall, & Borg, 2003; McMillian & Schumacher, 2006; Neuman, 2003). Cronbach's alpha coefficient, which measures the extent to which performance on any one item in an instrument indicates performance on any other item in that instrument, is the most preferred measure of internal consistency.

Interpretation of Reliability Coefficient Correlation

Reliability assessments are typically reported as correlation coefficients. It must be kept in mind that no universally accepted correlation values have been established for reliability; however, several schemes have been proposed. There is no simple answer as to how high the reliability of a research instrument should be. According to Nunnally (1978) and Nunnally and Bernstein (1994), the judgment of how high the reliability should be depends on the type of variable being measured and the stage of the development on the research instrument. The lowest limit for Cronbach's alpha coefficient, generally agreed upon, is .70, although a number between .60 to .69 is also considered an acceptable moderate range for a scale in its beginning stage of development (Hair, Anderson, Tatham, & Black, 1998; Nunnally, 1978; Nunnally & Burnstein, 1994). However, .80 or higher is acceptable for well-developed instruments, and 0.90 or higher is acceptable for important decision making (Nunnally, 1978).

Commonly Used Correlation Indexes

The two most commonly used correlation indexes are: the product-moment correlation coefficient (also referred to as Pearson's r), which is computed by interval or ratio measures; and Spearman's rank-order correlation (r_s), also referred to as Spearman's rho, which is computed with ordinal measures.

Reliability as Stability

Reliability as stability is captured in two forms: test-retest reliability and intra-rater reliability. The test-retest reliability is the correlation between scores from the same subjects tested at two different times. It involves giving a test twice to the same subjects and statistically comparing the two set of scores by calculating the correlation coefficient (see Figure 12-2).The closer the two sets of scores are to each other, the greater the test reliability. One of the major concerns for the researcher is the time intervals between the first and second test sessions. It is important that the time interval between the assessments be long enough that the subjects are not able to recall the items and inflate the reliability coefficient.

For example, Li (1993) examined job satisfaction and performance of coaches of the spare-time sports schools in China. He tested the test-retest reliability of 14 variables in the instrument using a pilot study. A pretest was administered, followed by a post-test 15 days later. The correlation coefficients for the variables ranged from .68 to .88. The intra-rater reliability refers to the correlations of scores by a single observer, rating the same behaviors on two or more occasions. It is also known as intra-coder reliability and intra-rater agreement.

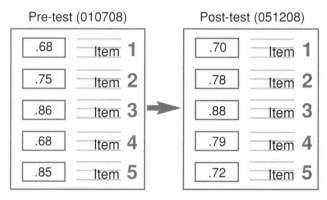

FIGURE 12-2. A Symbolic Illustration Test-retest Reliability (Fictitious pre- and post-tests)

Reliability as Equivalence

Reliability as equivalence has two forms: the parallel forms of reliability and inter-rater reliability. The parallel forms refer to the correlations of scores of two different instruments given to the subjects at the same time. The parallel forms extend from the development of two different tests that measure the same items in the same way. The correlation coefficient is based on the scores of the same individual taking two equivalent forms of the test, and the scores on form 1 are compared to the scores on form 2 (see Figure 12-3). After which, the correlation coefficient scores of each form are calculated. The higher the correlation coefficients between the two forms, the greater the test's reliability. The biggest concern for this type of reliability is that forms are difficult to construct. Parallel forms are used mostly for psychological constructs, self-esteem, self-image, and self-concepts.

The inter-rater reliability is also known as inter-coder reliability, inter-judge reliability, and inter-rater agreement. It refers to the correlations between

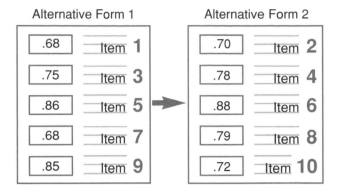

Alternative Form 1   Alternative Form 2

.68 — Item 1	.70 — Item 2
.75 — Item 3	.78 — Item 4
.86 — Item 5	.88 — Item 6
.68 — Item 7	.79 — Item 8
.85 — Item 9	.72 — Item 10

FIGURE 12-3. A Symbolic Illustration of the Alternative Form Reliability

two or more observers that independently rate the same behaviors on a single occasion of a particular subject or group of subjects. The inter-rater reliability can be assessed through the I_r coefficient developed by Perreault and Leigh (1989). It is established by comparing coding sheets for the same data completed by the same coder 24 hours apart, ranged from 96% to 100%. The 24-hour duration was chosen as an acceptable length of time for coders to lose awareness of their previous coding schemes on the same material (Stacks & Hocking, 1998). The inter-rater reliability is commonly used in sport management research. Illustrated in Table 12-2 are examples of recent studies in sport management using inter-rater reliability as reliability as equivalence.

Internal Consistency

Of the three forms of reliability, internal consistency is the most widely used in sport management research. Unlike stability and equivalence, it is a measure of an internal aspect of a scale or instrument. It refers to the degree of likeliness of items on a closed-ended questionnaire designed to measure a single research concept. For example, if a researcher developed a questionnaire of 30 items to measure job satisfaction among NCAA Division I athletic directors, the researcher would analyze the items on the instruments to evaluate the extent to which all 30 of the items measured the concept of job satisfaction.

The empirical approach most commonly used by researchers to estimate the internal consistency of instruments is known as Cronbach alpha (Cronbach, 1990; Nunnally, 1978; Nunnally & Berstein, 1994).

Cronbach alpha measures the extent to which performance on any one item in an instrument indicates performance on any other item in that instrument. In addition to Cronbach alpha, there are two other forms of reliability coefficients used as reliability consistency: Kuder-Richardson (KR) 20 and 21, and the Spearman Brown formula. For the split-half technique, the test items are divided into halves, usually odd and even numbered items and are then scored separately. The score on one half is compared to the score on the other half. The total number of test items are "split" into two groups (such as odd-even or first half-second half), and then each group is scored and a correlation coefficient is computed. The correlation is calculated based on the scores on each half of the test. The Spearman Brown formula is used to adjust the split-half correlation for the full-length test. It is based on the same procedures as the split-half technique. Unlike the split half technique, only the average scores from each of the split-halves are calculated for the Spearman Brown technique.

Internal consistency reliability is used in assessing tests that contain scalable items (such as Likert scales). It indicates how much of the measure is true and how much is based on error. An (alpha symbol) of .50 would indicate that half of the measure was based on error. The coefficient (alpha) is based on the average correlation among the items. McGuire and Trail (2002) investigated the extent to which three groups of university presidents (NCAA Divisions I-A, I-AA, I-AAA and III) differed on level of importance attributed to various intercollegiate athletic department goals and the level of satisfaction with such goals. The views of the presidents in the NCAA member institutions in each division were tested with the Scale of Athletic Department Goals (SADG). Internal consistency of the scale was evaluated using Cronbach's alpha. The mean score of each subscale was calculated to determine the president's satisfaction and important levels for each goal.

Validity as a Measurement Criterion in Sport Management Research

Reliability addresses the consistency and stability of the scores of the measurement scale(s) that is being utilized; *validity* addresses whether or not the

TABLE 12-2
Examples of inter-rater reliability by levels of coefficient correlations in sport management research

Source of Research Article Example	Estimated Reliability Coefficient Correlation	Purpose of Study and Description of the Validity Technique Used in the Article
Kelley, S. W., and Turley, L. W. (2004). The effect of content on perceived effect of Super Bowl commercials. *Journal of Sport Management*, 18(4), 398–420	The Ir values for the variables used in this study ranged from .77 for the slogan variable to .98 for the variables focusing on product type and price claims.	Kelly and Turley (2004) analyzed the content of the national advertisements that were telecast during the Super Bowl over a 7-year period from 1996 to 2002. Interjudge reliability was assessed through the calculation of the Ir Coefficient developed by Perreault and Leigh (1989). The Ir value for each of the qualitative nominally scaled variables included in our study is provided. The relatively high Ir coefficients associated with the variables included in this study are indicative of a high degree of inter-judge reliability for each of the variables encoded through our content analysis procedures.
Cuneen, G., and Sidwell, M.G. (1998). Gender portrayals in *Sports Illustrated* for kids' advertisements: A content analysis of prominent and supporting models. *Journal of Sport Management*, 12(1), 39–50.	Overall percentage of agreement between all subcomponents of analysis was .85. Reliability coefficient between coders for each subscale (.88 for advertisements 1989 issues, .84 for 1990 issues, .86 for 1991 issues, .87 for 1992 issues, .80 for 1993 issues, .82 for 1994 issues).	Cuneen and Sidwell (1998) analyzed gender portrayals in *Sports Illustrated* for kids' advertisements. Inter-coder reliability coefficients were examined to provide evidence of the agreement of the coder. All advertisements on which coders disagreed on prominent and/or supporting models were deleted from analyses.
Peterson, P. M., Whiserent, W. A., and Schneider, R. G. (2003). Using a content analysis to estimate the gendering of sports newspaper personnel and their coverage. *Journal of Sport Management*, 17(3), 376–393.	The agreement between the coders resulted in percentages that ranged from 89.1 to 97.2 with articles and from .845 to .965 with photographs.	Peterson, Whisement, and Schneider (2003) examined the gendering of sports newspaper personnel and then coverage. Inter-coder reliability coefficients were used to examine the percentage of agreement of the coders. Two trained individuals, independently of each other, coded the daily issues. After precoding sessions and a pilot test, the two coders independently examined the same 120 selected newspaper sport sections (20% of the sample) to test inter-coder reliability. According to the authors "high intercoder reliability percentages . . . for this study was manifest content . . . confirmed that the two coders had become thoroughly familiar with the coding protocol . . . by the time this study was conducted" (p. 383).

researchers are measuring what they think is supposed to be measured. In other words, it is the degree or extent to which items on a scale or research instrument measure what they are intended to measure. As such, the importance of validity shouldn't be overlooked. According to Nunnally and Bernstein (1994), no amount of statistical elegance or a sophisticated measurement strategy can be substituted for validity. If an instrument lacks validity, there is no point in establishing its reliability. This implies that reliability and validity are not independent characteristics of an instrument. An instrument that is not reliable cannot possible be valid. Overall, validity is concerned with instrument accuracy. The different ways for accumulating evidence of instrument validity usually have been classified and organized as face validity, content related validity, criterion-related validity, and construct-related validity (DePoy & Gitlin, 1994; McMillian & Schumacher, 2001; Gall, Gall, & Boy, 2003; Newman, 2003). As shown in Figure 12-4, judgment validity, criterion-related validity, and construct validity are the only three types of validity that will be discussed in this chapter.

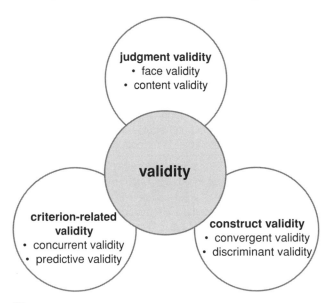

FIGURE 12-4. Major Dimensions of Instrument Validity

Judgment Validity

There are two dimensions of judgment validity: face validity and content validity. These two types of judgment validity are related to each other, but they are not the same. Face validity refers to a subjective judgment by a panel to determine if an instrument or scale appears to be measuring what it is supposed to measure. The panel usually is part of the population to be studied. Adams and Schvaneveldt (1991) stated: "Face validity refers to common sense content of the assessment device" (p. 96). Of the various types of validity being discussed in this chapter, face validity is the least empirical in nature. Its assessment relies primarily on the degree to which the panel agrees on how well a domain was sampled.

On the other hand, content validity refers to a judgment by a panel of scholarly or content experts and/or a review of related literature in determining if an instrument or scale appears to be measuring what it supposed to be measuring (see Figure 12-5). The content validity can be assessed and established

through a number of different approaches. Let us use examples in sport management research to illustrate the application of these approaches.

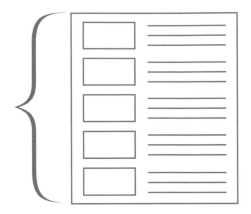

FIGURE 12-5. A Metaphor of Content Validity

To assess the economic and fiscal impacts generated by a state high school sport championship, Turco (1997) established an expert panel to generate content validity for the questionnaire used to gather the needed data in visitor group expenditures. Several key event officials and tourism researchers were asked to serve on the panel and to develop all possible categories of visitor spending. Based upon the recommendations of the panel, a number of minor revisions were made to the survey instrument. According to Turco (1997), the content validity of the instrument was enhanced through the critique provided by the panel of experts. Ridpath's (2006) study on the perceptions of college athletes about the degree of emphasis that their coaches placed on academic progress and graduation is another example that can illustrate the use of content validity in sport management research. "The content validity of the survey instrument used in the study was developed first through an extensive review of past and present related literature, then by the approval by a panel of eight experts in the higher education and intercollegiate athletic fields, and through a pilot test of a like population" (Ridpath, 2006, p. 21).

To examine both the face validity and content validity of their study designed to examine the differential effectiveness of television commercials, athlete endorsements, venue signage, and combined promotions as assessed by Generation-Y consumers, Cianfrone and Zhang (2006) created a panel of experts that included three professors in business, sport management, and measurement. Following the content validity guidelines suggested by Safrit and Wood (1989), the panel members were specifically instructed to look into content relevance, representatives, and clarity (p.331). To test the face validity, they utilized a group of university students (n = 10) who exhibited characteristics associated with the upper half of the Gen-Y age consumers to examine the face validity of the questionnaires. The improvements to the instrument were made with the input from the two panels.

Content validity can be measured with the application of a rigorous statistical approach developed by Lawshe (1975), who insisted the content validity of a measurement item can be reflected by the agreement among the members of an expert panel regarding how essential the item is in measuring the proposed construct. To use the method proposed by Lawshe, the researcher should ask the members of the panel if the item is essential to measure the construct under investigation. The following formula was suggested to use to determine the content validity of the item:

$$CVR = \frac{n_e - \dfrac{N}{2}}{\dfrac{N}{2}}$$

Where

> CVR = content validity ratio
> n_e = number of panel members indicating the item "essential"
> N = number of members on the expert panel

According to Lawshe (1975), an item will exhibit some content validity if more than half the panel members felt the item was essential. The higher the number of panel members who indicated the item to be essential, the higher the content validity of the item.

Criterion-related Validity

Criterion-related validity refers to the correlation of validating a new scale of an instrument with some other measure of a trait or interest (see Figure 12-6). It "examines the extent to which a measurement scale performs as expected in relation to some external variables considered to be meaningful criteria" (Kwon & Trail, 2003, p. 92). An instrument is said to possess criterion-related validity when there is a high degree of correlation between two measures of the same concept as measured (1) by the instrument being assessed and (2) by another established and presumed valid instrument or scale. There are two dimensions of criterion related validity, the concurrent validity and the predictive validity. The distinction between them pertains to the time period when data are gathered. In concurrent validity, both the test and criterion are measured about the same time. Concurrent validity is reflected by the correlation of scores between a measurement instrument or scale and the criterion instrument when administered at the same time. On the other hand, there is a time lapse between the two measures in determining the predictive validity. Predictive validity is indicated by the correlation of scores between a measurement instrument or scale and the criterion instrument or scale when administered at different times or for measuring future performance.

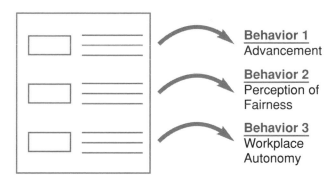

FIGURE 12-6. A Symbolic Illustration of Criterion Related Validity

The criterion-related validity of a measurement scale, like the assessment of reliability, is reported as a correlation coefficient. The correlation coefficient is an index for summarizing the degree of relationships between variables, usually ranging between +1.00 (for a perfect positive correlation) through 0.0 (for no relationship) to -100 (for a perfect negative correlation). The value of criterion-related validity

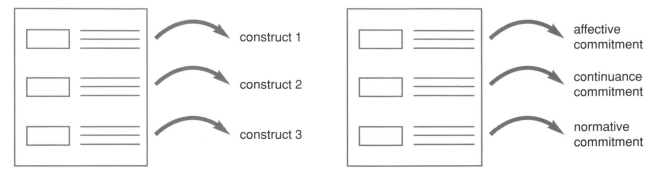

FIGURE 12-7. An Illustration of Construct Related Validity for the Organizational Commitment Scale)

is considered inadequate if below .70 and desirable if above .80. The following is an example illustrating the use of the criterion related validity in sport management research.

Mahony, Madrigal, and Howard (2000) examined the psychometric quality of a Psychological Commitment to Team (PCT) scale to be used in segmenting sport consumers based on their levels of loyalty in three measures. The correlations between the PCT scale and all three behavioral loyalty measures were examined to determine whether the scale demonstrated effective predictive validity. High correlation with these behavioral loyalty measures would indicate that the measure is appropriate for assessing attitudinal loyalty. The researchers confirmed strong relationships between the PCT scale and all three behavioral loyalty measures. First, there was a significant positive correlation between the PCT scale and the number of years as a fan of the favorite team, r = .426, p < .001. Second, there was a significant positive correlation between the PCT scale and the percentage of the favorite-team games respondents actually watched during the NFL season, r = .563, p < .001. Figure 12-7 is an illustration of criterion-related validity for the organizational commitment scale.

Construct-related Validity

Construct validity is regarded as the most theoretical form of validity. It has been defined in several ways by various researchers. Leary (1991) referred to it as subjective judgment of entities (hypothetical constructs) that cannot be directly observed but are inferred on the basis on empirical evidence by a panel

of experts in whether a test performance or results are related to the hypothetical construct (s) or set of related variables (p. 60). Babbie (2000) considered construct validity as the logical relationships within the questionnaire and whether a particular measure relates to other measures consistent with the content being examined. The principal aspect of construct validity is the determination of whether the items in a measurement scale have each been derived mainly from its underlying theoretical construct. More specifically, it measures whether each item contributes to the scale's underlying construct.

There are two procedures for assessing construct validity of a measurement scale or a questionnaire: the factor analysis procedure and multi-dimensional procedures (structural equation model), including the test of convergent construct validity and discriminant construct validity. The purpose of assessing convergent validity and discriminate validity is to determine whether the measures are indeed measures of the constructs they aim to assess and whether the measures are isolated to the construct that they are said to gauge and not to other constructs as well (Hair, Anderson, Tatham, & Black, 1998).

The study conducted by Koo, Quarterman, and Flynn (2006) is a good example of determining the convergent validity of a measurement scale. The purpose of the study was to assess the effect of perceived sport event and sponsor image fit on consumers' cognition, affect, and behavioral intentions. Evidence of convergent validity was sought by examining each construct's average variance extracted (AVE) (Hair et al., 1998). A construct was considered to exhibit convergent validity if the average vari-

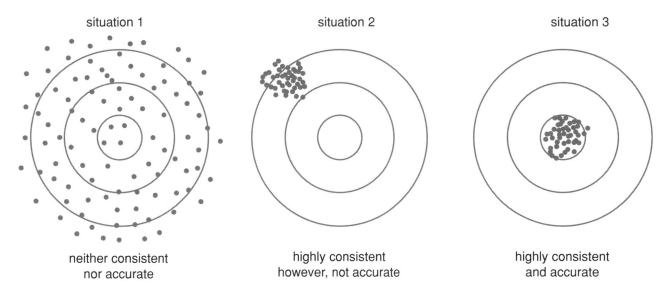

situation 1   situation 2   situation 3

neither consistent
nor accurate

highly consistent
however, not accurate

highly consistent
and accurate

FIGURE 12-8. A Metaphor of Reliability and Validity

ance extracted was .50 or greater (Fornell & Larcker, 1981). In their study, the AVE values for all constructs were between .55 and .84. Therefore, they concluded that the measurement scale possessed convergent validity.

RELATIONSHIPS BETWEEN RELIABILITY AND VALIDITY

Reliability is a precondition for validity because unreliable measurement cannot be valid. However, reliability does not guarantee validity. A metaphor of a marksman's shots on a target can be used to illustrate the relationships of reliability and validity (see Figure 12-8). In using this metaphor, reliability can be thought of as consistency, stability, or repeatability in measurement and validity can be described as accuracy for the claims to be measured. In situation 1, the shots are widely scattered. Thus, there is little or no consistency or accuracy. In situation 2, the shots are clustered around the most outer ring of the target, illustrating that consistency has been accomplished, but not accuracy. In situation 3, the shots are clustered around the bull's eye. As such, the marksman's shots are considered highly consistent and highly accurate. Although reliability and validity are two different procedures, each one is needed to compliment the other for credibility of research in sport management.

A CASE IN SPORT MANAGEMENT

An example in sport management that demonstrates the efforts of the researchers in establishing the credibility of the survey instrument is the study conducted by Fink, Pastore, and Riemer (2001). The study examined a framework of diversity initiatives as a basis for exploration top management beliefs and diversity management strategies of Division I-A intercollegiate athletic organizations. The researchers use a number of procedures, such as a panel of experts, a field test, and a pilot test, as well as internal consistency measures (Cronbach's alpha) and item-to-total correlations to evaluate the validity and reliability of the survey instrument.

First, the survey was sent to a panel of experts (14 individuals) who were provided directions for judging the instrument. They were asked to review the overall survey and provide suggestions for improvement. Most importantly, they were asked to look at the second portion of the instrument and rate each item on how well it represented the dimension it was intended to represent (compliance, reactive diversity management, proactive diversity management). Statements that were rated as "good" (as opposed to "poor" or "neutral") by at least 8 of the 14 judges were kept in the survey. After the initial survey was revised based on the panel of experts' comments, it was field tested by 25 sport management graduate students. They commented on the survey's clarity, wording, thoroughness, appropriateness, and ease of use. Again, the survey was revised based on these comments.

Finally, the survey was pilot tested as it was sent to athletic directors, senior women administrators, middle managers, baseball coaches, and softball coaches randomly selected from Division I-A and Division III institutions (N = 100). Thirty people responded to the pilot test. A Cronbach's alpha was calculated for the "beliefs" and the three subscales of the "diversity practices" sections of the survey. The Cronbach's alphas were: 0.88 for the beliefs section, 0.96 for compliance, 0.77 for reactive diversity management, and 0.73 for proactive diversity management. Item-to-total correlations were also analyzed. Based upon information from the pilot test, the survey was again revised (seven items were reworded and two were broken down into two items to avoid double-barreled questions). The final version of the survey was then sent to the sample noted previously.

Results from the analysis of the final survey indicated that it was a valid and reliable instrument. Cronbach's alpha for the beliefs section of the survey was 0.89. The Cronbach's alpha for the three subscales of the "diversity practices" section of the survey ranged from 0.83 (reactive diversity management) to 0.91 (proactive diversity management), while compliant diversity management had an alpha of 0.88. The results from the item-to-total correlation analysis indicated that 26 of the 29 items correlated at least 0.25 with the sum of the other items in its own dimension.

SUMMARY

The purpose of this chapter was to provide students with an understanding of the concepts of reliability and validity of measurement scales.

There are typically four classical levels of measurement, known as nominal, ordinal, interval, and ratio levels. The nominal level of measurement is considered the lowest degree of quantification, showing differences by names or categories. The ordinal level of measurement indicates differences in categories; however, it also shows differences by rank order without any specific distances between the ranks or order. The interval level of measurement is like the nominal and ordinal level variables, with an additional property for determining specific distances between the order and ranks of the data. The ratio level of measurement has a zero starting point and is considered the highest degree of quantification.

The criteria for determining how accurate or consistent repeated measurements are to describe phenomena in sport management are known as reliability (consistency) and validity (accuracy). Without validity and reliability, there would be no criteria by which the findings of a study could be judged as credible.

Reliability can be thought of as consistency, stability, or repeatability in measurement, and validity as accuracy. The reliability of an instrument refers to its level of being stable, being equivalent, and possessing internal consistency over time. Reliability has several different dimensions, which include stability, equivalence, and internal consistency. The concept of validity addresses whether or not a measurement scale measures what it is intended to measure. It consists of a number of dimensions, including judgment validity, criterion-related validity, and construct-related validity.

STUDY QUESTIONS

1. What are the differences among the four levels of measurement?
2. What is reliability, and what are the differences of the three types of reliability?
3. What is validity, and what are the three types of validity discussed in this chapter?
4. Why are validity and reliability critical attributes in evaluating a quantitative research report?

LEARNING ACTIVITIES

1. Evaluate the reliability and validity of the measurement scale used in an article published in a refereed sport management journal.
2. Review a nonexperimental research article that was published this year in one of the journals in sport management and argue for or against the type of reliability technique(s) used in the article.
3. Review a nonexperimental research article that was published this year in one of the journals in sport management and argue for or against the type of validity technique(s) used in the article.

References

Aaker, D. A., Kumar, V., & Day, G. S. (1998). *Marketing research* (6th ed.). New York: John Wiley & Sons, Inc.

Aczel, A. (1995). *Statistics: Concepts and applications*. Chicago, IL: Irwin.

Adams, G. R., & Schvaneveldt, J. D. (1991). *Understanding research methods*. White Plains, NY: Longman.

Babbie, E. (2000). *The practice of social research* (9th ed.). Belmont, CA: Wadsworth/Thomson Learning.

Cianfrone, B., & Zhang, J. (2006). Differential effects of television commercials, athlete endorsement and venue signage during a televised action sports event. *Journal of Sport Management, 20*(3), 322–344.

Cronbach, L. J. (1990). *Essentials of psychological testing* (5th ed.). New York, NY: Harper & Row.

Cuneen, G., & Sidwell, M.G. (1998). Gender portrayals in *Sports Illustrated* for kids' advertisements: A content analysis of prominent and supporting models. *Journal of Sport Management, 12*(1), 39–50.

DePoy, E., & Gitlin, L. N. (1994). *Introduction to research: Multiple strategies for health and human services*. St. Louis, MO: Mosby-Year Book, Inc.

Fink, J., Pastore, D. L., & Riemer, H. A. (2001). Do differences make a difference? Managing diversity in Division IA intercollegiate athletics. *Journal of Sport Management, 15*(1), 10–50.

Fornell, C., & Lacker, D. (1981). Evaluating structural equation models with unobservable variables and measurement error. *Journal of Marketing Research, 18*, 30–50.

Gall, M. D., Gall, J. P., & Borg, W. R. (2003). *Educational research and introduction* (7th ed.). Boston, MA: Allyn and Bacon.

Geisinger, K. F. (1992). The metamorphosis of test validation. *Educational Psychologist, 27*, 197–222.

Gill, D. L., Morrow, R. G., Collins, K. E., Lucey, A. B., & Schultz, A. M. (2006). Attitudes and sexual prejudice in sport and physical activity. *Journal of Sport Management, 20*, 554–564.

Hair, J. F., Anderson, R. E., Tatham, R .L., & Black, W. C. (1998). *Multivariate data analysis* (5th ed.). Upper Saddle River, NJ: Prentice Hall.

Koo, G., Quarterman, J., & Flynn, L. (2006). Effect of perceived sport event and sponsor image fit on consumers' cognition, affect, and behavioral intentions. *Sport Marketing Quarterly, 15*(2), 80–90.

Kwon, H. H., & Trail, G. T. (2003). Reexamination of the construct and concurrent validity of the Psychological Commitment to Team scale. *Sport Marketing Quarterly, 12*(2), 88–93.

Lawshe, C. H. (1975). A quantitative approach to content validity. *Personnel Psychology, 28*, 563–575.

Leary, M. (1991). *Introduction to behavioral research methods*. Belmont: Wadsworth Publishing Company.

Levine, D. M, Ramsey, P. P., & Berenson, M. (1995). *Business statistics for quality and productivity*. Englewood Cliffs, NJ: Prentice Hall, Inc.

Li, M. (1993). Job satisfaction and performance of coaches of the spare-time sports schools in China. *Journal of Sport Management, 1*(2), 134–135.

Lin, Y., Chen, C., & Chiu, P. (2005). An overview on issues on cross-cultural research and back-translation. *The Sport Journal, 8*(4). Retrieved March 31, 2008 from http://www.thesportjournal.org/article/cross-cultural-research-and-back-translation.

Mahony, D. F., Madrigal, R., & Howard, D. (2000). Using the psychological Commitment to Team (PCT) scale to segment sport consumers based on loyalty. *Sport Marketing Quarterly, 9* (1), 18.

McGuire, R., & Trail, G. (2002). Satisfaction and importance of athletic department goals: The views of university presidents. *International Journal of Sport Management, 3*(1), 53–60.

McMillian, J. H., & Schumacher, S. (2006). *Research in education* (6th ed.). Boston, MA: Pearson Education, Inc.

Neuman, W. L. (2003). *Social research methods: Qualitative and quantitative approaches* (5th ed.). Boston, MA: Pearson Education, Inc.

Nieswiadomy, R. M. (2002). *Foundations of nursing research* (4th ed.). Upper Saddle River, NJ: Prentice Hall.

Nunnally, J. C. (1978). *Psychometric theory* (2nd ed.). New York, NY: McGraw Hill.

Nunnally, J. C., & Bernstein, L. H. (1994). *Psychometric theory* (3rd ed.). New York: McGraw Hill.

Perreault, W. D., & Leigh, L. E. (1989). Reliability of nominal databased on qualitative judgments. *Journal of Marketing Research, 26*(2), 135–148.

Ridpath, B. D. (2006). College athletes' perceptions of the emphasis their coaches place on academic progress and graduation. *The SMART Journal, 3*(1), 14–27.

Safrit, M. J., & Wood, T. M. (1989). *Measurement concepts in physical education and exercise science*. Champaign, IL: Human Kinetics.

Shao, A. T. (2002). *Marketing research: An aid to decision making* (2nd ed.). Cincinnati: South-Western.

Stacks, D. W., & Hocking, J. E. (1998). *Communication research*. New York: Longman.

Triola, M. F., & Franklin, L. A. (1994). *Business statistics*. Reading, MA: Addison-Wesley Publishing Co.

Turco, D. M. (1997). Measuring the economic and fiscal impacts of state high school sport championships. *Sport Marketing Quarterly, 6*(3), 17–23.

Waltz, C. F., Strickland, O. L., & Lenz, E. R. (1984). *Measurement in nursing research*. Philadelphia, PA: Davis Company.

CHAPTER 13
ATTITUDE MEASUREMENT

OBJECTIVES FOR COMPLETING THIS CHAPTER ARE THAT STUDENTS WILL BE ABLE TO:

Understand the nature of attitude

Identify the three components of attitude and understand what each component entails

Identify the two main measurement techniques in attitude research

Identify the techniques used to measure the affective component of attitude

Apply any non-comparative scale to design a questionnaire used to measure the attitudes of sport consumers

Apply any comparative scale to design a questionnaire used to measure the attitudes of sport consumers

Apply either the categorical or the behavioral differential scale to evaluate sport costumers' behavioral intentions

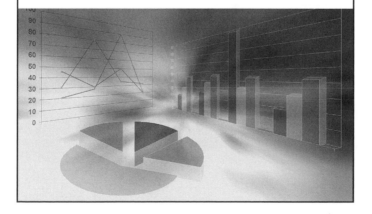

MOST OF THE RESEARCH IN sport management is conducted for the sake of obtaining information about the attitudes of those people who are involved in sport, such as sport consumers, sport participants, employees or employees of a sport organization, and so on. With the information, sport marketers are able to increase their sales with the adoption of effective strategies of sales and promotion. The information allows sport event organizers to make changes so as to enhance the experience of the sport participants, and it enables sport managers to identify and address the areas of concern expressed by the employees so as to improve their job satisfaction. To effectively measure attitude, it is imperative that students understand what it is, what its components are, and how it can be measured. This is the main purpose of this chapter.

NATURE OF ATTITUDE

There is a universally accepted definition of the term "attitude." Zikmund (2000) referred to attitude as "an enduring disposition to respond consistently in a given manner to various aspects of the world, including persons, events, and objects" (p. 288). Bradburn, Seymour and Wansink (2004, p. 121) defined it as "a bundle of opinions that are more or less coherent and are about some complex object." According to WorldWeb Online (2005), attitude is a complex mental state involving beliefs and feelings and values and dispositions to act in certain ways. A close review of these three definitions seems to suggest that attitudes are about consistent and lasting evaluative feelings toward an object. Here are some examples of attitudinal statements in sport: "The 2006 World Cup is boring due to the domination of European teams"; "Professional baseball players are over paid"; and "Professional athletes should be excluded from the Olympic Games to preserve amateurism."

In sport management, consumer attitude research typically looks at attitude-related issues from several angles. A common one is to examine consumers' attitudes toward a product (e.g., Taylor-Made's new r7 425, to determine if the product is well received by golf enthusiasts because of its new design and new shaft technology). Some research also focuses on consumers' attitudes toward a company. For example, the heated debate a few years ago regarding practices by Nike in Southeast Asia may affect consumers' perception of Nike, consequently affecting its bottom line. Sometimes, the researcher may be interested in consumer attitudes toward a retailer, such as the Foot Locker, Sports Authority, and Dick's Sporting Goods. Another angle of consumer attitude research is on the attitudes toward the attributes of a product, particularly, toward various types of brand associations of a product, such as logos (their design), symbols (their meanings, such as the five rings used for the Olympic Games), and product endorsers.

Components of Attitudes

It is generally believed by scholars (McDaniel & Gates, 1991; Zidmund, 2000) that attitudes are composed of an affective (feelings) component, a cognitive (beliefs) component, and a behavioral (actual actions) component. In sport management research, each of the components could be used for the researcher to gain an understanding of how persistent sport consumers evaluate, feel about, and react toward a specific object (e.g., products, organizations, advertisements, sponsorships) or issue. A detailed description and analysis of each of the attitudinal components with an example is provided in the following section.

The cognitive component of attitudes. The cognitive component represents a person's understanding of or knowledge and beliefs about an object. For instance, in the 2006 World Cup, adidas aired several commercials, one of which is *adidas +10* (including choose your team and dream team) in which kids in a sandlot pick a team of soccer stars for a game. Tiffany Cox, a sport management researcher, conducts a study to determine viewers' attitudes toward the commercial. Specifically, she is interested in knowing what the beliefs of viewers are about adidas. The results of her studies may reveal that viewers seem to hold such collective beliefs:

1. adidas is a brand that is widely endorsed and used by world class athletes
2. adidas is a brand that is full of imagination reflected in the slogan of the commercial, *impossible is nothing.*
3. adidas brings fun to life.
4. adidas is innovative and dares to dream.

Even through the above belief statements could be true or false, they may represent the viewers' general evaluation of adidas as a brand. Their positive evaluations may result in favorable impression of adidas.

A belief is a psychological association between an object and its attributes or features (and associated benefits). Beliefs are cognitive (based on knowledge, experience, perception, etc.). The stronger the association of features or attributes (and associated benefits) is with the object, the stronger is the individual's belief.

The affective component of attitudes. "What are the feelings or emotional reactions of viewers toward adidas?" is one of the research questions Tiffany wants to answer. The answers reflect the affective component of viewers' attitudes. Thus, the affective component of attitudes is a person's feeling or emotional reactions to an object. As attitudes are related to people's evaluations of an object, the affective component then elicits people's feelings. Tiffany's research may find that viewers generally feel adidas is a lovable brand and that the commercial makes them feel good.

It must be pointed out that the cognitive component and the affective component are not always consonant with each other. For example, many consumers may be aware that some of the sporting goods or athletic apparel companies have been accused of wrongfully exploiting workers in their foreign factories but still demonstrate a strong affectional attachment to the products made by those companies. That is, they may hold a negative cognitive evaluation of those companies but a positive affective evaluation of the products of those companies.

The affective component of attitude reflects the way in which we feel (e.g., like, dislike, are

neutral) in response to external stimuli. It is emotive rather than cognitive (i.e., beliefs). It is comprised of both a person's knowledge of stimuli and that individual's evaluations of the stimuli.

The behavioral component of attitudes. The intention of an individual to purchase a particular product reflects the behavioral component of the individual's attitude toward the product. The answer to such a question used in Tiffany's study, "What is the likelihood for viewers to purchase adidas branded products?" may reveal the viewers' predisposition to act. People may try to obtain an object about which they have a favorable impression; they may try to avoid or get rid of an object that they dislike or about which they have negative feelings.

People's intentions to act (e.g., purchase a particular product) positively, negatively, or neutrally toward an object are based on their affective evaluations of the object. As such, people's purchase decisions are often influenced by their affective response to the stimuli of an object. To obtain a comprehensive understanding of an individual's attitude toward an object or an issue, the researcher should approach it from the above-discussed three components.

Measurement Techniques in Attitude Research

In sport management research, rating and ranking are the two most common measurement techniques used by sport management researchers to measure attitudes. Even though both the sorting and choice techniques are among the options adopted by business professionals in measuring attitudes (Zikmund, 2000), they have rarely appeared in sport management-related literature.

Rating. The rating technique is used when respondents are asked to rate an idea, concept, individual, program, or product by providing their estimates on a measurement scale that typically has a number of choice points or response categories. The Likert scale, the most frequently utilized measurement scale, is a typical rating scale as respondents are presented with a series of statements and asked to indicate thier degree of agreement to the statements. The rating technique is used to elicit responses from respondents about their options or feelings.

Ranking. Ranking is a technique in which respondents are asked to rank a set of ideas, issues, or services, based on their relative importance or preference as perceived by the respondents. For example, in the study conducted by Li and Burden (2002) to explore the status of outsourcing of marketing operations in Division I intercollegiate athletics, they provided the respondents with a list of keys to maintaining an effective relationship between the outsourcing agency and an athletic department and then asked them to rank these keys in order of importance. The following are the actual questions used in the study, as well as the keys to maintaining an effective outsourcing relationship:

In your opinion, what is the major key to ensuring that the outsourced program will be successful? (Please rank each of the following keys in terms of their importance, with "1" being the most important one)

❏ Support from the administration of the institution
❏ A cooperative partnership between the institution and the contracted marketing company
❏ A well-thought-out strategic plan in outsourcing
❏ A long-term partnership between the institution and the contracted marketing company

In this research, it was more appropriate to use ranking than rating because of the nature of the issue at hand. The use of the ranking technique forced the respondents to prioritize the different choice options that were provided, in an attitude scale.

There are many types of scales using the ranking technique. The typical ranking scale is one that asks the respondent to rank given options in terms of either the importance or preference, such as the example given above about asking athletic administrators in NCAA Division I athletic departments to

rank keys to maintaining an effective relationship between the outsourcing agency and their departments. Each rank can be used only once. The researcher sometimes also asks the respondent to compare a pair of ideas, issues, or objects. A detailed description about attitude ranking scales is provided in the following section, "Techniques of Attitude Measurement."

TECHNIQUES OF ATTITUDE MEASUREMENT—THE AFFECTIVE COMPONENT

In general, the measurement techniques used in attitude research include two types of scales: non-comparative scales and comparative scales. In responding to questions designed with a non-comparative scale, respondents are asked to provide their evaluations of one object without reference to another object (McDaniel & Gates, 1991). The category scales, the graphic rating scales, the semantic scale and semantic differential scale, the Likert scale, and the staple scale are the non-comparative scales commonly used in sport management research. The comparative scale, on the other hand, is the type of scale that requires respondents to provide their judgments based on the results of comparison among or between objects. Examples of comparative scales include the rank order scale, the paired comparison scale, and the constant sum scale.

Non-comparative Scales

Category scales. Category scales are the most commonly used scales in sport management research. They are designed in such a way that the respondent is provided with a question usually having a set of 3 to 5 response choices. The response choices are listed in order of intensity. The commonly used category scales and their responses choices are shown in Figure 13-1.

The following are two examples of category scales. The first one is used to determine how frequently the respondents watch sports on TV. A scale used shows the five response choices of frequency from "Very Often" and "Never."

How often do you watch sports on TV?
❏ Very Often (every day)

Quality					
Excellent	Good	Fair	Poor		
Very Good	Fairly Good	Neither Good Nor Bad	Not Very Good	Not Good at All	

Importance				
Very Important	Fairly Important	Neutral	Not So Important	Not at All Important

Interest		
Very Interesting	Somewhat Interesting	Not Very Interesting

Satisfaction				
Very Satisfied	Somewhat Satisfied	Neither Satisfied Nor Dissatisfied	Somewhat Dissatisfied	Very Dissatisfied
Very Satisfied	Quite Satisfied	Somewhat Satisfied	Not At All Satisfied	

Frequency				
All of the Time	Very Often	Often	Sometimes	Hardly Ever
Very Often	Often	Sometimes	Rarely	Never
All of the Time	Most of the Time	Some of the Time	Just Now and Then	

Truth				
Very True	Somewhat True	Not Very True	Not at All True	Definitely True
More True Than False	More False Than True	Definitely Not True		

Sources:
Zikmund, W. G. (2000). *Business research methods* (6th ed.). Fort Worth, TX: Harcourt College Publishers (p. 292).
Wrenn, B., Stevens, R., & Loudon, D. (2002). *Marketing research: Text and cases.* Binghamton, NY: Best Business Books (pp. 132–133).

FIGURE 13-1. Commonly Used Category Scales and Their Response Choices

❏ Often (2–3 times a week)
❏ Sometimes (once a week)
❏ Rarely (once a month)
❏ Never

In the second example, the researcher desires to find out the level of interest in golf among college students. A set of three response choices are provided from which the respondents may choose.

Please place a check mark to the response choice that best reflects your level of interest in golf
❏ Very Interesed
❏ Somewhat Interesed
❏ Not Very Interested

The Importance-Performance Analysis (IPA) technique, a well-documented marketing technique used mostly in the analysis of (1) consumer expectations (importance) of attributes of a product and (2) consumer satisfaction (performance) with those attributes, combines two category scales in retrieving useful information. It has also been applied in other disciplines, such as recreation and sport management, since its introduction in 1977. Figure 13-2 shows an example using the IPA technique in designing a survey instrument to be used in identifying the areas of a bicycle path to which the management of the facility needs to pay attention.

To design a questionnaire using the IPA technique, the researcher first needs to review related literature and conduct focus groups to identify the basic design attributes of a facility (e.g., the bicycle path), such as accessibility, layout, length, lighting, etc. The identified design attributes or characteristics are then incorporated into a questionnaire that includes two category scales, the Importance Scale and the Performance Scale. The people who complete the questionnaire are asked to rate each attribute in terms of its importance (e.g., how important is this attribute in a bicycle path relative to participation in physical activity?) and performance (how satisfied are they with this attribute in the bicycle path they are currently using for participation in physical activity?). The mean values

Please rate the importance of each of the following physical environmental characteristics of a bicycle trail in Column I. Record your rating by circling one of the numbers listed in Column II, with "1" being "very unimportant" and "5" being "very important."

Column I	Column II				
1. Accessibility (to residential areas, schools, shopping, work, etc.)	1	2	3	4	5
2. Scenery enjoyability	1	2	3	4	5
3. Opportunities to observe wildlife	1	2	3	4	5
4. Level of crime	1	2	3	4	5
5. Connection between residential areas and schools	1	2	3	4	5
6. Connection between residential areas and shopping malls	1	2	3	4	5
7. Connection between residential areas and work	1	2	3	4	5
8. Connection between parks and other recreation facilities	1	2	3	4	5
9. Connection between communities	1	2	3	4	5
10. Connection to transit stops	1	2	3	4	5
11. The trail width accommodating various users (e.g., bikers, roller skaters, etc.)	1	2	3	4	5
12. Lights	1	2	3	4	5
13. Hills in the trail	1	2	3	4	5
14. The trail surface's suitability for various uses (e.g., biking, runners, etc.)	1	2	3	4	5
15. Signs for traffic control, warning, and information	1	2	3	4	5
16. Devices that slow or restrict traffic or speed	1	2	3	4	5
17. Maintenance of the trail (e.g., its surface is even and no holes, cracks, etc.)	1	2	3	4	5
18. Availability of parking along the trail for trail users	1	2	3	4	5
19. Roofed shelters/protected seating areas	1	2	3	4	5
20. Kiosks displaying trail information	1	2	3	4	5
21. Pavement markings warning trail users before intersections	1	2	3	4	5
22. Availability of restroom facilities	1	2	3	4	5
23. Fitness/exercise stations	1	2	3	4	5
24. Drinking fountains	1	2	3	4	5
25. Accessibility for people with disabilities	1	2	3	4	5

Please indicate the level of your satisfaction toward each physical environmental attribute of the bicycle trail that you are currently using in Column I. Record your rating by circling one of the numbers listed in Column II, with "1" being "very unsatisfied" and "5" being "very satisfied."

Column I	Column II				
1. Accessibility (to residential areas, schools, shopping, work, etc.)	1	2	3	4	5
2. Scenery enjoyability	1	2	3	4	5
3. Opportunities to observe wildlife	1	2	3	4	5
4. Level of crime	1	2	3	4	5
5. Connection between residential areas and schools	1	2	3	4	5
6. Connection between residential areas and shopping malls	1	2	3	4	5
7. Connection between residential areas and work	1	2	3	4	5
8. Connection between parks and other recreation facilities	1	2	3	4	5
9. Connection between communities	1	2	3	4	5
10. Connection to transit stops	1	2	3	4	5
11. The trail width accommodating various users (e.g., bikers, roller skaters, etc.)	1	2	3	4	5
12. Lights	1	2	3	4	5
13. Hills in the trail	1	2	3	4	5
14. The trail surface's suitability for various uses (e.g., biking, runners, etc.)	1	2	3	4	5
15. Signs for traffic control, warning, and information	1	2	3	4	5
16. Devices that slow or restrict traffic or speed	1	2	3	4	5
17. Maintenance of the trail (e.g., its surface is even and no holes, cracks, etc.)	1	2	3	4	5
18. Availability of parking along the trail for trail users	1	2	3	4	5
19. Roofed shelters/protected seating areas	1	2	3	4	5
20. Kiosks displaying trail information	1	2	3	4	5
21. Pavement markings warning trail users before intersections	1	2	3	4	5
22. Availability of restroom facilities	1	2	3	4	5
23. Fitness/exercise stations	1	2	3	4	5
24. Drinking fountains	1	2	3	4	5
25. Accessibility for people with disabilities	1	2	3	4	5

FIGURE 13-2. Example of IPA Technique

of each attribute in the two scales of the questionnaire are cross-tabulated and plotted on a four-quadrant grid according to its rated importance and performance as shown in Figure 13-3.

The horizontal axis of the grid presents bicycle path users' perceptions of the quality of performance, and the vertical axis indicates the importance of the attributes of bicycle path. As indicated in Figure 13-4, the labels for the four quadrants are "Keep Up the Good Work," "Concentrate Here," "Possible Overkill," and "Low Priority." The attributes in the "Keep Up the Good Work" areas are those that users consider to be important and are satisfied with in the path they use. The "Concentrate Here" quadrant represents attributes that receive low satisfaction scores from users but are perceived by them to be important. The "Possible Overkill" items are those with which users are happy but that they do not consider essential. The "Low Priority" quadrant includes path characteristics that receive low satisfaction evaluation and importance ratings.

In sport management, just like in many other social science-based disciplines, such as business, category rating scales are most commonly used to measure the affective domain of attitudes. Researchers often label them as "Likert-type" scales and treat them as interval scales so that they can use parametric statistics to analyze the data collected. Such practice is commonly acceptable; some scholars, however, insist that category scales measure only ordinal variables, not interval variables. Consequently, they believe that it is inappropriate to use interval-level statistics with ordinal-level data. The debate on whether or not category scales are interval scales has gone on for a long time. The purpose of mentioning such controversy here is to remind user of this type of scales that they should use them with care. In the following section, in which the Likert scale is described, a set of protocols is recommended for researchers to observe in order to collect interval data with the Likert scale.

Graphic rating scales. The graphic rating scales are the type of scales in which respondents are asked

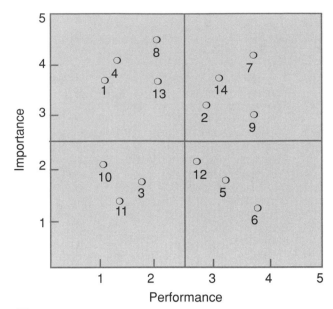

FIGURE 13-3. Cross-tabulating and Plotting on the Four-quadrant IPA Grid

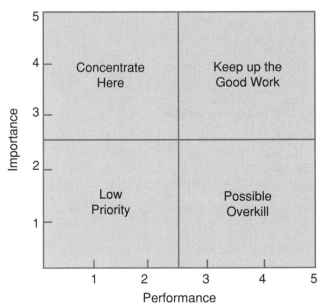

FIGURE 13-4. Interpretation of the Plotting and Labels of the Four Quadrants of the IPA Grid

to indicate their feelings by placing a check mark at any point on a graphic continuum that has two extreme adjectives anchored at each end. The most common form of the graphic rating scale is called the continuous rating scale. Once a check mark is made, the researcher measures the length of the checked point to the one end of the continuum to determine the score of the respondent. Let us use the following example to illustrate how it works.

In a study conducted to investigate viewers' reactions to one of the commercials shown in the recent Super Bowl, the surveyed viewers were asked to indicate how favorable they were in terms of the commercial with the following graphic scale:

Favorable   Unfavorable

❏   ❏   ❏

Assuming that the line is seven inches long, the measurement of the check mark placed by one of the respondents is about 2.1 inches away from "favorable." So, this respondent had a favorable reaction (scored 4.9 = 7 − 2.1) toward the commercial provided that starting point at the "favorable" end is coded "7."

There are graphic rating scales other than the continuous rating scale. An example of such an alternative is shown below. The respondent's score is determined either by dividing the line into as many categories as the researcher desires and assigning the respondent a score based on the category into which his or her mark falls, or by measuring the distance from either end of the scale as is done with the continuous rating scale.

Favorable   Unfavorable

❏   ❏   ❏   ❏   ❏   ❏   ❏   ❏   ❏   ❏   ❏

100   90   80   70   60   50   40   30   20   10   0

The graphic rating scales do not involve just a continuous line or continuum. One of the alternatives is the use of other forms of visual communication, as shown in Figure 13-5. The respondents are provided with a series of measuring tubs that are filled with liquid to a variety of levels. The respondents are asked to indicate the tubs that reflect their feelings about an object or issue. Whichever of these forms of the graphic rating scale is used, the results are normally analyzed as an interval scale.

Semantic differential scale. Using the semantic differential scales, the researcher uses a set of bipolar scales with semantic labels or adjectives placed at the end point of each of the scales to measure the respondents' reactions toward or feelings about an object or issue. The semantic differential scales use words rather than numbers. The following are examples of an attitude measurement scale with the use of the semantic differential scale.

The XYZ professional baseball team management conducted a survey to measure the fans' reactions to the new team logo:

Innovative   Conventional

     Quite   Neither   Quite

❏   ❏   ❏   ❏   ❏   ❏   ❏

Extremely   Slightly   Slightly   Extremely

Modern   Old Fashioned

     Quite   Neither   Quite

❏   ❏   ❏   ❏   ❏   ❏   ❏

Extremely   Slightly   Slightly   Extremely

Motivating   Discouraging

     Quite   Neither   Quite

❏   ❏   ❏   ❏   ❏   ❏   ❏

Extremely   Slightly   Slightly   Extremely

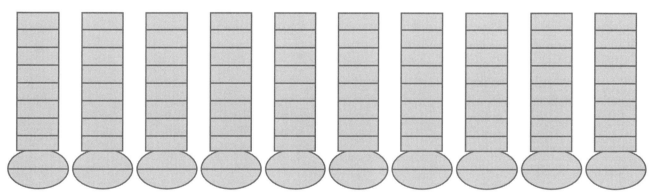

Very, Very, Favorable   Very, Very, Unfavorable

FIGURE 13-5. Graphic Rating Scale Using Measuring Tubs as a Tool of Visual Communication

Interesting						Boring
	Quite		Neither		Quite	
❑	❑	❑	❑	❑	❑	❑
Extremely		Slightly		Slightly		Extremely

Pleasant						Unpleasant
	Quite		Neither		Quite	
❑	❑	❑	❑	❑	❑	❑
Extremely		Slightly		Slightly		Extremely

The same scale can be modified without the use of the sematic labels.

Innovative						Conventional
❑	❑	❑	❑	❑	❑	❑

Modern						Old Fashioned
❑	❑	❑	❑	❑	❑	❑

Motivating						Discouraging
❑	❑	❑	❑	❑	❑	❑

Interesting						Boring
❑	❑	❑	❑	❑	❑	❑

Pleasant						Unpleasant
❑	❑	❑	❑	❑	❑	❑

The semantic differential scales are used more commonly in business and sport management research. Each semantic differential scale usually has seven response choices or positions. A weight is assigned to each position, 3, 2, 1, 0, -1, -2, -3. The middle one with "0" weight symbolizes the "neutral" position. The "1" positions (both 1 and -1) are labeled "slightly," the "2" positions "quite," and the "3" positions "extremely." A semantic differential scale measures directionality of a reaction (e.g., good versus bad), intensity (slight through extreme), and activity (active—passive). Ratings are combined in various ways to describe and analyze the respondent's feelings. So the researcher should attempt to identify adjectives along these three major factors or dimensions of judgment.

In a study designed to test a causal model revealing the relationship between consumer satisfaction and a number of such variables as pleasure, arousal, loyalty, and emotions, Caro and Garcia (2007) employed a semantic differential scale to measure emotions. The following shows the actual scale (p. 81):

Please circle the number that best reflects your emotions during the race based on a series of adjectives.

Pleased	1	2	3	4	5	Angry
Happy	1	2	3	4	5	Unhappy
Delighted	1	2	3	4	5	Undelighted
Glad	1	2	3	4	5	Sad
Hopeful	1	2	3	4	5	Disillusioned
Amused	1	2	3	4	5	Bored
Lively	1	2	3	4	5	Down
Excited	1	2	3	4	5	Calm
Active	1	2	3	4	5	Passive
Surprised	1	2	3	4	5	Indifferent

The Likert scale. The Likert scale is a special type of the category scale. It is known as a summated scale, which means that the attitudes making up a Likert scale are summed up to produce an index score. In that sense, a Likert scale is a composite of itemized attitude statements or scales. Typically, each statement has five categories, with scale values ranging from -2 to +2 with 0 as the neutral response, or from 5 to 1 with 3 as the neutral response. In other words, subjects are asked to express agreement or disagreement on a five-point scale. Each degree of agreement is given a numerical value. Thus a total numerical value can be calculated from all the responses. The following is an example of a questionnaire that is designed with the Likert scale technique.

For each of the statements below, please indicate the extent of your agreement or disagreement by placing a check mark in the appropriate box.	Strongly Agree	Agree	Neutral	Disagree	Strongly Disagree
1. A decrease in the number of television exposures will negatively affect ticket sales.					
2. A decrease in the number of television exposures will negatively affect boosters' contributions.					

Li and Burden (2002) conducted a study to investigate the perceptions of college athletic administrators toward outsourcing. The Likert scaling technique was used in constructing the section of the questionnaire that was drafted for assessing the perceived benefits on outsourcing of sport marketing operations in Division I-A athletic programs. The surveyed athletic administrators were asked indicate their agreement or disagreement to eighteen statements on benefits of outsourcing along four sub-scales. Figure 13-6 shows that particular section of the questionnaire.

As mentioned previously, it is still controversial as to whether or not the category scales, including the Likert scale, can be treated as inter-

The following are some statements describing the possible benefits of the outsourcing of sport marketing operations in Division I-A athletic programs. Please indicate your agreement or disagreement. For each statement, please check the appropriate box to indicate whether:

1 = Strongly Agree (SA)
2 = Agree (A)
3 = Neutral (N)
4 = Disagree (D)
5 = Strongly Disagree (SD)

Circle only one answer for each statement. There are no right or wrong answers to these questions.

	SA	A	N	D	SD
Outsourcing can broaden the media coverage of your athletic programs so as to enhance the public awareness of them.	❑	❑	❑	❑	❑
Outsourcing can help you build sustainable competitive advantage.	❑	❑	❑	❑	❑
It is less expensive for you to outsource your marketing operations than keep them in house.	❑	❑	❑	❑	❑
It is more efficient for you to outsource your marketing operations than keep them in house.	❑	❑	❑	❑	❑
Outsourcing of your marketing operations can bring in greater financial return than keep them in house.	❑	❑	❑	❑	❑
Outsourcing can help reduce bureaucracy and red tape in your marketing operations.	❑	❑	❑	❑	❑
Outsourcing can help you enhance the quality of your marketing operations.	❑	❑	❑	❑	❑
Outsourcing enables you to reallocate resources to other more critical areas within your department.	❑	❑	❑	❑	❑
Outsourcing allows you to access external specialized talent and expertise in marketing and promotion.	❑	❑	❑	❑	❑
Outsourcing enables you to cut down overhead expenses.	❑	❑	❑	❑	❑
Outsourcing can help you avoid the administrative complexity of in-house employment.	❑	❑	❑	❑	❑
Outsourcing enables you to use the contracted company as an extension of your overall marketing efforts.	❑	❑	❑	❑	❑
Outsourcing allows you to handle all aspects of your marketing operations in a more timely fashion.	❑	❑	❑	❑	❑
Outsourcing may cause loss of control of your marketing operations.	❑	❑	❑	❑	❑
Outsourcing may result in loss of opportunities to bring in more revenues for your athletic program.	❑	❑	❑	❑	❑
Outsourcing can provide you with opportunities to expand marketing efforts to non-revenue sports.	❑	❑	❑	❑	❑
Outsourcing can help you reduce capital expenses related to marketing operations.	❑	❑	❑	❑	❑
Outsourcing allows your department to be part of a marketing network and synergy.	❑	❑	❑	❑	❑

FIGURE 13-6.

val scales. Therefore, certain precautions need to be taken while using parametric statistics in analyzing the data obtained from the use of the Likert scale: (a) follow the required procedure to construct the Likert scale, (b) acquire a large sample size, and (c) ensure the sample is normally distributed. Specifically, to use the Likert scale in collecting interval data, the sport management researchers should follow a set of protocols:

1. A scale should include at least five, preferably more categories—the more the number of points, the more likely are the data collected meet the assumption of normal distribution. As Friedman and Amoo (1999) indicated, an 11-point scale may produce more valid results than a 3-, 5-, or 7-point scale. If the sample is large enough, the data collected could also meet the assumption of normal distribution.
2. The rating scale should be balanced. That is, it must offer the same number of favorable and unfavorable response choices (Friedman & Amoo, 1999).
3. To follow the recommended procedure for constructing a Likert scale, the index score should approximate the interval level of measurement (Sirkin, 1999). When scores from several items are summed to create an index, the process overwhelms minor differences and yields interval data (Sirkin, 1999).

According to Likert (1974, pp. 233–235), there are a few basic rules for constructing a Likert scale:

1. Each statement included in a Likert attitude scale should be of such a nature that persons with different points of view, so far as to the particular attitude is concerned, will respond to it differently.
2. It is essential that all statements be expressions of desired behavior and not statements of fact.
3. Each statement needs to be clear, concise, and straight-forward.

4. It would seem desirable to have each statement be worded such that the modal reaction to it is approximately in the middle of the possible responses.
5. It seems desirable to have the different statements so worded that about one-half of them have one end of the attitude continuum corresponding to the left or upper part of the reaction alternatives and the other half have the other end of the attitude continuum corresponding to the right or lower part of the reaction alternatives.
6. It is necessary to assign a value to the undecided positions on each statement. Example:

Strongly Agree (1)	Agree (2)	Neutral (3)	Disagree (4)	Strongly Disagree (5)

The staple scale. The staple scale is designed in such a way that a criterion that the researcher wants to assess is placed in the middle of the scale with typically five response choices or alternatives anchored on each side. The staple scale is used as an alternative to the semantic differential scale when it is difficult to find bipolar adjectives to meet the needs of the researcher. The following is a section of a questionnaire designed to assess spectators who are attending a professional football game in terms of the quality of food served by a concessionaire.

The following questions concern your ratings of the XYZ concessionaire, who sells food in the facility. You are asked to circle one number that best reflects your opinion in each of the quality measures.

-5	-4	-3	-2	-1	Taste	1	2	3	4	5
-5	-4	-3	-2	-1	Service Quality	1	2	3	4	5
-5	-4	-3	-2	-1	Cleanliness	1	2	3	4	5
-5	-4	-3	-2	-1	Price	1	2	3	4	5
-5	-4	-3	-2	-1	Variety	1	2	3	4	5

The following is another example using the staple scale in leadership assessment.

Please evaluate the leadership style demonstrated by the athletic director with the following scales:

+3	+3
+2	+2
+1	+1
Acceptability	Effectiveness
-1	-1
-2	-2
-3	-3

Comparative Scales

Rank-order scales. Rank-order scales require the respondent to make a judgment on one item against another. The biggest strengths of this type of scales are that (a) its is easy to use and form an ordinal scale of items, and (b) the respondent is forced to evaluate the object, idea, and product in a realistic manner. Results could be misleading if the choices provided are inclusive. Assuming that a researcher wants to know the brand preference of racquets by tennis enthusiasts, a rank-order scale can be applied to the survey instrument, which is shown as follows:

Rank the following brands of tennis racquets from 1 (best) to 5 (worst) according to your taste preference:

Dunlop   _____
Head   _____
Prince   _____
Prokennex   _____
Wilson   _____
Yonex   _____

The paired comparison scale. In a paired comparison scale, the researcher provides the respondent with a set of paired objects, and asks the respondent to pick one of the objects in each pair. The data collected with the use of the paired comparison scale are ordinal in nature. Compared to the ranking order scale, the biggest advantage of the paired comparison scale is the ease with which respondent can pick one of the two choices and then rank all the items provided in

a rank order scale. The disadvantage of this type of scale, on the other hand, is that it is very cumbersome to complete the list if there are a large number of paired items in the list. If the researcher who wants to obtain information about the brand preference of racquets by tennis enthusiasts uses the paired comparison scale in the survey, the question and the response choices will look like the following:

For each of the following pairs, which brand of tennis racquet do you think is better (please check one brand for each pair).

_____	Dunlop	_____	Head
_____	Head	_____	Prince
_____	Prince	_____	Prokennex
_____	Prokennex	_____	Wilson
_____	Wilson	_____	Yonex
_____	Yonex	_____	Dunlop
_____	Dunlop	_____	Prince
_____	Prince	_____	Wilson
_____	Wilson	_____	Dunlop
_____	Dunlop	_____	Prokennex
_____	Prokennex	_____	Yonex
_____	Yonex	_____	Head
_____	Head	_____	Prokennex
_____	Prince	_____	Yonex

The constant sum scale. The constant sum scales refer to the scaling method that requires the respondent to divide a given number of points, typically 100, among two or more attribute options based on their importance to the respondents. For example, in the study above, designed to determine the brand preference of racquets by tennis enthusiasts, instead of using the rank-order scale to design the survey instrument, the researcher employs the constant sum scaling technique. The questionnaire looks like this:

Allocate a total of 100 points among the following brands of tennis racquets depending on how favorable you feel toward each brand; the more highly you think of each brand, the more points you should allocate to it. (Please check that the allocated points add to 100.)

Dunlop _____ Points
Head _____ Points
Prince _____ Points
Prokennex _____ Points
Wilson _____ Points
Yonex _____ Points
100 Points

In another example, the purpose of a study is to evaluate how women runners view the nine characteristics of a newly designed women's jogging outfit. Each respondent is given 90 points and asked to allocate points to each of the characteristics based on its importance to her. The more important a characteristic, the more points she should allocate to it.

Characteristics	Number of Points
Is comfortable to wear	_____
Is durable	_____
Has the endorsement of famous athletes	_____
Is made in the United States	_____
Is made by well-known manufacturer	_____
Has up-to-date styling	_____
Gives freedom to movement	_____
Is not too expensive	_____
Authentic, like the pros wear	_____
	90 Points

TECHNIQUES OF ATTITUDE MEASUREMENT—BEHAVIORAL COMPONENT

The behavioral component of attitude can be assessed with either the category scales or the behavioral differential scales. The category scales are used to inquire a respondent's "likelihood" of action or intention to perform some action. Statements used in these scales often include action phrases such as "I would recommend," "I would buy," and "I would do" to indicate action tendencies. The following example illustrates how to use a category scale in assessing respondents' intention to renew their season tickets.

Please indicate how likely it is for you to renew your season ticket.
❑ I definitely will purchase.
❑ I probably will purchase.
❑ I might purchase.
❑ I probably will not purchase.
❑ I definitely will not purchase.

Sometimes, the researcher can use a question, "How likely are you . . ." instead of a statement to reflect the intention to act. As the likelihood to act is explicitly stated in the question itself, those action phrases as mentioned above do not have be included in the scale, as exemplified in the following example:

How likely are you to renew your season ticket?
❑ Extremely likely
❑ Very likely
❑ Somewhat likely
❑ Likely, about 50-50 chance
❑ Somewhat unlikely
❑ Very unlikely
❑ Extremely unlikely

The sport management researcher can also use the behavioral differential scale to measure the behavioral intentions of subjects toward any object or category of objects. The behavioral differential scale, similar to the semantic differential scale that has a pair of bipolar objectives placed in the two ends of the scale, has "would" and "would not" anchored in both sides of the scale. The researcher who wants to assess people's intention to renew their season tickets could use the behavioral differential scale to achieve the same purpose, as shown in the following example:

You would __:__:__:__:__:__:__: would not renew your season ticket.

SELECTION OF AN ATTITUDE MEASUREMENT SCALE

The most appropriate scale for a research project is the one that can yield the most useful information. Therefore, to select a right attitude measurement scale, the sport management researcher should closely review a number of factors, including

1. What are the preferred measurement techniques, the rating or ranking scale or the scale used to measure behavioral intention?

   Each measurement technique has one intended purpose. The rating scale is widely used in attitude-related research because of its applicability for use of parametric statistics. However, it usually does not provide the researcher with information about relativity of importance or preference among items. On the other hand, the ranking technique forces respondents to give their preferences about items evaluated. But the data collected can be analyzed only with the statistical procedures that are appropriate to ordinal data. If the main goal of a research project is to evaluate people's intention to act, the researcher should choose either category scales or the behavioral differential scale that are appropriate to measure behavioral intention.

2. Are the collected data nominal, ordinal, or interval?

The type of data collected dictates the type of statistical procedures (parametric or non-parametric) to be used in data analysis. The researcher should use the objectives of the study to select the type of statistical procedures to apply and, accordingly, the type of scale to use. For example, if the purpose of the study is to simply find out the education levels and occupations of the spectators attending a golf tournament, the researcher can just use the category scale technique to derive some nominal information (e.g., frequency and percentage) about them.

3. Does the issue to be investigated require a unidimensional or multidimensional scale?

A unidimensional scale refers to the scale used to only measure one attribute of an object. For example, the following scale designed to measure the service quality of athletic clubs is a unidimensional scale, as the question and all provided response choices measure the same thing, that is, service quality.

Compared with the service quality provided in Club A, the service quality in Club B is (seven-point semantic differential scale):

Favorable						Unfavorable
❑	❑	❑	❑	❑	❑	❑

Good						Bad
❑	❑	❑	❑	❑	❑	❑

Pleasant						Unpleasant
❑	❑	❑	❑	❑	❑	❑

On the other hand, there are phenomena or objects that have multiple attributes. To measure them, a multidimensional scaling approach is required. To assess how favorable youth skateboard enthusiasts are to a number of newly designed skateboard decks produced by several manufacturers, the researcher must choose a scale that measures a number of attributes of the skateboard deck, including size, shape, material, heaviness, length, structural strength (easiness to break), exterior design, etc. In other words, a multidimensional scale may contain a number of sub-scales with each measuring one attribute.

4. Should a balanced or an unbalanced scale be used?

A balanced rating scale has an equal number of positive and negative categories; a neutral or indifference point is at the center of the scale. The following is an example of such scale:

If you could not find a job in your chosen area in sport management, would you attempt to find a job in any other area in sport management?

Very Likely	Likely	Unsure	Unlikely	Very Unlikely
❑	❑	❑	❑	❑

On the other hand, an unbalanced rating scale refers to the scale that has more response categories piled up at one end of the scale. The positive categories do not equal negative categories in number. An example of the use of an unbalanced rating scale is shown below:

How would you rate the quality of service provided by the tournament organizer?
❑ Excellent
❑ Very Good
❑ Good
❑ Fair
❑ Poor

5. How many response choices or categories should be used?

As discussed in Chapter 12, one of the criteria to assess whether or not a survey instrument is a good measurement is its sensitivity, which is basically the ability of a survey instrument to catch the variability of responses (Zikmund, 2000). The more response choices provided in a scale, the more sensitive the scale will be. To answer the question of how many response choices or categories should be used, the researcher needs to decide how sensitive to make the scale. In general, five to nine response choices are appropriate. As mentioned in the section in which the Likert scale is discussed, the more response choices, the more likely the data collected will be normally distributed.

A related issue also should be addressed by researchers when deciding the number of response choices. That is, should the response choices be an even or odd number? Many scales, such as some category scales and the Likert scale, offer the respondent a neutral response choice in the middle of the scale. Typically, these scales have an odd number of response choices. The neutral option provides those respondents who may not have an opinion toward the object or issue one way or the other with the opportunity to express their opinion (i.e., "neutral"). Some scholars believe that having a neutral response choice could be problematic as it gives the respondent the option of hiding their opinions or not thinking hard on the question. It is commonly the case that responses tend to regress to the middle point of the scale if there is a neutral answer choice.

6. Is a forced choice scale a better option than a non-forced choice scale?

A forced-choice scale is a scale that does not provide such response choices as "do not know" or "can't tell" for the respondent to choose from the fixed alternatives. The se-

mantic differential scaling technique is a typical example of a forced-choice scale, as it does not have an option for the respondent to indicate "no opinion." The following are two examples, one of the forced-choice scale and the other one of the non-forced-choice scale.

How reliable is the treadmill produced by the XYZ sporting company?

(Forced Choice Scale)	(Non-Forced Scale)
Extremely _____ Reliable	Extremely _____ Reliable
Very _____ Reliable	Very _____ Reliable
Somewhat _____ Reliable	Somewhat _____ Reliable
Somewhat _____ Unreliable	Somewhat _____ Unreliable
Very _____ Unreliable	Very _____ Unreliable
Extremely _____ Unreliable	Extremely _____ Unreliable
	Can't Tell _____

There is not a consensus in terms of whether or not the researcher should use or not use the non-forced choice scale in attitude research (McDaniel & Gates, 1991), but a large majority of research conducted in sport management uses the forced-choice format.

7. Should it be a labeled or end-anchored scale?

The following is a labeled scale, in which each response choice is labeled.

Excellent	Very Good	Fair	Poor	Very Poor
❏	❏	❏	❏	❏

The semantic differential scale is an end-anchored scale, as it has only a pair of polarized adjectives placed in two ends of the scale. There are no labels given to each response choice in the middle of the scale between two anchored adjectives.

Excellent __ __ __ __ __ __ __ __ Poor

Summary

This chapter discussed the basic issues of which sport management researchers should be aware while choosing a scale or scales to measure attitudes. In general, among the four types of measurement techniques that can be used to assess attitudes, sport management researchers prefer rating and ranking more than sorting and choice techniques.

All the measurement techniques used in attitude research can be categorized as either the noncomparative scales or comparative scales. The noncomparative scales that are commonly employed by sport management researchers include category scales, graphic rating scales, semantic scale and semantic differential scale, the Likert scale, and the staple scale. The rank-order scale, the paired comparison scale, and the constant sum scale are examples of comparative scales.

Sport management researchers also use either category scales or behavioral differential scales to measure the behavioral component of attitude. While assessing the behavioral component of attitude, the researcher typically asks the respondent to indicate the "likelihood" or "intention" of doing something. "I would recommend," "I would buy," and "I would do," are some of common phrases provided in the answer choices.

To choose an appropriate scaling technique to yield the most meaningful information, the sport management researcher must carefully consider a number of factors. Such factors include the following:

- What are the preferred measurement techniques, the rating or ranking scale, or the scale used to measure behavioral intention?
- Are the collected data nominal, ordinal, or interval?
- Does the issue to be investigated require a unidimensional or multidimensional scale?
- Should a balanced or an unbalanced scale to be used?
- How many response choices or categories should be used?
- Is a forced choice scale better option than a non-forced choice scale?
- Should it be a labeled or an end-anchored scale?

STUDY QUESTIONS

1. What are the three components of attitudes? Explain each of them with an example.
2. What are the four basic measurement techniques in attitude research? Which technique is the most common one used in sport management research?
3. What are the differences between the non-comparative scales and comparative scales?
4. What are advantages and disadvantages of the following pairs of scaling techniques?
   a. The category scales and the semantic differential scales
   b. The Likert scale and the staple scale
   c. The rank-order scale and the constant sum scale
5. What are the scaling techniques that can be used to measure behavioral component of attitudes?
6. What are the factors that need to be considered when choosing a particular type of scaling technique in questionnaire design?

LEARNING ACTIVITIES

1. Assume that the Marketing Department of the Red Devil, an arena football team, wishes to understand how fans react to the half-time show the team just unveiled, specifically around four attributes: excitement, creativity, attractiveness, and satisfaction. You are asked to design a questionnaire to be used as a survey to obtain the information. What will the questionnaire look like:
   - if it is designed with one of the category scales?
   - if it is designed with the Likert scale?
   - if it is designed with the semantic differential scale?

2. Assume that you were just hired as assistant ticker manager in a sports facility. One of the things you have been assigned to do is to design a short questionnaire, using either the categorical or the behavioral differential scale, to evaluate customers' behavioral intentions to purchase season tickets and tickets to other events to be held in the facility in the near future. What will the questionnaire look like? Be sure to include at least four questions.

References

Bradburn, N. M., Seymour, S., & Wansink, B. (2004). *Asking questions: The definitive guide to questionnaire design— for market research, political polls, and social and health questionnaires* (rev. ed.). San Francisco, CA: Jossy-Bass.

Caro, L. M., & Garcia, J. A. M. (2007). Consumer satisfaction with a periodic reoccurring sport event and the moderating effect of motivations. *Sport Marketing Quarterly*, *16*(2), 70–81.

Friedman, H. H., & Amoo, T. (1999). Rating the rating scales. *Journal of Marketing Management*, *9*, 114–123.

Li, M., & Burden, W. (2002). Outsourcing sport marketing operations by NCAA Division I athletic programs: An exploratory study. *Sport Marketing Quarterly*, *11*(4), 227–232.

Likert, R. (1974). The method of constructing an attitude scale. In G. M. Maranell (Ed.), *Scaling: A sourcebook for behavioral scientists* (pp. 233–243). Chicago, IL: Aldine Publishing Company.

McDaniel, C., & Gates, R. (1991). *Contemporary marketing research*. St. Paul, MN: West Publishing Company.

Sirkin, R. (1999). *Statistics for the social sciences* (2nd ed.). Thousand Oaks, CA: Sage Publications.

WordWeb Online (2005). *Attitude*. Retrieved on September 23, 2006, from *http://www.wordwebonline.com/en/ ATTITUDE*

Zikmund, W. G. (2000). *Business research methods* (6th ed.). Fort Worth, TX: Harcourt College Publishers.

CHAPTER 14
QUESTIONNAIRE DESIGN

OBJECTIVES FOR COMPLETING THIS
CHAPTER ARE THAT STUDENTS WILL
BE ABLE TO:

Describe the process of developing
a questionnaire

Understand the importance of a draft plan
in questionnaire development

Explain the advantages and disadvantages
of both open-ended questions and
closed-ended questions

Explain the criteria of a "good question"

Understand the factors that sport management
researchers should consider when determining
the order of questions and answer choices

Explain how to deal with the "Don't Know"
or "Not Applicable" answer choices

Indicate the criteria that sport management
researchers use to determine the usability of
a questionnaire during the pretesting phase
of questionnaire development

Explain the methods that can be used
to increase response rate

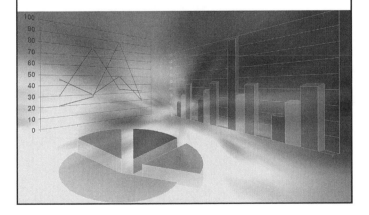

A S MENTIONED PREVIOUSLY, sport management researchers have used questionnaires to gather data in most studies. Because of the importance of questionnaires, students should develop a clear understanding and skills in proper questionnaire design. A questionnaire is a form that contains a number of questions used to gather information from a statistically significant number of subjects in a survey (Robson, 2002). As such, it is also referred to as a survey instrument.

In this chapter, a number of important issues pertaining to questionnaire design will be discussed. Specifically, the questionnaire development process and other practical issues related to questionnaire design, such as the order of questions and answer choices, the ways to deal with "Don't Know" or "Not Applicable" answer choices, the length of a questionnaire, and ways to increase response rate will be examined.

The Questionnaire Development Process

Designing an effective questionnaire is both an art and a science, and it requires time and careful thought (Bradburn, Sudman, & Wansink, 2004). Before a sport management researcher decides to de-sign a questionnaire to solve a particular issue (e.g., to determine whether or not fans' satisfaction affect their intention to attend a sport event), the researcher should find out if questionnaires already exist that could be used or modified to gather the required information. It will save a lot of time and work if the researcher does not need to develop an entirely new questionnaire. If such a questionnaire is not available, the researcher then should follow the necessary process to design the instrument.

The development of a questionnaire is a multi-stage process that begins with defining the objectives of the survey research and ends with revising and finalizing the questionnaire before use (McDaniel & Gates, 1991; Patten, 2001). Every step needs to be executed carefully, as it ultimately affects the quality of the final product. Although questionnaires may be less expensive to administer than other data collection methods, they can be costly in terms of the time required to design them.

The questionnaire development process includes these six steps: (a) defining the objectives of the survey research, (b) determining a format of questioning, (c) writing the questions, (d) reviewing the questionnaire, (e) pretesting the questionnaire, and (f) revising and finalizing the questionnaire (Swanson & Holton, 2005). In the following section, descriptions of the six steps and actions that should be taken in each step will be provided in detail.

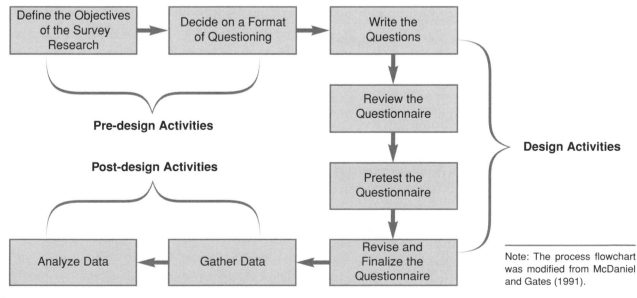

FIGURE 14-1. The Questionnaire Development Process

Defining the Objectives of the Survey Research

The importance of well-defined objectives can not be overemphasized. A questionnaire that is designed without clear objectives is inevitably going to overlook important issues and waste participants' time by asking useless questions. The researcher often comes to realize that the objectives of the survey research have not been specified precisely when the questionnaire is being developed. Consequently, the questionnaire may lack a logical flow and cause the participant to lose interest, ultimately compromising the data that it is intended to collect. All questions to be included in the questionnaire must be consistent with the objectives of the research (Bradburn, Sudman, & Wansink, 2004). Thus, the biggest challenge in developing an effective questionnaire is to translate the objectives of the survey research into a well-conceptualized and methodologically sound survey instrument. To accomplish this goal, the researcher should ask such questions as: Why is this survey being conducted? What do I need to know? How will the information be used? How accurate and timely does the information have to be (Ghauri, Gronhaug, & Kristianslund, 1995)?

Most of the problems found in the analysis of survey results can be traced back to the design phase of the questionnaire. Well-defined objectives are the best way to assure a good questionnaire design (Bradburn, Sudman, & Wansink, 2004). When the objectives of a survey research can be expressed in a few clear and concise sentences, the process in designing the questionnaire becomes considerably easier, because the questionnaire is developed to directly address the objectives of the research. Therefore, it is necessary for the researcher to put the survey objectives in writing. A good rule of thumb in this regard is that if the researcher finds it difficult to write a question, then the researcher has not spent enough time defining the objectives of the survey research (Ghauri, Gronhaug, & Kristianslund, 1995). At this point, the researcher needs to go back to review the objective again. The review will give the researcher more clues of how to phrase the question as the question should always be derived naturally from the objective. Researchers should resist the temptation to ask a question because it would be "interesting to know" and should guard themselves with the principle of "optimal ignorance"—collect only information that is really needed.

Before designing a questionnaire, it is suggested that the researcher develop a draft plan that outlines the objectives of the survey research, the data requirements, and the analysis plan. This document will determine the variables to be measured, and ultimately, the survey questions and response alternatives. The analysis plan will describe the target audience and provide a list of the units to be sampled (e.g., athletes, facilities, managers). In addition, the analysis plan will also state the method of data collection to be used (e.g., face-to-face interview, telephone interview, mailed questionnaire) and explain how the questionnaire content, wording, format, and pretesting process will be developed. The methods to be used during the data processing (e.g., coding, editing) are also described in the plan. Finally, the last two important issues to be considered are the time required to complete the entire process and the budget that has been allotted to it (Ghauri, Gronhaug, & Kristianslund, 1995).

Determining the Formats of Questioning

Before determining the formats of questioning and subsequently writing specific questions, the researcher must decide the mode of information collection: whether or not the questionnaire will be (a) self-administered or interviewer-administered, and (b) delivered by mail, email, fax, telephone, in person, or posted on the Internet. The mode of information collection will determine how questions and response options are constructed. Also, the overall questionnaire length, question complexity, and question sensitivity must be weighed in determining the mode of information collection besides financial constraints. For example, long questionnaires may not work well on the telephone, complex questions may require an interviewer to be sure that they are understood, and sensitive questions may be best done in a self-administered format. Review the discussion in Chapter 9 about factors affecting the choice of particular survey methods.

After the mode of information collection has been

decided, the researcher can proceed to determining the formats of questioning. In general, sport management researchers use two types of formats in asking questions, open-ended or closed-ended (Yates, 2004). Most questionnaires contain both types of questioning formats. However, open and closed question formats are appropriate in different contexts and provide different kinds of information.

Open-ended Questions

Open-ended questions are questions that allow respondents to answer freely, however they choose, so as to receive unprompted opinions (Johnson & Christensen, 2000; Yates, 2004). There are no predetermined responses. For example, a fan attending a NBA game might be asked to respond to the following open-ended question:

> Do you like tonight's game and why?

Open-ended questions are often used when the issue is complex. An obvious advantage of an open-ended question is its flexibility, as respondents can answer in any way they wish. Another advantage is that it is good for soliciting subjective data when the range of responses is not tightly defined. Accordingly, the variety of responses is wider and more truly reflects the opinions of the respondents (Johnson & Christensen, 2000). This increases the likelihood of receiving unexpected and insightful suggestions, for it is impossible to predict the full range of opinions. It is common for a questionnaire to end with an open-ended question asking respondents for their unabashed ideas for changes or improvements. They may be a better means of eliciting true opinions and attitudes and of identifying how strongly attitudes are held or not. The open-ended question is often used in the exploratory stage of a research project.

One main concern of open-ended questions is that they require more thought and time on the part of both the respondent and researcher (Johnson & Christensen, 2000). When respondents feel like they have been asked to answer a lot of questions, it increases the chance that they will become tired or bored. This may dramatically reduce the number of questions that the questionnaire can realistically ask. And because the researcher must read all the responses individually, open-ended questions can be costly in both time and money, and they may not be practical for lower budget or time-sensitive evaluations. Another concern about the use of open-ended questions is that it is more difficult to pool opinions across the sample, and respondents may sometimes answer in unhelpful ways (Yates, 2004). Obviously, there is no way to automatically tabulate or perform a statistical analysis on open-ended questions. The third concern of open-ended questions is that they are also open to the influence of the reader, for no two people will interpret an answer in precisely the same way. This conflict can be eliminated by using a single reader, but a large number of responses can make this impossible (Yates, 2004).

Closed-ended Questions

Closed-ended questions are questions in which all possible answers are identified and the respondent is asked to choose one of the answers provided (Yates, 2004). They are commonly used situations in which answers are known, are limited in number, and are clear-cut. In other words, closed-format questions are an appropriate means of asking questions that have a finite set of answers of a clear-cut nature. As such, they usually take the form of a multiple-choice question. The following is an example of a closed-ended question:

> Based on your observation, what is the level of international sport management education training that your faculty members have received?
> ❏ None or minimal training
> ❏ Moderate training
> ❏ Advanced/adequate training

There is no clear consensus on the number of answer choices that should be given in a closed-format question. Obviously, a sufficient number of answer choices need to be provided to fully cover the range of answers but not so many as to blur the distinction between them. Usually, five to nine possible answer choices are included for each question. For questions that measure a single variable or opinion, conventional wisdom says that there should be an odd number of answer choices as it allows for a neutral or no opinion response. Other schools of thought contend that an even number of answer choices is best because it forces the respondent to get off the fence (Bradburn, Sudman, & Wansink, 2004). It may, nevertheless, induce some inaccuracies as the respondent may actually have no opinion. Professional wisdom in questionnaire design supports the theory that it is best to use an even number of choices to prevent large numbers of neutral answers for larger questionnaires that examine opinions on a large number of items (Robson, 2002; Yates, 2004; Zikmund, 2000).

Closed-ended questions offer many advantages in terms of time and money. First, they involve minimal effort on the part of the respondent. Second, they provide the researcher with greater control over the outcomes of the survey as the respondent is forced to answer particular questions. Third, restricting the answer set makes it is easy to calculate percentages and other hard statistical data over the whole group or over any subgroup of participants (Johnson & Christensen, 2000). Modern scanners and computers make it possible to administer, tabulate, and perform preliminary analysis in a relatively short period of time. Fourth, closed-ended questions also make it easier to track opinion over time by administering the same questionnaire to different but similar participant groups at regular intervals. Finally, closed-ended questions allow the researcher to filter out useless or extreme answers that might occur in an open-ended question (Yates, 2004).

Closed-ended questions are not problem-free. Closed-ended questions are appropriate only when the set of possible answers are known and clear-cut. If poorly designed, closed-ended questions may be misleading and frustrate respondents. Examples of inappropriately drafted closed-ended questions can be found in the "Writing the Questions" section.

Writing the Questions

Criteria of a good question. The wording of questions will influence the answers that the respondent will provide. As such, the sport management researcher should keep in mind the basic principles or criteria used to write good questions in questionnaire design. The following are important criteria recommended by professional wisdom in questionnaire design to consider when phrasing questions. These criteria are used to judge whether or not a question is appropriately written (Johnson & Christensen, 2000; Schwab, 1999; Zikmund, 2000).

Be simple. The three most important things for anyone involved in designing a questionnaire to remember are simplicity, simplicity, and simplicity (Johnson & Christensen, 2000). Ideas need to be conveyed clearly and questions should be easy to comprehend. There must be no guesswork for the respondent when it comes to understanding exactly what information is being asked. Otherwise, the reliability of the question will be questionable.

Evoke the truth in a non-threatening manner. When a respondent is concerned about the consequences of answering a question in a particular manner (i.e., feels threatened), there is a good possibility that the answer will not be truthful. For example, the following question will put the respondent in a very uncomfortable position to answer:

The use of illegal substances is rampant among players on your team. Yes ❏ No ❏

Anonymous questionnaires that contain no identifying information are more likely to produce honest responses than those that identify the respondent. If the questionnaire does contain sensitive items, the researcher must clearly state the policy on confidentiality to ease concerns (Bradburn, Sudman, & Wansink, 2004).

Ask for an answer on only one dimension. The purpose of a survey is to find out information. A question that asks for a response on more than one dimension will not provide the information the researcher wants (Bradburn, Sudman, & Wansink, 2004). For example, a researcher interested in finding out if the users of an athletic club are satisfied with the club asks, "Are you satisfied with the programming and services provided by this club"? If a respondent answers "no," there is no way for the researcher to know whether the programming or service, or both, were unsatisfactory. This kind of question is often referred as a "double-barreled question," A good solution to the problem is to obtain the information with two separate questions.

Accommodate all possible answers. Multiple choice items are the most popular type of survey questions because they are generally the easiest for a respondent to answer and the easiest to analyze. Asking a question that does not accommodate all possible responses not only can confuse and frustrate the respondent, but can also introduce bias (McDaniel & Gates, 1991). The following question is an example of questions that do not accommodate all possible answers:

What brand of tennis racquet do you own?
❏ Wilson
❏ Yonex

Clearly, there are many problems with this question. What if the respondent doesn't play tennis and thus does not own a tennis racquet? What if the respondent owns a different brand of tennis racquet other than those listed? What if the respondent owns tennis racquets in both brands? There are two ways to correct the problem. The first way is to make each response a separate dichotomous item on the questionnaire. For example:

Do you own a Wilson tennis racquet? (circle: Yes or No)

Do you own a Yonex tennis racquet? (circle: Yes or No)

Another way to correct the problem is to add the necessary response categories and allow multiple responses. This is the preferable method because it provides more information than the previous method.

What brand of tennis racquet do you own? (Check all that apply)
❏ Do not own a tennis racquet
❏ Wilson
❏ Yonex
❏ Other (specify _____)

The most common example for not accommodating all possible answers is to leave out such responses as "neutral" or "don't know" when, in fact, respondents may well be neutral or may actually not know. More discussion on this particular phenomenon can be found in the "Dealing with Don't Know or Not Applicable Answer Choices" section later in the chapter.

Have mutually exclusive options. A good question leaves no ambiguity in the mind of the respondent. There should be only one correct or appropriate choice for the respondent to make (Bradburn, Sudman, & Wansink, 2004). Bias could be introduced if the answer choices are not mutually exclusive and only one choice may be selected. An obvious example is:

Where did you grow up?
❏ country
❏ farm
❏ city

A person who grew up on a farm in the country would not know whether to select choice A or B. This question not only would not provide meaningful information, but also could frustrate the respondent. There is a great possibility that the respondent may stop completing the questionnaire while frustrated.

Produce variability of responses. When a question produces no variability in responses, it leaves considerable uncertainty about why this question is asked and what the researcher wants to learn from the information. If a question does not produce variability in responses, it will not be possible to perform any statistical analyses on the item (McDaniel & Gates, 1991). For example:

What do you think about this game?
❏ It is the worst game I have watched
❏ It is somewhere between the worst and best
❏ It is the best game I have watched

Because the respondents will most likely choose B, the question yields very little information. So, the researcher should phrase sensitive questions to allow for differences between respondents.

Again, the following is another example of a question with very little variability in responses as most of the respondents will choose "yes":

Are you against drug use by professional athletes? Yes ❑ No ❑

Follow comfortably from the previous question. Writing a questionnaire is similar to writing anything else. Transitions between questions should be smooth. Grouping questions that are similar will make the questionnaire easier to complete, and the respondent will feel more comfortable. Questionnaires that jump from one unrelated topic to another feel disjointed and are not likely to produce high response rates.

Do not assume a certain state of affairs. Among the most subtle mistakes in phrasing questions is to make an unwarranted assumption. An example of this type of mistake is:

Are you satisfied with your tennis racquet? Yes ❑ No ❑

This question will present a problem for someone who does not currently have a tennis racquet. The researcher should write the questions that will apply to everyone. This often means simply adding an additional response category.

Are you satisfied with your tennis racquet?
❑ Yes
❑ No
❑ Do not have a tennis racquet

One of the most common assumptions is that the respondent knows the correct answer to the question. Industry surveys often contain very specific questions that the respondent may not know the answer to. For example:

What percent of your budget do you spend on participating in sport?

Very few people would know the answer to this question without looking it up, and very few respondents will take the time and effort to look it up. If researchers ask questions similar to this, it is important that they understand that the responses are rough estimates and there is a strong

likelihood of error. So, it is essential for researchers to look at each question and decide if all respondents will be able to answer it. Researchers must be careful not to assume anything. For example, the following question assumes the respondent knows what GO bond is about.

Are you in favor of the use of GO Bond in facility financing?
❑ Yes
❑ No
❑ Undecided

If there is any possibility that the respondent may not know the answer to the question, researchers should include a "don't know" response category.

Do not use unfamiliar words, colloquial expressions, or abbreviations. The researcher must have a clear understanding of the target population of the survey research, thus writing questions particularly for them. With that in mind, the researcher should avoid using uncommon words or compound sentences and should write short sentences (Bradburn, Sudman, & Wansink, 2004). The researcher should also avoid using colloquial or ethnic expressions that might not be equally used by all participants. Abbreviations or technical terms can be used only if the researcher is absolutely certain that all respondents understand the meanings of those terms or abbreviations. Otherwise, abbreviations should be avoided. The following question, for instance, might be okay if all the respondents are golf enthusiasts, but it would not be a good question for the general public:

What is your handicap? _____

Do not imply a desired answer. People sometimes have a desire to give the "right" answer to a question whether or not it is actually true. This type of question is referred to as a "leading" question. Researchers should strive for objectivity in the survey and must be careful not to lead the respondent into giving the answer they would like to receive. Leading questions are usually easily spotted because they use negative phraseology. For example:

The city has spent too much taxpayers' money in building sports facilities.
❏ Strongly Agree
❏ Agree
❏ Neutral
❏ Disagree
❏ Strongly Disagree

The researcher should consider asking the question in less obvious way:

Should the city spend money in building sports facilities? Yes ❏ No ❏

Here is another example. The spectators attending to a professional football game were asked to express their overall impression of the game:

Is this the best game you have ever watched? Yes ❏ No ❏

In this case, even if the spectators enjoyed the game, but had a favorite game that was preferred, they would be forced to answer "no." Clearly, the negative response covers too wide a range of opinions. A better way would be to ask the same question but supply the following choices:

This is the best game you have ever watched.
❏ Strongly Agree
❏ Agree
❏ Neither Agree or Disagree
❏ Disagree
❏ Strongly Disagree

Also, the word "best" has strong overtones that deny the spectators an objective environment to consider the game. The signal sent to the respondent is that the researcher thinks it is the best game, and so should everyone else. Though this may seem like an extreme example, this kind of superlative question is common practice in sport management research.

Do not use emotionally loaded or vaguely defined words. This is one of the areas often overlooked by researchers. Quantifying adjectives (e.g., most, least, majority) are frequently used in questions. It is important to understand that these adjectives mean different things to different people. Accordingly, the researcher should try to be as precise as possible in wring the questions to ensure that respondents understand exactly what is being asked. In other words, it is best to phrase the question empirically if possible and to avoid the use of unnecessary adjectives. For example, a question asks about frequency, but supplying choices that are open to interpretation such as:

How frequently do you exercise?
❏ Very Often
❏ Often
❏ Sometimes
❏ Rarely
❏ Never

This question is fairly vague. How many times or days a person exercises is considered "very often"? A better way to ask the question is to provide the respondents with quantifiable choices, such as:
❏ Every Day or More
❏ 2–6 Times a Week
❏ About Once a Week
❏ About Once a Month
❏ Never

This example illustrates a dilemma: when questions are made more precise, they often become more limited in scope.

Do not ask hypothetical questions. This type of question forces respondents to give thought to something they may never have considered. It does not produce clear and consistent data representing real opinion. The following is an example of a hypothetical question:

If you were David Stern, what would you do to stop players from fighting in NBA?

Try to prevent prestige bias. Prestige bias is the tendency of respondents to answer a question in a way that makes them feel better. People may not lie directly but may try to put a better light on themselves. For example, a survey on alumni contributions includes this question: "Did you donate any money to XYZ University during its annual campaign last year?" To deal with prestige bias, the researcher should try to make the questionnaire as private as possible and assure the respondents of absolute confidentiality.

Do not make the questions dependent on responses to previous questions. Branching in written questionnaires should be avoided. Although branching can be used as an effective probing technique in telephone and face-to-face interviews, it should not be used in written questionnaires because it sometimes confuses respondents. An example of branching is:

1. Do you play golf? Yes ❑ No ❑
   If no, go to question 3

2. How much did you spend on playing golf?
   _____

3. Why don't you play golf?

If the purpose of the survey is to find out how much golfers spent on average, these questions could easily be rewritten as one question that applies to everyone:

How much did you spend last year on playing golf? _____ (write 0 if none)

Do not ask the respondent to order or rank a series of more than five items. The researcher should avoid asking respondents to rank items by importance. This becomes increasingly difficult as the number of items increases, and the answers become less reliable. This becomes especially problematic when asking respondents to assign a percentage to a series of items. In order to successfully complete this task, the respondents must mentally continue to re-adjust their answers until they total 100 percent. Limiting the number of items to no more than five will make it easier for the respondent to answer.

In attitude assessment, how many alternatives should be given has been an issue debated among scholars. Five alternatives are the most common set, typically ranging from "strongly agree" to "strongly disagree," unless one wishes to deny the respondent the lazy choice of a mid-point, which sometimes has no meaning. Careful thought is needed to synthesize the attitude measures into a meaningful indicator or "profile." Often informants ought to participate directly in deciding the importance of profile elements.

Question and Answer Choice Order

After writing all of the questions, the researcher's next task is to determine the question and answer choice order. The order of the questions and the order of the answer choices not only encourage people to complete the survey but also affect the results of the survey (Schwab, 1999).

The order of question affects the outcome of the survey. An idea mentioned early in one question can make the respondents to think of it while they answer a later question. Habituation is the other way the order of questions can affect the outcome of a survey. Habituation is what has occurred when respondents give the same answer to all questions without really considering them, after having been asked a series of similar questions that have the same answer choices.

There are a few principles that experts in survey research generally have a consensus on in terms of the question and answer choice order (Bradburn, Sudman, & Wansink, 2004):

1. The questions in the early sections of the survey should be easy to answer. These kinds of questions encourage respondents to continue the survey.
2. Place the most important items in the first half of the questionnaire. Respondents often send back partially completed questionnaires. By putting the most important items near the beginning, the partially completed questionnaires will still contain important information.
3. Grouping together questions on the same topic makes the questionnaire easier to answer.
4. Difficult or sensitive questions should be asked in the end of the questionnaire. The advantage of such an arrangement is that the

respondents would have already answered most of the questions if they decided to quit at that point.

5. One way to reduce habitation is to ask only a short series of similar questions at a particular point in the questionnaire. Then ask one or more different kinds of questions, and then another short series if needed.

6. To reduce habitation in survey instruments that contain questions asking respondents to indicate their levels of agreement, researchers can phrase some statements in such a way so that a high level of agreement means satisfaction (e.g., "My supervisor gives me positive feedback") and some others so that a high level of agreement means dissatisfaction (e.g., "My supervisor usually ignores my suggestions"). This technique forces the respondents to think more about each question.

Answer choice order can make individual questions easier or more difficult to answer. Whenever there is a logical or natural order to answer choices, researchers should use it. They should also always present agree-disagree choices in that order. Presenting them in disagree-agree order will seem odd. For the same reason, positive to negative and excellent to poor scales should be presented in those orders. When using numeric rating scales, higher numbers should mean a more positive or more agreeing answer.

The order in which answer choices are presented can also affect the answers given. People tend to pick the choices nearest the start of a list when they read the list themselves on paper or a computer screen. People tend to pick the most recent answer when they hear a list of choices read to them.

As mentioned previously, sometimes answer choices have a natural order (e.g., Yes followed by No; or Excellent—Good—Fair—Poor). If so, researchers should use that order. At other times, questions have answers that are obvious to the person who is answering them. In these cases, the order in which the answer choices are presented is not likely to affect the answers given. However, there are kinds of questions, particularly questions about preference or recall or questions with relatively long

answer choices that express an idea or opinion, in which the answer choice order is more likely to affect which choice is picked. Researchers who are using telephone, computer direct, or Internet interviewing should have their software present these kinds of answer choices in a random order.

There are different schools of thought in terms of whether or not demographic data should be collected at the beginning of the questionnaire, at the end, or scattered throughout. The proponents for having this type of question collected at the beginning of the questionnaire argue that normally background questions are easier to answer and can ease the respondent into the questionnaire. On the other hand, it is also believed that demographic questions such as age, gender, income, and education should be asked at the end of the questionnaire. By then the researcher may have collected enough information even if the respondent refuses to complete the demographic questions. Some exceptions exist. If a demographic question qualifies someone to be included in the survey, it should be placed near the beginning as a filter question. For example, sport economic impact studies often exclude local residents from their studies.

It is important to ask only those background questions that are necessary. Researchers should not ask the income of the respondent unless there is at least some rationale for suspecting a variance across income levels. There is often only a fine line between background and personal information. Researchers do not want to cross over into the personal realm unless absolutely necessary. If they need to solicit personal information, they should phrase the questions as unobtrusively as possible to avoid ruffling the participants and causing them to answer less than truthfully (Bradburn, Sudman, & Wansink, 2004).

Dealing with "Don't Know" or "Not Applicable" Answer Choices

It is recommended that a "Don't Know" or "Not Applicable" answer choice be available for questions that the researchers are not sure the respondents will be able to answer (Patten, 2001). In most cases, these are wasted answers as far as the researcher is concerned, but they are necessary alternatives to avoid frustrated respondents. Sometimes "Don't Know" or "Not Applicable" will really represent some respondents' most honest answers to some questions. Respondents who feel they are being coerced into giving an answer they do not want to give often do not complete the questionnaire. For example, many people will abandon a questionnaire that asks them to specify their income but does not offer a "decline to state" choice. When the researcher decides to include "Don't Know" or "Not Applicable" as an answer choice, it should be treated as a legitimate response in data analysis and reporting (Huisman & van der Zouwen, 1998). For the same reason, the researcher should include "Other" or "None" as a logically possible answer if the circumstance warrants.

Reviewing the Questionnaire

After the initial draft is completed, the researcher should carefully examine the questionnaire to determine that each of the questions included in the instrument meets certain standards (Fraenkel & Wallen, 2000). Extra time and resources are often wasted asking for information that will never be put to use. Reviewing the questionnaire is a fundamental step in developing a questionnaire. The following is a list of some key points for researchers to consider when reviewing questionnaires:

1. Is the introduction informative?
2. Does it stimulate respondent interest?
3. Are the words simple, direct, and familiar to all respondents?
4. Do the questions read well?
5. Does the overall questionnaire flow?
6. Are the questions clear and as specific as possible?
7. Does the questionnaire begin with easy and interesting questions?
8. Does the question specify a time reference?
9. If the questions are closed-ended, are the response categories mutually exclusive and exhaustive?
10. Are the questions applicable to all respondents?
11. Are the questions included in the question-naire clearly linked to the objectives of the survey research?
12. Do the questions directly address the issues under the investigation?

While reviewing the questionnaire, the researcher should pay close attention to the last two questions as they are the most critical ones to ask. To address them, the researcher should first review the objectives of the study, and then write down each question number next to the objective that the particular question will accomplish. After that has been done, the researcher can determine the need to either add more questions or drop some from the questionnaire.

Pretesting the Questionnaire

Although the questionnaire has gone through a few steps in its design process, it is not ready to be sent out yet. It needs to be pretested. Pretesting is considered an essential step in questionnaire design (Fraenkel & Wallen, 2000; Johnson & Christensen, 2000). Even though the researcher has tried to ensure that all questions are clear and concise in writing the questions, invariably some items are ambiguous and some bias and error still exist in the questionnaire. Thus, it is important to conduct two pretests to see how it works. Specifically, pretesting helps discover poor wording or ordering of questions, identify errors in the questionnaire layout and instructions, determine problems caused by the respondent's inability or unwillingness to answer the questions, suggest additional response categories that can be precoded on the questionnaire, and provide a preliminary indication of the length of the interview and any refusal problems.

Testing can include the entire questionnaire or only a portion of it. A questionnaire will at some point in time have to be fully tested. The pretesting can be done by a small number of people (number from 25 to 75), preferably including some of the people for whom the questionnaire was designed. Prior to the first pretest, the questionnaire usually has more questions than the final version as a key purpose of the first pretest is to identify weaker or inappropriate questions and drop them from the questionnaire. The second pretest is used simply for polishing, trimming, rearranging, and other refinements, but not for adding new questions or making major substantive changes to the questionnaire. It is possible that this step may need to be repeated more than twice depending on resources and the need for accuracy. The main purpose to re-test the questionnaire is to determine its face validity. (See Chapter 12 for detailed information about face validity.)

There are a few evaluative criteria that can be used during the pretesting to determine the usability of the questionnaire:

1. The researcher needs to obtain information about whether or not the questionnaire is easy to administer, score, and interpret. In other words, what are the practicalities of implementing and using a questionnaire?
2. Is the questionnaire capable of producing reliable results or data? It is a crucial for the researcher to obtain an answer to this question during the pretesting process.
3. A questionnaire should actually measure what it is designed to measure. It depends greatly on the quality of the questioning.

It should be kept in mind that no questionnaire is perfect. Therefore, a little extra time and care in the pretesting step of a questionnaire can avoid many problems and greatly improve the quality of information sought.

Finalizing the Questionnaire

After the pretest, the researcher should review the questionnaire with the respondents in terms of how they felt about the questionnaire. Review questions include:

- Does the questionnaire miss some key information?
- Should multiple-choice questions include other possible answers?
- Can respondents follow the questionnaire or do they get confused or frustrated?
- Are questions repeated unnecessarily?
- Are questions understood and answered properly, or are there confusing words or phrases?
- Is the questionnaire too long?

Based on the feedback and comments obtained from the respondents, the researcher can revise the questionnaire before putting it into use.

OTHER PRACTICAL ISSUES RELATED TO QUESTIONNAIRE DESIGN

How Long Should the Questionnaire Be?

It has been proven in sport management research that long questionnaires in general get less response than short questionnaires. So, the researchers should keep their questionnaires short, particularly those to be sent to sport management practitioners to complete. Response rate is the single most important indicator of the level of confidence of the results. A low response rate can be destructive to the quality of a study; therefore, researchers should try to do whatever they can to maximize the response rate. One of the most effective methods of maximizing response is to shorten the questionnaire.

If a survey instrument is more than a few pages, the researcher should shorten it by eliminating questions. To determine which questions to eliminate, the researcher might read each question and then ask, "Is this question critical to answer the research question?" If the information will be important to solve the research problem or to use in a decision-making process, then the question should be kept. If not, it could be omitted.

Even though long questionnaires often have fewer responses than short questionnaires, some studies have shown that the length of a questionnaire does not necessarily affect response (StatPac Inc., 2007). More important than length is question content. Subjects are more likely to respond if they are involved and interested in the research topic.

The Order of the Questions

No definitive empirical evidence suggests that the order of questions affects response in survey research; however, it is believed that the order effect may exist in interviews but not in written questionnaires (Bradburn, Sudman, & Wansink, 2004).

Regardless, the sport management researcher should attempt to order the questions in a logical manner. Grouping questions that are similar will facilitate the respondent's completion of the questionnaire as the order makes the respondent feel more comfortable. Questions that use the same response formats, or those that cover a specific topic, should appear together. Also, the order of questions should be designed so that the questions appearing earlier hold the interest of the respondents and accordingly motivate them to complete the questions in the latter part of the questionnaire (Bradburn, Sudman, & Wansink, 2004). Also, the transitions between questions should be smooth. A questionnaire with questions that jump from one topic to another may frustrate respondents and discourage them from completing the questionnaire, thus leading to low response rates.

Ways to Increase the Response Rate

In addition to those techniques discussed in the Survey Research chapter, sport management researchers can also use the following 12 ways relative to questionnaire design to increase the response rate of a survey:

Include experts in the questionnaire design process. Their suggestions will improve the questionnaire. Researchers should form a panel of sport management experts who have expertise in the area of relative research and ask this group to review the questions. This will ultimately validate the questionnaire.

Keep the questionnaire short. Long questionnaires will deter respondents. So, the researcher needs to always ask what to do with the information collected from each question. Based on the examination, questions can be placed into three groups: must know, useful to know, and nice to know. The "nice questions" should be dropped unless the total number of questions in the previous two groups is very low.

Hold the respondent's interest. Researchers want the respondent to complete the questionnaire. One way to keep a questionnaire interesting is to provide variety in the type of items used. Varying the questioning format will also prevent respondents from falling into "response sets." At

the same time, it is important to group items into coherent categories. All items should flow smoothly from one to the next. The questionnaire should start with a few non-threatening and interesting questions. Respondents may be discouraged to complete the survey instrument if threatening or "boring" questions are provided at the beginning of the questionnaire. Respondents generally make a decision of whether or not they will continue to answer the questions in the questionnaire by reviewing the first few questions.

Use the supporting text throughout the questionnaire wisely. The supporting text (1) should be used to communicate clearly to the respondents about the purpose of the survey, (2) should address the confidentiality of responses, and (3) must instruct the respondents on how to complete the questionnaire. The instruction provided in terms of how to complete each section of the questionnaire is very important.

Be logical and coherent. A good questionnaire has a coherent structure. Where possible, researchers should collect questions under definable subject areas and develop a logical order of questions.

Make the envelope unique. The first impression of the respondents is very important. Their first impression of the survey research comes from the envelope containing the questionnaire. The best envelopes use commemorative postage stamps. Envelopes with bulk mail permits or gummed labels are perceived as unimportant. This perception will generally be reflected in a lower response rate.

Use a short and meaningful title for the questionnaire. A questionnaire with a title is generally perceived to be more credible than one without.

Use professional production methods for the questionnaire. Researchers should be creative and consider trying different colored inks and paper. The objective is to make the questionnaire stand out from all the others that the respondent receives. Each page of a mail questionnaire should be numbered.

Leave adequate space for respondents to make comments. One criticism of questionnaires is their inability to retain the "flavor" of a response. Leaving space for comments will provide valuable information not captured by the response categories. Leaving white space also makes the questionnaire look easier, and this increases response.

Use the tablet form instead of a staple to hold the questionnaire. If a questionnaire is more than a few pages and is held together by a staple, include some identifying data on each page (such as a respondent ID number). Pages often accidentally separate.

Print the return address on the questionnaire. It often happens that the questionnaires get separated from the reply envelopes and the cover letter. By printing the return address on the questionnaire, it gives another assurance that the respondents will send back the survey instrument.

Make it convenient. The researcher should always include a self-addressed postage-paid envelope in the mail survey. Envelopes with postage stamps get better response than business reply envelopes.

The Layout of a Questionnaire

The layout of a questionnaire is also an important part of the questionnaire design. The general principles for the layout of a questionnaire are that the layout must be attractive, easy to understand, and easy to complete. Also, it should be easy for data entry.

The researcher should try to keep the answer spaces in a straight line, either horizontally or vertically. A single answer choice on each line is best. It is easier for a respondent to follow a logical flow across or down a page.

As shown in the second of the following examples, researchers like to use question-and-answer choice grids in the layout of their questionnaires. The grids not only look attractive, but also save paper or computer screen space. They also can avoid a long series of very repetitive question-and-answer choice lists. The researchers, however, must realize that such layouts may be more difficult than the repeated lists for some people to understand. As always, the researchers need to consider their subjects when creating the questionnaire.

Look at the following layouts and decide which you would prefer to use:

Do you agree, disagree or have no opinion that the benefits of outsourcing for a sport organization include:

It helps the sport organization build sustainable competitive advantage—agree/not sure/disagree.

It brings in greater financial return than keeping them in house—agree/not sure /disagree.

It helps the sport organization enhance the quality of its marketing operations—agree/not sure/disagree.

It allows the sport organization to handle all aspects of your marketing operations in a more timely fashion—agree/not sure/disagree.

An alternative layout is:

Do you agree, disagree or have no opinion that the benefits of outsourcing for a sport organization include

It helps the sport organization build sustainable competitive advantage.

Agree	Not Sure	Disagree
3	2	1

It brings in greater financial return than keeping them in house.

Agree	Not Sure	Disagree
3	2	1

It helps the sport organization enhance the quality of its marketing operations.

Agree	Not Sure	Disagree
3	2	1

It allows the sport organization to handle all aspects of its marketing operations in a more timely fashion.

Agree	Not Sure	Disagree
3	2	1

The second example shows the answer choices in neat columns and has more space between the lines. It is easier to read. The numbers in the second example will also speed data entry, if a paper questionnaire is used.

Tips for Designing Web-Based Questionnaires

Because of the advantages of online surveys in the areas of research costs, access to subjects, the scope of the research, and the nature of behavior under study, they are becoming an increasingly popular choice of researchers in collecting data with a questionnaire, over paper-pencil surveys (Andrews, Nonnecke, & Preece, 2003). Although the principles used in designing paper-pencil surveys can be applicable to the construction of online questionnaires, it is important to remember that the latter requires some special attention because of the distinctive differences that exist between email and online surveys. Figure 14-2 is an example of an online questionnaire used in sport management.

Web Questionnaire Design. There are several important rules for researchers to keep in mind while drafting online questionnaires (Andrews, Nonnecke & Preece, 2003; Bhaskaran, 2007; Lumsden, 2005, pp. 6–7).

1. The first rule is precision and concision. The respondent may lose interest in completing the questionnaire if the questions are complicated and long. This rule implies that the questionnaire should not be so long as to displease the respondent. It is suggested that the total number of questions included in an online questionnaire should be less than 60 (Lumsden, 2005).

2. The question and answering process should be attractive—that is, uncluttered and easy to complete.

3. A question should never be divorced from its response set—that is, a question and all elements of its response should appear on the same page or screen.

4. Questions relating to a given topic should be presented together and clearly sectioned from questions related to other topics. Section headings and sub-headings that are meaningful and well designed should be used to clearly differentiate sections.

5. Avoid using too many sections in any one questionnaire because this is likely to become confusing to respondents; it also reflects poor questionnaire design and lack of focus.

6. Unless for very specific reasons, respondents should be able to interrupt and re-enter responses and move backward and forward throughout the entire questionnaire.

7. To avoid excessive scrolling, list only a few questions per page and provide clear and easy links to the preceding and succeeding pages of a questionnaire. On the other hand, simply having one question per page is not a good idea either as it will increase the time to complete the survey, which may increase the possibility for the respondent to quit the survey.

8. Avoid excessive numbers of pages with complex navigational aids. As a general rule, the decision to scroll or to segment a questionnaire into a series of pages should be determined on the basis of the content and size of a questionnaire.

9. Frames should not be used for online-questionnaires as they increase loading time.

Formatting is also an important aspect of online questionnaire design. Text, color, graphics, and tables are several aspects of formatting that deserve attention from sport management researchers. Table 14-1 shows the basic guidelines for online questionnaire design, as suggested by Lumsden (2005, pp. 9–11).

Online Survey Software. A number of companies are specialized in providing online survey services, such as SurveyMonkey.com, QuestionPro, Zoomerang, and Survey Gold. The services include online survey creation and programming, data analysis, product training, and so on.

1. XYZ Widcat Club Young Alumni Program

The Athletic Department Office at XYZ University is in the process of creating a young alumni program for the students of XYZ University. The program's goal is to keep the recent alumni connected to the Athletic Department at XYZ University through the Wildcat Club. All information gathered in this survey will be kept anonymous and used in the development of the young alumni program.

1. After graduation, do you plan on moving away from the XYZ area?
   - ○ Yes
   - ○ No

2. Following graduation, do you plan on returning to campus for any of the following next year? (Please check all that apply)
   - ○ Homecoming (football)
   - ○ Football game (non-homecoming)
   - ○ Men's basketball game
   - ○ Any other athletic event
   - ○ Halloween
   - ○ Graduation

3. Do you plan on checking your XYZ University email account upon graduation?
   - ○ Yes
   - ○ No

4. What is your preferred method of contact?
   - ○ Mail
   - ○ Phone
   - ○ Text message
   - ○ Email

5. Do you know what the XYZ Wildcat Club is?
   - ○ Yes
   - ○ No

6. Do you plan on joining the XYZ Wildcat Club upon graduation?
   - ○ Yes
   - ○ No

7. Are you willing to join the XYZ Wildcat Club for $25 to achieve the $100 membership level?
   - ○ Yes
   - ○ No

8. Please rate the following benefits in order of importance for membership (most important on left side and declining in importance to the right)

	Most important								Least Important
Opportunity to purchase away game tickets	○	○	○	○	○	○	○	○	○
Lapel pin	○	○	○	○	○	○	○	○	○
Access to website content	○	○	○	○	○	○	○	○	○
Priority for football season tickets	○	○	○	○	○	○	○	○	○
Priority for tickets for Championships/Bowl Games	○	○	○	○	○	○	○	○	○
Wildcat newsletter	○	○	○	○	○	○	○	○	○
Homecoming (football) ticket	○	○	○	○	○	○	○	○	○
Wildcat priority points	○	○	○	○	○	○	○	○	○
Priority for men's basketball season tickets	○	○	○	○	○	○	○	○	○

9. Please list any other benefits that would be of importance to you

_____

_____

FIGURE 14-2. Example of an Online Questionnaire in Sport Management

TABLE 14-1
Guidelines for Text, Color, Graphics, and Tables

Text

1. Sentences should not exceed 20 words and should be presented with no more than 75 characters per line. If elderly respondents are anticipated, then this limit should be reduced to between 50 and 65 characters per line. Paragraphs should not exceed five sentences in length.
2. Technical instructions (instructions related to the basic technical operation of the website delivering the questionnaire) should be written in such a way that non-technical people can understand them.
3. Questions should be easily distinguishable, in terms of formatting, from instructions and answers.
4. Each question type should be consistent in terms of the visual appearance of all instances of that type and the associated instructions concerning how they are to be answered; in particular, the relative position of the question and answer should be kept consistent throughout the questionnaire. Where different types of questions are to be included in the same questionnaire, each question type should have a unique visual appearance.

Color

1. Use consistent color coding throughout the questionnaire to reinforce meaning or information in an unambiguous fashion.
2. Use a neutral background color that excludes patterns that can make text very hard to read.
3. When pairing colors or using two colors in close proximity, endeavor to use colors of high contrast to ensure maximum discernability across the target audience. This is particularly important for questionnaires targeted at audiences over 35 years of age.

Graphics

1. Avoid cluttering the questionnaire with graphics.
2. When using graphics, try to use small graphics that will download quickly. Individual images should not exceed 5KB in size and no single web-page should exceed 20KB of graphics in total.
3. Wherever a graphic is used, it is essential to provide a text-only version of the web page.
4. Minimize the number of colors that are used in any single graphic, and do not use graphics that mimic (or resemble) other items on a typical website.
5. Do not blur pictures, gray out information, or overlap menus; use crisp, clear images to maximize accessibility for users with visual disabilities.
6. Do not associate multimedia and audio clips with graphics if plug-ins would typically have to be downloaded by the respondents in order to access the associated media. Make it easy for users to skip, without penalty, multimedia content.

SUMMARY

Questionnaire design is an important process that demands careful attention. A questionnaire is a powerful evaluation tool and should not be taken lightly. Design begins with an understanding of the capabilities of a questionnaire and how they can help the research. If it is determined that a questionnaire is to be used, the greatest care should go into the planning of the objectives. Questionnaires are like any scientific experiment. Researchers do not collect data and then see if they found something interesting.

Questionnaires are versatile, allowing the collection of both subjective and objective data through the use of open- or closed-format questions. Modern computers have only made the task of collecting and extracting valuable material more efficient. However, a questionnaire is only as good as the questions it contains. There are many guidelines that must be met before a questionnaire can be considered a sound research tool. The majority deal with making the questionnaire understandable and free of bias. Mindful review and testing are necessary to weed out minor mistakes that can cause confusion in meaning and interpretation. When these guidelines are followed, the questionnaire becomes a powerful and economic evaluation tool.

Online survey has gradually replaced paper-pencil survey because of its quick distribution and lower cost. Although the general principles in questionnaire design can be applied to both the paper-pencil survey and the online survey, the latter has some special characteristics.

1. Elaborate on the process in developing a questionnaire.
2. What is a draft plan in questionnaire development?
3. Compare and contrast the open-ended questions and closed format questions in terms of their advantages and disadvantages.
4. What are the criteria of a good question?
5. What should sport management researchers consider when determining the order of questions and answer choices?
6. Explain how to deal with the "Don't Know" or "Not Applicable" answer choice.
7. What are the criteria that sport management researchers use to determine the usability of a questionnaire during the pretesting phase of questionnaire development?
8. Explain the methods that can be used to increase response rate.

LEARNING ACTIVITIES

1. The following are questions taken from several survey instruments. Based on the criteria of asking good questions, provide your critique of each of the questions. Be sure to indicate the problem first and then revise it. If you believe that a question is well stated, just write "OK" next to the question.

   a. Questions developed by the XYZ sport marketing firm for the solicitation of public opinions about the quality of services provided at a sports facility:

   (1) The services staff is courteous and knowledgeable about the facility.

Strongly Agree	Agree	Neutral	Disagree	Strongly Disagree
❏	❏	❏	❏	❏

   (2) The food served by ARMARK, a company whose products are highly recognized by the sport industry as excellent food provider, is incredible.

Strongly Agree	Agree	Neutral	Disagree	Strongly Disagree
❏	❏	❏	❏	❏

   b. How many football home games you have attended in the last five years?

   ❏ 1–5   ❏ 5–10   ❏ 1–15   ❏ 6–20   ❏ 21–25   ❏ Every Game

   c. What or who makes you believe that our football home games suffer from a lack of excitement?

   ❏ The media   ❏ My peers   ❏ My own observations   ❏ Other source (specify)

   d. In a study conducted to examine consumers' preference of athletic shoes, one of the questions asked is "Do you have a pair of Nike shoes?"

   e. Should the team trade John Smith, who is too old and overpaid, for a younger player?

   Yes ( )   No ( )

2. The following is a questionnaire drafted by the staff in the athletic department of XYZ University. It is intended to determine local residents' levels of awareness

of XYZ University athletics in general. You are asked to evaluate the survey instrument and accordingly provide feedback to them on how to revise it. Show your critique.

XYZ University Athletics Awareness Survey

Level of Athletic Involvement

1. Approximately how often have you attended the following XYZ University athletic events over the past 12 months? Please circle one for each sport.
    1 = Almost all games/matches
    2 = More than half of the games/matches
    3 = More than two but less than one-half of the games/matches
    4 = Once in a great while
    5 = Have not attended
    The number in parentheses indicates the number of home games in that sport.

Football (6)	1	2	3	4	5
Men's Basketball (13)	1	2	3	4	5
Women's Basketball (12)	1	2	3	4	5
Baseball (30)	1	2	3	4	5
Women's Softball (18)	1	2	3	4	5
Men's Golf (3)	1	2	3	4	5
Women's Volleyball (12)	1	2	3	4	5
Men's Tennis (5)	1	2	3	4	5
Women's Tennis (5)	1	2	3	4	5
Men's Cross Country (2)	1	2	3	4	5
Women's Cross Country (2)	1	2	3	4	5
Men's Soccer (12)	1	2	3	4	5
Women's Soccer (12)	1	2	3	4	5
Men's Swimming (4)	1	2	3	4	5
Women's Swimming (4)	1	2	3	4	5
Other_____	1	2	3	4	5

Please check *one* for each question.

2. How long have you attended XYZ University athletic events?
    ___ Less than a year ___ 1–2 years ___ 2–3 years ___ 3–5 years ___ More than 5 years

3. Will you spend any nights away from home attending an XYZ University athletic event?
    ___ Yes ___ No   If yes, how many? ___ 1 night ___ 2 nights ___ 3 or more nights

4. Why do you attend XYZ University athletic events?
    ___ Interest in that particular sport
    ___ Social/family activity
    ___ Business
    ___ Support the school
    ___ Other (please specify) _____

5. When was the last time you attended an XYZ University athletic event?
    ___Week or less ___ 1–4 weeks ___ 1–6 months ___ 6 months–year ___ Over a year

6. How often do you plan your schedule around XYZ University athletic events?
    ___All the time ___ Often ___ Sometimes ___ Rarely ___ Never

7. How far are you willing to travel to attend an XYZ University athletic event?
___ 50–99 miles ___ 100–250 miles ___ 251–500 miles ___ 500 + miles; ___ Would not travel

Info-bits

8. Can you name the new Athletic Director at XYZ University?
___ Yes ___ No   If yes, who? _____

9. Can you name two head coaches at XYZ University, besides Joe Jones?
___ Yes ___ No   If yes, who? _____
1._____   2._____

10. Can you name the Marketing/Promotions Director at XYZ University?
___ Yes ___ No   If yes, who? _____

11. Can you name the new Sports Information Director at XYZ University?
___ Yes ___ No   If yes, who? _____

12. Do you know the schedule for XYZ University athletic events?
___ Yes ___ No
If yes, from what media?
___ Newspaper ___ Radio ___ TV ___ Mail ___ Word of mouth ___ Pocket schedules

13. Does XYZ University have a coach's show on television for football? ___ Yes ___ No
for basketball? ___ Yes ___ No

14. How often do you listen to XYZ University athletic events on the radio?
___ All the time ___ Often ___ Sometimes ___ Rarely ___ Never

15. How many Great Sky Conference Championships did XYZ University win in 2002–2003?
Please circle **one**.
0   1   2   3   4 or more

16. Can you identify an XYZ University athletic marketing promotion or advertising program
to which you have been exposed in the past year?
___ Yes ___ No   If yes, what? _____

Level of Athletic Support

17. When did you last purchase XYZ University merchandise? (hats, shirts, etc.)
___ Less than a month ago ___ 1–6 months ___ 6–12 months ___ Over 12 months ___ Never

18. If Yes to #17, how much did you spend in the last year?
___ $1–$20 ___ $21–$50 ___ $51–$75 ___ $76–$100 ___ $100 +

19. If Yes to #17, where did you make your purchase?
___ University store
___ Discount Store (Wal-Mart, K-Mart, etc.)
___ At the event
___ Sports store (Athletic Attic, etc.)
___ Other (specify) _____

20. Do you donate money to XYZ University? ___ Yes ___ No
If yes, in what area?
___ General funds
___ Endowments
___ Athletics
If Yes to #20, please answer #21 and #22, if No to #20, please move on to #23.

21. How often do you donate money to XYZ University?
    ___ Once a month
    ___ Once every 3–6 months
    ___ Once every 6–12 months
    ___ Once a year
    ___ Once every 1–5 years

22. Approximately how much money have you donated in the last year?
    ___ $1–$100 ___ $101–$500 ___ $501–$1000 ___ $1,001–$5,000 ___ $5,000+ ___ Zero last year

23. Have you volunteered in any capacity in the last 12 months for XYZ University athletics?
    ___ Yes ___ No   If yes, how much time?
    ___ 1 hour ___ 1–4 hours ___ 4–8 hours ___ More than a day ___ Other _____

24. What is the likelihood that you can donate any items such as labor, equipment (maintenance, landscape), materials (uniforms, athletic equipment), or other resources?
    ___ Very likely ___ Somewhat likely ___ Likely (50-50) ___ Somewhat unlikely ___ Very unlikely

Level of Satisfaction

25. Please rate the following XYZ University attributes on a 5-point scale, with 1 representing *totally unsatisfactory* and 5 representing *totally satisfactory*. Please circle one for each attribute.

All athletics win-loss record	1	2	3	4	5
Schedule strength (all sports)	1	2	3	4	5
Women's athletics	1	2	3	4	5
Ticket prices	1	2	3	4	5
Ticket availability	1	2	3	4	5
Availability of "good seats"	1	2	3	4	5
Concession prices	1	2	3	4	5
Concession quality	1	2	3	4	5
Parking situation/facilities (all sports)	1	2	3	4	5
Overall service	1	2	3	4	5
Academic reputation	1	2	3	4	5
Community relations	1	2	3	4	5
Pregame publicity (advertising)	1	2	3	4	5
Promotions/Activities at games	1	2	3	4	5
Game times/days	1	2	3	4	5
Corporate sponsorships	1	2	3	4	5
Location of venues	1	2	3	4	5

26. If you could change one thing about XYZ University athletics, what would it be? Explain.

    _____
    _____
    _____
    _____

27. ___ Male ___ Female

28. Age? ___

29. Level of education: ___ High school ___ Some college experience ___ College graduate
    ___ Master's/Ph.D., etc.

Thank you for your help and participation!

References

Andrews, D., Nonnecke, B., & Preece, J. (2003). Electronic survey methodology: A case study in reaching hard to involve Internet users. *International Journal of Human-Computer Interaction, 16*(2), 185–210.

Bhaskaran, V. (n.d.). Preparing an online questionnaire—How to conduct an online survey. Retrieved May 3, 2007, from http://www.questionpro.com/akira/showArticle.do?articleID=build01

Bradburn, N., Sudman, S., & Wansink, B. (2004). *Asking questions: The definitive guide to questionnaire design—for market research, political polls, and social and health questionnaires.* San Francisco, CA: Jossey-Bass.

Fraenkel, J. R., & Wallen, N. E. (2000). *How to design and evaluate research in education* (4th ed.). Boston, MA: McGraw Hill.

Ghauri, P. N., Gronhaug, K., & Kristianslund, I. (1995). *Research methods in business studies: A practical guide.* New York: Prentice Hall.

Huisman, M., & van der Zouwen, J. (1998). *Item nonresponse in scale data from surveys: Types, determinants, and measures.* Technical report, University of Groningen.

Johnson, B., & Christensen, L. (2000). *Educational research: Quantitative and qualitative approaches.* Boston, MA: Allyn and Bacon.

Lumsden, J. (2005). *Guidelines for the design of online-questionnaires.* Fredericton, NB: National Research Council of Canada.

McDaniel, C., & Gates, R. (1991). *Contemporary marketing research.* St. Paul, MN: West Publishing Company.

Patten, M. L. (2001). *Questionnaire research: A practical guide* (2nd ed.). Los Angeles, CA: Pyrczak Publishing.

Robson, C. (2002). *Real world research: A resource for social scientists and practitioners-researchers* (2nd ed.). Oxford, UK: Blackwell Publisher.

Schwab, D. P. (1999). *Research methods for organizational studies.* Mahwah, NJ: Lawrence Erlbaum Associates, Publishers.

StatPac Inc. (2007). *Length of a questionnaire.* Retrieved January 20, 2008 from http://www.statpac.com/surveys/length.htm.

Swanson, R. A., & Holton, E. F., III. (2005). *Research in organizations.* San Francisco, CA: Berrett-Koehler Publishers, Inc.

Yates, S. J. (2004). *Doing social science research.* London, UK: Sage Publications.

Zikmund, W. G. (2000). *Business research methods* (6th ed.). Fort Worth, TX: Harcourt College Publishers.

CHAPTER 15
SAMPLING METHODS AND PROCEDURES IN SPORT MANAGEMENT RESEARCH

OBJECTIVES FOR COMPLETING THIS
CHAPTER ARE THAT STUDENTS WILL
BE ABLE TO:

Define population, sample, and sampling

Explain the differences between two terms used
in sampling, such as population versus sample,
a target population versus accessible population,
random sampling versus non-random sampling

Differentiate nonprobability and probability
sampling procedures

Compare the advantages and disadvantages of
specific nonprobability and probability
sampling procedures

Compare and contrast the four basic methods
of probability sampling

Explain how to use a table of random numbers
to select a sample

Identify the sampling procedure used in a sport
management study

Discuss the factors that influence the
determination of sample size

SPORT MANAGEMENT researchers often collect data from a representative sample of the population in which they are interested. There are numerous sampling procedures that are available for them to choose. In this chapter, these sampling procedures will be reviewed, and examples in sport management will also be provided to illustrate how each of the procedures is used in the selection of a proper sample. Prior to the review, basic terms relevant to the topic of sampling procedures will be discussed. In the last section of this chapter, the method that can be used to determine sample size in sport management research will be discussed briefly.

NATURE OF POPULATION AND SAMPLES

Prior to a discussion about the processes of sampling methods and techniques, one must have an understanding of relevant terms and each of their meanings for such processes. These terms are essential for a better understanding of sampling methods and sampling techniques. The terms are: population, target population, accessible population, sample, census, universe, sampling frame, data, sample data, census, parameter, statistic, sampling error, statistical relationship, representative, and generalizability (Johnson & Christensen 2004; Levine, Berenson, & Stephan, 1998; Triola & Franklin 1994).

A population (also called the universe or census) refers to the entire group of units, elements, or individuals to be studied. The makeup of the data may consist of the observations of events, places, individuals, or groups. For example, Reese and Mittelstaedt (2001) used the population of ticket operators to investigate ticket pricing strategies in the National Football League. "Subjects consisted of the entire population of individuals responsible for ticket operations in the NFL (n = 31). This population was selected due to the expertise of each subject in the areas of establishing ticket prices and identifying variables that affect the decision-making process" (p. 225). Academically, a census refers to an investigation of all the units, elements, or individuals of a population.

In general, there are two types of populations: a target population and an accessible population. The target population refers to the population that the investigators want to generalize the major finding of the investigation. For example, a target population is all of the NCAA Division I head women volleyball coaches in the U.S. from both private and public universities. An accessible population would be the sector of the target population that is available to the researcher during the time of the investigation.

Unlike a population, a sample refers to a subset of units, elements, or individuals selected that represents a population of interest. There are several advantages of using a sample, such as low cost, less time, being more accurate by making less errors, feasibility of having the core of the population of interest, and the possibility of gathering more extensive of information (Levine, Rampsey, & Berenson, 1995). Sampling is a complex but critical process. So, it is important for the investigator to ensure that the sample is representative of the population under study.

The list of all units, elements, or subjects in a population is referred to as a sampling frame. For example, if Florida State University (FSU) students were defined as the population, the sampling frame would be the university registrar's student records that show all the students at FSU.

An example of a sampling frame was used by Kwon and Trail (2001) when they compared the differences between American and international student's motivation for attending intercollegiate sports events. The sample was collected from a Midwestern university in the U.S. The Office of the Registrar of that university provided the list of all the students. The sample was then drawn from the list or the sampling frame. The survey was sent to 600 students, divided into two strata, including 300 American students and 300 international students. The sample for each stratum was created using systematic random sampling. If the Office of the Registrar had omitted a student's name from the list, the list would not be representative of all students of the university as a sampling frame. Tables 15-1 and 15-2 show comparisons of the advantages of using a sample versus a census.

TABLE 15-1
Census Survey

Advantages

Eliminates the risks of uncertainty of sample representativeness.

Promotes a better quality study.

Allows for better control of statistical procedures for determining a meaningful sample size.

Disadvantages

Data collection and analysis will be more time consuming.

Data collection and analysis will be more expensive.

Larger data sets present the opportunity for less control of errors.

More than likely, it is just not feasible to survey the entire population.

TABLE 15-2
Sample Survey

Advantages

Data collection and analysis will be less time consuming.

Data collection and analysis will be less expensive.

Modern sampling techniques of small data sets can provide results to a great degree of precision.

It is feasible to survey the core of the population of interest.

Disadvantages

Involves risk of uncertainty of sample representativeness.

The study may not be of high quality.

Statistical procedure for determining a meaningful sample size is complex.

Basic Approaches to Sampling

There are two basic approaches to sampling: nonprobability sampling and probability sampling. Both approaches strive to be representative of the population and/or the phenomenon under study but employ entirely different methods to do so. Both have their strengths and weaknesses.

Nonprobability Sampling

Unlike probability sampling, nonprobability sampling is based on judgment of the researcher. As such, the selection process is subjective. The primary advantages of nonprobability sampling are that they require less time and are less expensive, more economical, and more administratively feasible. For example, Boyd and Krehbiel (1999) conducted a study to analyze the effect of promotion timing on Major League Baseball attendance. Data were selected from a nonprobability-based sample for only six of the teams (Chicago Cubs, New York Mets, Cincinnati Reds, Detroit Tigers, Kansas City Royals, and the Boston Red Sox). These were the teams willing to provide the needed data, had outdoor stadiums, and were located in climates that were subjected to cool springs, fall weather, and hot muggy summers. Therefore, the research was not applicable to teams that played in domed stadiums (e.g., Minnesota Twins or Seattle Mariners) or in warm climates (e.g., Florida Marlins or Los Angeles Dodgers, Anaheim Angels, or Arizona Diamondbacks). The sample was administratively feasible for the researcher; however, it was not stratified and "coincidentally northeastern and Midwestern teams were overrepresented" (p. 26).

The major disadvantage of this non-probability sampling approach is that there is no way to analyze the probability of a unit of information, element, or individual being selected for an investigation. This approach is not considered as sophisticated as probability sampling (Cozby, 2001).

There are several types of nonprobability sampling: (a) purposive or judgmental sampling, (b) convenience sampling, and (c) quota sampling (DePoy & Gitlin 1994; Levine, Berenson, & Stephan, 1998; Levine, Rampsey, & Berenson, 1995; McMillan & Schumacher, 2001; Neuman 2003; Shiffler & Adams, 1990; Triola & Franklin, 1994). In the following section, each of them will be discussed within the context of sport management research.

Probability Sampling

In probability sampling, every person, unit, or element of the population has an equal chance to be selected for an investigation. The major advantages of this approach to sampling are is that it allows for more accurate representation and generalization of the population being studied. It is free of sampling bias because no population members are favored, and each unit, element, or individual has an equal chance of being selected for a study. It is not subjected to the conscious bias of the researcher. Also, the probability of choosing a representative sample increases as the size of the sample increases.

The major disadvantage is that it may be time consuming. Cost also may be a factor. To execute the probability sampling procedure, the researcher must specifically define the population, list all units or elements of the population, and then randomly select samples of units from the population. For example, Branch and Crow (2002) investigated *Sport Marketing Quarterly* (*SMQ*) readership profiles (current and potential) and usage by related academic and sport industry persons/communities, and rated the usage and value of each SMQ topical section. Subjects for this study were derived from two groups: academics (sport marketing professors) and sport marketing practitioners. For academics, the researchers randomly selected 50 individuals who listed marketing as their main teaching and research interest from the professional membership roster of the North American Society for Sport Management (NASSM). For the sport marketing practitioner group, the researchers randomly selected 50 sport marketing practitioners, representing four distinct sport industry segments, from the Sports Business Directory Online (http://directory.sportsummit.com). Segments represented included sport marketing firms, major professional sport organizations, minor professional organizations, and university/college athletic programs.

Convenience Sampling

In a convenience sampling, the most accessible units (individuals, places, groups, objects, or organizations) are used in the research investigation. It is the most common method of nonprobability samples. The major advantages of a convenience sample are the ease of conducting the investigation and the savings in both time and money. For example, Park (2001) used a convenience sample to explore the involvement profiles in selected recreational activities in Korea. Boyd and Shank (2004) used convenience sampling to explore how the gender of the athlete endorsers and type of product that they are endorsing (sport- related versus non-sport related) is related to respondents' perceptions of source expertise, trustworthiness, and attractiveness.

Swanson, Gwinner, Larson, and Janda (2003) used convenience sampling procedures to explore four individual psychological motivations of college student game attendance and word-of-mouth behavior for attending sporting events. A table was set up in a high-traffic area of the university student center during dining hours for four consecutive days. Individuals walking by the data collection table were invited to participate in the survey and were offered either a button or pen that promoted the university's football team. A total of 537 usable surveys were collected.

Quota Sampling

Quota sampling refers to a nonprobability sampling procedure in which the population as a whole is split into a number of groups or strata. It requires the researcher to take steps to ensure that certain kinds of subjects are obtained in designated proportions for the study. It is analogous to stratified random sampling (to be discussed later in this chapter) in that the population is divided into subgroups or strata. It differs from stratified random sampling because it obtains subjects through convenience samples, whereas stratified sampling obtains its subjects through a random sample method. The researcher must specify in advance that the sample will include certain percentages or particular kind of subjects.

There are several steps in formulating quota. The researcher first determines which strata are to be studied. A stratum can be an attribute variable or an independent variable of the study. Common variables are age, gender, race, and geographic location. The researcher then computes a quota (or number of participants) needed for each stratum. The quota is computed proportionally or disproportionally to the population under study. After a quota for each stratum has been determined, the subjects are solicited via a convenience sampling method. Like convenience samples, quota samples are relative easy to administer and are not expensive.

Matsuoka, Chelladurai, and Harada (2003) assessed the direct and interaction effects of team identification on spectators' intent to attend future games. In order to obtain a sample representing all spectators, a quota sampling method was used in each game. Each data collector selected subjects from each seating block of the stadium according to the approximate proportions of age and sex of spectators in that block. Before the game, the selected individuals were administered the first questionnaire containing items on demographic characteristics (age, gender, occupation, and city/town of residence), team identification ,and intent to attend future games This procedure yielded a sample of 2,845 respondents (p. 247).

Purposive or Judgmental Sampling

When using the purposive sampling procedure, a researcher "hand-picks" the units or subjects. Purposive sampling is well suited for exploratory studies. Thus it is used for both qualitative and quantitative research. In purposive sampling, the investigators use their judgment and prior knowledge to choose the group of subjects who best serve the purpose of a study. For example, an investigator is interested in finding out how male intercollegiate athletic directors of NCAA Division I member institutions differ from their female counterparts in terms of their intent to remain in their jobs. The primary advantage of purposive sampling is that the researcher is allowed to choose the sample based on knowledge of the purpose of the study. The disadvantage is the potential of sampling bias, use of a sample that does may not represent the population, and the very limited generalizability of the results that can be made.

A number of sport management studies that have employed this type of sampling technique are found in the literature (Danylchuk & Chelladurai, 1999; Kropp, Lavack, Holden, & Dalakas, 1999). Let's use Kwon and Armstrong's study (2002), designed to examine factors influencing impulse buying of team-licensed merchandise by a sample of college students, as an example to see how sport management researchers use this technique. They used purposive sampling by selecting subjects from related disciplines in sport/physical education and textile classes. "One hundred forty-five students (48 male and the rest female) at a large mid-western university participated in the study. Among the 145 students, 82.8% were white, and 10 subjects were African-American. The average number of years the participants had been enrolled in the university was 2.39, with approximately 41% of the subjects having been enrolled for more than 2 years" (p. 155).

PROBABILITY SAMPLING PROCEDURES

There are four distinct types of probability sampling procedures that are commonly used in social science-based research: (a) simple random sampling, (b) stratified random sampling, (c) systematic random sampling, and (d) cluster random sampling (drawing from the works of contemporary scholars of standardized research methods and statistics such as DePoy & Gitlin, 1994; Levine, Berenson, & Stephan, 1998; Levine, Rampsey, & Berenson, 1995; McMillan & Schumacher, 2001; Neuman 2003; Shiffler & Adams, 1990; Triola & Franklin, 1994). Each

of the procedures has been selected for discussion within the context of sport management research.

Simple Random Sampling

Simple random sampling is a probability sampling technique in which every subject, element, or unit of a population has an equal chance to be selected for an investigation. The major advantages of this procedure are that little knowledge of the study population is needed, it is easy to analyze, and it is less biased than the three other probability procedures. The major disadvantages are that it is time consuming and expensive. Also, it can be insufficient for obtaining a representative random sample (Aczel, 1995; Hamburg, 1985; Shao, 2002). Let us look at an example to illustrate the use of this type of probability sampling procedure in sport management research. Danylchuk (2000) used simple random sampling to survey spectator perceptions of tobacco sponsorship at an LPGA event.

There are three means to randomly select the subjects, elements, or units when using this procedure: (a) by placing the numbers or ID of each participant in a container and drawing the numbers out one at a time; (b) using a table of random numbers; and (c) using a computer-generated selection of random numbers. Of the three ways, the table of random numbers has been most frequently used. A table can be found in most standard research methods and statistics textbooks or can be generated by computer programs as illustrated in Table 15-3. When using this method, the researcher starts out by

TABLE 15-3									
A Fictitious Table of Numbers for Random Sampling									
38	17	42	63	41	33	34	63	7	23
49	18	46	44	62	70	67	20	48	61
14	48	59	28	51	71	10	30	8	27
46	71	66	18	57	29	53	61	81	60
53	25	40	19	11	56	18	41	29	29
68	66	37	76	46	77	50	45	13	75
69	28	15	86	55	81	19	29	74	21
78	80	79	33	39	88	72	69	35	92
64	81	72	17	9	55	42	49	87	16
24	39	41	28	48	86	52	6	35	21

pointing to a number on the table without looking. This number is the first selected element. The researcher will continue pointing to numbers on the table in a variety of directions until the desired sample size is accomplished.

Stratified Random Sampling

Stratified random sampling is the probability sampling procedure in which the population is first divided into subpopulations identified as strata, followed by randomly selecting a sample from each stratum. The primary goal of stratified random sampling is to guarantee that all groups in the population are adequately represented in proportion to the size of each stratum. The major advantage of stratified random sampling is that it ensures the representation of a particular segment of the population. This is obtained by dividing the population into groups based on such demographic variables as race, age, gender, educational level, marital status, type of work performed, and years of work experience and taking a random sample from each stratum. The major disadvantage of stratified random sampling is that it requires accurate knowledge of the population and the more advanced statistical data analyses techniques. It may be expensive, too. When using stratified random sampling, it is necessary for the researcher to make certain to avoid the problem of disproportionate representation of subgroups in a sample. There are several steps the researcher must perform when dividing the population into strata of interest.

To use this type of probability sampling procedure, the researcher must first clearly identify the strata of interest. A second step is to construct a sampling frame for each stratum. The third step involves the selection of a simple random sample or systematic sample from each of the sampling frame. The study conducted by Stoldt, Miller, and Comfort (2001) shows an example of a recent study in sport management study using a stratified random sample:

> A stratified, random sample of ADs at NCAA institutions was selected based on the institutions' levels of affiliation (Division I, II, or III). A list of NCAA members was obtained from the organization's website (NCAA, 2000). According to that list, of the 973 institutions that were active NCAA members, 32.6% competed in Division I, 26.9% competed in Division II, and 40.4% competed in Division III. The sample was stratified accordingly. ADs at one of every three institutions at each level were randomly selected for inclusion in the sample. Names and addresses were gathered from *The National Directory of College Sports* (1999). (p. 47)

Systematic Random Sampling

While applying the systematic random sampling, the sample is obtained by taking every nth unit, element, or subject on the list of all units in the population. Systematic random sampling can be classified as either a probability or nonprobability process of sampling. It is used when a lengthy list of the population exists.

The major advantage of systematic random sampling is that it is not only easy, but also economical to obtain a sample as it requires less time than simple or stratified random sampling techniques. There are two major disadvantages of this technique. First, the samples may be biased when the units, elements, or subjects in the population are not in order. Second, it does not allow for random sampling replacement. After the first sampling units, elements, or subjects are selected, population members no longer have an equal chance to be selected. Many sport management researchers utilize this technique in selecting a sample in their studies. Torco and Navarro (1993) assessed the economic impact and financial return on investment of a national sporting event. The researchers conducted interviews with a random sample of spectators on the tournament grounds during each of the event's nine days of operation. Every 11th spectator was selected to participate in the survey as that individual entered the tournament grounds. This procedure controlled the distribution of the survey to event spectators; avoided personal bias in sample selection and self-selection by attendee; and assured total numbers contacted. An official tournament program was offered as an incentive to sampled spectators to complete the questionnaire. A total of 448 completed spectator interviews were obtained during the nine days of the tournament and, based on the average visitor group's size, are representative of over 1,300 persons.

Random Cluster Sampling

When groups are selected from the population rather than individuals, the researcher uses the random cluster sampling technique. Random cluster sampling is analogous to quota sampling in that the population is divided into subgroups or strata. However, it differs from quota sampling because it obtains groups of subjects through a random sample method, whereas quota sampling obtains its subjects through a convenience sampling method. The primary purpose of random cluster sampling is to assist the researcher to gather data in the most meaningful way for large scale studies when the population is geographically spread out. Like stratified and systematic random sampling techniques, it is economical and time-saving. The major disadvantage is that it may allow for more sampling errors than the other probability sampling techniques.

Cluster sampling differs from stratified random sampling. In stratified random sampling, stratum is sampled. However, in cluster sampling, data are not collected from each cluster. Instead, only the final elements derived from among the clusters are tested.

Random cluster sampling is conducted by stages. Let us use an example to illustrate the use of the cluster sampling procedure. Assuming a researcher wants to conduct a study to solicit college football fans' opinions about the recently implemented "under review" measure. The researcher first randomly picks 10 out of 50 clusters or states. In the next stage, the researcher may treat each Division I-A institutions in those chosen states as clusters and selects half of them to participate in the survey. Zhang, Pease, Lam, Bellervive, Pham, Williamson, Lee, and Wall (2001) used this technique when they examined the relationship between five sociomotivational factors (stress and entertainment, achievement seeking, catharsis and aggression, salubrious effects, and community image) and attendance at minor league hockey games. "Subjects (N = 257)

were spectators from three 1994–1995 season home games of an international Hockey League team located in a major southern city. A random cluster sampling procedure was applied in selecting subjects to include spectators of various backgrounds and ticket types" (Zhang et al., 2001, p. 45).

DETERMINING THE SAMPLE SIZE

When using quantitative methods, a researcher is expected to determine how many subjects will be necessary to answer the research questions or hypothesis before a study in undertaken. The determination of sample size is a very important process as the researcher does not want to waste time and resources to collect a sample that is unnecessarily large. By the same token, the researcher also does not want to obtain a sample that is too small and will lead to inaccurate results. Nevertheless, the process to determine an appropriate sample size is complicated. This chapter will briefly review the process.

To determine how big a sample must be, the researcher should first determine the sample mean and the population mean. The sample mean is typically different from the population mean. The difference between them is viewed as an error. The margin of error (E) is the maximum difference between the observed sample mean and the true value of the population mean. The error is sought with the use of the following mathematical expression:

$$E = Z \frac{S}{\sqrt{n}}$$

Where

Z = the standardized value corresponding to a confidence level
S = the standard deviation of the population
n = the sample size

Rearranging this mathematical expression yields a new equation that shows how the sample size is necessary to produce results accurate to a specified confidence and margin of error. The new equation is as follows:

$$n = \left(\frac{ZS}{\sqrt{E}}\right)^2$$

Let us use an example in sport management to illustrate how to put this formula to use. Assuming the manager of Red Tigers Sports Authority, a specialized store for winter sport gear and equipment wants to use a 95% confidence level (the 95% confidence level is almost universally taken as the standard, which is equivalent to Z value of 1.96) and a range of error of less than $15 to estimate the average price of skis. The estimated standard deviation is $20. How many different types of skis should the manager survey?

$$n = \left(\frac{ZS}{\sqrt{E}}\right)^2 = \left(\frac{1.96 \times 20}{\sqrt{15}}\right)^2 = \left(\frac{39.2}{\sqrt{15}}\right)^2 = (26.1)^2 = 601$$

A close examination of this equation may yield a number of implications. First, the more precise (less error) the estimate must be, the bigger the sample size must be. Second, doubling sample size increases the degree of precision by one fourth (Zikmund, 2000).

Although the researchers can use the above-mentioned equation to determine the sample size for their studies, there are some practical issues that they need to consider. In general, the bigger the sample size is, the more accurate the results will be. However, researchers should be aware of the so-called "law of diminishing returns," which means additional units may become less and less meaningful. Of course, the time and cost factors should also be considered in the determination of how big the sample needs to be. The type of statistical procedures to be used in data analysis is another consideration. Multivariate statistics usually require a large sample. The researcher must keep in mind that to a certain extent, quality of the sample is more important than its size.

Appropriateness of Sampling Design: Practical Pointers

A number of factors may affect the determination of the appropriate sampling design for a particular study. These factors include the degree of accuracy, resources, time, degree of homogeneity, advance knowledge of the population, national versus local project, and need for statistical analysis (McDaniel & Gates, 1991; Zikmund, 2000). As mentioned previously, the accuracy of the research outcome correlates with the size of the sample and the sampling

method used in the study. However, the more sophisticatic the sampling design, the more resources required; the more sophisticatic the sampling design, the more time for the researcher to execute the sampling plan. There is always some trade off between sampling design, and accuracy, resources, and time, respectively.

If the population to be investigated is somewhat homogeneous, a small sample size and relative simple sampling design could suffice to yield accurate and reliable results. Also, whether or not the population elements are clearly defined and available to study are some of the issues that researchers should consider while choosing their sampling plan. Obviously, it will require a complex and multi-staged sampling design if a research project is to be conducted nationally. The last factor that may influence the selection of a sampling design is the needs of the researcher for statistical analysis. The sample taken with a non-probability sampling technique does not give the freedom for the researcher to make projection beyond the sample (Zikmund, 2000).

The Sampling Process

Before attempting to select a sample, the researcher must first develop a sampling plan that outlines the steps that should be taken in order to acquire a sample appropriate for the research design. Recommended by scholars (McDaniel & Gates, 1991; Zikmund, 2000), the following are the steps including in the sampling plans:

1. Define the population of interest
2. Choose data collection method
3. Choose sampling frame
4. Select a sampling method
5. Determine the sample size
6. Develop operational procedures to select the sample
7. Execute the sampling plan

Summary

This chapter reviews the key concepts of qualitative research in context of sport management research. An understanding of the terminology will facilitate the comprehension of various sampling procedures discussed in this chapter. Basic terminology includes population, target population, accessible population, sample, census, sampling frame, data, sample data, census, parameter, statistic, sampling error, statistical relationship, representative, and generalizability. Sampling can be categorized under two major groupings: nonprobability and probability. The primary advantages of nonprobability sampling are less time, less cost, more economical, and more administratively feasible. The three types of nonprobability sampling techniques that are commonly seen in sport management research are purposive sampling, convenient sampling, and quota sampling. Purposive sampling is utilized in both quantitative and qualitative studies. Convenience sampling is a nonprobability sampling procedure in which the most accessible units (individuals, places, groups, objects or organizations) are used in a research investigation. Quota sampling differs from stratified random sampling in that the participants are not randomly selected from each stratum.

The process of probability sampling requires that every person, unit or element of the population have an equal chance to be selected for the investigation. Simple random sampling, stratified random sampling, systematic random sampling, and cluster random sampling are four probability sampling procedures that sport management researchers can use in their selection of a sample. The process of simple random sampling allows for all elements or participants of a population to have an equal chance of being selected for a study. On the other hand, the primary goal of stratified random sampling is to guarantee that all groups in the population are adequately represented in proportion to the size of each stratum. The major advantages of systematic random sampling include: easy to obtain a sample, economical, and requires less time than simple or stratified random sampling techniques. The primary purpose of cluster random sampling is to assist the researcher in gathering data in the most meaningful way for large-scale studies when the population is geographically spread out.

Sample size could be determined based on three parameters: the margin of error, the estimated standard deviation, and the standardized value corresponding to a confidence level. There are a number of issues that can affect the determination of sample size. They are time, cost, and application of statistical procedures.

When determining the appropriate sampling design for a particular study, the researcher should consider these factors: degree of accuracy, resources, time, degree of homogeneity, advance knowledge of the population, national versus local project, and need for statistical analysis.

The researcher should follow these seven steps to execute the sampling plan: (a) define the population of interest, (b) choose data collection method, (c) choose sampling frame, (d) select a sampling method, (e) determine the sample size, (f) develop operational procedures to select the sample, and (g) execute the sampling plan.

STUDY QUESTIONS

1. What is a population? What is a sample? What is a sampling frame?
2. What are differences between these terms used in sampling?
   a. population versus sample
   b. target population versus accessible population
   c. random sampling versus non-random sampling
3. What are the differences between nonprobability and probability sampling procedures?
4. What are the advantages and disadvantages of specific nonprobability and probability sampling procedures?
5. What are the four basic methods of probability sampling?
6. How is a table of random numbers used to select a sample?
7. What are the factors that influence the determination of sample size?

LEARNING ACTIVITIES

1. Review an article that was published this year in one of the journals in sport management that has used the non-random sampling technique(s) in selecting the sample for the study. Comment on its sampling design.

2. Review an article that was published this year in one of the journals in sport management and provide your critique on the random sampling technique(s) used in the study in terms of its appropriateness.

3. Discuss the sampling designs employed in the following studies. Which sampling methods are used for the journals? How would you classify these?

    a. O'Rourke, S. M., & Chelladurai, P. (2006). Effectiveness of the national collegiate athletic association: Perceptions of intercollegiate athletic administrations. *Internal Journal of Sport Management, 7*(1), 82–101.

    b. Cunningham, G. B., & Sagas, M. (2005). Diversified dyads in the coaching profession. *Internal Journal of Sport Management, 6*(4), 305–323.

    c. Mahony, D. F., Riemer, H. A., Breeding, J. L., and Hums, M. A. (2006). Organizational justice in sport organizations: Perceptions of college athletes and other college students. *Journal of Sport Management, 20*(2), 159–188.

    d. Kahle, L., Duncan, M., Dalakas, V., and Aikon, D. (2001). The social values of fans for men's versus women's university basketball. *Sport Marketing Quarterly, 10*(2), 36–42.

4. Find a study that utilizes one of the following sampling techniques in a sport management related journal published in a 2007 or 2008 issue:

    a. Cluster random sampling
    b. Stratified random sampling

References

Aczel, A. (1995). *Statistics: Concepts and applications.* Chicago, IL: Irwin.

Boyd, T. C., & Krehbiel, T. C. (1999). The effect of promotion timing on Major League Baseball attendance. *Sport Marketing Quarterly, 8*(4), 23–34.

Boyd, T. C., & Shank, M. D (2004). Athletes as product endorsers: The effect of gender and product relatedness. *Sport Marketing Quarterly, 13*(2), 82–93.

Branch, C., & Crow, B. (2002). Ten years of *Sport Marketing Quarterly*: Comparing research and practice perspectives. *Sport Marketing Quarterly, 11*(2), 93–94.

Cozby, P. C. (2001). *Methods in behavioral research* (8th ed.). Boston, MA: McGraw Hill.

Danylchuk, K .E. (2000). Tobacco sponsorship: Spectator perceptions at an LPGA event. *Sport Marketing Quarterly, 9*(2), 103–111.

Danylchuk, K. E., & Chelladurai, P. (1999). The nature of managerial work in Canadian intercollegiate athletics. *Journal of Sport Management, 13*, 148–166.

DePoy, E., & Gitlin, L. N. (1994). *Introduction to research: Multiple strategies for health and human services.* St. Louis, MO: Mosby-Year Book, Inc., p. 195.

Hamburg, M. (1985). *Basic statistics: A modern approach.* New York: Harcourt, Brace Jovanovich.

Johnson, B., & Christensen, L. (2000). *Educational research: Quantitative and qualitative approaches.* Boston, MA: Allyn and Bacon.

Kropp, F., Lavack, A. M, Holden, S. J. S., & Dalakas, V. (1999). Attitudes toward beer and tobacco sports sponsorships. *Sport Marketing Quarterly, 8*(3), 49–58.

Kwon, H. H., & Armstrong, K. L. (2002). Factors influencing impulse buying of sport team licensed merchandise. *Sport Marketing Quarterly, 11*(3), 151–162.

Kwon, H., & Trail, G. (2001). Sport fan motivation: A comparison of American students and international students. *Sport Marketing Quarterly, 10*(2), 27–35.

Levine, D. M., Berenson, M. L., & Stephan, D. (1998). *Statistics for managers using Microsoft Excel.* Upper Saddle River, NJ: Prentice Hall Inc.

Levine, D. M., Ramsey, P. R., & Berenson, M. L. (1995). *Business statistics for quality and productivity.* Englewood Cliffs, NJ: Prentice Hall Inc.

Matsuoka, H., Chelladurai, P., & Harada, M. (2003). Direct and interaction effects of team identification and satisfaction on intention to attend games. *Sport Marketing Quarterly, 12*(4), 244–253.

McDaniel, C., & Gates, R. (1991). *Contemporary marketing research*. St. Paul, MN: West Publishing Company.

McMillian, J. H., & Schumacher, S. (2006). *Research in education* (6th ed.). Boston, MA: Pearson Education, Inc.

Neuman, W. L. (2003). *Social research methods: Qualitative and quantitative approaches* (5th ed.). Boston, MA: Allyn and Bacon.

Park, S. (2001). A further exploration of the involvement profiles in selected recreational sport activities: Results from a study in Korea. *Sport Marketing Quarterly*, *10*(2), 77–82.

Reese, J. T., & Mittelstaedt, R. D. (2001). An exploratory study of the criteria used to establish NFL tickets prices. *Sport Marketing Quarterly*, *10*(4), 223–230.

Shao, A. T. (2002). *Marketing research* (2nd ed.). Cincinnati, OH: South-Western, p. 371.

Stoldt, G. C., Miller, L. K., & Comfort, P. G. (2001). Through the eyes of athletics directors: Perceptions of sports information directors, and other public relations issues. *Sport Marketing Quarterly 10*(3), 44–52.

Swanson, S. R., Gwinner, K., Larson, B. V., & Janda, S. (2003). Motivation of college student game attendance and word-of-mouth behavior: The impact of gender differences. *Sport Marketing Quarterly 12*(3), 151–162.

Triola, M. F., & Franklin, L. A. (1994). *Business statistics*. Reading, MA: Addison-Wesley Publishing Co.

Zhang, J. J., Pease, D. G., Lam, E. T. C., Bellerive, L. M., Pham, U. L., Williamson, D. P., Lee, J. T., & Wall, K. A. (2001). Sociomotivational factors affecting spectator attendance at minor league hockey games. *Sport Marketing Quarterly*, *10*(1), 43–54.

Zikmund, W. G. (2000). *Business research methods* (6th ed.). Fort Worth, TX: Harcourt College Publishers.

CHAPTER 16
DATA EDITING, CODING, AND TRANSFORMING

OBJECTIVES FOR COMPLETING THIS CHAPTER ARE THAT STUDENTS WILL BE ABLE TO:

Define and explain editing and coding

Explain the tasks involved in editing

Explain the reasons or causes of missing data

Explain how to deal with the "I Don't Know" answer

Elaborate on the four principles that researchers should use in data coding

Use the content analysis technique to conduct a research project

THE PURPOSE OF THIS CHAPTER is to present information about how to prepare the data collected so as to facilitate the data analysis process. Specifically, this chapter will cover two major topics: data preparation and analysis and content analysis. In discussing the topic on data preparation and analysis, attention will be given to the review of the activities in which the researcher is engaged at different stages in the data preparation and analysis process. The primary aim of those activities, such validating, editing, coding, and data entry, is to ensure the accuracy of the data while transforming them from the raw data form to a new arrangement that can be analyzed easily.

The other topic to be covered in this chapter is content analysis. It is introduced in the hope that students will find a useful technique to create a new set of data while analyzing available documents or other materials.

AN OVERVIEW OF THE STAGES OF DATA PREPARATION AND ANALYSIS

Data preparation and analysis is the act of transforming data with the aim of extracting useful information and facilitating conclusions (McDaniel & Gates, 1991). Depending on the type of data and the question, this might include the application of statistical methods, curve fitting, selecting or discarding certain subsets based on specific criteria, or other techniques. In general, the data preparation and analysis process involved four stages: validating, editing, coding, and data entry and analysis.

Validating

Data validating has been seen as an integral step of data process. It is used to make sure that the data collection process, such as interviews (including those conducted by phone, by intercepting respondents at a sport facility, etc.), in fact took place. The main goal is to determine whether or not the survey instrument did in fact measure what it was intended to measure or whether or not "each of the questionnaires to be processed represents a valid interview"

(McDaniel & Gates, 1991, p. 482). The manner of how an interview is conducted affects the validity of an interview. For example, an unskilled interviewer may forget to provide proper instruction to the interviewees in terms of how to complete the survey instrument. Interviewer fraud or cheating, a common phenomenon in research involving interviews, also affects the validity of an interview. Unethical interviewers may complete the survey instruments themselves by filling in fabricated numbers and answers to the questionnaires.

To validate the data, it is recommended that 10% to 20% of participants interviewed be contacted again to provide information about (a) whether or not they were interviewed, (b) whether or not the interviewees were in fact qualified to be interviewed, (c) whether or not the interviewer followed a proper interview protocol to conduct the interview, (d) whether or not the interviewee was presented with all the questions included in the survey instrument, and (e) whether or not the interviewee believed the interviewer was courteous, and so on. (McDaniel & Gates, 1991).

Editing

"Editing is the process of ascertaining that questionnaires were filled out properly and completely" (McDaniel & Gates, 1991, p. 482). Editing involves two stages. The first stage is called "field editing" as it is often completed by the researcher who personally conducts the data collection with an interview or field survey. Its purpose is to examine the collected raw data in order to be sure that it is accurate, complete, and usable. When interviews are used in data collection, the main task of field editing is to check for incomplete sentences and to make sense of the abbreviations used by the interviewer.

Central editing follows the field editing process. Its aim is to complete the remaining editing tasks. Specifically, the researcher finishes the final editing of the questionnaire to ensure that there will be no ambiguity in each question before coding and data entry. Central editing often occurs in a central location.

Green and Tull (1978) stated that editing usually involves several tasks, including the verification of legibility of entries, completeness of entries, consistency of entries, and accuracy of entries. The following is a brief description of each of the tasks.

Legibility of entries. The first step of the field editing is to make sure the recorded data are clear and legible. This process is especially important in research that involves data recording by human beings, such as interviews and observations. It is very common that the recorded information was drafted in a hurry so that the handwriting is illegible, because the researcher tried to note quickly every piece of information during the interview or observation. In order for the data to be useful, they must be reviewed and clarified if there is any doubt about their clarity. The researcher who recorded the data should be the individual involved in the first order of editing for legibility.

Completeness of entries. It happens frequently that not all the questions are completed if a questionnaire is used in data collection in a mail or online survey or in a personal interview. The incompleteness could be attributed to a number of reasons, such as the unwillingness of the participant to provide the information, the unintentional omission of the respondent, or the failure of the interviewer to record the data.

Consistency of entries. Discrepancies may exist between the answers provided by the respondent to the questions included in a survey or an interview. For example, in a questionnaire designed to examine consumer purchasing behavior related to golf, the following question was included: *What is the amount of discretionary income (i.e., the amount of your income available for spending after the essentials, such as food, clothing, and home mortgage payment, have been taken care of)?* A respondent indicated that his discretionary income was "less than $500." However, while responding to another question, *"Please provide your estimate in terms of how much money you spend monthly on average on playing golf or purchasing golf-related products,"* the same respondent said he usually spent at least $600 a month on playing golf or purchas-

ing golf-related products. Such inconsistency should be detected during the editing phase.

Accuracy of entries. One of the major sources of inaccuracy is caused by the respondent's selection of more than one answer in a question with exclusive answer choices. The following is an example to illustrate this commonly committed error.

What is your marital status?
❑ Single
❑ Widow
❑ Separated
❑ Divorced
❑ Married
❑ Cohabited

When a situation like this occurs, the researcher should determine which answer choice is more logical and accurate to the respondent.

Scholars in research methods in social sciences have identified a number of reasons why data might be missing in survey instruments (Huisman & van der Zouwen, 1999; McDaniel & Gates, 1991). These reasons include:

Missing by logic. The missing data is caused by the inapplicability of the survey question to the respondent. For example, one of the questions in a questionnaire distributed at the entrance of a professional football stadium reads: "To what extent has the commercial influenced your decision to purchase a season ticket?" A respondent skipped the question as this individual was not a season ticket holder. Asking the participant to respond to all the questions included in a questionnaire regardless of their background is one of the most commonly committed errors by new or unskillful questionnaire designers. To avoid missing data caused by this reason, the researcher could us the routing or branching technique or with a response choice of "not a season ticket holder."

Missing by design. Often, the interviewer can decide not to ask the respondent a particular subset of questions because the interviewer feels that the characteristics of the subject do not match the intended purpose of those questions.

For instance, there is a particular section in the exit survey on Discover Hong Kong Year Campaign that is devoted to those tourists who have visited any of the new tourist attractions during their trips. If a respondent interviewed did not visit the new attractions, the interviewer will skip to another part of the survey instrument.

Item omission. There are many reasons causing item omission in interviews or in a mailed or online survey. A respondent may omit a certain section of the questionnaire unintentionally if that section was laid out in such a way that it could be skipped easily. Sometimes, the omission results from a missing page in the questionnaire. The illegibility of some questions in the survey instrument caused by poor printing quality could also irritate the respondent, who then decides not to respond to those questions. The inappropriate use of the branching technique can lead to item omission as well (discussion of the branching technique can be found in Chapter 14).

Refusal to respond. The willingness of the respondent to answer a survey question is influenced by several factors, including the topic of the question, the way the question was phrased and presented, and the presence of the interviewer. A respondent may refuse to respond to a question under the following circumstance: (a) the question asked is threatening or invasive of privacy; (b) the question is testing the respondent's knowledge of certain issues to which that individual would be embarrassed not to know the answer; (c) the question asked is cognitively too difficult for the respondent to answer; (d) the question asked is perceived to be either unclear or irrelevant; (e) the answer provided to the question could be socially undesirable and the presence of an interviewer leads to the decision of not answering the question.

The following is an example illustrating the type of question that could be considered too threatening. A survey conducted to determine alcohol consumption behavior in tailgate parties before college football games may include a question such as, "Do you frequently use alcoholic beverages such as liquor, wine, or beer during tailgating?" This type of question could be perceived as threatening if the respondent is either a faculty member or a university administrator.

Don't know. It happens all the time that a respondent decides to use the phrase "I don't know" during an interview. As Huisman and van der Zouwen (1999) stated, "[I don't know] is the abbreviation representing the group of nonsubstantive responses like 'No Idea,' 'No Opinion,' or 'I Don't Know'" (p. 6). Sometimes, it also means "It is hard to say" or "It depends." The researchers must decide how to treat them. Specifically, they need to decide whether or not the "I don't know" answer in fact means that the respondent truly did not know the answer or, rather, that the question asked was irrelevant to the respondent so that individual chose not to answer (i.e., missing by logic) or the respondent wanted to hide certain feelings (equivalent to the effect of refusal to respond).

As mentioned in Chapter 14, the researcher must understand the pros and cons of using this type of response choice in a mailed or online survey. The basic reason for its usage is to give the respondent an opportunity to indicate true feelings (i.e., "I don't know") about a particular issue when the respondent in fact does not have sufficient information to formulate an opinion.

The following are some questions that could potentially be answered by the respondents in an interview.

a. Who is the current NFL commissioner who succeeded Paul Tagliabue last year?
b. Do you think the new drug policy imposed recently by the MLB is acceptable?
c. Do you like your current job as a sales representative?
d. What brand of athletic shoes do you like the most?
e. How many times did you attend professional sport games last year?

To question A, the "I don't know" answer is logical, as the intention of the question is to determine if the respondent knows the name of the new NFL commissioner. There is no reason why respondents would give the "I don't know" answer unless they were not aware of the switch in power in that association. If the "I don't know" answer is given to question B, however, it is difficult to judge whether or not the respondent really either did not know the MLB's new drug policy or was aware but had not formed a particular opinion yet. To the remaining questions, C to E, the "I don't know" answer could imply the inappropriateness in drafting those questions. The meaning of "I don't know" may be multifaceted: "I don't want to answer the question," and "I don't want to answer the question, as the question is not important to me."

Inadequate response. "An inadequate response is a response which does not fall within the accepted range of values" (Huisman and van der Zouwen, 1999, p. 7). For example, one of the questions included in a mailed survey reads "Do you play golf?" and a dichotomous set of answer choices (i.e., "Yes" or "No") is provided. A respondent might ignore the answer choices and write "sometimes" in the space between "Yes" and "No." The effect of inadequate response is similar to that of item omission. The researcher should decide if it is legitimate to choose one of the two answer choices immediately next to the mark or to simply treat it as a missing answer. Choosing more than one answer to a question that requires only one of the response choices provided is another type of inadequate response. The same treatments suggested to deal with the problem mentioned previously can also be applied to edit this type of inadequate response.

The above discussion implies that the causes of missing data or the "determinants of item non-response" as referred to by Huisman and van der Zouwen (1999) are multidimensional. The researcher, the respondent, and the individual who conducts the interview can all contributors to the problem. First, the researcher can be a cause of missing data. Asking the respon-

dents to complete a questionnaire that contains questions that are utterly irrelevant to them is one of the errors that could be committed by the researcher, which will inevitably lead to many questions not being answered adequately. The way the questionnaire is designed may affect the response behavior of the respondent. Huisman and van der Zouwen (1999) noted the areas in a questionnaire that can potentially cause the respondent not to answer certain questions:

> The structure of the questionnaire (e.g., the incorrect use of the branching technique may confuse the respondent and increase item non-response), the position of the item in the questionnaire (e.g., items placed early in the survey instrument are more likely to be completed), the item wording (the terminology used in a question is unknown to the respondent), the topic and questions in the scale (e.g., questions concerning income, sexual behaviors, etc. have a higher rate of item non-response), the task involved in the questions (e.g., the difficult questions are more likely to be unanswered than easier ones), the format of the questions (e.g., the number of answer choices provided in a close-ended question may affect the response behavior of the respondent. (p. 9)

The respondent can be another cause of missing data. The demographic characteristics and the level of motivation and interest of the respondents influence their response behavior. Previous research found that less educated respondents are more likely to commit item non-response (Huisman and van der Zouwen, 1999, p. 11). When respondents are approached with topics with which they are not familiar or in which they have little interest, they are more likely to be apathetic and less willing to complete the questionnaire.

The interviewer can also be a cause of missing data. Unskillful interviewers tend to have a higher rate of missing data as they often make mistakes, including skipping questions, noting nswers in the wrong place, presenting questions incorrectly, and forgetting to record responses. To prevent interviewers from making these mistakes, it is important to provide adequate training for them.

Simply put, the purpose of editing is to prepare the survey instrument for the next stages of analysis, coding and tabulating. Even though "the editing process is extremely tedious and time consuming . . . [it] is an important step in the processing stage" (McDaniel & Gates, 1991, p. 488).

Coding

Coding refers to the process of grouping and assigning numeric codes to the various responses to a particular question (McDaniel & Gates, 1991; Ghauri, Gronhaug, & Kristianslund, 1995). As mentioned in Chapter 14, questions in a questionnaire are presented either in an open-ended format or a closed-ended format. Most of the survey instruments in sport management research use the closed-ended format.

Coding for closed-ended questions is a relatively simple process. The researcher often precodes the questionnaire prior to putting it into use (see Table 16-1 for an example of a precoded questionnaire). The precoding practice simplifies the coding process, as the researcher can directly enter the data from the questionnaire that has been through the editing process. If a respondent circles "2" in response to question A, the researcher can input the number "2" on the computer directly, without the need to go through the coding process.

The purpose of coding the responses collected with an open-ended format is to make them processable and analyzable with statistic procedures. The process of coding open-ended questions involves four steps (McDaniel & Gates, 1991, pp. 489–491):

Step 1: The researcher lists all the responses provided by the respondents to each of the open-ended questions on the same piece of paper. If the number of respondents is large and makes the task cumbersome, the researcher may randomly select a manageable number of responses

---

TABLE 16-1
Example of a Precoded Questionnaire

Please check the box in front of the answer choice that best represents your situation.

A. What is the division designation of your conference?
 1. ❑ Division I-A
 2. ❑ Division I-AA
 3. ❑ Division I-AAA
 4. ❑ Division II
 5. ❑ Division III
 6. ❑ Other (explain) _____

B. If your conference competes at the Division I level, is your conference commonly referred to as:
 1. ❑ Equity Conference
 2. ❑ Mid-Major Conference
 3. ❑ Other (explain) _____

C. How many institutions are affiliated with your conference?

D. How many conference tournaments are currently sponsored by your conference?

E. How many years has your conference been in existence?
 1. ❑ Fewer than 5
 2. ❑ 6–10
 3. ❑ 11–15
 4. ❑ 16–20
 5. ❑ More than 20

F. Has your conference outsourced any part of its marketing operations and rights?
 1. ❑ Yes
 2. ❑ No

---

to complete the coding process.

Step 2: The researcher reviews all the responses and consolidates those responses that essentially have the same meaning into a particular category. A name is given to each of the newly created categories.

Step 3: After the consolidation, the researcher assigns a numeric code to each of the categories.

Step 4: To complete the tasks in the final step, the researcher first associates all the responses that belong to the same category created in step 2. Based on the results of Step 3, the researcher then assigns a numeric code to all of them by writing the code in the questionnaire.

Following is an example illustrating how to employ this four-step process to provide coding to open-ended questions. In a recent survey conducted with a group of several senior sport facility executives, an open-ended question was asked: "In your opinion, what skills are important for a sports facility manager to perform the job effectively?" The 26 skills identified are shown in Table 16-2. The questions were consolidated and accordingly coded. Table 16-3 shows the results.

As Table 16-3 indicates, the 26 responses can be consolidated into six categories: policies and procedures; accounting, budgeting, and purchasing; sales and service contracts; marketing, promotion, and public relations; personnel management; and facility management. Each category is given a numeric code from 1 to 6. Based on the code assignment sheet, the researcher can then assign a numeric code to each of the 26 responses to facilitate data entry.

It is suggested that a number of principles be followed while coding all questions, regardless of whether or not they are closed-ended or open-ended, to achieve optimal outcomes (Luck & Rubin, 1987):

1. Sufficiency. The number of categories should be sufficient to include all the themes represented by the responses but not too many to hamper the statistical process. It is impractical to have fewer than three categories, as much important information could be hidden in so few categories.

2. Appropriateness. The created categories should fit well with the purpose of the research. In other words, the responses should be categorized to facilitate the approval of the research hypothesis or causal relationship between variables.

3. Exclusiveness. The researcher must make sure that the categories created are mutually exclusive, meaning that the categories should not overlap in the themes and meanings they represent. Mutual exclusivity also means that a response can be placed appropriately into only one category, but also different responses are grouped into different categories (interclass heterogeneity, Luck & Rubin, 1987,

---

TABLE 16–2
Responses from Sport Facility Executives Important Skills

Question: In your opinion, what skills are important for a sports facility manager to perform the job effectively?

Responses:
a. Develop and manage standard operating procedures for all operational functions of the facility
b. Develop organizational structures and personnel staffing requirements
c. Develop marketing, advertising, and public relations plans
d. Manage booking and scheduling
e. Generate accurate projections for attendance and revenue
f. Develop contracts with lessees and promoters/performers
g. Develop and manage emergency preparedness procedures
h. Manage security personnel and develop crowd management plans
i. Handle procurement of products and services
j. Develop contracts and agreements with vendors for products and services
k. Oversee novelty sales and contract negotiations
l. Oversee equipment and supply purchases
m. Operate the facility in accordance with applicable local, state and federal regulations
n. Manage personnel assigned to various facility functions
o. Develop job descriptions, duties, responsibilities and performance standards for employees
p. Oversee the compliance of state and federal regulations regarding personnel practices
q. Negotiate with unions for all outside services
r. Assess the quality of services and the facility's effectiveness
s. Handle and settle grievances of employees
t. Develop financial reports and manage audit activities
u. Oversee innovative improvements in facility and facility services
v. Communicate effectively with clients, subordinates, and the public
w. Manage catering activities for food and alcoholic beverages to ensure quality of service
x. Oversee food preparation and concession sales
y. Develop management plans for safety of the facility and equipment
z. Develop operational budgets

TABLE 16-3
Consolidated Response Categories and Codes for the Open-Ended Responses to Important Skills in Table 16-2

Response Categories	Response Number From Table 16-1	Assigned Numeric Code
Policies and Procedures	1, 7, 8, 13	1
Accounting, Budgeting, and Purchasing	4, 5, 9, 12, 20, 26	2
Sales and Service Contracts	6, 10, 11, 23, 24	3
Marketing, Promotion, and PR	3, 22	4
Personnel Management	2, 14, 15, 16, 17, 19	5
Facility Management	13, 18, 21, 25	6

p. 348). For example, in a survey, the respondent was asked to indicate an occupation. The following occupation categories were provided: (a) Professional, (b) Manager, (c) Sales Representative, (d) Priest/Pastor/Minister, (e) Artist, (f) Technician, (g) Unemployed. Due to the nature of the categories, the respondent could easily have chosen more than one response. Those who thought artists were professionals, or instance, would have chosen both (a) and (e).

4. Single-dimensionality. Each category should represent only one dimension conceptually. All the homogenous responses placed in a specific category should be similar ("intra-class homogeneity" (Luck & Rubin, 1987, p. 348) to cluster around one single dimension. The occupation case discussed previously can be used to illustrate the single-dimensional rule in coding. Asked to indicate an occupation, a respondent who used to be a manager of a sporting goods store but is currently unemployed might have chosen both "manager" and "unemployed," as these two answer choices represent two concepts that are in different dimensions. The "unemployed" category shows the current status of the respondent, but it is not an occupational category.

If the desire of the researcher is to prepare and code the open-ended responses so that they can be analyzed with parametric statistical procedures, the following three rules, as recommended by Luck and Rubin (1987) should be observed:

1. Avoid open-ended class intervals.
2. Choose class interval of the same width.
3. Deal with mid-points of class intervals.

There is a consensus that the coding process should be handled by one person for each open-ended question to ensure consistency (Huisman & van der Zouwen, 1999). When more than one coder is needed to code a particular question, it is strongly encouraged that they consult with each other during the coding process, particularly during the step involving consolidation of responses that essentially have the same meaning into a particular category.

In large-scale projects, and especially in cases in which the data entry is performed by a subcontractor, researchers utilize a data code book. The data code book contains every variable used in the research, including its variable name, and the code number associated with each possible response to each question that makes up the data set. Table 16-4 shows an example of the data code book for a project that examines the attitudes of American adults toward sport participation.

Data Entry and Analysis

Data entry refers to the creation of a computer file that holds the raw data taken from all of the questionnaires deemed suitable for analysis. It is the last step before data analysis in which the researcher

TABLE 16-4
A Section of a Data Code Book for a National Survey of Adult Attitudes to Sport Participation

Question	Variable Number	Code Description	Variable Name
	1	Record Number	RECNUM
	2	Respondent Number	RESPID
1	3	5-Digit Zip Code	ZIP
		99999 = Missing	
2	4	2-Digit Birth Year	BIRTH
3	5	Gender	GENDER
		1 = Male	
		2 = Female	
		9 = Missing	
4	6	Marital Status	MARITAL
		1 = Married	
		2 = Widowed	
		3 = Divorced	
		4 = Married but Separated	
		5 = Unmarried	
		9 = Missing	
5	7	Household Income	INCOME
		1 = Below $20,000	
		2 = $20,001–$40,000	
		3 = $40,001–$60,000	
		4 = $60,001–$80,000	
		5 = $80,001–$100,000	
		6 = Above $100,000	

keys in the coded data on the computer. The online survey has shortened the data entry process considerably. In some cases, it eliminates it entirely as the researcher can simply download the answers or data sheet to a preformatted spreadsheet sheet and process it with a specific type of statistical computer software, such as the SPSS, SAS, and so on.

USING CONTENT ANALYSIS ON CODING OPEN-ENDED QUESTIONS

Content analysis is one of the methods that sport management researchers have used in analyzing the collected information to achieve their research objectives. For example, Pedersen and Pitts (2001) used content analysis as a method to analyze all the articles published in the *Sport Marketing Quarterly* to determine the frequency of various types of research methods and statistical procedures utilized by sport marketing researchers. To determine how gender was portrayed in *Sports Illustrated for Kids*, Cuneen and Sidewell (1998) conducted a content analysis of the advertisements included in the magazine over a six-year period.

Content analysis is defined as "the systematic,

quantitative description of the composition of the object of the study" (Gay & Diebl, 1992). The object described here may include a whole array of things, including the minutes of meetings, letters, memoranda, diaries, speeches, newspapers, magazine or journal articles, films, television programs, and photographs (Robson, 2002).

Steps to Execute a Content Analysis

As mentioned above, content analysis is a systematic process that involves several steps (Fraenkel & Wallen, 2000). The steps will be described briefly in the following section.

Step 1: Determination of Objectives. It is critically important for sport management researchers desiring to use the content analysis technique to determine what is to be accomplished. For example, Pederson, Whisenant and Schneider (2003) yielded some descriptive information about the gender of the journalists (reporters, photographers, editors, etc.) who provided the coverage of interscholastic athletics in the state of Florida. Table 16-5 shows the percentages of male and female journalists working in the newspaper sports departments during a certain period of time. In general, content analysis is adopted to "obtain descriptive information about a topic" (Fraenkel & Wallen, 2000, p. 472).

Other reasons to use the content analysis technique are to verify other research findings and to test hypotheses. Sport management researchers can use the content analysis technique to validate the results of studies utilizing other research methodologies, such as observation and survey. In the aforementioned study, Whisenant and Schneider (2003) developed four hypotheses, one of which is: "Female reporters will give greater coverage to girls' interscholastic athletics than will male reporters" (p. 382). Some scholars also believe that content analysis can be used to identify a new research idea as an exploratory technique when large numbers of documents are available for the researchers to review and study (Robson, 2002). Through the review process and the application of the content analysis method, the researchers may hope to generate an actionable research theme.

Step 2: Definition of Terms of Interest. It is also essential for the sport management researcher to operationally define the concepts or terms that will be under investigation. For example, in the study conducted by Cuneen and Sidewell (1998) to investigate how gender was portrayed in *Sports Illustrated for Kids*, they operationalized several key terms, such as prominent models and supporting models.

TABLE 16-5
Percentages of Male and Female Journalists Working in the Newspaper Sport Departments during a Certain Period of Time

	Male	Female	Other	Total
Editors				
Executive Sports	43 (100%)	0 (0%)	0 (0%)	43 (100%)
Prep Sports Editors	41 (95.3%)	2 (4%)	0 (0%)	43 (100%)
Written Articles				
Editorial Guidance	1636 (91.3%)	156 (8.7%)	0 (0%)	1792 (100%)
Journalists	276 (91.4%)	26 (8.6%)	0 (0%)	302 (100%)
Articles	953 (53.2%)	93 (5.2%)	746 (41.6%)	1792 (100%)
Photographs				
Editorial Guidance	721 (87.2%)	106 (12.8%)	0 (0%)	827 (100%)
Photographers	132 (78.6%)	36 (21.4%)	0 (0%)	168 (100%)
Photographs	396 (47.9%)	90 (10.9)	341 (41.2)	827 (100%)

Step 3: Identification of the Unit of Analysis. In this step, the sport management researcher must decide what is to be analyzed: words, phrases, sentences, abstract meanings, and so on. "The unit most commonly used is probably the individual word" (Robson, 2002, p. 351). The unit of analysis could be syntactical, referential, or thematic. A word or phrase is a syntactical unit. Robson (2002) maintained that the syntactical unit could be the number of stories on a topic, the column inches, or the size of headlines, in analyzing newspaper, magazine, or journal articles.

On the other hand, a referential unit could be something that is referred to with different expressions, but the meanings of those expressions are the same. For example, expenses and expenditure are terms used interchangeably by sport marketers. In using the thematic unit, the researcher attempts to extract a number of themes from the content.

Step 4: Selection of a Sampling Plan. After the units of analysis have been identified, the sport management researcher should determine how to obtain the needed sample(s) for analysis. The samples could be the publications of a particular journal or newspaper over a certain period of time (e.g., five years) or all the commercials aired during a particular TV program. For example, all the advertisements appearing during Super Bowl games from the years 1996 to 2002 were included in the sample for a study conducted by Kelley and Turley (2004) that was designed to investigate the relationship between advertising content and the effect of the advertisement. All of the sampling techniques discussed in Chapter 15 can be employed to select samples for studies using the content analysis technique.

Step 5: Data Recording and Analysis. Counting is the basic method of data recording. Each time a unit of analysis appears, it is counted. When the counting process is complete, the collected data is tabulated and analyzed. The most commonly used statistical data analysis techniques in con-tent analysis are descriptive statistics, particularly the frequency (e.g., the number of times a particular unit of analysis appears) and percentage and/or proportion that a particular term appeared in the total occurrence of all the units of analysis. The P^2 test is also commonly used by sport management researchers to determine the degree of association between two units of analysis.

Advantages and Disadvantages of Content Analysis

Content analysis can be used to collect information that is often difficult or impossible to collect through the use of other traditional research methods because of its unobtrusive nature. This is its major advantage. The other advantage is that it can be used to obtain information about events that happened in the past so as to enable the researcher to make comparisons between the historical information and data collection from present events. Another reason why content analysis is advantageous over other means of data collection is that the needed data (journals, newspapers, books, photos, videotapes, etc.) are readily available so that it is relatively economical to acquire the data. Content analysis can be repeated and replicated (Fraenkel & Wallen, 2000).

A major disadvantage of content analysis is that it is extremely time consuming, as the systematic nature of the method requires the commitment of human resources to record the data carefully. The other disadvantage is that "there is a temptation among researchers to consider that the interpretations gleaned from a particular content analysis indicate the causes of a phenomenon rather than being reflection of it" (Fraenkel & Wallen, 2000, p. 481).

A Content Analysis Case

Green, Costa, and Fitzgerald (2003) conducted a content analysis on 2002 NCAA Women's Final Four telecasts. The purpose of the study was to determine the nature and extent of the television exposure generated for the city of San Antonio by hosting the 2002 NCAA Women's Final Four basketball tournament. The ESPN coverage of the tournament was content analyzed for any verbal mentions of San Antonio or its associated images and for the variety and duration of San Antonio imagery that appeared in the ESPN broadcast coverage. Two research questions were raised for the study: (1) How extensive is the host city's exposure during the telecast of a large and nationally significant sport event? and (2) What kinds of city mentions and city images occur during the telecast?

All coders involved in the study engaged in code training for both verbal mentions and imagery. During this stage, the coders developed lists of the types of verbal mentions and visual images appearing in the broadcasts. The coders shared their lists and discussed the emerging categories and assignment rules with the other coders. This initial process allowed for the clarification of some ambiguous rules, the development of more precise definitions, and the addition of new categories. Definitions for each coding category were agreed upon and compiled in a coding manual. Coding matrices were developed for each analysis—visual and verbal. Specific image or verbal types were listed down the left side of the matrix, and each occurrence was listed along the top. Coders then entered the duration of each occurrence by its image type.

The second phase consisted of pilot coding. During this phase, coders individually analyzed a sample of the telecasts. Inter-coder reliability assessed at the pilot-coding phase yielded a coefficient of reliability greater than .90 for all variables.

In the final analysis, two researchers independently coded each telecast twice. First, the telecast was coded for the number and type of verbal name mentions of San Antonio or San Antonio-related words (e.g. Alamodome, Alamo, River Walk). In the second analysis, coders recorded the types of San Antonio-related images (i.e., what was shown), and the duration of those images (i.e., how many seconds the image appeared on the screen). The achieved coefficient of reliability was greater than .90 for all but two variables. In both cases, the broadcast was then analyzed by a third researcher. The two scores that correlated at .90 or higher were used to calculate aggregate scores.

Ten programs (11 hours and 46 minutes of coverage) were analyzed: (1) the *Selection Show*; (2) *ESPN Sports Center* broadcasts on the Friday, Saturday, and Sunday of the tournament weekend; (3) pregame show for each of the semi-final games and for the championship game; (4) both semi-final games; and (5) the national championship game.

Overall, the findings of the study question the value of the exposure generated by events as a tool for place marketing.

SUMMARY

Data editing, coding, and transforming play key roles in ensuring the accuracy and quality of a research project. The importance of this research phase should not be overlooked.

Editing, whose purpose is to ensure the completeness of a survey instrument, involves two stages: field editing and central editing. Regardless of where editing takes place, the researcher involved in the editing process typically has to complete four tasks: (a) ensure the legibility of entries, (b) check the completeness of entries, (c) ascertain the consistency of entries, and (d) ensure accuracy of entries.

Coding is the process immediately following editing, and it involves grouping and assigning numeric codes to the various responses to a particular question. The coding procedures used to process open-ended or closed-ended questions are different. Coding for closed-ended questions is a relatively simple process, but the coding process for responses collected with an open-ended format is somewhat time consuming and tedious. The goal of coding is to make data processable and analyzable with statistical procedures. A four-step model is commonly used by sport management professionals in coding open-ended questions. The four steps include reviewing and listing responses, consolidating responses, setting codes, and entering codes.

It is suggested that four basic rules be observed while coding questions, regardless of whether or not they are closed-ended or open-ended. These four rules are: sufficiency, appropriateness, exclusiveness, and single-dimensionality. While handling a large-scale project, researchers often utilize a data code book, which contains every variable used in the research, including variable names and the code number associated with each possible response to each question that makes up the data set.

Data entry, the last step before data analysis, is the process of creating a computer file that holds the raw data taken from all of the questionnaires deemed suitable for analysis.

STUDY QUESTIONS

1. Can you define and explain the following two terms in your own words?
   a. Editing
   b. Coding
2. What are the tasks involved in editing? Explain them.
3. According to scholars in research methods, what are the reasons or causes of missing data?
4. How can researchers deal with the "I don't know" answer?
5. What are the four principles the researcher should use in data coding? Explain each.
6. What are the steps or stages in executing a study using the content analysis technique?

LEARNING ACTIVITIES

1. In a study conducted by Li and Burden (2001), they asked the athletic directors in all NCAA Division I institutions the question, "What are the benefits of outsourcing of sport marketing operations in intercollegiate athletics?" The following are 18 reasons the surveyed athletic directors provided. You are asked to use the four-step coding process for open-ended questions to complete the coding task. The end product of your coding should be a table like Table 16-3 that shows the consolidated response categories and codes, and the response associated with each category.
   a. Outsourcing can help broaden the media coverage of your institution so as to enhance the public awareness.
   b. Outsourcing can help your institution build a sustainable competitive advantage.
   c. It is less expensive for your conference to outsource your marketing operations and rights than to keep them in-house.
   d. It is more efficient for your institution to outsource your marketing operations and rights than to keep them in-house.
   e. Outsourcing of your marketing operations and rights can bring in a greater financial return than keeping them in-house.
   f. Outsourcing can help reduce bureaucracy and red tape in your marketing operations.
   g. Outsourcing can help your institution enhance the quality of its marketing operations.
   h. Outsourcing enables your institution to reallocate resources to other more critical areas.
   i. Outsourcing allows your institution to access external specialized talent and expertise in marketing and promotion.

j. Outsourcing enables your institution to reduce overhead expenses.

k. Outsourcing can help your institution avoid the administrative complexity of in-house employment.

l. Outsourcing enables your institution to use the contracted company as an extension of your overall marketing efforts.

m. Outsourcing allows your institution to handle all aspects of your marketing operations in a more timely fashion.

n. Outsourcing may cause loss of control of your marketing operations and rights.

o. Outsourcing may result in loss of opportunities to bring in more revenues for your institution.

p. Outsourcing can provide your institution with opportunities to expand marketing efforts to non-revenue sports.

q. Outsourcing can help your institution reduce capital expenses related to marketing operations.

r. Outsourcing allows your institution to be part of a marketing network and synergy.

2. Ask 10 of your classmates this question: "Where would you like to see yourself 10 years from now?" Using one of the basic steps of content analysis, analyze their answers and then describe the frequency of the answers.

References

Cuneen, J., & Sidwell, M. J. (1998). Gender portrayals in *Sports Illustrated for Kids* advertisements: A content analysis of prominent and supporting models. *Journal of Sport Management, 12*(1), 39–50.

Fraenkel, J. R., & Wallen, N. E. (2000). *How to design and evaluate research in education* (4th ed.). Boston, MA: McGraw Hill.

Gay, L. R., & Diebl, P. L. (1992). *Research methods for business and management*. New York: Macmillan Publishing Company.

Ghauri, P. N., Gronhaug, K., & Kristianslund, I. (1995). *Research methods in business studies: A practical guide*. New York: Prentice Hall.

Green, B. C., Costa, C., & Fitzgerald, M. (2003). Marketing the host city: Analyzing exposure generated by a sport event. *International Journal of Sports Marketing and Sponsorship, 4*, 335–353.

Green, P. E., & Tull, D. S. (1978). *Research for marketing directions* (4th ed.). Englewood Cliffs, NJ: Prentice Hall.

Huisman, M., & van der Zouwen, J. (1999). Item nonresponse in scale data from surveys: Types, determinants, and measures. In M. Huisman (Ed.), *Item nonresponse: Occurrence, causes, and imputation of missing answers to test items* (pp. 63–90). Leiden: DSWO-press.

Kelley, S. W., & Turley, L. W. (2004). The effect of content on perceived affect of Super Bowl commercials. *Journal of Sport Management, 18*(4), 398–420.

Luck, D. J., & Rubin, R. S. (1987). *Marketing research* (7th ed.). Englewood Cliffs, NJ: Prentice Hall.

McDaniel, C., & Gates, R. (1991). *Contemporary marketing research*. St. Paul, MN: West Publishing Company.

Pedersen, P. M., & Pitts, B. G. (2001). Investigating the body of knowledge in sport management: A content analysis of *Sport Marketing Quarterly*. *The Chronicle of Physical Education in Higher Education, 12*(3), 8–9, 22–23.

Pedersen, P. M., Whisenant, W. A., & Schneider, R. G. (2003). Using a content analysis to examine the gendering of sports newspaper personnel and their coverage. *Journal of Sport Management, 17*(4), 376–393.

Robson, C. (2002). *Real world research: A resource for social scientists and practitioners-researchers* (2nd ed.). Oxford, UK: Blackwell Publisher.

Wiseman, D. C. (1999). *Research strategies for education*. Belmont, CA: Wadsworth Publishing Company.

CHAPTER 17
INTRODUCTION TO STATISTICAL DATA ANALYSIS IN SPORT MANAGEMENT RESEARCH

OBJECTIVES FOR COMPLETING THIS CHAPTER ARE THAT STUDENTS WILL BE ABLE TO:

Define statistics

Differentiate between descriptive statistics and inferential statistics

Differentiate between parametric statistics and non-parametric statistics

Understand and differentiate between the dependent variable and the independent variable

Understand the nature and scope of hypothesis and hypothesis testing

Properly state a null hypothesis

Differentiate between the two types of alternative hypotheses

Properly apply either type of alternative hypothesis in a research situation

Understand the nature and scope of research questions

Differentiate between difference questions and relationship questions

Understand the concept of statistical significance

Understand the difference between Type I error and Type II error

SPORT MANAGEMENT RESEARCHERS use statistics and statistical analysis procedures to answer research questions, test hypotheses, and develop new knowledge in their specific area or focus of study. The language of research and statistics can be cumbersome when beginners attempt to interpret statistics and statistical data analysis.

The intention of this chapter is to introduce several fundamental elements that will aid beginning researchers in better interpreting and critiquing statistics in sport management research. Like any other scheme for selecting such elements, the list is not an exhaustive one, nor is it perfect; however, it is important for aiding beginners to better understand statistics and statistical analysis techniques in the sport management literature.

NATURE OF STATISTICAL ANALYSIS

One of the first tasks for beginning researchers is to understand clearly a working definition of the term "statistics." The term has been defined by a variety of scholars in research methods and statistics. One of many examples is the one by Keller, Warreck, and Bartel (1990), who defined statistics as "a body of principles and methods concerned with extracting useful information from a set of numerical data" (p. 2). Another definition is by Kiess (1996) who defined statistics "as methods, techniques or procedures used to summarize, analyze, and draw inferences from data of a sample" (p. 5). For this book, statistics refer to a body of rules, procedures, and standards directed to extract units of information from a set of numerical data. It is the science that uses mathematical methods to collect, organize, analyze, summarize, and interpret quantitative data. Statistics is a group of methods, procedures, and techniques that are used to collect, analyze, present, and interpret data and to make decisions. In Figure 17-1, an umbrella concept of statistics is used to illustrate the major statistical dimensions: descriptive statistics and inferential statistics.

Descriptive Statistics and Inferential Statistics

In general, descriptive statistics are procedures used to describe and summarize large volumes of data. More comprehensively, they are a major dimension of statistics for describing, organizing, condensing, summarizing, and displaying numerical data for a population or a sample (DePoy & Gitlin, 1994; Gall, Gall, & Borg, 2003; Howell, 1997; Keller, Warrack, & Bartel, 1990; Leedy & Ormrod, 2001; McMillan & Schumacher, 2001; Neuman, 2003; Shiffler & Adams, 1990, 2003).

Inferential statistics are the second way of grouping statistics by function or use. They are more sophisticated than descriptive statistics and have a primary goal of drawing conclusions about a large body of data called a population. Inferential statistics have been defined by several authorities of research and statistics. Keller, Warrack, and Bartel (1990) have defined inferential statistics as "a group of statistical data analysis techniques for drawing conclusions or making inferences about a characteristics of a population, based on information available in a sample taken from the population" (p. 2). The goal of inferential statistics is to make a statement about a population based on information from a sample (Levine, Ramsey, & Berenson, 1995; Shiffler & Adams, 1990).

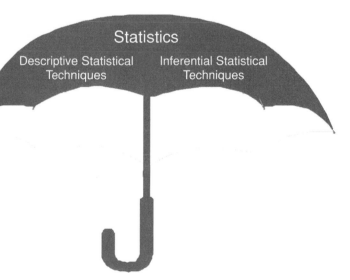

FIGURE 17-1. The Umbrella of Statistics Analysis Techniques

Unlike descriptive statistics, inferential statistics consist of a variety of procedures that permit a researcher to make judgments or inferences about a population based on information collected from a sample. More specifically, they enable the researcher to make judgments about the accuracy of a given sample in reflecting the characteristics of the population from which it is drawn. For example, in a random sample of 300 men aged 25 to 45 years, 30% of the men were smokers. This dimension of statistics allow us to generalize from this limited sample to the larger population and draw conclusions about the percentage of male smokers in the population based on the sample data. Given the sample size, we can be 95% certain that the true population mean will be 30% plus or minus 4%. In other words, we can be 95% certain that the true population mean falls between 26 and 34% (Levine, Ramsey, & Berenson, 1995).

Parametric Statistics and Nonparametric Statistics

Beginning researchers must keep in mind that both parametric and nonparametric statistics allow researchers to make assumptions about random samples taken from populations. Parametric techniques are used for deriving logical conclusions about the characteristics of a population when (a) data taken from the populations are normally distributed, (b) they have equal variances on the variable(s) that is being measured, and (c) the levels of measurements are interval or ratio. Parametric statistical procedures are the most powerful in testing questions and hypotheses about the differences of groups or set of values.

Unlike parametric techniques, nonparametric techniques are used for deriving conclusions about the characteristics of a sample; however, they do not make assumptions about the population and the levels of measurements are primarily ordinal or normal (Gall, Gall, & Borg, 2003; McMillan & Schumacher, 2001; Neuman, 2003). Nonparametric statistical procedures are recognized as the most useful in testing questions and hypotheses about relationships and associations of groups or set of values. Figure 17-2 shows the classifications of these two types of inferential statistics.

Outlined in Table 17-1 is the list of the names of the different types of statistical tests as captured under the major dimensions of descriptive, inferential, parametric, and nonparametric techniques. The list shows the grouping of statistical analysis procedures. Presenting this holistic view of statistics to beginning researchers may help eliminate some of the fear about the nature and scope of statistics.

INDEPENDENT AND DEPENDENT VARIABLES

The relationship between independent variables and dependent variables is another important issue for beginning researcher to understand. In order to better understand inferential statistical tests, one must understand how to interpret dependent and independent variables in a study. First, researchers must recognize that the language is different when interpreting independent and dependent variables for experimental research than for non-experimental research (Kerlinger & Lee, 2000). This can be a confusing process because different researchers refer to the terms in different ways. For example, independent variables are referred to as predictor or treatment variables in correlational studies, and dependent variables are referred to as criterion, effect, or response

Parametric Statistical Tests	Nonparametric Statistical Tests
1. most powerful testing questions and hypotheses about the differences of groups or sets of values	1. most powerful in testing questions and hypotheses about relationships and associations of groups or set of values
2. via the use of interval and ratio measurement	2. via the use of nominal or ordinal measurement scales
3. primarily via the use of the mean and median	3. primarily via the use of frequencies, percentages, and proportions

FIGURE 17-2. Two Major Classifications of Inferential Statistics

TABLE 17-1 Grouping Statistical Analysis Procedures		
Descriptive Statistics	**Inferential Statistics**	
	Parametric	Nonparametric
percentages frequency mean standard deviation range ranking median mode	ANOVA regression MANOVA T-test factor analysis (EFA) Pearson product-moment correlation factor analysis (CFA) discriminant analysis canonical correlation cluster analysis structural equation model Fishers Z score MANCOVA ANCOVA path analysis trend analysis	Chi Square Mann-Whitney Wilcoxon signed rank test Kruskal-Wallis Spearman rank correlation Fisher's exact test conjoint analysis

variables. As shown in Figure 17-3, independent variables are easier to identify in experimental studies because they are the variables manipulated by the researcher to see if such manipulation causes change in the dependent (criterion) variable(s).

The variable that is influenced by the treatment variable is the dependent variable. It is the outcome variable, or the one that the researcher is trying to explain. Such a variable is determined by the researcher prior to the research investigation and is dependent on data collection. For example, a researcher may ask, "What effect will different colors of players' uniforms have on high school men's basketball players' attitude when playing home games?" In this case the independent (or treatment) variable is the color of the players' uniforms and the dependent (outcome) variable is the players' attitudes.

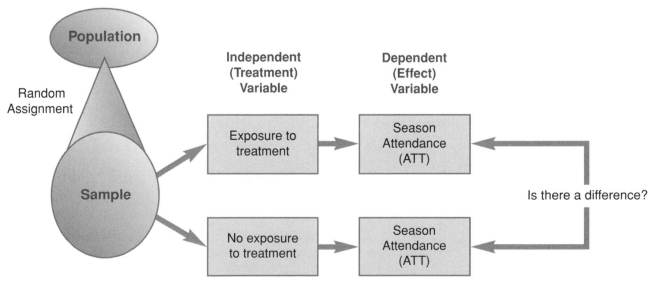

FIGURE 17-3. Interpretation of Independent and Dependent Variables

Defining the Independent and Dependent Variables for Non-experimental Designs

In non-experimental research, the independent (predictor) variable is not manipulated or controlled as in experimental research, but is observed in its natural setting to see if it can be correlated or causally compared with the dependent (criterion) variable (Wimmer & Dominick, 2000). The independent variable describes the characteristic by which the alternative groups being studied are distinguished. Usually, the independent variable is divided into a few discrete groups distinguished from each other in meaningful ways. This is illustrated in Figure 17-4, as there is no manipulation of the presumed independent variable (bright color uniforms and white uniforms) on the presumed dependent variable (players' attitude) is inferred or speculated from our observations that the two vary together (are correlated) (Kerlinger & Lee, 2003).

One must keep in mind that dependent variables

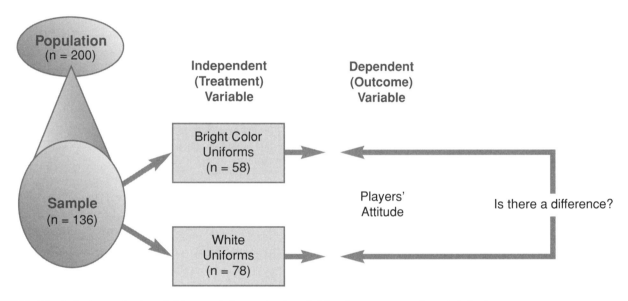

FIGURE 17-4. Independent variables and dependent variables for non-experimental designs

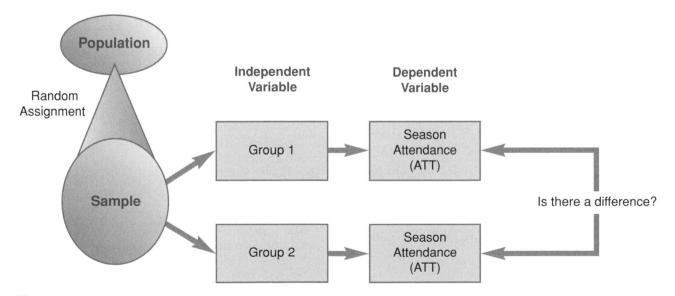

FIGURE 17-5. Independent variables and dependent variables for non-experimental designs

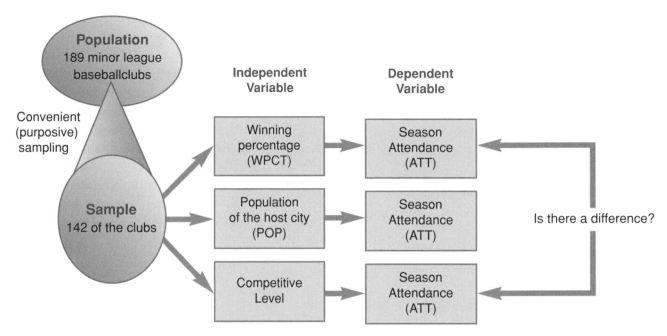

FIGURE 17-6. Example: independent variables and dependent variables for non-experimental designs

are not determined by the researcher prior to the research investigation. They are dependent on the data collection. They are the outcome variables or the ones that the researcher is trying to explain. For example, Buxton, Lankford, and Noda (1992) examined the motivational congruencies and discrepancies (*dependent variables*) between certified athletic trainers and noncertified student trainers (*independent variables*) in the state of Hawaii (p. 320). The dependent variables (motivational congruencies and discrepancies) are dependent or contingent upon data collection. They were not determined by the researcher prior the research investigation. They are the outcome variables or the ones that the researcher will be trying to explain after the data have been analyzed. The independent (or predictor) variables (athletic trainers) have been determined prior to and are independent of the collection of data (The athletic trainer's responses are the key factors in determining the dependent variables).

THE NATURE AND SCOPE OF HYPOTHESIS AND HYPOTHESIS TESTING

Hypothesis testing provides objective criteria for researchers to decide whether or not a research hypothesis should be accepted as true or rejected as false. The rules of statistical hypothesis testing are based on what might at first seem to be strange logic. They allow the researcher to reject the idea that any difference found between groups is due to chance or error, rather than allowing the researcher to prove that there is a real relationship between the variables that are being studied. Generally speaking, a hypothesis is an educated prediction or a logical assumption that is based on prior research or known facts and that can be tested by experimental or nonexperimental strategies. The logic is that hypotheses are neither proved nor disproved and that they can only be supported or not supported by statistical analysis. "Hypotheses have nothing to do with proof. . . . their acceptance or rejection is dependent on what the data—and the data alone—ultimately reveal" (Leedy & Ormrod, 2001, p. 60). That is the function of any statistical test. The two main types of hypotheses testing are (a) the null hypothesis, and (b) the alternative hypothesis. Alternative testing may take the form of being directional or nondirectional (Bork, 1993; Leedy & Ormrod, 2001; McMillan & Shumacher, 2006).

Conceptually, the term "null" means without value or without significance. The null hypothesis is a statement of no difference and it is tested statistically. It is usually symbolized as H_0. This statement basically tells us that there will be no difference, relationship, association, or pattern between the independent and dependent variables based on the results of statistical testing. If there is a statistical difference or relationship between the variables, the null hypothesis is *rejected*. When no differences are found between the variables, the null hypothesis is *accepted*. The following are a few examples of null hypothesis:

■ At the $p \le 0.05$ level of confidence, no relationship exists between organizational commitment and age.

■ At the $p \le 0.05$ level of confidence, no relationship exists between organizational commitment and gender.

■ At the $p \le 0.05$ level of confidence, no relationship exists between organizational commitment and levels of education.

■ At the $p \le 0.05$ level of confidence, no relationship exists between organizational commitment and marital status.

■ At the $p \le 0.05$ level of confidence, no relationship exists between organizational commitment and length of service.

The alternative hypothesis (H_a), or research hypothesis, generally states that there will be a statistically significant difference between the dependent and independent variables, but it does not state the magnitude or direction of the differences. As the null hypothesis, it is subjected to statistical analysis. Unlike the null hypothesis, it states that a statistically significant difference, pattern, or relationship exists between the independent and dependent variables, and it identifies under what conditions that the differences or relationships will occur. It is a form of the statement of hypothesis that represents the expectation of the researcher.

Alternative (research) hypotheses can be formulated in two ways: directional and nondirectional. The directional hypothesis (H_d) not only states that there will be statistically significant difference but, in fact, identifies where or under what conditions that difference will occur. Directional hypotheses predict differences or relationships between independent variables and dependent variables and specify the directions of such differences and relationships. For the alternative hypothesis stated earlier, a corresponding research hypothesis would be that certified athletic trainers will rate the factors that motivate them in the workplace higher than would the noncertified student athletic trainers. The study conducted by Kwon & Armstrong (2002) provides a good illustration of directional hypotheses. The following are the four directional hypotheses they used to answer the research questions focusing on the examination of factors influencing impulse buying of sport team licensed merchandise (p. 154–155):

■ Hypothesis 1: The higher the consumer's level of shopping enjoyment, the greater the likelihood of the consumer making an impulse purchase of sport team licensed merchandise.

■ Hypothesis 2: The higher the level of identification the consumer has with the respective sport team, the greater the likelihood of the consumer making an impulse purchase of the team's merchandise.

■ Hypothesis 3: The more time available to sport consumers in shopping situations, the greater the likelihood of the consumer making an impulse purchase of sport team-licensed merchandise.

■ Hypothesis 4: The more money available to sport consumers in shopping situations, the greater the likelihood of the consumers making an impulse purchase of sport team-licensed merchandise.

Like directional hypotheses, nondirectional hypotheses predict differences or relationships between the independent variables and the dependent variables; however, they do not specify the directions of such differences or relationships. For the directional hypothesis stated earlier, a corresponding nondirectional hypothesis would be that there will be significant differences (or relationships) between certified athletic trainers and noncertified student athletic trainers when rating the factors that motivate them in the workplace. In the example below, there are six directional hypotheses that can be used as relationship questions (Triola & Franklin, 1995):

- There are significant relationships between male and female athletic directors of NCAA Division II when ranking occupational affective commitment.
- There are no significant relationships between male and female athletic directors of NCAA Division II when ranking occupational affective commitment.
- There are significant relationships between male and female athletic directors of NCAA Division II when ranking occupational normative commitment.
- There are no significant relationships between male and female athletic directors of NCAA Division II when ranking occupational normative commitment.
- There are significant relationships between male and female athletic directors of NCAA Division II when ranking occupational continuance commitment.
- There are no significant relationships between male and female athletic directors of NCAA Division II when ranking occupational continuance commitment.

THE NATURE AND SCOPE OF RESEARCH QUESTIONS

Research does not always contain hypotheses. For first time or exploratory studies of a particular area of interest, the researcher would more than likely use research questions. The use of research questions is common where there is an absence of literature or related research studies in a particular area of interest to the researcher. One must understand the nature of research question to better understand inferential statistical techniques. There are two types of research questions written relevant to inferential statistics: difference questions and relationship questions (McMillan & Schumacher, 2006).

Difference Questions

Difference questions are typically used in the measurements for comparing differences between two or more groups and are primarily answered via parametric statistics. A difference question asks: Are there differences between two or more sets of data?

This type of question has been the basis for much of the nonexperimental research conducted in sport management in which the researcher was interested in comparing one group to another group on the basis of their existing characteristics. In the example below, there are three research questions that can be answered as differences questions (Triola & Franklin, 1995):

- Are there significant differences between male and female athletic directors of NCAA Division II when rating occupational affective commitment?
- Are there significant differences between male and female athletic directors of NCAA Division II when rating occupational normative commitment?
- Are there significant differences between male and female athletic directors of NCAA Division II when rating occupational continuance commitment?

Relationship Questions

Unlike differences questions, relationship questions are raised in the study that assess the degree of relationship or association between two or more groups and are usually associated with nonparametric statistics. The typical question is: Are there significant relations or associations between two or more variables for a group of subjects? A mathematical equation is used to show how one variable is related to one or more variables and calculated through correlation coefficients. In the example below, there are three research questions that can be answered as relationship questions (Triola & Franklin, 1995):

- Are there significant relationships between male and female athletic directors of NCAA Division II when ranking occupational affective commitment?
- Are there significant relationships between male and female athletic directors of NCAA Division II when ranking occupational normative commitment?
- Are there significant relationships between male and female athletic directors of NCAA Division II when ranking occupational continuance commitment?

THE CONCEPT OF STATISTICAL SIGNIFICANCE

Researchers should realize that sampling is not perfect in that researchers can never select a sample of subjects that exactly matches all of those in the profile of a population. Additionally, it is impractical to test hypotheses on populations because they are too large (Salkind, 2000). After choosing the research questions and/or hypotheses, the researcher must be able to interpret the risk of being wrong in reference to the variables being measured. This calls for understanding of credence, credibility, and acceptance of observed differences or relationships in the statistical findings of the variables being analyzed.

Statistical significance is a term used to refer to a result that is extremely unlikely to have occurred by chance. After all data have been collected, the results are statistically analyzed. Statistical significance helps us to determine how confident researchers are that their results are real and did not occur by chance alone. It means that results are not likely to be due to chance factors and indicates the probability of finding a relationship in the sample when there is none in the population.

Statistical significance estimates the probability (p calculated) of sample results from those specified by the null hypothesis for population, given the sample size (Cohen, 1994). Statistical significance tests operate under the assumption that the null hypothesis exactly describes the population and then tests the sample's probability. Such logic is convoluted and does not tell us what we need to know regarding population values and the likelihood of result replication for future samples drawn from the same population.

Statistical significance tests do not tell us what we want to know nor do they evaluate whether or not our results are important. They tell us only whether or not the results of a study were due to chance. How do researchers go about doing this? After collecting all data, the researcher is required to state beforehand how willing the researcher is to be wrong when declaring that one group of variables is really different from another group of variables being measured. The level of significance values are symbolized as p. The p stands for probability. By rule of thumb or convention, the two most frequently used levels of significance are .05 and .01.

With a .05 significance level, the researcher accepts the risk that out of 100 samples, a true null hypothesis would be wrongly rejected five times. More specifically, this means that the researcher feels safe in concluding that two variables are different or related when a statistical analysis shows that there is less than a 5% probability that such findings were due to chance or a "fluke." Another way of saying this is that the results are significant at .05 level or "the point of fine" level. A p value of 0.05 means that the probability of the findings being caused by chance alone is 5 in 100 (McMillian & Schumacher, 2006). It also implies that there is a 5% chance that such differences or relationships did occur by chance. There is nothing magical about the 0.05 level. Other levels can be used. A p value of 0.05 or 5% is the most conventional level of chance.

If researchers want to have a stricter criterion, that is, they want to be even more assured that the results have not occurred by chance, then they set the significance level at 0.01, which is a 1 in 100 chance of having occurred by chance. If researchers wanted to be more certain that the results of their studies were not a fluke or did not occur merely by chance, they would select a more stringent level of statistical significance. For example, when a study is concerned with matters of vital importance to the health and welfare of human beings, or if decisions based on the study would involve great expense, the need would be to select a 0.01 or even a 0.001 level of statistical significance. On the other hand, if the researcher was less concerned about rejecting the null hypotheses when it was really true, a less stringent level, such as 0.05 or 0.10 (the most permissive level of chance) could be selected.

In sport management research, p is evaluated using two levels of credence or credibility: the 5% or .05 level or the 1% or .01 level. The 5% (.05) is the most commonly used level of chance employed in sport management research.

Generally, researchers report the probability level at which they were able to reject the null hypothesis. For example, if the level of significance was .05, the researcher rejects the null hypothesis at a probability that is less than .05. Instead of writing this out in words, the researcher uses the equation $p < .05$ (p meaning probability, the symbol $<$ meaning "less than"). In other words, the symbolic statement $p < .05$ means that (a) if the null hypothesis were true, the chances are less than five out of 100 that the researcher would have gotten the particular sample data results, and (b) because the sample is so different from what would be expected under the condition of a true null hypothesis, the researcher concludes that the null hypothesis was probably incorrect to begin with.

The level of significance is a probability that tells the researchers how unlikely the sample data must be before they can reject the null hypothesis. In other words, when the researchers reject a null hypothesis, they need to know what chances they are taking in doing so. They can make two kinds of mistakes: Type I error (alpha error) is committed when they conclude that the null hypothesis is false when it is really true. Type II (beta) errors occur when researchers conclude that the differences were due to chance when in fact they were not.

For most studies, a level of significance of $p = .05$ (a 1 in 20 chance of being wrong) is the maximum risk researchers are willing to accept for making a Type I error. A level of .01 (1 in 100 chance of being wrong) or .001 (1 in 1000 chance of being wrong) means that the likelihood that the researchers are mistaken in rejecting the null hypothesis is lower. In journal articles, the level of statistical significance is sometimes called the *level of probability*. Finally, the .95 *level of confidence* refers to the same thing as the .05 level significance, except it is stated backward. As it should be clear from the preceding discussion, the harder a researcher tries to lower the risk of committing a Type I error, the greater the risk of

committing a Type II error. In other words, if the researchers use strict criteria to reject the null hypotheses, they increase the chance that they will accept a false one.

An Understanding of Type I and Type II Errors

Beginning researchers must be able to interpret Type I and Type II errors, which can be made when researchers make decisions about the meaning of the value obtained from a statistical test. Both types of errors are defined in reference to the null hypothesis. A Type I error is committed when the researcher rejects the null hypothesis when in fact it is true. A Type II error is committed when the researcher accepts the null hypothesis when in fact it is false. Beginning researchers should memorize: "Type I *reject*" and "Type II *accept*." When researchers are overly careful not to reject a Type I error (mistakenly rejecting the null hypothesis), they increase the likelihood of committing a Type II error (mistakenly failing to reject the null hypothesis). When researchers are overly careful to avoid committing a Type II error, they increase the likelihood of increasing a Type I error. It is the researcher's prerogative to decide which error, Type I or Type II, is more acceptable when this occurs. Rejecting the null hypothesis implies that significant differences have been found. It must be kept in mind that the level of significance selected in the test of significance is the risk of committing the error. For example, if the significance level is set at 0.05 there is probability of 0.05 (five chances out of 100) that the sample data will be extreme enough for the researcher to reject the null hypothesis when it is obviously true. When the researcher is primarily interested in avoiding a Type I error, efforts should be made to use the 0.01 or 0.001

Null hypothesis			True	False
Decision	Accept the null		Type A Correct decision	Type II error (false negative)
	Reject the null		Type I error (false positive)	Type B Correct decision
(Cozby, 1997; DePoy & Gitlin, 2005; Leary, 1991).				

FIGURE 17-7. Statistical decision making: Type I and Type II errors

levels of significance. However, there is greater risk of a Type II error with 0.01 or 0.001 levels of significance than with a 0.05 level of significance. Figure 17-7 shows the relationship between a statistical decision and the risk of committing an error.

Shown in Figure 17-7 and Table 17-2 are a summary of the statistical data analysis methods used in three of the leading sport management journals. Of the three methods, parametric statistical techniques were most frequently used, accounting for slightly more than half of the techniques as primary to the research purpose, questions, and/or hypotheses. A technique was considered primary when it was used to directly answer a study research purpose, questions, and/or hypotheses (Quarterman, Pitts, Jackson, Kim & Kim, 2005). Descriptive statistics were the second most frequently used techniques, accounting for more than one third, or 37.8%, of the

techniques primary to the questions and hypotheses. Nonparametric statistical techniques were least frequently coded (10.2%) as primary to the research purpose, questions, and/or hypothesis.

SUMMARY

The introduction of critical concepts and issues in statistical analysis is the focal point of this chapter. Specifically, a number of paired concepts were reviewed and compared. They include descriptive statistics and inferential statistics, parametric statistics and nonparametric statistics, and dependent variable and independent variable.

The nature and scope of hypothesis testing is another topic of discussion. The two main types of hypotheses testing are (a) the null hypothesis and (b) the alternative hypothesis. The null hypothesis is a statement of no difference and it is tested statistically. On

TABLE 17-2
A numerical summary of the types of statistical data analysis techniques used in JSM, IJSM, and SMQ, 1987–2006

Technique	Operational Definition	N	%
Descriptive statistics	Techniques for describing, organizing, and summarizing numerical (mean, mode, median, variance, standard deviation, range, percentage, frequency, and rank)	381	37.8
Parametric statistics	Techniques for deriving logical conclusions about the characteristics of a population from corresponding characteristics of a sample or the population itself when the level of measurement of data is primarily interval or ratio (t test, ANOVA, MANOVA, ANCOVA, MANCOVA, exploratory factor analysis, confirmatory factor analysis, the Pearson product-moment correlation, regression analysis, trend analysis, discriminant analysis, cluster analysis, canonical correlation, path analysis, structural equation model, and Fisher's Z score)	523	51.9
Nonparametric statistics	Techniques for deriving logical conclusions about the characteristics of a population from corresponding characteristics of a sample or the population itself when the level of measurement of data is primarily nominal or ordinal scale (Chi-square, Mann-Whitney, Kruskal-Wallis, conjoint analysis, Wilcoxon's Sign Rank test, Fisher's Exact test, and Spearman rank correlation).	103	10.2
Total		1007	100.0

Source: Quarterman, J., Pitts, B., Jackson, N., Han, K., Haung, J., & Ahn, T. (2007). Statistical data analysis techniques employed in the *Journal of Sport Management, Sport Marketing Quarterly, & International Journal of Sport Management:* 1987 to 2006. Unpublished manuscript.
The categories of statistical analysis were adapted from textbooks by Gall, Gall, & Borg, 2003; Howell, 1999; McMillan & Schumacher, 2001; Neuman, 2003.

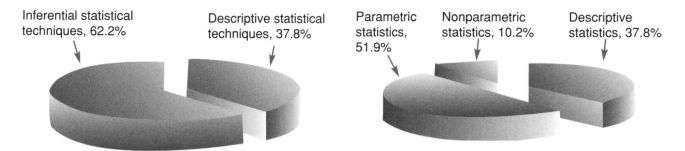

Inferential statistical techniques, 62.2%

Descriptive statistical techniques, 37.8%

Parametric statistics, 51.9%

Nonparametric statistics, 10.2%

Descriptive statistics, 37.8%

FIGURE 17-8. A summary of the statistical data analysis methods used in JSM, SMQ, and IJSM, 1987–2004

Source: Quarterman, J., Pitts, B., Jackson, N., Han, K., Haung, J., & Ahn, T. (2007). Statistical data analysis techniques employed in the *Journal of Sport Management, Sport Marketing Quarterly, & International Journal of Sport Management:* 1987 to 2006. Unpublished manuscript.

the other hand, the alternative hypothesis generally states that there will be a statistically significant difference between the dependent and independent variables, but it does not state the magnitude or direction of the differences. There are two ways that alternative hypotheses can be formulated, the directional hypothesis and the nondirectional hypothesis.

The third topic of discussion in this chapter is the concept of statistical significance. There are two types of research questions written in relevance to inferential statistics: difference questions and relationship questions. Difference questions are typically used in the measurements for comparing differences between two or more groups and are primarily answered via parametric statistics. Rela-

tionship questions are raised in studies that assess the degree of relationship or association between two or more groups, and they are usually associated with nonparametric statistics.

The concept of statistical significance is also examined. It is an important statistical procedure that tests operate under the assumption that the null hypothesis exactly describe the population and then test the sample's probability. The two most frequently used levels of statistical significance are .05 and .01.

This chapter also gives a brief overview of the Type I and Type II errors that could be committed in research. Sport management researchers carry the responsibility of deciding which error is more acceptable in their studies.

STUDY QUESTIONS

1. What does the term "statistics" mean?
2. What are the differences between descriptive statistics and inferential statistics?
3. What are the differences between parametric statistics and nonparametric statistics?
4. What are the differences between the dependent variable and the independent variable?
5. Properly state a null hypothesis.
6. What are the differences between the two types of alternative hypotheses?
7. Properly state an alternative hypothesis in a research situation.
8. What are the differences between the difference questions and the relationship questions?
9. Explain the concept of statistical significance.
10. What are the differences between Type I errors and Type II errors?
11. How can researchers reduce the probability of committing Type I errors and Type II errors?

References

Bork, C. E. (1993). *Research in physical therapy*. Philadelphia, PA: J. B. Lippincott Company.

Buxton, B. A., Lankford, S. V., & Noda, J. E. (1992). Motivational congruency between certified athletic trainers and noncertified student athletic trainers in the State of Hawaii. *Journal of Athletic Training, 27*(4), 20, 22, 24.

Cohen, J. (1992). A power primer. *Psychological Bulletin, 112*, 115–159.

Crowl, T .K. (1996). *Fundamentals of education research* (2nd ed.). Boston, MA: McGraw Hill, pp. 182–183.

DePoy, E., & Gitlin, L. N. (2005). *Introduction to research; Understanding and applying multiple strategies* (3rd ed.). St. Louis, MO: Elsevier.

Cozby, P. C. (2001). *Methods in behavioral research* (8th ed.). Boston, MA: McGraw Hill.

Gall M. D., Gall J. P., & Borg W. R. (2003). *Educational research: An introduction* (7th ed.). Boston, MA: Allyn and Bacon.

Howell, D. C. (1997). *Statistical methods for psychology* (4th ed.). Belmont, CA: Duxbury Press.

Keller, G., Warrack, B., & Bartel, H. (1990). *Statistics for management and economics* (2nd ed.). Belmont, CA: Wadsworth.

Kerlinger, F. D., & Lee, H. B. (2000). *Foundations of behavioral research* (4th ed.). Fort Worth, TX: Harcourt Collegiate Publishers.

Kwon, H. H., & Armstrong, K. L. (2002). Factors influencing impulse buying of sport team licensed merchandise. *Sport Marketing Quarterly, 11*(3), 151–162.

Leary, M. (1991). *Behavioral research methods*. New York: Wadsworth.

Leedy, P. D., & Ormrod, J. E. (2001). *Practical research; Planning and design* (7th ed.). Upper Saddle River, NJ: Prentice Hall, Inc.

Levine, D. M., Ramsey, P. R., & Berenson, M. L. (1995). *Business statistics for quality and productivity*. Englewood Cliffs, NJ: Prentice Hall Inc.

Lyberger, M. R., & Pastore, D. L. (1998). Health club facility operators' perceived level of compliance with the Americans with Disabilities Act. *Journal of Sport Management, 12*(1), 138–145.

McMillan, J. H., & Schumacher, S. (2006). *Research in education; Evidence-based inquiry* (6th ed.). Boston, MA: Allyn and Bacon.

Neuman, W. L. (2003). *Social research methods: Qualitative and quantitative approaches* (5th ed.). Boston, MA: Allyn and Bacon.

Quarterman, J., Jackson, E. N., Kim, K., Yoo, E., Koo, G. Y., Prugger, B., & Han, K. (2006). Statistical data analysis techniques employed in the *Journal of Sport Management* January 1987 to October 2004. *International Journal of Sport Management, 7*(1), 13–30.

Quarterman, J., Pitts, B. G., Jackson, E. N., Kim, K., & Kim, J. (2005). Statistical data analysis techniques employed in the *Sport Marketing Quarterly* January 1982 to October 2004. *Sport Marketing Quarterly, 14*(1), 158–167.

Salkind, N. J. (2000). *Exploring research* (4th ed.). Upper Saddle River, NJ: Prentice Hall Inc.

Shiffler, R. E., & Adams, A. J. (2003). *Introductory business statistics with microcomputer applications*. Boston, MA: PWS-Kent Publishing Company.

Triola, M. F., & Franklin, L. A. (1994). *Business statistics*. Reading, MA: Addison-Wesley Publishing Co.

Wimmer, R. D., & Dominick, J. R. (2000). *Mass media research: An introduction* (6th ed.). Wadsworth Publishing Company: Belmont, CA.

CHAPTER 18
DESCRIPTIVE STATISTICS IN SPORT MANAGEMENT RESEARCH

OBJECTIVES FOR COMPLETING THIS CHAPTER ARE THAT STUDENTS WILL BE ABLE TO:

Describe the characteristics and uses of frequency polygons, histograms, bar diagrams, and be able to interpret them

Recognize distributions by their shapes and name them

Define "correlation"

Interpret correlation coefficient

Determine when Pearson and Spearman correlation procedures are to be utilized

Define measures of central tendency and dispersion

Name the three measures of central tendency and determine which one is most commonly used in sport management research

Define what is meant by the measures of variability

Explain the differences between the mean and the standard deviation

THE PURPOSE OF THIS CHAPTER is to introduce the general nature of descriptive statistical data analysis techniques and the ways in which such techniques are used to organize, describe, and summarize data. Specifically, the text introduces the techniques commonly used in the descriptive statistical data analysis, such as mean, median, and mode (measures of central tendency), range, variance, and standard deviation (measures of variability), and percentiles, percentile ranges, and quartiles (measures of relative proportions). The graphic presentations of descriptive data, including frequency polygons, histograms, bar diagrams, are also reviewed in this chapter.

Major Approaches for Presenting and Measuring Relationship of Descriptive Statistical Data

Contemporary scholars (DePoy & Gitlin, 1994; Gall, Gall, & Borg, 2003; Hunter & Brown, 1991; McMillian & Schumacher, 2004; Neuman, 2003) have identified six distinct categories of descriptive statistical data analysis techniques that are applicable to sport management research: (a) describing statistical data as frequency distributions, (b) describing statistical data by graphic presentations, (c) describing statistical data as measures of central tendency, (d) describing statistical data as measures of variability, (e) describing statistical data as measures of relative proportions, and (f) measuring statistical data by correlations.

A major reason for calculating statistics is to describe and summarize a set of data. A collection of numbers, the raw data, is not very informative, so the researcher needs to find ways of picking out and presenting the key information in a clear, concise, and comprehensible format. The following section introduces a variety of methods used to present data and to summarize data.

Describing Statistical Data by Frequency Distributions

Beginning researchers must to take time to learn how to make sense of a large amount of numerical data and learn how to formulate *frequency distributions*. A frequency distribution is used to group and display quantitative data. It is an initial way of arranging data so that we can know how often a particular score or unit of information occurs. In order to introduce the relevant ways of applying frequency tables, a demonstration of an example of a large set of data will be organized and presented in several tables and charts in the most logical and coherent manner.

Frequency distributions are usually presented as tables or graphs that present the number of times (frequency) different values of a variable occur in a group of observations or scores. Frequency distributions are used to make large groups of data more manageable by showing how often a score occurs from a set of scores (Weinbach & Grinnell, 2007; Huck, Cormier, & Bounds, 1974).

For an analysis of a large set of scores, such as those listed in Table 18-1, there is a need to organize and summarize the data within tables and graphs. The table shows the list of ungrouped data for the ages of high school girls' basketball coaches. The age obtained from each of the coaches has been recorded alphabetically. The State High School Activities Association wants to analyze the demographic characteristics of its high school girl's basketball coaches. The sample of 100 coaches was selected and the age at nearest birthday of each coach was collected from the Board of Education office. This initial list of scores for each of the coaches is referred to as raw data.

As currently listed in the Table 18-1, it is difficult to determine and summarize the raw data as collected. How would you go about extracting meaningful information from the data for the Association? One simple way to gain some order is simply to list the scores in a descending or ascending order. This technique is called an *ordered array*, and the result is given in Table 18-2. When the data is sorted into an ordered array, it is easier to locate the extremes. According to the ordered array, the oldest coach is 63 and the youngest coach is 23. This information is not readily seen in the raw data in Table 18-1. Although this technique has helped us to understand how the scores were distributed, it is

TABLE 18-1
Ages of 100 Interscholastic Head Coaches of Female Basketball Teams

39	37	32	52	46	35	25	28	33	33
30	63	23	30	29	26	29	41	40	32
58	26	24	55	51	28	28	40	44	38
35	25	42	34	29	43	41	31	30	36
43	34	35	37	33	38	34	34	33	34
32	32	30	31	25	49	31	26	33	36
43	25	27	35	53	25	38	33	37	33
23	51	57	23	26	36	39	31	35	34
34	51	40	50	35	45	28	36	32	39
26	48	27	45	45	25	25	30	36	60

still quite cumbersome because of the number of scores. Therefore, there is still a need for the data to be further consolidated. The most common way to consolidate the data is to create a frequency distribution table.

A frequency distribution table refers to a summary table in which the data are arranged into conveniently established numerical ordered class groupings or categories (Levine, Berensen, & Stephan, 1999). The ordered array of data (Table 18-2) of the ages for the 100 interscholastic head coaches can be used to illustrate the construction of a frequency distribution table. To construct a frequency distribution table, a four-step process is recommended (Daniel & Terrell, 1995; Groebner, Shannon, Fry, & Smith, 2007):

Step 1: Determine the number of groups or classes. There is no binding rule for grouping the number of class intervals. However, according to a rule of thumb, a frequency distribution table should have at least five class intervals and no more than 15. When selecting the number of intervals, the researcher must consider two things: First, the effects of having too few intervals will result in the loss of too much specific and detail information about the scores. Second, the effects of having too many class intervals would not allow for condensing the original data enough to make clear the information they contain. In this example, nine classes were formulated.

Step 2: Establish the width of each class grouping (class intervals). When determining the width of

TABLE 18-2
An Ordered Array of Ages of 100 Interscholastic Head Coaches of Female Basketball Teams

63	50	43	38	36	34	33	30	28	25
60	49	42	38	35	34	32	30	28	25
58	48	41	38	35	34	32	30	27	25
57	46	41	37	35	34	32	30	27	25
55	45	40	37	35	33	32	30	26	25
53	45	40	37	35	33	32	29	26	25
52	45	40	36	35	33	31	29	26	24
51	44	39	36	34	33	31	29	26	23
51	43	39	36	34	33	31	28	26	23
51	43	39	36	34	33	31	28	25	23

TABLE 18-3 Frequency Distribution for the Ages of 100 Interscholastic Head Basketball Coaches of Female Teams		
Age Intervals	Tally	Frequency
20–24	1111	4
25–29	1111111111111111111	21
30–34	1111111111111111111111111111	28
35–39	11111111111111111111	20
40–44	1111111111	10
45–49	111111	6
50–54	111111	6
55–59	111	3
60–64	11	2

the class intervals, the researcher should bear in mind that the primary purpose of the interval is to make the data relevant and meaningful to the reader. Given the class width equation of:

$$W = \frac{\text{Largest value–Smallest value}}{\text{Number of classes}}$$

In applying this formula for the 100 coaches, we discover that the highest number is 63 and the lowest one is 23. Since there are nine classes, we then could construct nine classes that included five years each.

Step 3: Determine the class boundaries for each class interval. The class boundary refers to the lower and upper values of each class interval. Class boundaries for the first interval begin with 20 and end with 24; for the last interval, they begin with 60 and end with 64.

Step 4: Count the number of values in each of the class intervals. From the ordered array in Table 18-2, or the raw data in Table 18-1, at this point we count the number of coaches in each class. The results are shown in Table 18-3.

Shown in Table 18-3 is a frequency table that uses the data already presented in Table 18-2. When observing the frequency table, one can get a better feel for the distribution of the ages of the coaches.

Describing Data by Graphic Presentations

Graphic presentations are unique ways of providing a picture of the differences that exist in the statistical data being presented. At times it may be difficult to

conceive the overall meaning of frequency distribution tables; however, a picture can better communicate the overall meaning of the data being presented. It is important for beginners in research methods to understand the concepts of frequency graphic methods used for describing statistics in condensed forms. Typically, bar graphs, histograms, frequency polygons, and pie charts are the four types of graphic methods frequently used by researchers (Shao, 2002; Cozby, 2001). Histograms are simply extensions of the frequency distributions previously discussed and are used with continuous rather than categorical data, that is, usually they are used with interval and ratio-type data.

Bar Graph (also known as a bar chart). A bar graph is used to give visual presentation of data when the scale of measurement is nominal. Bar graphs (which use horizontal or vertical rectangles) are often used to display categorical data where there is no emphasis on the percentage of a total represented by each category. The scale of measurement is nominal or ordinal (Aczel, 1995). The units of measure for the bar graphs are arranged from lowest to highest. The bar graph differs from the histogram in that it is the height of the bar that indicates the value, not the area of the bar. Bar charts or graphs are used for discrete variables. They can have either a vertical or horizontal orientation with a small space between the bars. As shown in Figure 18-1 and Figure 18-2, the traditional form

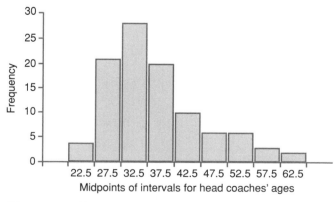

FIGURE 18-1. Example of Bar Chart

of a bar graph is a series of disjointed or separated rectangles; each rectangle represents a category of a qualitative variable, and the height of each rectangle corresponds to the frequency of such category. There is a distinct bar for each piece of information (Cozby, 1997).

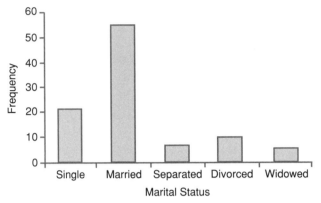

FIGURE 18-2. Example of Bar Chart

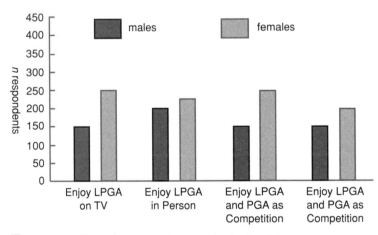

FIGURE 18-3. Spectator interest in the LPGA

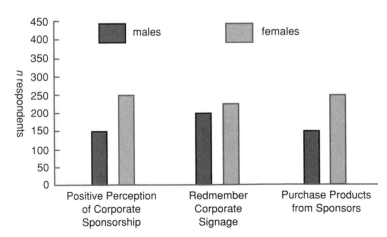

FIGURE 18-4. Perceptions of LPGA Corporate Sponsors

The choice of using a vertical or horizontal bar graph is one of aesthetics.

Dixon (2002) examined gender differences in perceptions and attitudes toward the Ladies Professional Golf Association (LPGA) and its tour professionals. As presented in Figure 18-3 and Figure 18-4, she used a bar graph to summarize the perceptions of the LPGA corporate sponsors between males and females.

Histogram. A histogram is a graphical display of ordinal data on ordinal, interval, or ratio scales of measurement (Aczel, 1995). Unlike in a bar graph, the bars in a histogram touch each other. When analyzing ordinal data, the bars of a histogram are all equal in width; however, when analyzing interval or ratio measurements, the bars may or may not be of the same width. When grouped frequencies of unequal intervals are displayed, the bars must be constructed to show the different widths to correspond to the different sizes of the intervals. Histograms are simply extensions of the frequency distributions previously discussed. Like the frequency distributions, they can be used to analyze categorical (ordinal) data; unlike frequency distributions, they can be used with continuous (interval and ratio-type) data (Aczel, 1995).

Frequency Polygon. The frequency polygon refers to a type of line graph that shows frequency distributions. It can be created with interval or ratio data (Aczel, 1995; Cozby, 1997). Using this procedure, the bars in a histogram are removed and a line is used to represent the frequencies (known as a line graph). The line is drawn at each end of the distribution of scores or values to connect it to the horizontal axis. Figure 18-5 is an illustration of a frequency polygon.

Pie Chart. A pie chart consists of a circle representing the total data, or 100%, with each slice of "pie" being proportional to the percentage in a particular category. Thus, a pie chart can convey the infor-

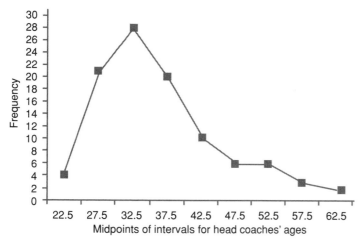

FIGURE 18-5. Frequency polygon with ends of polygon open

mation in a table at a glance. Pie charts are useful for displaying nominal scale information. It is recognized as the most illustrative way for displaying quantities as percentages of a given total (Aczel, 1995). Usually the raw frequencies are converted into percentages. Pie charts are useful as long as they are clearly labeled and limited to an easily readable number of slices (Shao, 2002). Figure 18-6 shows the applications of a pie chart.

Describing Data by Measures of Central Tendency

The measures of central tendency refer to a numerical index of the average score of a distribution of scores. Such measures describe the center of distribution of data, denoting where most of the subjects lie. The most common measures of central tendency include the mean, median, and mode. The measures of central tendency assist in condensing a large set of scores to a single numerical index for the mean, median, or the mode. Of the three measures, the mean is most commonly known to the lay person and is the most preferred measure of central tendency because it includes all of the scores. However, when there are extreme scores in the set of scores, the mean score will be affected. The median would be reported in this case, because it is not affected by extreme scores.

Mean. The mean is the most familiar and useful measure used to describe the central tendency or average of a distribution of scores for any set of data. It is calculated by adding the values of all scores in a dataset and then dividing that sum by the number of scores in the set. This provides the average score of all the data. Consider the following numerical values each of the per-team payout for each of the seventeen 2005–06 football bowl games. The mean is the measure of central tendency closest to the everyday meaning of the term. The mean of the per-team payout is $3,331,411 and is calculated by adding all of the figures together and dividing by the number of figures. If a researcher were to rely on the mean alone in a report of the per-team payouts, the readers would be misled, since there was no mention of the wide range of payouts ($750,000 to $14,500,000). The mean is distorted

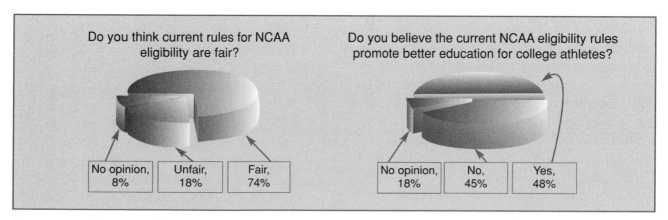

FIGURE 18-6. Sample Pie Charts

when there are extreme total values at either the high or low end of a scale: it is more accurate when the extremes are not widely separated.

Median. The median is the number that lies at the mid-point of the distribution of scores and divides the distribution of scores into two equal halves. Medians are the most representative measurement for ordinal data and skewed distributions. It is often referred to as the 50th percentile because it is the score that divides the group of scores in half (50% of the scores are below the median and 50% of the scores are above the median). Placing the scores in order is a more manageable way to locate median. For an odd number of scores, the median is the middle score in the set of scores; for an even number of scores, the median is the mean of the two middle scores. Unlike the mean, the median is not distorted by extreme values. When presented in a journal article, median is usually illustrated by the word itself or by the symbol *Mdn*.

Mode. The mode is the most frequently occurring score(s) in a distribution of scores. It is the simplest measure of variability. Unlike the mean and median, it is not calculated. It is the quickest method of calculating the measure of central tendency when appropriate. There may be no mode if none of the scores appear more often than any other. There may also be bimodal (having two modes), trimodal (having three modes), or multimodal (having four or more modes).

Sport management researchers frequently use these three measures of central tendency to report their data. Armstrong-Doherty (1995) used the mean, standard deviation, median, and range to describe the profile of funding practices in Canadian interuniversity athletics and to examine any changes from previous reports, particularly in light of recent financial constraints.

Pitts and Ayers (2001) conducted an analysis of visitor spending in Amsterdam from the Gay Games V: 1998. They used the median to describe the average daily spending in U.S. dollars per visitor and to describe the total spending by visiting participants and visiting spectators.

Describing Data by Measures of Variability

The measures of central tendency describe the middle or central characteristics of a distribution of a set of data. Unlike the measures of central tendency, the measures of variability characterize the amount of spread in a distribution of scores. The three most common measures of variability include the range, variance, and standard deviation.

Range. The range of a set of scores is the difference between the highest and lowest scores in a distribution of scores. It is the simplest measure of variability. It is the least complicated because it is a measure of scatter. When presented in a journal article, it is usually illustrated by the word itself or by the symbol *R*. Parks and Bartley (1996) utilized range to examine "gender and salary ranges of the sport management professoriate" (p.126; also see Table 5).

Variance. The variance is one of several measures of variability used to describe the dispersion among the measures in a given population. It is equal to the square of the standard deviation. In other words, to determine the variance, one must first calculate the mean of the scores, measure the amount that each score deviates from the mean, and then square that deviation. The variance is the arithmetic average of the squared differences between the values and the mean in the data collected.

Standard deviation. The standard deviation indicates the average by which scores deviate from the mean. It is commonly symbolized as *SD* or *s* or *o*, or by writing out the word "sigma." The *SD* is the most frequently used measure of variability in sport management. Standard deviation is the measure of spread most commonly used in statistical practice when the mean is used to calculate central tendency. Thus, it measures spread around the mean. Because of its close links with the mean, standard deviation can be greatly affected if the mean gives a poor measure of central tendency. Here is an example illustrating the use of standard deviation in sport management research. Baird (2004) calculated the number of standard deviations each team's record is over .500 to investigate "the relationship between player compensation in college football and competitive balance on the field" (p. 217).

Describing Data by Measures of Relative Proportions

The measures of relative proportions describe the spread of scores based on relative positions. Percentiles, percentile ranges, and quartiles are the most common ways to spread scores that measure relative positions of such scores in a sample of data. The measures of relative proportions are rarely found in sport management research.

Percentile. A percentile is the score of a set of data that divide the frequency into hundredths or 100 equal parts. Percentile is a descriptive statistic that is used to tell the relative position of a given score in a distribution of scores. For example, if a student's test score was at the 80th percentile in a class, it means that 80% of the other students in the class had lower scores, or 20% of the students had higher scores. The study conducted by Colyer (2000) is an example from the sport management literature that shows the application of this type of measure of relative proportion. In the study, the researcher investigated the organizational culture of a selected group of state sport organizations in Western Australia. The results were presented with the use of percentile scores to compare a gender ratio of sport employees and volunteers in the sport organizations.

Percentile range. Percentile range is a descriptive statistic that is used to describe the interquartile range (IQR) of values extending from 25th to 75th percentile. The 50th percentile means a median. The 1st quartile is middle value of all scores below median and the 3rd quartile is some distance above mean. IQR is a vital statistic in determining consensus because the median was used as the measurement of central tendency. The IQR is a logical choice to determine consensus. The IQR can be statistically calculated by determining the difference between the 75th and 25th percentiles.

Drain and Ashley (2000) utilized interquartile range (IQR) to determine the degree of consensus for each critical issue facing intercollegiate athletics at the NCAA Division I-A level in the following 15 years that may lead to reforms in intercollegiate athletics. The Delphi Technique was used to derive the consensus of the panel.

The IQR was a vital statistic in determining consensus. Because the media was used as the measurement of central tendency, the IQR was a logical choice to determine consensus. The IQR can be calculated by determining the difference between the 75th and the 25th percentiles. It was deemed that an IQR score of one or less would show consensus, meaning that at the minimum, 50% of the answers were within one point of each other (Drain & Ashley, 2000, p.80).

The results showed that the 13 Division I-A athletic directors who participated in the panel forecasted 31 critical issues facing Division I-A athletics in the next 15 years. "These 31 issues fell into eight broad categories: funding issues, NCAA, bowl games versus play-offs, amateurism, academics, gender equity, facilities, and student-athlete issues" (p. 80).

Measuring Relationships of Data by Correlational Statistical Techniques

It is important for students to understand tools and techniques used to measure relationships. First, it must be understood that the word "correlation" is also used as a synonym for "relationship" and "association." Unlike descriptive research, correlational statistical techniques are used to measure relationships between two variables. As explained in the beginning of this chapter, descriptive statistical techniques are used for describing, organizing, condensing, summarizing, and displaying numerical data for a population or a sample. A correlation is a numerical measure of strength of the relationship between two or more things. Researchers use correlation to determine how two variables are similar or distinct. For example, the researcher may use this technique to determine how related are years of work experience and organizational trust or loyalty among a group of workers in organizations of the sport industry. Researchers can also use the techniques to determine how well one variable can be used to predict the other variable (for instance, using grade point averages and scores of standardized examinations such the Graduate Record Examination (GRE) and Miller Analogy Exam to predict how successful a candidate will be in completing the academic requirements for earning a graduate degree in a sport management program).

A positive correlation means that high values of one variable are associated with high values of the other, and that low values of one variable are associated with low values of the other. A positive correlation exhibits a direct relationship between two variables. For example, if we measured the GRE scores of students entering a master's degree in sport management and found that the students graduating from the program with the highest grade point averages (GPAs) also had the higher GRE scores when entering the program, this would lead us to believe there is a positive correlation between high GRE scores and high GPAs for this group of students. This would illustrate a systematic direct relationship between the two sets of variables.

In contrast, a negative correlation exhibits an inverse relationship between two variables. Considering the same example, if students entering the program with high GRE scores in fact graduated with lower GPAs, this would illustrate a systematic negative correlation since high values of one set of variables (high GRE scores) paired with the other set of variables (low GPAs upon graduation). Zero correlation occurs when no systematic relationship exists between the two sets of variables (Cozby, 2001; Salkind 1999). If there is no relationship between two variables, then they are uncorrelated. For example, shoe sizes and IQ scores are probably uncorrelated.

Correlation Coefficients

A correlation coefficient is often used to show the degree of relationship. It is a statistical measure of the strength and direction of the relationship or associations that exist between two variables. Unlike the measures of central tendency, variability, and relative proportions, correlation coefficient is used to explore relationships between two variables. Correlation coefficient tells us (a) how strongly related the two variables are, and (b) the direction (positive or negative) of the relationship. There are three types of relationships interpreted by correlation: positive correlations; negative correlations; and zero or no correlations (Huck, Cormier, & Bounds, 1974).

Correlation coefficient is expressed as a decimal fraction that is preceded by either a plus (+) or minus (-) sign. The degree of the relationships range along a continuum and is usually illustrated by three types of patterns. The patterns usually range between +1.00 (as positive correlation) through 0.0 (for no relationship) to -1.00 (as negative correlation). Very few variables are perfectly related to each other and, therefore, most correlation coefficients are not +1.00 or -1.00, but have more moderate values, such as +.70 and -.41. However, the closer the correlation coefficient is to +1.00 or -1.00, the stronger the correlation. The closer the coefficient is to zero, the lower or weaker the correlation (Huck, Cormier, & Bounds, 1974). Shown in Figure 18-7 are five graphs representing hypothetical correlation coefficients

Interpretation of Correlation Coefficients in Sport Management Research

No universally accepted correlation values have been established by researchers; therefore, several schemes have been proposed. The terminology for describing strength of the relationship varies by author and across different research investigations. The following represents the most common descriptors for interpreting relationships in sport management research.

0.00–0.24 extremely low relationship
0.25–0.49 low relationship
0.50–0.69 moderate relationship
0.70–0.89 high relationship
0.90–1.00 extremely high relationship

There is no simple answer to how high the reliability of a research instrument should be. According to Nunnally (1967) and Nunnally and Bernstein (1994), the judgment of how high the reliability should be is based on the type of variable being measured and the

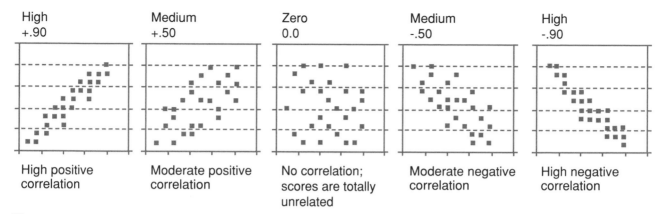

High +.90	Medium +.50	Zero 0.0	Medium -.50	High -.90
High positive correlation	Moderate positive correlation	No correlation; scores are totally unrelated	Moderate negative correlation	High negative correlation

FIGURE 18-7. Five graphs representing hypothetical correlation coefficient

stage of the development on the research instrument. A value of r of 0.8 is a high correlation. However, in order to state with confidence that there is a positive association between two sets of data, researchers need to refer to a statistical probability table that tells them whether the correlation has statistical significance at a defined confidence level. The level of confidence will depend on the size on the sample used.

Statistical Techniques for Determining Correlations

The two most common statistical techniques for determining relationships of variables are the Pearson product-moment correlation and Spearman's rho.

The Pearson product-moment correlation. The Pearson product-moment correlation refers to a parametric statistical test using continuous data to analysis the strength and nature of a relationship between two variables. It is the parametric equivalent of the Spearman's rho correlation. Let us look at an example of a recent study in sport management research to illustrate the use of the Pearson product-moment correlation. Branvold, Pan, and Gabert (1997) examined the effects of winning percentage and market size on attendance in Minor League Baseball (MiLB). The data were examined using correlation and hierarchical multiple regression procedures for winning percentage and host city population by competition levels on season attendance for a recent five-year period. The data were collected on 142 MiLB clubs from the National Association of Professional Baseball Leagues (NAPBL).

The researchers examined the relationship between attendance and winning percentage as well as market size using correlation analysis. A significant but low relationship between attendance and winning percentage (r = 0.1041, p < 0.01) and a moderate relationship between attendance and market size (r = 0.5152, p < 0.001) were found in the overall analysis.

Spearman's rank order correlation (Rho). The Spearman's rho is the nonparametric equivalent of the Pearson product-moment correlation. It is a nonparametric statistical test used to analyze rank-ordered variables to analyze the strength and nature of a relationship between two variables. Armstrong-Doherty (1996) conducted a study to examine whether athletic departments are perceived to be controlled by the funding sources in their environment according to their relative resource dependence upon those sources. Spearman rank order calculations revealed the resource dependence-based, perceived control of the university central administration, corporate sponsors, and provincial/federal sport organizations and ministries (p < .05).

Shown in Table 18-4 is a cross-tabulation of descriptive statistical techniques used by the journals between 2000 and 2004. Seven types of descriptive statistical techniques were identified that were directly related to answering the research purposes, questions, and/or hypotheses. Of this amount, two of the techniques including percentages and frequencies each accounted for more than a fourth of the techniques. Percentage was the most dominant statis-

TABLE 18-4
A summary of descriptive statistical techniques primary to the research questions and hypotheses in *JSM*, *SMQ*, and *IJSM* by journal: 1987 to 2006

DESCRIPTIVE	Journal							
	JSM (1987–2006)		SMQ (1992–2006)		IJSM (2000–2006)		Total	
STATISTICS	N	%	N	%	N	%	N	%
Percentages	45	26.79%	54	38.57%	21	28.77%	120	31.50%
Frequency	39	23.21%	40	28.57%	22	30.14%	101	26.51%
Mean	36	21.43%	21	15.00%	15	20.55%	72	18.90%
Standard Deviation	35	20.83%	5	3.57%	12	16.44%	52	13.65%
Range	5	2.98%	5	3.57%	2	2.74%	12	3.15%
Ranking	4	2.38%	10	7.14%	0	0.00%	14	3.67%
Mode	0	0.00%	2	1.43%	0	0.00%	2	0.52%
Median	4	2.38%	3	2.14%	1	1.37%	8	2.10%
Column Total	168	100%	140	100%	73	100%	381	100%

Note: More than one statistical technique was used in some articles.
Source: Quarterman, J., Pitts, B., Jackson, N., Han, K., Haung, J., & Ahn, T. (2007). Statistical data analysis techniques employed in the *Journal of Sport Management, Sport Marketing Quarterly, & International Journal of Sport Management:* 1987 to 2006. Unpublished manuscript.

tical technique to emerge, accounting for 28.37% of the techniques, followed by frequencies (26.96%) and the means (21.99%) used in the three journals. The range, ranking, and median were the least used descriptive techniques; however, the mode was not used by any of the researchers during this time period.

SUMMARY

This chapter explains the techniques that are essential for understanding descriptive statistical data analysis techniques. Statistics are a body of rules, procedures, and standards directed to extract units of information from a set of numerical data.

Descriptive statistics are used to analyze data for descriptions about existing demographic variables such as age, sex, marital status, ethnicity, income, occupation, and religious status. The measures of central tendency, including mean, median, and mode, refer to a numerical index of the average score of a distribution of scores. Unlike the measures of central tendency, the measures of variability indicate a degree of dispersion or spread of a set of data. The three most common measures of variability are range, variance, and standard deviation. The measures of relative proportions describe the spread of scores based on relative positions.

The measures of relationships use coefficient of correlation to explore relationships between two or more variables. Two of the most common statistical techniques for determining relationships of variables in sport management research have been the Pearson product-moment correlation and Spearman's rho.

Charts in different forms are used for condensing and displaying statistical data in sport management research. Five of the most common charts used for describing statistics in graphical condensed forms are (1) pie charts, (2) bar graphs. (3), histograms (4), frequency polygons, and (5) picture grams.

STUDY QUESTIONS

1. Explain how to use frequency polygons, histograms, and bar diagrams, and interpret each of them.
2. Describe distributions by their shapes and name them.
3. Define measures of central tendency and dispersion.
4. What are the three measures of central tendency? Which one is most commonly used in sport management research?
5. What do the measures of variability mean?
6. What are the differences between the mean and the standard deviation?
7. Define correlation and interpret correlation coefficient.
8. Under what circumstances can the Pearson and Spearman correlation procedures be utilized?

LEARNING ACTIVITIES

1. Shown in the following table are the salaries of head football coaches of NCAA Division IA member institutions (*USA Today* [2006, November 16]). Construct a frequency table for this data using the procedures outlined in this chapter.

Compensation for NCAA Division I-A head football coaches (2006)

Coach	Total	Coach	Total	Coach	Total
F. DeBerry	755,370	K. Ferentz	2,840,000	J. Paterno	NA
J. Brookhart	207,500	D. McCarney	1,107,000	D. Wannstedt	NA
M. Shula	1,766,853	M. Mangino	1,501,241	J. Tiller	1,364,785
W. Brown	371,500	R. Prince	750,000	T. Graham	NA
M. Stoops	865,000	D. Martin	150,200	G. Schiano	911,000
D. Koetter	991,000	R. Brooks	729,165	C. Long	701,500
H. Nutt	1,049,644	L. Miles	1,450,000	D. Tomey	342,100
S. Roberts	189,655	J. Bicknell III	208,500	S. Spurrier	1,300,000
B. Ross	NA	R. Bustle	194,250	J. Leavitt	1,117,500
T. Tuberville	2,231,000	C. Weatherbie	130,000	P. Carroll	2,782,320
B. Hoke	159,220	B. Petrino	1,743,000	P. Bennett	495,602
G. Morriss	1,144,236	M. Snyder	390,603	J. Bower	349,983
C. Petersen	511,800	R. Friedgen	1,691,864	W. Harris	NA
T. O'Brien	733,626	T. West	925,000	G. Robinson	638,441
G. Brandon	150,000	L. Coker	1,800,000	A. Golden	NA

continued on next page

B. Mendenhall	NA	S. Montgomery	139,500	P. Fulmer	2,050,000
T. Gill	183,000	L. Carr	1,454,619	M. Brown	2,664,000
Jeff Tedford	1,505,300	J. Smith	1,545,834	D. Franchione	2,012,200
G. O'Leary	1,035,000	R. Stockstill	254,800	G. Patterson	952,162
B. Kelly	184,897	G. Mason	1,210,000	M. Leach	1,600,000
M. Dantonio	495,000	E. Orgeron	905,000	M. Price	543,000
T. Bowden	1,198,028	S. Croom	940,000	T. Amstutz	376,400
D. Hawkins	1,098,500	G. Pinkel	1,095,000	L. Blakeney	226,750
S. Lubick	529,900	P. Johnson	1,003,309	C. Scelfo	NA
R. Edsall	845,000	B. Callahan	1,690,317	S. Kragthorpe	438,533
T. Roof	370,200	C. Ault	360,000	K. Dorrell	881,000
S. Holtz	425,000	R. Long	431,175	M. Sanford	435,000
J. Genyk	154,442	H. Mumme	283,800	K. Whittingham	672,000
U. Meyer	1,524,550	J. Bunting	311,200	B. Guy	241,900
H. Schnellenberger	353,147	C. Amato	995,000	B. Johnson	NA
D. Strock	282,100	D. Dickey	266,625	A. Groh	1,785,000
B. Bowden	1,691,900	J. Novak	212,496	F. Beamer	2,008,000
P. Hill	1,253,982	P. Fitzgerald	NA	J. Grobe	987,843
M. Richt	1,713,000	C. Weis	NA	T. Willingham	1,414,772
C. Gailey	1,009,191	F. Solich	262,172	B. Doba	559,042
J. Jones	820,008	J. Tressel	2,012,700	R. Rodriguea	1,100,000
A. Briles	550,000	B. Stoops	3,450,000	B. Cubit	188,000
D. Erickson	214,643	M. Gundy	800,000	B. Bielerna	761,600
R. Zook	1,241,750	M. Bellotti	1,160,000	J. Glenn	505,100
T. Hoeppner	600,000	M. Riley	835,000		

Source: *USA Today* (2006, November 16). Compensation for NCAA Division I-A head football coaches. *USA Today, 25*(45), 16A.

2. Shown in the following table is information on college football bowl game per-team payout in 2006–2007. Apply the central tendency techniques (i.e., mean, median, and mode) discussed in this chapter to analyze the payouts.

Bowl	Site	Per-team payout
Poinsettia	San Diego	$750,000
Pioneer Pure Vision Las Vegas	Las Vegas	$950,000
R+L Carriers New Orleans	New Orleans	$325,000
Papajohns.com	Birmingham, Ala.	$300,000
New Mexico	Albuquerque	$750,000
Bell Helicopter Armed Forces	Fort Worth	$600,000
Sheraton Hawaii	Honolulu	$398,000

Motor City	Detroit	$750,000
Emerald	San Francisco	$850,000
Petro Sun Independence	Shreveport, La.	$1,100,000
Texas (for Big East)	Houston	$500,000
Texas (for Big 12)	Houston	$750,000
Pacific Life Holiday	San Diego	$2,200,000
Gaylord Hotels Music City	Nashville	$1,600,000
Brut Sun	El Paso	$1,900,000
AutoZone Liberty	Memphis	$1,500,000
Insight	Tempe, Ariz.	$1,200,000
Champs Sports	Orlando	$2,250,000
Meineke Car Care	Charlotte	$750,000
Alamo	San Antonio	$2,200,000
Chick-fil-A (for ACC)	Atlanta	$3,250,000
Chick-fil-A (for SEC)	Atlanta	$2,400,000
MPC Computers	Boise	$250,000
Outback	Tampa	$3,000,000
AT&T Cotton	Dallas	$3,000,000
Toyota Gator	Jacksonville	$2,250,000
Capital One	Orlando	$4,250,000
Rose	Pasadena, Calif.	$17,000,000
Tostitos Fiesta	Glendale, Ariz.	$17,000,000
FedEx Orange	Miami	$17,000,000
Allstate Sugar	New Orleans	$17,000,000
International	Toronto	$750,000
GMAC	Mobile, Ala.	$750,000
Tostitos BCS Championship	Glendale, Ariz.	$17,000,000
Total		$126,523,000

References

Aczel, A. (1995). *Statistics: Concepts and applications.* Chicago, IL: Irwin.

Armstrong-Doherty, A. (1995). The structure of funding in Canadian interuniversity athletics. *Journal of Sport Management, 9*(1), 59–69.

Baird, K. (2004). Dominance in college football and the role of scholarship restrictions. *Journal of Sport Management, 18*(3), 217–235.

Branvold, S. E., Pan, D. W., & Gabert, T. E. (1997). Effects of winning percentage and market size on attendance in minor league baseball. *Sport Marketing Quarterly, 6*(4), 35–42.

Colyer, S. (2000). Organizational culture in selected western Australian sport organizations. *Journal of Sport Management, 14*(4), 321–341.

Cozby, P. C. (1997). *Methods in behavioral research* (6th ed.). Mountain View, CA: Mayfield Publishing Company.

Cozby, P. C. (2001). *Methods in behavioral research* (8th ed.). Boston, MA: McGraw- Hill.

Daniel, W. W., & Terrell, J. C. (1995). *Business statistics: Basic concepts and methodology* (7th ed.). Boston, MA: Houghton Mifflin Company.

DePoy, E., & Gitlin, L. N. (1994). *Introduction to research: Multiple strategies for health and human services.* St. Louis, MO: Mosby-Year Book, Inc., p. 195.

Dixon, M. (2002). Gender differences in perceptions and attitudes toward the LPGA and its tour professionals: An empirical investigation. *Sport Marketing Quarterly*, *11*(1), 44–54.

Drain, T. S., & Ashley, F. B. (2000). Intercollegiate athletics: Back to the future II: A comparison with branch and crow five years later. *Sport Marketing Quarterly*, *9*(2), 77–84.

Gall, M. D., Gall, J. P., & Borg, W. R. (2003). *Educational research and introduction* (7th ed.). Boston, MA: Allyn and Bacon.

Groebner, D. F., Shannon, P. W., Fry, P. C., & Smith, K. D. (2007). *Business statistics: A decision-making approach* (7th ed.). Upper Saddle River, NJ: Prentice Hall.

Huck, S. W., Cormier, W. H., & Bounds, W. G., Jr. (1974). *Reading statistics and research*. Cherry Valley, CA: D & S Martin.

Hunter, R., & Brown, R. (1991). The application of inferential statistics with non-probability type samples. *Journal of Applied Recreation Research*, *16*(3), 234–243.

Levine, D. M., Berenson, M. L., & Stephan, D. (1999). *Statistics for managers using Microsoft Excel* (2nd ed.). Upper Saddle River, NJ: Prentice-Hall.

McMillan, J. H., & Schumacher, S. (2006). *Research in education: Evidence-based inquiry* (6th ed.). Boston, MA: Allyn and Bacon.

Neuman, W. L. (2003). *Social research methods: Qualitative and quantitative approaches* (5th ed.). Boston, MA: Allyn and Bacon.

Nunnally, J. C. (1976). *Psychometric theory*. New York: McGraw-Hill.

Nunnally, J. C., & Bernstein, I. (1994). *Psychometric theory* (3rd ed.). New York: McGraw Hill.

Parks, J. B., & Bartley, M. E. (1996). Sport management scholarship: A professoriate in transition? *Journal of Sport Management*, *10*(2), 119–130.

Pitts, B. G., & Ayers, E. K. (2001). An analysis of visitor spending and economic scale on Amsterdam from the Gay Games V, 1998. *International Journal of Sport Management*, *2*(2), 134–151.

Salkind, N. J. (2000). *Exploring research* (4th ed.). Upper Saddle River, NJ: Prentice Hall Inc.

Shao, A. T. (2002). *Marketing research: An aid to decision making* (2nd ed.). Cincinnati, OH: South-Western.

Weinbach, R., & Grinnell, R. M. (2007). *Statistics for social workers*. Boston, MA: Pearson Allyn & Bacon.

CHAPTER 19
STATISTICAL TESTING OF DIFFERENCES

OBJECTIVES FOR COMPLETING THIS
CHAPTER ARE THAT STUDENTS WILL
BE ABLE TO:

Distinguish between parametric and
nonparametric statistical techniques

Understand the circumstances under which
each of the two types of t-test can be used

Explain the differences between the two types
of analysis of variance

Explain the differences between a t-test
and an analysis of variance

List reasons for utilizing nonparametric
techniques versus parametric techniques

Identify the assumptions of the Chi square test

Explain the difference between a t-test
and a Mann-Whitney U-test

Explain the differences between an ANOVA
and a Kruskal-Wallis test

Explain the differences between a Chi square
test and a Fisher's Exact test

THE PURPOSE OF THIS CHAPTER is to provide students with an overview of the most commonly used techniques of statistical testing of differences in sport management research. The main intent is to present a conceptual rather than numerical review of inferential statistics and to describe in the most logical ways the statistical procedures that investigators use to analyze data in sport management research. As such, the numerical description of various statistical analysis procedures is purposefully omitted and deemphasized.

The nature and scope of parametric statistical techniques will first be discussed. Particularly, the t-test and the analysis of variance (ANOVA), two most commonly used parametric statistical techniques that assess differences between univariate means, will be reviewed.

In the second half of this chapter, some nonparametric statistical data analysis techniques that are used in sport management research will be discussed. Such techniques include the Chi square test, the Mann Whitney U-test, the Wilcoxon Sign Rank Test, and the Kruskal-Wallis test.

PARAMETRIC STATISTICAL TECHNIQUES

For better interpretation of parametric statistical techniques, the researcher must be cognizant that it exists as one of the major dimensions of inferential statistics. There are two major dimensions of statistical techniques within the domain of inferential statistics: parametric statistical techniques and nonparametric statistical techniques. As a dimension of inferential statistics, parametric statistical techniques are used for deriving logical conclusions about the characteristics of a population when (a) data taken from the populations are normally distributed, (b) data have equal variances on the variable(s) that is(are) being measured, and (c) the levels of measurements of the data are interval or ratio.

Ways to Subdivide Parametric Statistical Techniques

There is no one way to subdivide the categories of parametric statistical techniques. For the purpose of this book, parametric statistical techniques are divided into eight categories. Such categories are shown in Table 19-1. Table 19-2 presents a summary of the parametric statistical analysis techniques used to address research questions and prove hypotheses in sport management studies published in such publications as *Journal of Sport Management*, *Sport Marketing Quarterly* and *International Journal of Sport Management* from 1987–2006. As shown in Table 19-2, ANOVA, regression analysis, and MANOVA, t-test, and factor analysis are the five parametric statistical analysis methods used most frequently by sport management researchers.

Parametric statistics are used for making assumptions about the characteristics of a sample or population when the level of measurement of data is primarily interval or ratio. They are the most powerful tools in testing questions and hypotheses about the differences of groups or a set of values via the use of interval and ratio scales, and primarily via the use of means. More specifically, parametric techniques are used for deriving logical assumptions or conclusions about the characteristics of a population when data:

- are taken from the populations are normally distributed,
- have equal variances on the variable(s) that is being measured, and
- are interval or ratio.

Parametric techniques are credited as most powerful for testing research questions and hypotheses about the differences of groups or set of values.

Table 19-3 illustrates the use of the level of measurement to select an appropriate parametric statistical procedure for testing of differences. For example, as shown in Table 19-3, the t-test should be selected when the dependent variable is either interval or ratio in nature and is a nominal measurement, and the independent variable contains two categories.

TABLE 19-1
A summary of parametric statistical techniques

Assessing differences between univariate and multivariate means	T-tests
	Analysis of Variance (ANOVA)
	Analysis of Covariance (ANCOVA)
	Multiple Analysis of Variance (MANOVA)
	Multiple Analysis of Covariance (MANCOVA)
	Discriminant Analysis
Assessing bivariate and multivariate means of observed variables	Canonical Correlation Analysis
	Path Analysis
	Cluster Analysis
	Trend Analysis
Regression analysis techniques	Simple Regression Analysis
	Multiple Regression Analysis
	Stepwise Regression Analysis
	Logistic Regression
	Hierarchical Regression Analysis
Parametric statistical techniques to determine degree of relationship of two sets of variables	Pearson Product-Moment Correlation
	Spearman rho
Factor analysis	Exploratory Factor Analysis (EFA)
	Confirmatory Factory Analysis (CFA)
Structural equation modeling	Structural Equation Model (SEM)
Z-score	Z-score

The T-test as a Parametric Statistical Technique

The t-test (also known as the t-statistics) is a group of related parametric tests used when we want to determine the statistical significance of a difference between the means of two groups. As the t-test compares the means of two groups, the dependent variable must have the characteristics that make calculation of a mean appropriate. In other words, the t-test is used when the dependent variable is at the interval or ratio level of measurement and the independent variable has two categories.

The t-test produces a t value that is compared with a standardized table to determine whether or not it was justifiable to reject the null hypothesis. There are two different forms of the t-test for comparing group means: the t-test for independent groups or variables and the t-test for dependent groups or variables. Both forms of the t-test compare the two means of interval or ratio level data within a research sample with each other. They ask the question: "Is the mean of one sample different enough from the mean of the other sample that it would be safe to conclude that there is a statistically

TABLE 19-2

A Summary of Parametric Statistical Techniques Used by Sport Management Researchers as Reflected by the Manuscripts Published in *JSM*, *SMQ*, and *IJSM* by Journal: 1987 to 2006

| PARAMETRIC | Journal | | | | | | | |
| | JSM (1987–2006) | | SMQ (1992–2006) | | IJSM (2000–2006) | | Total | |
	N	%	N	%	N	%	N	%
ANOVA	50	21.19%	37	21.14%	26	23.21%	113	21.61%
Regression	46	19.49%	33	18.86%	21	18.75%	100	19.12%
MANOVA	32	13.56%	23	13.14%	12	10.71%	67	12.81%
T-test	28	11.86%	20	11.43%	16	14.29%	64	12.24%
Factor Analysis (EFA)	26	11.02%	12	6.86%	10	8.93%	48	9.18%
Pearson Product-Moment Correlation	14	5.93%	15	8.57%	9	8.04%	38	7.27%
Factor Analysis (CFA)	14	5.93%	17	9.71%	5	4.64%	36	6.88%
Discriminatory Analysis	5	2.19%	4	2.29%	2	1.79%	11	2.10%
Canonical Correlation	5	2.19%	0	0.00%	1	0.89%	6	1.15%
Cluster Analysis	2	0.85%	1	0.57%	0	0.00%	3	0.57%
Structural Equation Model	5	2.19%	8	4.57%	7	6.25%	20	3.82%
Fishers Z score	3	1.27%	3	1.71%	0	0.00%	6	1.15%
MANCOVA	2	0.85%	0	0.00%	3	2.68%	5	0.96%
ANCOVA	1	0.42%	1	0.57%	0	0.00%	2	0.38%
Path Analysis	1	0.42%	1	0.57%	0	0.00%	2	0.38%
Trend Analysis	1	0.42%	0	0.00%	0	0.00%	1	0.19%
Hierarchical Linear Modeling (HLM)	1	0.42%	0	0.00%	0	0.00%	1	0.19%
Column Total	236	100%	175	100%	112	100%	523	100.00%

Note: More than one statistical technique was used in some articles.
Source: Quarterman, J., Pitts, B., Jackson, N., Han, K., Haung, J., & Ahn, T. (2007). Statistical data analysis techniques employed in the *Journal of Sport Management, Sport Marketing Quarterly, & International Journal of Sport Management*: 1987 to 2006. Unpublished manuscript.

TABLE 19-3

Selection of an Appropriate Parametric Statistical Procedure to Test Differences

Parametric Statistical Procedures		
Test	**Dependent (Criterion) Variable**	**Independent (Predictor) Variable**
Independent t-test	Interval/ratio	Nominal (2 categories)
Paired t-test	Interval/ratio	(2 repeated measures)
One-way ANOVA	Interval/ratio	Nominal (3 or more categories)
Within subject one-way ANOVA	Interval/ratio	(2 or more repeated measures)
Pearson	Interval/ratio	Interval/ratio

Adapted from the work of Weinbach and Grinnell (1995)

significant difference between the two samples in relation to the dependent variable?" (Weinbach & Grinnell, 1995, p. 174).

McGehee, Yoon, and Cardenas (2003) examined relationships between recreational runners' involvement in travel to road races and behavioral characteristics. The subjects of the study were 444 members of three North Carolina running clubs. Based on the degree of sport involvement, they were divided into two groups: cluster 1 (low involvement group) and cluster 2 (high involvement group) based on nine involvement items. A number of t-tests were conducted to see if differences could be found in several dependent variables, including participation in road races, preparation for road races, travel behavior, and running-related expenditures. The study found statically significant differences between the high involvement group and low involvement group in terms of travel behavior and running-related expenditures. Also, the authors concluded that involvement should be considered by sport and tourism agencies when planning, marketing, and managing events targeted at traveling recreational runners.

Stoldt and Narasimhan (2005) examined how collegiate sports information professionals assessed their expertise levels relative to a variety of public relations tasks. They used a paired-samples t-test to test for differences in managerial and technical expertise assessments and for differences in managerial and technical task importance assessments. Three hundred thirty-nine collegiate sports information professionals participated in the study. Results indicated collegiate sport information professionals assess themselves as having significantly greater levels of expertise in technical tasks than managerial tasks. They also deem technical tasks to be significantly more important to their organization's well being than managerial tasks.

Analysis of Variance (ANOVA) as a Parametric Statistical Technique

Analysis of variance (ANOVA) is a parametric test used when the researcher wants to determine the statistical significance of a difference between the means of three or more groups. ANOVA allows researchers to investigate the mean differences of one dependent variable on three or more independent variables. When ANOVA technique is employed, the dependent variable must be at the interval or ratio level of measurement and the independent variable must be at the nominal or ordinal level of measurement with three or more categories. ANOVA tests whether several populations have the same

mean by comparing how far apart the sample means are with how much variation there is within the samples. It is an extension of the t-test, but it avoids the error inherent in performing multiple t-tests. The ANOVA are useful to researchers for detecting the differences and for testing hypotheses when the t-tests are not appropriate.

There are two forms of ANOVA used by sport management researchers for answering research questions and hypothesis testing: one-way ANOVA and two-way ANOVA. The one-way ANOVA is the more commonly used method.

One-way ANOVA. A one-way ANOVA is used to analyze one independent variable when the dependent variable has more than two categories. It is an extension of the independent t-test. An F value is computed and compared with a standardized table to determine whether or not it is justifiable to reject the null hypothesis. To use this particular statistical procedure, a number of the following assumptions must be met:

- the populations from which the samples were obtained must be normally or approximately normally distributed,
- the samples must be independent, and
- the variances of the populations must be equal.

The study conducted by Mahony and Moorman (2000) is a good illustration of how the one-way ANOVA technique can be used by sport management professionals in meeting their research needs. The two researchers applied one-way ANOVA to see if there were significant differences among the mean of strong positive and strong negative attitudes on NFL and NBA viewing intentions of a pool of undergraduate and graduate students at a large Midwestern university. The NFL sample included 161 students and the NBA sample included 157 students. The independent variables were the teams that the students reported watching and the dependent variables were the self-reported intentions made by the students regarding their preferences for watching their favorite team. The major finding revealed that the students preferred to watch their favorite team. Their secondary choice was a team they disliked if this team threatened the success of their favorite team; otherwise, they would also watch a neutral game.

Two-way ANOVA. A two-way ANOVA is used to analyze the mean differences of two independent variables. Each independent variable has more than two categories or levels. A two-way ANOVA is an extension of the independent t-test and the one-way ANOVA. In addition to the three assumptions that must be met before the one-way ANOVA can be employed, there is one additional assumption for the use of two-way ANOVA. That is, the groups must have the same sample size.

Sport management researchers use two-way ANOVA much less frequently than they use one-way ANOVA. Nevertheless, it is still worthwhile to briefly discuss this particular statistical technique. Let us use the study conducted by London and Boucher (2000) to exemplify how sport management researcher can take advantage of two-way ANOVA in their studies. The purpose of the study was to determine whether or not there was any statistically significant difference among the athletic directors in Canadian universities in terms of their use of either transformational or transactional leadership with regard to the organizational effectiveness of their respective athletic programs. The researchers utilized the two-way ANOVA technique to analyze the collected data. The results of the analysis showed that transformational leadership has significant effects on organizational effectiveness. Interestingly, no significant effect resulted from transactional leadership on athletic program organizational effectiveness.

Post Hoc Tests of Statistical Significance for ANOVA

When an ANOVA yields a significant result (i.e., a significant value for the F-ratio), additional statistical analysis is necessary. Thus, the researcher can further compare various pairs of means with the use of what is known as post hoc comparisons of means.

Post hoc comparisons (also known as multiple comparison procedures) are computed in an ANOVA by what is called the F ratio (F-test). The computed F value is compared with a standardized table to determine whether or not it was justifiable to reject the null hypothesis. A significant F indicates that at least one of the means of one or more of the three or more groups are significantly different. Because there are at least three groups of means, it is impossible to determine which means are statistically different from each other simply by visually comparing their relative magnitudes. To determine precisely the group means that are significantly different from the other group means, it is necessary to carry out a post hoc test of statistical significance. The post hoc comparisons have been developed to assist researchers to locate exactly where the significant differences lie after a significant F ratio has been obtained (Crowl, 1996). There are several commonly used post hoc tests that can be used to locate the significant differences:

- Fisher LSD
- Newman-Keulis test
- Scheffe's test
- Tukey's test

Among these post hoc tests, Sheffe's test and Tukey's test are the most stringent methods but least likely to make a Type I error. Fisher LSD is at the other end of the spectrum but most powerful in calling the comparison groups statistically significant different.

Z-test

Z-test is used to express a score in terms of its distance from the mean and in terms of the normal curve. It is calculated by subtracting the mean score and dividing by standard deviation of that distribution of scores. A z-score is a standard score frequently used in educational research that is derived from standard deviation units. Also, z-scores are continuous and have equality units. Thus, a person's relative standing on two or more measurements can be compared by converting the raw scores to z-scores. The z-distribution is used when samples are large and is used to determine the level of statistical significance of an observed difference between the groups (Gall, Gall, & Borg, & Gall, 2003; Huck, 2000).

NONPARAMETRIC STATISTICAL TECHNIQUES

Unlike parametric statistics, nonparametric statistics are used for deriving conclusions about the characteristics of a sample when the level of measurement of data is primarily nominal or ordinal. Nonparametric statistics do not make assumptions about the population (Gall, Gall, & Borg, 2003; Hollander & Wolf, 1999; Leedy & Ormrod, 2001; McMillan & Schumacher, 2001; Neuman, 2003). Nonparametric statistics have been recognized as the most powerful in testing questions and hypotheses about relationships and associations of groups or sets of values, via the use of nominal or ordinal measurement scales, and primarily via the use of frequencies, percentages, and proportions.

Common Nonparametric Statistical Techniques

Table 19-4 is a list of the nonparametric statistical procedures that sport management researchers may use. Presented in Table 19-5 is a summary of the nonparametric statistical analysis techniques used to address research questions and prove hypotheses in sport management studies published in such publications as *Journal of Sport Management*, *Sport Marketing Quarterly* and *International Journal of*

Sport Management from 1987–2006. As shown in Table 19-5, Chi square overwhelmingly is the most frequently used nonparametric statistical method by sport management researchers.

Table 19-6 illustrates the use of the level of measurement to select an appropriate nonparametric statistical procedure for testing of differences. For example, to properly use the χ^2 test, both the independent and dependent variables must be nominal in nature with two or more categories. In the use of the Mann-Whitney U-test, the dependent variable needs to be ordinal data, and the independent variable is a nominal measurement.

When the data take the form of categories (male vs. female, undergraduate vs. graduate), ordinal groups (mild vs. moderate vs. severe), or rankings (academic standing in one's class), nonparametric statistics will be needed. It is also appropriate to use nonparametric statistics when numerical data are not normally distributed. Among the more popular parametric tests are the χ^2 test, which is used with categorical or ordinal data, and the Mann-Whitney U-test, which is used when the data are rankings.

Chi square (χ^2) as a Nonparametric Statistical Technique

The χ^2 test is used to test the differences in proportion in two or more independent groups of which the levels of measurement for independent variable is the nominal level. It determines whether the two variables being examined are independent or related

TABLE 19-4 Common nonparametric statistical data analysis techniques	
Nonparametric statistical data analysis techniques	Chi Square
	Spearman-Rank Order Correlation
	Mann-Whitney U
	Kruskal-Wallis One-Way ANOVA
	Fisher's Exact Test
	Wilcoxon's Sign Ranked Test
	Conjoint Analysis
	Friedman's Two-Way ANOVA by Rank
	Kendall's Tau

TABLE 19-5
A Summary of Nonparametric Statistical Techniques Used by Sport Management Researchers as Reflected by the Manuscripts Published in *JSM*, *SMQ*, and *IJSM* by Journal: 1987 to 2006

Nonparametric statistical techniques	JSM (1987–2006)		SMQ (1992–2006)		IJSM (2000–2006)		Total	
	N	%	N	%	N	%	N	%
Chi Square	37	77.08%	31	79.49%	13	81.25%	81	78.64%
Mann-Whitney	1	2.08%	2	5.13%	1	6.25%	4	3.88%
Kruskal-Wallis	2	4.17%	1	2.56%	1	6.25%	4	3.88%
Spearman Rank Correlation	8	16.67%	0	0.00%	0	0.00%	8	7.77%
Fisher's Exact Test	0	0.00%	1	2.56%	0	0.00%	1	0.97%
Wilcoxon Signed Rank Test	0	0.00%	2	5.13%	0	0.00%	2	1.94%
Conjoint Analysis	0	0.00%	2	5.13%	1	6.25%	3	2.91%
Column Total	48	100%	39	100%	16	100%	103	100%

Note: more than one statistical technique was used in some articles.
Source: Quarterman, J., Pitts, B., Jackson, N., Han, K., Haung, J., & Ahn, T. (2007). Statistical data analysis techniques employed in the *Journal of Sport Management, Sport Marketing Quarterly, & International Journal of Sport Management:* 1987 to 2006. Unpublished manuscript.

TABLE 19-6
Selection of an Appropriate Nonparametric Statistical Procedure to Test Differences

Nonparametric Statistical Tests		
Test	**Dependent (Criterion) Variable**	**Independent (Predictor) Variable**
Chi square test	Nominal (2 or more categories)	Nominal (2 or more categories)
Fisher's exact test	Nominal (2 categories)	Nominal (2 categories)
McNemar's test	Nominal (2 categories)	(2 repeated measures)
Mann-Whitney U test	Ordinal	Nominal (2 categories)
Wilcoxon Sign test	Ordinal	(2 repeated measures)
Kruskal-Wallis test	Ordinal	Nominal (3 or more categories)
Friedman's test	Ordinal	(2 or more repeated measures)
Spearman rho test	Ordinal	Ordinal
Kendall's tau test	Ordinal	Ordinal

Adapted from the work of Weinbach and Grinnell (1995).

and whether the difference in frequencies of observed data exists with the comparison of the frequencies that could be expected to occur if the data categories were actually independent of each other.

The P^2 test is the most popular nonparametric statistical test. It requires only nominal level data which means the values for each variable need only represent distinct categories and a difference of kind. In other words, the P^2 test is commonly used to analyze nominal (categorical) data among groups. It is computed by summing differences between the observed frequencies in each cell and the expected frequencies—the frequencies that would be expected if there were no relationship between the two variables.

The formula for computing the P^2 is based on the comparison of the observed frequencies and the expected or theoretical frequencies. For example, suppose a master's program in sport management had two concentrations: event management and fitness management. Of the 200 enrolled students, 120 (60%) chose event management, and 80 (40%) chose fitness management. A question that might be addressed would be whether the sex of the student is related to the choice of specialty area. See Figure 19-1 for a breakdown of enrollment by gender. The percentages are in parentheses. The null hypothesis would be that there is no difference between males and females in relation to choice of a specialty area. Then the expectation would be that the frequencies would be the same for males and females. In this case, because 120 or 60% of the entire sample selected event management, we would expect that approximately 60% of the females and 60% of the males would select event management. Instead we see that 56% of the females and 75% of the males choose event management. Obviously, proportionately fewer males chose fitness management than did females. What P^2 does is to test whether or not the difference is statistically significant. It compares the numbers we have observed with the numbers we would expect if the two groups were equal. For this example, the P^2 value is significant at the 0.05 level. That is, there are fewer than five chances in 100 that a difference as great as this would have occurred by chance alone.

Let us use two examples in sport management to illustrate the use of this type of nonparametric statistics. Li and Burden (2002) applied the P^2 test when they examined the current status of marketing operations outsourcing in collegiate athletics. They used the P^2 test to determine whether or not there was some difference between each of the areas of out-sourcing and the football designations, and whether or not the difference was statistically significant. One-hundred twenty seven athletic directors from Division I-A and Division I-AA athletic programs participated in the study. The results of the study indicated that more than half of Division I athletic programs have been exercising the outsourcing option partially or entirely. Results of the study also showed that 11 out of the sixteen areas of marketing operations that could be possibly outsourced, a significant difference was observed. They believed these were the areas where athletic programs in Division I-A usually placed more of their marketing efforts. Also, those are the areas where Division I-A programs generate most of the revenues. On the other hand, athletic programs in Division I-AA were not engaged in those areas as intensively as their counterparts in Division I-A due to the size of their marketing staff. Thus, outsourcing was not a logical option for most of the athletic programs at this level because of the degree of utilization of those areas.

Robinson and Carpenter (2002) conducted a study to determine if the day of the week impacted select socio-demographic characteristics and consumption patterns of spectators attending a Ladies Professional Golf Association (LPGA) event. A P^2 test was utilized to determine if statistically significant differences existed on the days attended using the variables of spectator's gender, age, income, employment status, how they acquired their tickets, and frequency of play. Significant differences did exist for variables of age [P^2 (33) = 60.04, p = .003]. The "(33)" means the test had 33 degree of freedom. The "60.04" is the value of the test statistic. The test

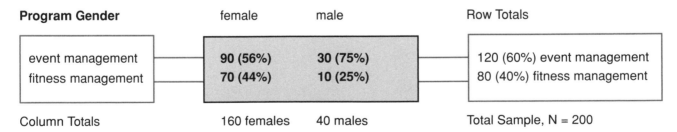

Program Gender	female	male	Row Totals
event management	90 (56%)	30 (75%)	120 (60%) event management
fitness management	70 (44%)	10 (25%)	80 (40%) fitness management
Column Totals	160 females	40 males	Total Sample, N = 200

A statistical interpretation of the Chi square (χ^2) test
χ^2 = 60.04; p = .003

FIGURE 19-1
A Fictitious Specialty of Sport Management Programs by Gender of Student

statistic represents the ratio of differences between the groups to measurement error. The "*p*" refers to the probability of making a Type I error, or the probability that the result occurred by chance. The ".003" means that the probability of a Type I error was less than .03%.

Mann-Whitney U-test as a Nonparametric Statistical Technique

The Mann-Whitney U-test uses ordinal data (ranks) to determine whether two independent samples come from the same distribution. It is a distribution-free test for statistical significance and does not utilize means, medians, modes, or standard deviations in the computation of the U-value.

To perform the Mann-Whitney U-test, the basic requirement is that the two samples be independent, and that the observations be ordinal or continuous measurements. It is one of the best-known nonparametric significance tests. The Mann-Whitney U-test is analogous to the parametric independent t-test. It is often presented as an alternative to a t-test when the data are not normally distributed. In general, the Mann-Whitney U-test technique is used when these three conditions are met: (a) when the researchers want to avoid the assumptions of the t-test, (b) when random selection has not occurred, and (c) when the measurement variables generate categorical or ordinal data and when the sample sizes are small (Huck, Cormier, & Bounds, 1974; Witte, 1985).

Shown in Table 19-7 is an illustration of the Mann-Whitney U-test to measure motivational congruency and discrepancy between certified athletic trainers and noncertified student athletic trainers in the state of Hawaii (Buxton, Lankford, & Noda, 1992). The technique was used to determine differences between the two groups of trainers in ranking 16 motivational statements. Because this was research that used rank order data, the Mann-Whitney U-test is the appropriate statistical measure (Huck, Cormier, & Bounds, 1974; Weinbach & Grunnell, 1995).

As illustrated in the Table 19-7, significant differences (p < .05) were found in the hierarchical rankings of the motivational statements between the two groups of trainers. The noncertified student athletic trainers ranked job growth (item G) as their

	Certified Athletic Trainers (I) (N = 20)	Noncertified Athletic Trainers (II) (N = 16)
TABLE 19-7 Example of the Mann-Whitney U-test		
Motivational Statement		
A. Designated as a leader	3.50 (± 0.76)	3.19 (± 0.83)
B. Importance of work	4.90 (± 0.31)	4.75 (± 0.45)
C. Freedom on the job	4.50 (± 0.61)	3.75 (± 0.86) *
D. Achieving work-related goals	4.70 (± 0.47)	4.44 (± 0.51)
E. Getting along with others	4.70 (± 0.57)	4.81 (± 0.40)
F. Opportunities for advancement	4.55 (± 0.61)	4.00 (± 0.82) *
G. Job growth	4.85 (± 0.37)	5.00 (± 0.00)
H. Good work condition	4.50 (± 0.51)	4.44 (± 0.51)
I. Good benefits and wages	4.75 (± 0.44)	3.75 (± 1.00) *
J. Being appreciated	4.25 (± 0.72)	4.50 (± 0.63)
K. Helping organization obtain goals	4.30 (± 0.47)	4.56 (± 0.51)
L. Receiving raises	3.95 (± 0.67)	3.44 (± 1.03)
M. Being an integral part of work team	4.55 (± 0.61)	4.75 (± 0.45)
N. Job security	4.75 (± 0.55)	3.94 (± 0.85) *
O. Feedback on performance	4.25 (± 0.55)	4.38 (± 0.62)
P. Role in decision making	4.65 (± 0.49)	4.13 (± 0.50)

Scale: 1 = Extremely Unimportant; 2 = Unimportant; 3 = Neutral; 4 = Important; 5= Extremely Important
* Significant p < .05

number one motivator. Additionally, differences (p < .05) were found between the two groups for the rankings of freedom on the job (item C), job growth (item G), good benefits and wages (item I), being appreciated (item J), helping the organization to obtain its goals (item K), being an integral part of the work team (item M), job security (item N), and feedback on performance (item O).

Another example of the use of Mann-Whitney U-test in sport management is the study conducted by Zhang, Wall, and Smith (2000). The three researchers utilized Mann-Whitney U-test to examine the relationship between gender and game attendance variables. Season home game ticket holders of a major Western Conference NBA team (n = 924) were the subjects of the study. Gender was the independent variable. Game attendance variables, number of home games, number of playoff games in the previous season are the dependent variables. The results of the Mann-Whitney U test revealed that gender was not significantly (p > .05) related to game attendance variables.

Westerbeek (2000) tested "the relationship between five place-specific factors of service quality in spectator sport settings (the dependent variable) and two critical demographic variables, frequency of attendance and age (the independent variables)" (p. 194). "A Mann-Whitney test, performed to determine if older spectators differed from young spectators in relation to frequency of attendance (Z = -.757, p > .05), delivered no significant results. The results of the Mann-Whitney test showed no difference in frequency of attendance between young and old spectators, indicating that when older spectators continue to attend football matches, they do so as often as younger spectators" (Westerbeek, 2000, p. 2000).

Kruskal-Wallis Test as a Nonparametric Statistical Technique

The Kruskal-Wallis test is analogous to the parametric one-way ANOVA. It uses mean ranks rather than mean scores, and provides a statistical measure of the differences between means for both rank order and ratings among three or more groups. Intu-

TABLE 19-8
Rank order of motivational statements by groups with the Kruskall-Wallis Values

Motivational Statement	High School	Rank Order University	Clinic	K-W[a]
A. Designation as a leader	16	16	15	1.26
B. Importance of work	2	1	1	0.90
C. Freedom on the job	9	11	4	2.56
D. Achieving work-related goals	10	5	2	2.11
E. Getting along with others	8	2	6	0.95
F. Opportunities for advancement	7	10	11	0.99
G. Job growth	4	4	5	0.72
H. Good work conditions	5	6	7	0.51
I. Good benefits and wages	1	9	3	5.58
J. Being appreciated	14	12	10	0.58
K. Helping organization obtain goals	11	13	14	2.79
L. Receiving raises	15	14	13	0.84
M. Being an integral part of work team	13	3	12	8.34+
N. Job security	3	8	9	1.04
O. Feedback on performance	12	15	16	2.88
P. Role in decision making	6	7	8	0.56

[a] Value required for significance at the .05 level, df = 2, is 5.99
+ Significant p < .05; whereas High School differs from University (Mann-Whitney U)

itively, the Kruskal-Wallis test is identical to a one-way analysis of variance with the data replaced by their ranks. It is an extension of the Mann-Whitney U test to three or more groups. As a nonparametric technique, it does not assume a normal population and the population variabilities among groups do not have to be equal. So, the Kruskal-Wallis test can be applied to the situation where the ANOVA normality assumptions may not apply.

Table 19-8 provides one example of the Kruskal-Wallis test. In the same study mentioned previously, Buxton, Lankford, & Noda (1992) utilized the Kruskal-Wallis test to determine if any statistically significant differences existed between the certified athletic trainers who worked in high schools and those who were employed by colleges and universities in the state of Hawaii in terms of their job motivations.

The study conducted by Zhang, Wall, and Smith (2000) shows another example of a sport management research project that applied the Kruskal-Wallis test. The study examined the relationship of selected variables to game attendance level of NBA season ticket holders in the following four areas: sociodemographics, decision making, special program, and customer service. The season home game ticket holders of a major Western Conference NBA team (n = 924) were the subject of the study. To conduct the Kruskal-Wallis test, the researchers used a number of sociodemographic variables such as age, ethnicity, income, and education as independent variable. Each of these variables had more than two categories or groups. The dependent variables examined were the number of home games attended and the number of playoff games in the previous season attended. The Kruskal-Wallis test revealed that age and household income were significantly ($p < .05$) related to two attendance variables. Educational background was also found to be significantly ($p < .05$) related to the number of season home games that the respondents intended to attend next season.

Fisher's Exact Test as a Nonparametric Statistical Technique

The Fisher's exact test is a procedure that the researcher can use for categorical (i.e., nominal) data

in a two by two contingency table. It is an alternative to the test. It is mainly used when the sample size is small and the application of the P^2 test becomes inappropriate.

An example of the use of the Fisher's exact test is provided by Cuneen and Spencer (2003), who analyzed the milk mustache ads of sport celebrities (n = 34) to ascertain if there were differences in gender separation. Fisher's exact test was used in the study to measure relationships between sport celebrity gender and the units of analysis. The test was used in place of the regular test of relationship model because the small sample size rendered several under-filled cells, and Fisher's exact is the appropriate test to use when the conditions of small sample size and unexpected counts exist in the cells (Agresti, 1996). Using Fisher's exact test, the researchers found that there was a significant relationship between model gender and activity type ($p = 0.0174$). Examples of their findings included: (1) seven times more males (n = 14 or 88%) than females (n = 2 or 12%) represented the milk mustache ads; (2) two times more females (n = 8 or 62%) than males (n = 4 or 31%) represented the ads for individual sports; and (3) there were no females associated with extreme (n = 2 or 100%) and motor sports (n = 2 or 100%). All the sport celebrities pictured in these sports were males.

Wilcoxon Signed Ranks Test

As a nonparametric statistical procedure, the Wilcoxon Signed Ranks test is used to examine the differences between two related groups of participants for which the level of measurement for the dependent variables is of the ordinal level. Most specifically, it is used to measure the effect of a treatment on pre- and post-treatment observations, where the same subjects are measured twice (Zikmund, 2000, p. 542). It is a test used for comparing two paired groups. The Wilcoxon Signed Rank test is a nonparametric alternative to the paired Student's t-test.

Let us look at an example in sport management research to which we can apply this statistical technique. Brown, Nagel, McEvoy, and Rascher (2004) conducted a cross-sectional study to determine if a significant difference in net revenue change existed in NFL teams that moved into new facilities and to determine if there was a significant change in valuation for these franchises. The subjects of the study were NFL franchises that opened new stadia during the 1995–1999 timeframe. The Wilcoxon Signed Rank test was employed in data analysis. The variables compared included ticket sales, local TV and radio, loge boxes, concessions, advertising/parking/other, and total local revenue. The results of the study indicated that there was a significant difference between pre-stadium opening revenue and post-stadium opening revenue at the .05 level in the areas of ticket sales, loge box revenue, advertising/parking/other, and total local revenue.

Summary

The focus of this chapter was on the testing of differences. The commonly used procedures in both parametric and nonparametric statistics were reviewed. The t-test, the analysis of variance or ANOVA, and the z score are the three types of parametric statistical testing procedures discussed.

The t-test is used when the dependent variable is at the interval or ratio level of measurement and the independent variable has two categories. There are two different forms of the t-test for comparing group means: the t-test for independent groups or variables and the t-test for dependent groups or variables. On the other hand, ANOVA is used when the researcher wants to determine the statistical significance of a difference between the means of three or more groups. One-way ANOVA and two-way ANOVA are the two forms of ANOVA that are used by sport management researchers for answering research questions and hypothesis testing. It must be pointed out that, however, the one-way ANOVA is the more commonly used method. A number of post hoc comparison tests are typically run to determine which means are statistically different from each other when an ANOVA yields a statistically significant result. These tests include the Fisher LSD, the Newman-Keulis test, the Tukey's test, and the Scheffe's test.

Four types of nonparametric testing procedures are introduced in this chapter (i.e., the χ^2 test, the Mann Whitney U-test, the Kruskal-Wallis test, the Wilcoxon Signed Ranks test, and the Fisher Exact test). The χ^2 test is the nonparametric statistical method most frequently used by sport management researchers.

The χ^2 test is used to analyze nominal (categorical) data among groups. The Mann-Whitney U-test uses ordinal data (ranks) to determine whether two independent samples come from the same distribution. It is a distribution-free test for statistical significance. The Kruskal-Wallis test is analogous to the parametric one-way ANOVA and an extension of the Mann-Whitney U test to three or more groups. The Fisher's exact test is used for categorical (i.e., nominal) data in a two by two contingency table when the sample size is small and the application of the P^2 test becomes inappropriate. The Wilcoxon Signed Rank test is a nonparametric alternative to the paired Student's t-test for two related groups of subjects.

STUDY QUESTIONS

1. What are the differences between parametric and nonparametric statistical techniques?
2. Under what circumstances can each of the two types of t-test be used?
3. What are the differences between the two types of analysis of variance?
4. What are the differences between a t-test and an analysis of variance?
5. What are the reasons for utilizing nonparametric techniques versus parametric techniques?
6. What are the assumptions of the Chi square test?
7. What are the differences between a t-test and a Mann-Whitney U-test?
8. What are the differences between an ANOVA and a Kruskal-Wallis test?
9. What are the differences between a Chi square test and a Fisher's Exact test?

LEARNING ACTIVITIES

1. Identify an article published this year in one of the sport management related journals that used a parametric test procedure, and give your justification of why such a procedure was an appropriate one to use in that study.
2. Identify an article published this year in one of the sport management related journals that used a t-test in data analysis, and give your justification of why the t-test was an appropriate statistical procedure to use in that study.
3. Identify an article published this year in one of the sport management related journals that used ANOVA in data analysis, and give your justification of why ANOVA was an appropriate statistical procedure to use in that study.
4. Identify an article published this year in one of the sport management related journals that used one of the nonparametric test procedures to find out the justification given by the author in terms of why this type of nonparametric test was used.

References

Agresti, A. (1996). *An introduction to categorical data analysis*. New York: John Wiley & Sons.

Brown, M., Nagel, M., & McEvoy, C. (2004). Revenue and wealth maximization in the National Football League: The impact of stadia. *Sport Marketing Quarterly*, *13*(4), 227–235.

Buxton, B. A., Lankford, S. V., & Noda, J. E.(1992). Motivational congruency between certified athletic trainers and noncertified student athletic trainers in the State of Hawaii. *Journal of Athletic Training*, *27*(4) 20, 22, 24.

Crowl, T. K. (1996). *Fundamentals of education research* (2nd ed.). Boston, MA: McGraw Hill. pp. 182–183.

Cuneen, J., & Spencer, N. (2003). Gender representations related to sport celebrity portrayals in the milk mustache advertising campaign. *Sport Marketing Quarterly*, *12*(3), 140–150.

Gall, M. D., Gall, J. P., & Borg, W. R. (2003). *Educational research* (7th ed.). Boston, MA: Pearson Education, Inc.

Hollander, M., & Wolfe, D. A. (1999). Nonparametric statistical methods (2nd ed.). New York: Wiley.

Howell, D. C. (1997). *Statistical methods for psychology* (4th ed.). Belmont, CA: Duxbury Press.

Huck, S. (2000). *Reading statistics and research* (3rd ed.). New York: Longman.

Huck, S. W., Cormier, W. H., Bounds, & W. G., Jr. (1974). *Reading statistics and research*. New York: Harper & Row, pp. 68–69.

Leedy, P. D., & Ormrod, J. E. (2001). *Practical research: Planning and design* (7th ed.). Upper Saddle River, NJ: Prentice Hall.

Li, M., & Burden, W. (2002). Outsourcing sport marketing operations by NCAA Division I athletic programs: An exploratory study. *Journal of Sport Management*, *11*(4), 226–232.

London, C., & Boucher, R. (2000). Leadership and organizational effectiveness in Canadian university athletics. *International Journal of Sport Management*, *1*(1), 70–87.

Mahony, D. F., & Moorman, A. M. (2000). The relationship between the attitude of professional sport fans and their intentions to watch televised games. *Sport Marketing Quarterly*, *9*(3), 131–139.

McGehee, N.G., Yoon, Y., & Cardenas, D. (2003). Involvement and travel for recreational runners in North Carolina. *Journal of Sport Management*, *17*(3), 305–324.

McMillan, J. H., & Schumacher, S. (2006). *Research in education; Evidence-based inquiry* (6th ed.). Boston, MA: Allyn and Bacon.

Neuman, W. L. (2003). *Social research methods: Qualitative and quantitative approaches* (5th ed.). Boston, MA: Allyn and Bacon.

Robinson, M. J., & Carpenter, J. R. (2002). The day of the week's impact on selected socio-demographic characteristics and consumption patterns of spectators at a Ladies Professional Golf Association event. *Sport Marketing Quarterly*, *11*(4), 242–247.

Stoldt, G. C., & Narasimhan, V. (2005). Self assessments of collegiate sports information practitioners regarding their professional expertise. *International Sport Journal*, *6*(3), 252–269.

Weinbach, R. W., & Grinnell, R. M., Jr. (1995). *Statistics for social workers* (3rd ed.). White Plains, NY: Longman Publishers USA.

Westerbeek, H. M. (2000). The influence of frequency of attendance and age on "place"-specific dimensions of service quality at Australian rules football matches. *Sport Marketing Quarterly*, *9*(4), 194–202.

Zhang, J. J., Wall, K. A., & Smith, D. W. (2000). To go or not? Relationship of selected variables to game attendance of professional basketball season ticket holders. *International Journal of Sport Management*, *1*(3), 200–226.

Zikmund, W. G. (2000). *Business research methods* (6th ed.). Fort Worth, TX: Harcourt College Publishers.

CHAPTER 20
MULTIVARIATE DATA ANALYSIS

OBJECTIVES FOR COMPLETING THIS CHAPTER ARE THAT STUDENTS WILL BE ABLE TO:

Understand the decision-making criteria used in the selection of a bivariate or multivariate analysis method

Understand how to classify multivariate analysis techniques

Understand the decision-making criteria in terms of how to select an appropriate technique of multivariate analysis

Explain the differences between simple regression analysis and multiple regression analysis

Explain under what circumstances a sport management researcher can use the disciminant analysis technique to solve a research problem

Explain the differences between an ANOVA and MANOVA

Understand the circumstances under which conjoint analysis is a preferred statistical analysis technique

Differentiate cluster analysis and factor analysis

Explain the differences between exploratory factor analysis and confirmatory factor analysis

TO ANALYZE PROBLEMS that have three or more variables or are multi-dimensional, sport management researchers often use statistical procedures that are called *multivariate analyses* (McDaniel & Gates, 1991). The biggest advantage of multivariate analysis is that it allows the effects of more than one variable to be considered at one time. In this chapter, the commonly utilized multivariate analysis techniques by sport management researchers will be briefly reviewed. The chapter has three sections. The first section will focus on the classification of multivariate statistical analysis methods followed by a section that examines the statistical procedures used to analyze the data that are involved with only one dependent variable. The third section will deal with the analysis of interdependence of all the variables involved. This last section will showcase a case in sport management research that exemplifies the application of a major statistical procedure of multivariate analysis.

CLASSIFICATION OF MULTIVARIATE ANALYSIS TECHNIQUES

As mentioned above, sport management researchers use a variety of multivariate analysis techniques to analyze collected data that involve more than two variables (in other words, when the complexity of the research situation exceeds the abilities of those statistical procedures discussed in Chapters 18 and 19).

To determine which multivariate analysis technique to use, a sport management researcher should ask this question: Does the research situation include one or more dependent variables? If the answer is yes, the researcher should choose a dependence analysis technique. Otherwise, an interdependence analysis technique, which can be applied to determine the interdependence of all the variables under investigation, should be chosen. Figure 20-1 shows how all the multivariate analysis techniques are divided into these two classifications.

As Figure 20-1 demonstrates, the sport management researcher will choose one of the dependence analysis techniques if the research situation requiring the use of multivariate analysis techniques involves at least one dependent variable. If there is only one dependent variable, the multivariate analysis options available to the researcher include multiple regression analysis (if the dependent variable is interval-scaled) or discriminate analysis (if the data collected on the dependent variable is either nominal or ordinal in nature.) When more than one dependent variable is involved, multivariate analysis of variance (MANOVA) should be chosen if the dependent variables are interval-scaled. Otherwise, conjoint analysis is the option.

If the structural relationship among all the variables being invested is the interest of an investigation, the researcher can select one of the interdependence analysis techniques. Again, depending on the nature of the data collected, either factor analysis or cluster analysis can be chosen if the variables are interval-scaled. If not, the researcher can use other special multivariate methods, such as multidimensional scaling with nominal or ordinal data.

TECHNIQUES OF DEPENDENCE ANALYSIS

Multiple Regression Analysis

As discussed in Chapter 19, sport management researchers use simple regression analysis to test the relationships between two variables (one independent variable and one dependent) and use the independent variable to predict the dependent variable. They, however, may have to employ multiple regression analysis to research situations in which there are several independent variables and only one dependent variable that is interval-scaled (Zikmund, 2000). Specifically, multiple regression analysis is a parametric statistical technique used to test the relationships between two or more independent (predictor) variables and one dependent (criterion or outcome variable) to predict a dependent variable from two or more independent variables. The following is a mathematical expression of a multiple regression equation:

$$Y = \alpha + \beta_1 X_1 + \beta_2 X_2 + \beta_3 X_3 \quad \beta\eta X\eta$$

Multiple regression analysis has been widely utilized by sport management researchers to study multiple

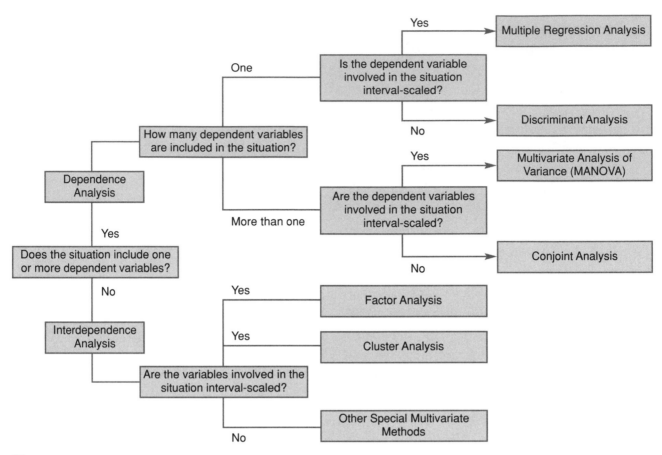

FIGURE 20-1. Classification of Multivariate Analysis Techniques

independent variables simultaneously to identify a pattern or patterns (Wells, Southall, & Peng, 2000; Pikul & Mayo, 1999; Lee, Ryder, & Shin, 2003). Such statistical procedure provides the researcher with a way to explore causal relationships between independent and dependent variables. The intent of a multiple regression analysis is to relate a response variable to a set of predictor variables by using a multiple regression model. Ultimately, the goal is to be able to estimate the mean value of Y and/or predict particular values of Y to be observed in the future when the predictor variables assume specific values (Mendenhall & Beaver, 1995). It is used to analyze the relationship between predictive variables and outcome variables. The study conducted by Funk, Mahony, and Ridinger (2001), as shown in Table 20-1, is an example to illustrate the use of multiple regression analysis in sport management research.

There are a number of different methods of entering variables into the multiple regression equations (George & Mallery, 2001, p. 185), such as the enter, forward, backward, stepwise, and remove methods. Of them, the stepwise entering method is the most popular (George & Mallery, 2001). It is also the case in sport management research (Kwon & Armstrong, 2002; McDaniel, 2002; Zhang, Smith, Pease, & Jambor, 1997). The enter method is used in a standard multiple regression analysis, in which the sport management researcher determines the number of predicting variables or predictors to enter the equation. All the predictors will enter the regression model simultaneously. In a stepwise multiple regression analysis, however, variables are entered one at a time based on a p value (typically less than 0.05 or 0.10) of each of the variables. When a new variable enters into the equation, the variance explained by the variables that have already included in the equa-

TABLE 20-1
An Example of Multiple Regression Analysis in Sport Management Studies

Type	Source and purpose of the study	Sample	Independent variables	Dependent variables	Major findings
Multiple Regression	Funk, Mahony, and Ridinger (2001) examined how individual difference factors could be used to explain various levels of consumer support for a specific sport property.	Spectators attending the 1999 U.S. Nike Cup on October 10, 1999, in Louisville, Kentucky (n = 580)	Fourteen Motives: Aesthetics, Family bonding, Drama, Excitement, Entertainment value, Interest in players, National pride, Role modeling, Interest in soccer, Social opportunities, Support for women's opportunities, Interest in team, Vicarious achievement, Wholesome environment	Spectator support level	Multiple linear regression analysis revealed that five motivational characteristics—sport interest, team interest, vicarious achievement, role modeling, and entertainment value—explained 54% of variance in level of spectator support for women's professional soccer. The results suggest that augmenting traditional spectator measures offers a better understanding of motivational characteristics in different sport situations and of the impact these motivations have on behavior. (p. 33)

tion may change. The stepwise method will eliminate those variables that become none-significant as other new variables are added.

Kwon and Armstrong (2002) conducted a study using the stepwise regression analysis technique to investigate the impulsive tendencies to purchase sport team-licensed merchandise. This research illustrates the essence of this particular data entering method.

Using a survey method, they obtained data from 145 college students (48 males and 97 females) at a large Midwestern university). The impulse of buying sport team licensed merchandise was examined as a dependent variable. They wanted to see if any of the predicting variables, including shopping enjoyment, time availability, money availability, and sport team identification is a significant predictor of the impulse of buying sport team licensed merchandise. The results of the stepwise multiple regression analysis revealed that the only significant antecedent to impulse buying of sport team licensed merchandise was the students' identification with the univer-

sity's sport team. Sport team identification also influenced the amount of money spent on impulsive sport purchases. (p.151)

Sport management researchers have also applied a number of advanced regression analysis procedures to meet their research needs (Gladden & Milne, 1999; Harrison, Lee & Belcher, 1999). Such advanced procedures include logistic regression analysis, hierarchical loglinear models, and so on. In the following section, a brief review of each of these procedures is provided.

Logistic regression analysis. Logistic regression analysis is a parametric statistical technique used to predict the probability of a dichotomous dependent variable (e.g., success/failure), typically using a combination of nominal (categorical) ability of two or more independent variables to predict the probability of an event, to estimate relative risk (odds ratios) when the independent variables are nominal level data. Logistic regression analysis is "an extension of multiple regression [analysis]"

(George & Mallery, 2001, p. 306). Logistic regression provides a way for studying the prediction of a criterion variable when the independent variables cannot be assumed to have a normal distribution. The independent variable can be continuous or categorical.

Peetz, Park, and Spencer (2004) used logic regression analysis to examine the role of gender in the transfer of meaning from athlete endorsers to products and to purchase intentions of a select sample of undergraduate students. The overall description of the study is provided in Table 20-2.

Hierarchical linear regression analysis. Hierarchical loglinear regression analysis examines the predictive ability of several independent variables on one dependent variable when a given variable is selectively controlled. It provides the re-

TABLE 20-2
An Example of Logistic Regression in Sport Management Studies

Type	Source and purpose of the study	Sample	Independent variables	Dependent variables	Major findings
Logistic Regression	Peetz, Park, and Spencer (2004) examined the role of gender in the transfer of meaning from athlete endorsers to products and to purchase intentions of a select sample of undergraduate students.	Sport management and kinesiology students at a midsize university located in the Midwestern United States (n = 150; 102 males and 48 females)	Group by gender; male, female	Identification of endorsers Athlete expertise Intention to purchase	Male endorsers were more likely to be identified correctly and to influence participants' purchase intentions. Gender differences also existed in participants' perceptions of endorsers' expertise and influence on purchase intentions. These findings suggest that gender plays an important role in the transfer of meaning for the members of the Generation Y market segment.

TABLE 20-3
An Example of Hierarchical Regression in Sport Management Studies

Type	Source and purpose of the study	Sample	Independent variables	Dependent variables	Major findings
Hierarchical Regression	Matsuoka, Chelladurai, and Harada (2003) investigated the direct and interaction effects of team identification and satisfaction with facets of a game on intentions to attend future games.	1,256 spectators in seven J-League (Japan professional football/soccer league)	Team identification, satisfaction	Intention to attend games	Correlational and regression analyses showed that both team identification and facets of satisfaction were significantly correlated with intention to attend future games, with team identification correlating at a higher level. The significance of the interaction of identification and satisfaction indicated that the intentions of highly identified fans relative to low-identified fans were less influenced by any of the facets of satisfaction.

searcher with strategies for exploring causal relationships between independent and dependent variables. A number of studies using hierarchical linear regression analysis are found in sport management literature (Carptner, 2001; McDaniel & Chalip, 2002). The case described in Table 20-3 exemplifies the use of such a statistical procedure.

Discriminant analysis. Discriminant analysis is a multiple analysis procedure used when the dependent variable is categorical (nominal or ordinal in nature) and the independent variables are continuous. It allows sport management researchers to study the difference between two or more groups of objects with respect to several variables simultaneously, determining whether a meaningful difference exists between the groups and identifying the discriminating power of each variable (Klecka, 1980). In addition, multiple discriminant analysis allows sport management researchers to "establish a model for classfying individuals or objects into groups on the basis of their values on the dependent variable" (McDaniel & Gates, 1991) or specifically, "to predict membership into two or more mutually exclusive groups" from a set of predicting variables (George & Mallery, 2001, p. 264). For example, Li and Burden (2004) examined such variables as institutional control, relationship with the local community, perceived product attractiveness, availability of in-house equipment, institutional support and facilities, and competency of athletic marketing staff to determine whether they affected athletic administrators' outsourcing decisions (outsourcing vs. in-house operations). Table 20-4 provides a detailed description of this study.

TABLE 20-4
An Example of Discriminant Analysis in Sport Management Studies

Type	Source and purpose of the study	Sample	Independent variables	Dependent variables	Major findings
Discriminant analysis	Li and Burden (2004) examined whether institutional control, relationship with the local community, perceived product attractiveness, availability of in-house equipment, institutional support and facilities, and competency of athletic marketing staff affect athletic administrators' outsourcing decisions.	Athletic directors from NCAA Division I-A, Division I-AA and Division I-AAA athletic programs from the National Directory of Collegiate Directors (n = 236)	Degree of control over the right to athletic properties Perceived product attractiveness	Outsourcing In-house operations	1. The degree of control over the rights to market the athletic properties did affect athletic administrators' decisions regarding outsourcing. 2. The relationship between the athletic department and its local business community did not have an effect on the athletic administrator's decisions regarding outsourcing. 3. The athletic administrators' perception of the attractiveness of the sports product was one of the factors affecting their decisions regarding outsourcing. 4. The competency of marketing staff was a factor influencing the athletic administrator's decisions regarding outsourcing.

A number of other sport management research found in the sport management literature also applied the multiple discriminant analysis technique (Granzin & Olsen, 1989; Straub, Martin, Williams, & Ramsey, 2003). The mathematical expression of a discriminant analysis equation is shown as follows:

$$Z = b_1X_1 + b_2X_2 + b\eta X\eta$$

Where

Z = discrimant score
b = discrimant weight or coefficient
X = independent variable

MANOVA

The multivariate analysis of variance, also known as MANOVA, is a multivariate analysis technique that is used to test the group difference simultaneously across several interval-scaled dependent variables on one or more categorical (i.e., nominally-scaled) variables serving as independent variables. This technique overcomes the limitation and drawback of the bivariate analysis of variance, including a higher error due to separate tests or lack of accuracy (George & Mallery, 2001).

Sport management researchers usually apply MANOVA under the following circumstances:

■ to compare the difference among groups formed by categorical independent variables in a number of interval-scaled dependent variables;
■ to identify the independent variables that can best differentiate the dependent variables.

The sport management researchers have adopted the MANOVA technique for a number of research purposes, such as to determine divisional differences in the methods of employee evaluation used by collegiate athletic directors (Barber & Eckrich, 1998); to investigate the relationships among gender, type of sport, motives, and points of attachment to a team for spectators of selected intercollegiate sports (Robinson & Trail, 2005); to analyze differences in perception of leadership and climate related to division of competition in college athletics (Scott, 1999); to assess the efforts of gender, membership of college divisions, and mentor status on the member of promotion and salary (Weaver & Chelladurai, 2002). The study conducted by Robinson, Trail, Dick, and Gillentine (2005) is a good showcase of how MANOVA can be used in solving problems in sport management. Table 20-5 provides a summative description of the study.

TABLE 20-5
An Example of Multivariate Analysis of Variance (MANOVA) in Sport Management Studies

Type	Source and purpose of the study	Sample	Independent variables	Dependent variables	Major findings
MANOVA	Using the model developed by Trail, Robinson, Gillentine, and Dick (2003) Robinson, Trail, Dick, and Gillentine conducted a study to determine how individuals who attend college football games should be classified at the four NCAA divisions of college football.	Data were collected from spectators at four intercollegiate football games during the 2001–2002 academic year. Out of 910 questionnaires distributed, 861 usable questionnaires were returned, for a return rate of 94%. The selection of the schools for the study was based on the geographic proximity to the researchers. The data were collected at one game in each of the divisions. (n = 236)	Collegiate Division levels	Overarching Motives, Spectator Motives, Vicarious Achievement Motive, Organizational Identification, Sport Identification, and Player Identification	Differences do exist among the divisions based on the motive variables and the points of attachment variables.

Conjoint Analysis

Conjoint analysis is one of the "many [statistical] techniques for dealing with situation in which a decision maker has to choose among options that simultaneously vary across two or more attributes" (Geen, Wind, & Rao, 1999, pp. 12–65). Such technique has been very popular in marketing research (Daniel & Johnson, 2004) and used to determine what attributes a new product should have and how it should be priced (Curry, 1996). For example, a tennis racquet has a number of attributes, such as color, price, stiffness, length, head size, weight, design, and reputation. Before purchasing a tennis racquet, consumers typically examine those attributes and then make trade-off judgments (e.g., picking reputation over pricing) to determine their final purchase choice. The conjoint analysis technique helps analyze these trade-off judgments to determine the combination of attributes that will satisfy the consumers most. The results of the analysis can provide the tennis manufacturers with information about how they can present their consumers with a product that combines all the attributes that will be most satisfying to them.

A review of sport management-related literature has found a few studies that applied the conjoint analysis technique to answer their research questions (Chalip & McGuirty, 2004; Chang & Johnson, 1995; Daniel & Johnson, 2004). A close analysis of the study, conducted by Daniel and Johnson (2004), who employed conjoint analysis to determine whether or not it is viable to bundle benefits with different pricing structures in an Australian professional football team, is provided in Table 20-6.

TECHNIQUES OF INTERDEPENDENCE ANALYSIS

Cluster Analysis

Cluster analysis is an exploratory data analysis technique used to identify objects or people with similar attributes and put the similar objects or people into clusters according to well-defined similarity rules (McDaniel & Gates, 1991; Vermetten, 1999). Never-

---

TABLE 20-6
An Example of Conjoint Analysis in Sport Management Studies

Type	Source and purpose of the study	Sample	Variables Investigated	Major Findings
Conjoint Analysis	To investigate the viability of bundling benefits with different pricing structures so as to provide better service and encourage retention while increasing prices.	A questionnaire was sent to a random sample of 1500 members of an Australian professional football team, 500 for each of the three membership categories (standard members, full club members—concourse seating, and full club members—grandstand seating). About 35% of the surveyed responded.	The respondents were asked to rate their probability of renewal of their membership under each of the sixteen scenarios or hypothetical membership packages provided. The packages included one of the three price levels and various combinations of the five benefit attributes, such as grand final ticket preference, ticket resale program, an official glossy yearbook, discount on public transport, and entry to newly improved social club facilities.	1. The members in the standard membership group were the most price sensitive of the three groups surveyed. However, they were prepared to extend to the medium price level to full club members—concourse seating. 2. The full club members—concourse seating group—found the access to grand final ticket option appealing and were interested in the newly improved social club facilities. This group seemed to be prepared for moving up to the next price level. 3. The full club members—grandstand seating group was least sensitive to price increase. In fact, they were prepared to pay more for superior services.

theless, it only discovers structures in data without explaining why those structures exist. The identified structures are referred to as clusters. There are various methods to group objects or people into clusters. Different methods will result in different cluster patterns (George & Mallery, 2001; McDaniel & Gates, 1991; Nicol & Pexman, 1999). There are three generally used approaches of cluster analysis: hierarchical clustering, k-means clustering, and two-step clustering.

Hierarchical clustering is also referred to as agglomerative hierarchical clustering. It allows researchers to first define a distance criterion, and then use the criterion to form clusters, ultimately determining how many clusters will fit the data best. Hierarchical clustering is more appropriate for a study with a smaller sample. The hierarchical clustering method starts with the consideration of each object of interest as a cluster. Then, based on the criterion, two or more similar objects (i.e., those with the lowest distance or highest similarity) are combined into a cluster. Next, the object with the highest similarity to either of the first two is considered. If that third object is more similar to a fourth one than it is to either of the first two, the third and fourth ob-

jects form another cluster. Otherwise, the third object is added to the first cluster. As the clustering process goes on, either more and more objects are added to the existing clusters or more and more new clusters are created or combined. If the process continues, all objects are joined together. When will the process stop, or when is the number of clusters is optimal? It depends on the research purpose. Figure 20-2 is an example of the hierarchical tree clustering plots.

K-means clustering. In k-means clustering, the number of clusters is first specified by the researcher. The researcher then decides how to assign objects into the clusters. K-means clustering uses Euclidean distance as decision criterion. *Euclidean distance* is the most common distance measure. A given pair of objects is plotted on two variables, which form the x and y axes. The Euclidean distance is the square root of the sum of the square of the x difference plus the square of the y distance. The initial cluster centers are chosen randomly in a first pass of the data, then each additional iteration groups observations based on nearest Euclidean distance to the mean of the cluster. That is, the algorithm seeks to

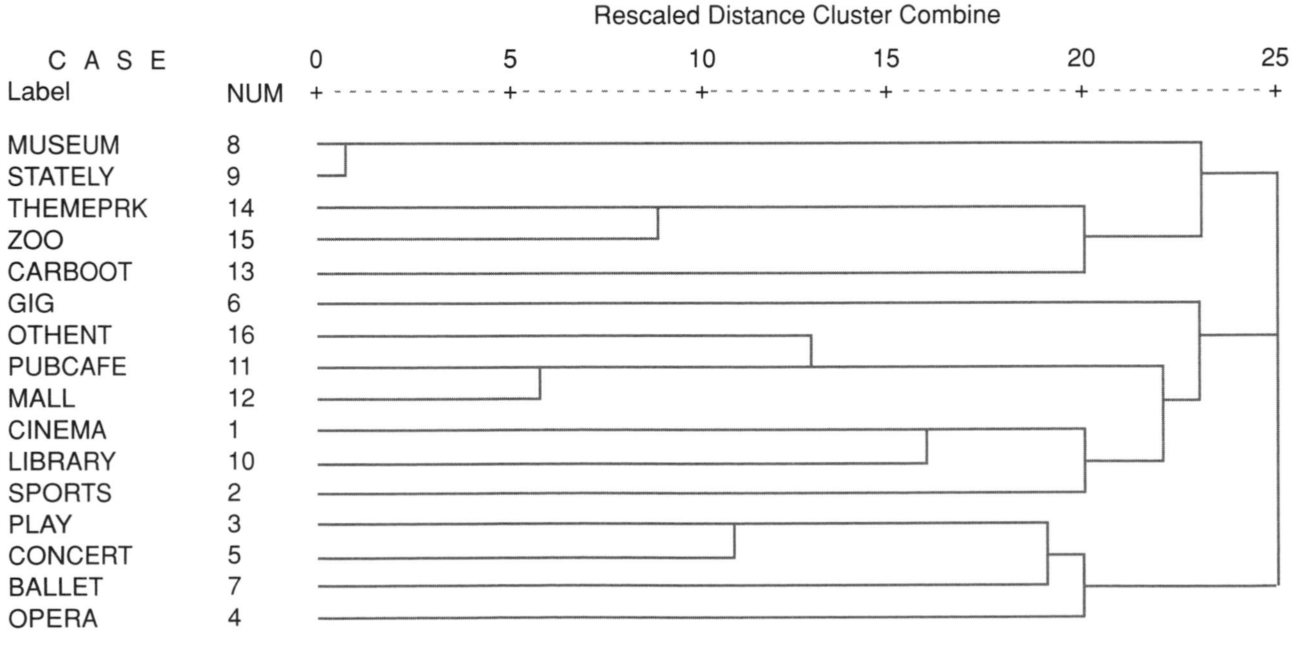

FIGURE 20-2 An Example of Cluster Analysis

Source: Sturgis, P., & Jackson, J. (2003). Examining participation in sporting and cultural activities: Analysis of the UK 2000 Time Use Survey. London, UK: Department for Culture, Media and Sport.

minimize within-cluster variance and maximize variability between clusters in an ANOVA-like fashion. Cluster centers change at each pass. The process continues until cluster means do not shift more than a given cut-off value or the iteration limit is reached. k-means clustering is much less computer-intensive and is therefore sometimes preferred when data sets are very large.

Two-step clustering. When using this method, the researcher first creates a number of pre-clusters and then the researcher clusters the pre-clusters. Standard hierarchical clustering is then applied to the pre-clusters in the second step. This is the method used when one or more of the variables are categorical (not interval or dichotomous). Also, because it is a method requiring neither a proximity table like hierarchical classification nor an iterative process like k-means clustering, but rather is a one-pass-through-the-data-set method, and as such is recommended for very large data sets.

The primary use of cluster analysis in business is to segment the population of interest (Ross, 2007). In sport management-related research, cluster analysis has been used in strategy studies to identify homogenous groups of amateur sport organizations (Kikulis, Slack, Hinings, & Zimmerman, 1989), to classify recreational runners into mutually exclusive segmented groups based on their perceptions and attitudes on a list of involvement items (McGehee, Yoon, and Cardenas, 2003), and to identify segments of spectators based upon the brand associations held for a professional sport team (Ross, 2007).

The following is a brief description of the application of cluster analysis by Ross (2007) in identifying segments of spectators. Six hundred sixty-five season ticket holders in the 2004–2005 NBA season participated in the study. Data were collected on 11 measures of team brand associations for professional sport teams, including (1) non-player personnel, (2) team success, (3) team history, (4) stadium community, (5) team-play characteristics, (6) brand mark, (7) organizational attributes, (8) concessions, (9) social interaction, (10) rivalry, and (11) commitment. The hierarchical tree clustering method was

applied to determine how many clusters in brand association were contained within the surveyed participants. Such determination followed a number of diagnostic steps. Specifically, the clustering coefficients or the within-cluster sum of squares in the agglomeration schedule were examined. Homogenous clusters with small coefficients were then merged. This process continued until the largest difference among clustering coefficients appeared. Two clusters finally emerged.

Factor Analysis

Factor analysis is a multivariate analysis technique for reducing a large set of variables into a smaller set of variables with common characteristics or underlying dimensions. Factor analysis is used by researchers to develop underlying commonality or dimensions among variables. The idea is that some variables belong together, and they are referred to as factors. The primary goals of factor analysis are "to discover the factors that best explain a group of measures and describe the relation of each measure to the factor of underlying construct" (Thomas & Nelson, 1996, p. 184). In most instances, factor analysis is the starting point for examining the factor structure of a research instrument. This procedure identifies underlying patterns of procedures (Kline, 1994). It involves the application of complex statistical procedures; however, when used appropriately and effectively, it is an excellent starting point for the interested researcher. Factor analysis attempts to place variables in groups. The groups are named, permitting variables in the group to be considered together. Grouping of the data makes interpretation more distinctive.

There are two different types of factor analyses: exploratory factor analysis and confirmatory factor analysis. The computation of the factors is a complex process. When employing factor analysis, researchers use a variety of factoring or data reduction techniques for reducing data to smaller and more manageable sets of underlying concepts. Four commonly used techniques include the principal axis factoring (PAF), principal components analysis (PCA), image factor extraction, and alpha factoring (Portney & Watkins, 2000; Tabachnick & Fidell,

2001). Of the four techniques, principal components extraction is the most commonly used technique (Portney & Watkins, 2000). A number of criteria are used when making decisions about variables to be retained in a data set. Using "rules of thumb analogy" the typical factor loading cutoff criteria range of .30 to .55 is considered to be a strong factor loading coefficient (Stevens, 1996).

For example, Zhang, Penninghton-Gray, Connaughton, Braunstein, Ellis, Lam, and Williamson (2003) examined the hierarchical relationships among sociodemographics, lifestyle, and level of game consumption of women's professional basketball spectators. The authors used a principal axis analysis to reduce the number of independent variables from 27 items to four. In reducing the data sets and calculating the factor scores, factor analyses were conducted for six game consumption variables and 19 lifestyle variables. Principal axis was used as the extraction method; one factor emerged for the level of spectator participation variables (game consumption) and four factors emerged for the lifestyle variables (professional sports, amusement activities, amateur sports, and recreational sports). Items were retained using the criteria of an item with a factor loading equal to or greater than .30. The typical

loading in most sport management studies is at least .40 on a variable.

In computing factors, researchers also use what are called rotation strategies. The two most common strategies are the orthogonal rotation and the oblique rotation strategies (George & Mallery, 2001). The orthogonal rotation strategy operates under the assumption that each of the factors clustered are independent of each other. The oblique rotation is most appropriate when the factors are not perceived as independent of each other. There are several approaches to the orthogonal rotation (for example, varimax, equimax, and quartimax). Varimax is one of the most commonly used approaches.

There are several important decisions for researchers to make when using factor analysis: (1) make clear the purpose of the instrument that is being developed, (2) test the construct validity of the variables for the proposed instrument, (3) make certain the sample size is adequate when testing the instrument, (4) select the most appropriate type of data reduction technique, (5) select the most appropriate type of rotation, and (6) stipulate how much loading a variable should have on each factor. Table 20-7 is an example of factor and scale loadings in a factor analysis.

TABLE 20-7
Oblique Factor Analysis of the Specialization Variables: Factor and Scale Loadings

Specialization Variables	Factor 1 (Investment)	Factor 2 (Experience)	Factor 3 (Lifestyle)
Amount of Equipment	.57	.07.	-.04
Overall Investment in Related Expenses	.72	.13	.23
Subscription to Related Sport Magazines	.64	.29	.37
Self-Reported Skill Level	.17	.54	.17
Development of Skills	.08	.52	.21
Days Engaged in an Activity	.12	.62	.11
Percent/Leisure Time	.27	.18	.53
Importance of Activity	.43	.29	.48
Eigenvalue	3.43	1.52	1.25
% of Total Variance	38.80	10.90	6.70
Cumulative %	38.80	49.70	56.40

Note: Factor loadings greater than .45 are underlined.

Exploratory factor analysis (EFA). The primary purpose of exploratory factor analysis is to summarize all of the information that exist in a data set and present it in a more manageable form with minimal loss of the variables. Typically, there is no underlying theory in exploratory factor analysis about which variables should be quantitatively associated with which factors. The factors are simply empirically associated. The clusters of variables (or factors) that emerge are statistically rather than theoretically derived. Exploratory factor is used because it describes and summarizes data by grouping together variables that are correlated (Tabachnick & Fidell, 2001). It is most often implemented to identify a small number of parts that may be used to represent relationships among sets of interrelated variables (George & Mallery, 2001).

The application of exploratory factor analysis has been the most common used in sport management research (Quarterman, Pitts, Jackson, Han, Haung, & Ahn, 2007). Table 20-8 provides an example of a study conducted by Ferreira and Armstrong (2004), who used EFA to explore the factors that may influence aspects of the purchase cycle regarding individual evaluations of sport products as a multi-attribute choice problem using student sample.

Confirmatory factor analysis (CFA). Unlike exploratory factor analysis, the objective of confirmatory factor analysis is to test a hypothesized factor or model and to assess its fit to the data (Bryant & Yarnold, 1995). The goal of confirmatory analysis is to clearly identify whether a priori specified scale items are appropriately related to their specified factors (Nunnally, 1978). In most instances, it is used to test a proposed theory underlying an instrument or to confirm the model of an instrument used in a different context or population. The clusters of variables (or factors) that emerge are theoretically rather than statistically derived. Typically, it is based on a strong theoretical foundation that allows the researcher to specify the factor structure in advance. The major question is: Are the correlations or covariances among the variables consistent with the hypothesized factor structure?

The appropriate use of confirmatory factor analysis is theory testing. Using "rules of thumb analogy," the typical factor loading cutoff criteria range of .30 to .40 is considered to be a strong factor loading coefficient. Confirmatory factor analysis is quite useful for studying the factorial validity of data obtained with multiple-item and multiple-subscale instruments (Stevens, 1996). For a more comprehensive discussion on factor analysis see the books written by Kim and Mueller (1978a, 1978b).

As an interdependence analysis technique, CFA has often been adopted by sport management researchers in their determination as to whether the collected data fit the proposed con-

TABLE 20-8
An Example of Exploratory Factor Analysis in Sport Management Studies

Type	Source and purpose of the study	Sample	Type of Analysis	Rotation	Major findings
Exploratory Factor Analysis (EFA)	Ferreira and Armstrong (2004) explored the factors that may influence aspects of the purchase cycle regarding individual evaluations of sport products as a multiattribute choice problem.	Students enrolled in three sport-related classes offered by the School of Physical Activity and Educational Services at a large Midwestern university (n = 53)	Principal components	Orthogonal (Varimax)	The result of EFA suggested that some attributes may not be sport-specific and may be included in the individual's general evoked set for different sport events. (p. 207)

TABLE 20-9			
An Example of Confirmatory Factor Analysis (CFA) in Sport Management Studies			

Type	Source and purpose of the study	Sample	Type of Analysis	Rotation
Confirmatory Factor Analysis (CFA)	James and Ross (2004) investigated research under two purposes of study: first, to extend understanding of sport consumers by identifying the motives that help explain an individual's interest in nonrevenue collegiate sports; second, to ascertain whether similar motives influence consumption across multiple nonrevenue sports.	People attending wrestling matches, baseball games, and softball games at a large Midwestern university (n = 947; wrestling matches = 292, baseball games = 354, softball games = 301)	Principal components	Orthogonal (Varimax)

ceptual framework (Gladden & Funk, 2002; Kwon & Trail, 2003). Table 20-9 provides one example of confirmatory factor analysis in sport management studies. It was conducted by James and Ross (2004), who were interested in identifying the motives that help explain an individual's interest in nonrevenue collegiate sports and to ascertain whether similar motives influence consumption across multiple nonrevenue sports.

A CASE USING MULTIVARIATE ANALYSIS TECHNIQUES IN SPORT MANAGEMENT RESEARCH

Caro and Garcia (2007) conducted a study to measure consumer satisfaction in a popular long-distance race event and to examine the role of sport motivations on the "cognitive affective relationships that drive satisfaction evaluation" (p. 70). The study employed a number of multivariate analysis techniques, including exploratory factor analysis, confirmatory factor analysis, cluster analysis, and MANOVA.

A survey was used in data collection. Out of 352 questionnaires sent, 137 were returned. The response rate was approximately 38%. Two conceptual models of satisfaction were proposed. Both the models contained the same constructs, but each had different structural relationships among the constructs. The constructs in the models, which included disconfirmation (two items), pleasure (six items), arousal (four items), overall satisfaction, loyalty (five items), and sport motivations (eight items), were first measured. Then, the researchers used exploratory factor analysis to evaluate the items included in the proposed model. To improve the quality of the psychometric properties of the measures, a number of the original items were deleted from the model after the performance of exploratory factor analysis. After that, a confirmatory factor analysis was followed. Figure 20-3 summaries the results of the confirmatory factor analysis,

Cluster analysis was also used in the study to analyze the moderating effect of sport motivation. A

	DIS	PLE	ARO	SAT	LOY
Disconfirmation (DIS)	.747	.174	.213	.341	.334
Pleasure (PLE)	.441	.747	.736	.323	.209
Arousal (ARO)	.462	.858	.514	.508	.318
Satisfaction (SAT)	.584	.568	.713	.616	.593
Loyalty (LOY)	.578	.457	.564	.770	.611
Composite reliability	.855	.897	.759	.865	.823

Note: Intercorrelations are presented in the lower triangle of the matrix. The average variance extracted (AVE) is depicted on the diagonal. Shared variances are given in the upper triangle of the matrix.

FIGURE 20-3. Summary of the Results of the Confirmatory Factor Analysis

	Mean				Brown		
	High motivated	Low motivated	Porsythe statistic	P value	Effect size[1]	Power
Factors positive effect	4.23	3.70	6.69	< .05	.24	.75
Social contact	3.53	2.25	56.07	< .001	.57	1.00
Body image	3.44	2.98	6.67	< .05	.23	.71
Competition	3.47	2.25	33.36	< .001	.47	1.00
Challenge	4.57	3.81	20.93	< .001	.40	.99
Physical exercise	4.65	4.59	.24	n.s.	.04	.07
Entertainment	4.44	3.40	32.82	< .001	.48	1.00
Coping strategy	3.52	2.07	48.62	< .001	.54	1.00

[1] Effect size conventions for the F test (Cohen, 1998); small: .10; medium: .25; large: .40.

FIGURE 20-4. Results of the MANOVA Used to Determine if Differences Exist among Members of the Two Clusters in Each of the Eight Motivation Factors

two-cluster solution was derived. In other words, all the respondents were different enough to be put into two groups or clusters based on their scores on all the motivation factors. A MANOVA was then applied, with the cluster membership as the independent variable, and the eight motivation measures as the dependent variables, to verify that differences indeed existed among members of the two clusters. Figure 20-4 shows the results of the MANOVA.

SUMMARY

There are a number of multivariate analysis techniques that are commonly used in sport management research. These techniques include multiple regression analysis, discriminant analysis, MANOVA, conjoint analysis, factor analysis, cluster analysis, and so on. To use each of the techniques, the sport management researcher should understand the circumstances or prerequisites under which it should be used.

In general, all the multivariate analysis techniques can be categorized as either methods dealing with the explanation or prediction of the dependent variable (referred to as methods of dependence analysis), or methods used to depict the structure of all the variables under investigation when there is no dependent variable involved, which are called methods of interdependence analysis. Multiple regression analysis, discriminant analysis, MANOVA, and conjoint analysis are some of the methods of dependence analysis discussed in this book. Factor analysis and cluster analysis are two techniques reviewed in this chapter.

STUDY QUESTIONS

1. What are the decision-making criteria used in the selection of a bivariate or multivariate analysis method?
2. How can multivariate analysis techniques be classified?
3. What are the decision-making criteria in terms of how to select an appropriate technique of multivariate analysis?
4. What are the differences between simple regression analysis and multiple regression analysis?
5. Under what circumstances can sport management researchers use the disciminant analysis technique to solve their research problems?

(continued on next page

STUDY QUESTIONS (continued)

6. What are the differences between an ANOVA and a MANOVA?
7. Under what circumstances is conjoint analysis a preferred statistical analysis technique?
8. What are the differences between cluster analysis and factor analysis?
9. What are the differences between exploratory factor analysis and confirmatory factor analysis?

LEARNING ACTIVITIES

1. Identify a research article in one of the sport management-related journals published this year that employed the multiple analysis of variance (MANOVA) technique and describe the variables involved in the study.
2. Design a research project that will use multiple regression analysis to predict the attendance of college football games at your school with a number of independent variables. What are those variables?
3. Design a study that involves the use of the cluster analysis technique.

References

Barber, H., & Eckrich, J. (1998). Methods and criteria employed in the evaluation of intercollegiate coaches. *Journal of Sport Management, 12*(4), 301–322.

Bryant, F. B., & Yarnold, P. R. (1995). Principal-components analysis and exploratory and confirmatory factor analysis. In L. C. Grimm & P. R. Yarnold (Eds.), *Reading and understanding multivariate statistics* (pp. 99–106). Washington, DC: American Psychological Association.

Caro, L. M., García, J. A. M. (2007), Measuring perceived service quality in urgent transport service. *Journal of Retailing and Consumer Services, 14*(1), 60–72.

Carpenter, P. (2001). The importance of a church youth club's sport provision to continued church involvement. *Journal of Sport & Social Issues, 25*(3), 283–300.

Chalip, L., & McGuirty, J. (2004). Bundling sport events with the host destination. *Journal of Sport Tourism, 9*(3), 267–282.

Chang, M. G. S. J., & Johnson, L. W. (1995). Segmenting the triathlon association membership market: An Australian example. *Sport Marketing Quarterly, 4*(4), 25–28.

Curry, J. (1996).*Understanding conjoint analysis in 15 minutes.* Technical report. Evanston, IL: Sawtooth Technologies, Inc.

Daniel, K., & Johnson, L. W. (2004). Pricing a sporting club membership package. *Sport Marketing Quarterly, 13*, 113–116.

Ferreira, M., & Armstrong, K. L. (2004). An exploratory examination of attributes influencing students' decisions to attend college sport events. *Sport Marketing Quarterly, 13*(4), 194–208.

Funk, D. C., Mahony, D. F., & Ridinger, L. L. (2001). Characterizing consumer motivation as individual difference factors: Augmenting the Sport Interest Inventory (SII) to explain level of spectator support. *Sport Marketing Quarterly, 11*(1), 33–43.

George, D., & Mallery, P. (2001). *SPSS for Windows step by step: A simple guide and reference 10.0 update.* Boston, MA: Allyn and Bacon.

Gladden, J. M., & Funk, D. C. (2002). Developing an understanding of brand associations in team sport: Empirical evidence from consumers of professional sport. *Journal of Sport Management, 16*(1), 54–81.

Gladden, J. M., & Milne, G. R. (1999). Examining the importance of brand equity in professional sport. *Sport Marketing Quarterly, 8*(1), 21–29.

Granzin, K. L., & Olsen, J. E. (1989). Identifying those ready to make a voluntary commitment to fitness. *Journal of Sport Management, 3*(2), 116–128.

Green, P. E., Wind, J., & Rao, V. R. (1999). Conjoint analysis: Methods and applications. In R. C. Darf (Ed.), *Technology management handbook.* Boca Raton, FL: CRC Press.

Harrison, L., Jr., Lee, A., & Belcher, D. (1999). Self-schemata for specific sports and physical activities: The influence of race and gender. *Journal of Sport and Social Issues, 23*(3), 287–307.

James, J. D., & Ross, S. D. (2004). Comparing sport consumer motivations across multiple sports. *Sport Marketing Quarterly, 13*(1), 17–25.

Kikulis, L.M., Slack, T., Hinings, B., & Zimmerman, A. (1989). A structural taxonomy of amateur sport organizations. *Journal of Sport Management, 3*(2), 129–150.

Kim, J., & Mueller, C. W. (1978a). *Introduction to factor analysis: What it is and how to do it.* Quantitative Applications in the Social Sciences Series, No. 13. Thousand Oaks, CA: Sage Publications.

Kim, J., & Mueller, C. W. (1978b). *Factor analysis: Statistical methods and practical issues.* Quantitative Applications in the Social Sciences Series, No. 14. Thousand Oaks, CA: Sage Publications.

Klecka, W. R. (1980). *Discriminant analysis*. Thousand Oaks, CA: Sage Publications.

Kline, P. (1994). *An easy guide to factor analysis*. London, UK: Routledge.

Ko, Y. J., & Pastore, D. L. (2005). A hierarchical model of service quality for the recreational sport industry. *Sport Marketing Quarterly, 14*(2), 84–97.

Kwon, H. H., & Armstrong, K. L. (2002). Factors influencing impulse buying of sport team licensed merchandise. *Sport Marketing Quarterly, 11*(3), 151–162.

Kwon, H. H., & Trail, G .T. (2003). A reexamination of the construct and concurrent validity of the Psychological Commitment to Team Scale. *Sport Marketing Quarterly, 12*(3), 88–93.

Lee, S., Ryder, C., & Shin, H. (2003). An investigation of environmental motivation factors among Minor League Baseball (MiLB) fans. *The Sport Journal, 6*(3). Retrieved March 31, 2008, from http://www.thesportjournal.org/article/investigation-environmental-motivation-factors-among-minor-league-baseball-milb-fans.

Li, M., & Burden, W. (2004). Institutional control, perceived product attractiveness, and other related variables in affecting athletic administrators' outsourcing decisions. *International Journal of Sport Management, 5*(4), 295–305.

McDaniel, C., & Gates, R. (1991). *Contemporary marketing research*. St. Paul, MN: West Publishing Company.

McDaniel, S. R. (2002). An exploration of audience demographics, personal values, and lifestyle: Influences on viewing network coverage of the 1996 summer Olympic Games. *Journal of Sport Management, 16*(2), 117–131.

McDaniel, S. R., & Chalip, L. (2002). Effects of commercialism and nationalism on enjoyment of an event telecast: Lessons from the Atlanta Olympics. *European Sport Management Quarterly, 2*(1), 3–22.

McGehee, N. G., Yoon, Y., & Cardenas, D. (2003). Involvement and travel for recreational runners in North Carolina. *Journal of Sport Management, 17*(3), 305–324.

Mendenhall, W., & Beaver, R. J. (1995). *A brief course in business statistics*. Belmont, CA: Wadsworth Publishing Company.

Nicol, A. A. M., & Pexman, P. M. (1999). *Presenting your findings: A practical guide for creating tables*. Washington, DC: The American Psychological Association.

Nunnally, J. C. (1978). *Psychometric theory* (2nd ed.). New York: McGraw-Hill.

Peetz, T. B., Parks, J. B., & Spencer, N. E. (2004). Sport heroes as sport product endorser: The role of gender in the transfer of meaning process for selected undergraduate students. *Sport Marketing Quarterly, 13*(3), 141–150

Pikul, J., & Mayo, H. (1999). Performance and eligibility for arbitration or free agency and salaries of professional Major League Baseball players, the 1994–1995 experience. *Journal of Sport and Social Issues, 23*(3), 353–361.

Portney, L. C., & Watkins, M. P. (2000). *Foundations of clinical research: Applications to research* (2nd ed.). Upper Saddle River, NJ: Prentice Hall Health.

Quarterman, J., Pitts, B., Jackson, N., Han, K., Haung, J., & Ahn, T. (2007). Statistical data analysis techniques employed in the *Journal of Sport Management, Sport Marketing Quarterly, & International Journal of Management: 1987 to 2006*. Unpublished manuscript.

Robinson, M. J., & Trail, G. T. (2005). Relationships among spectator gender, motives, points of attachment, and sport preference. *Journal of Sport Management, 19*, 58–80.

Robinson, M. J., Trail, G. T., Dick, R. J., & Gillentine, A. J. (2005). Fans vs. spectators: An analysis of those who attend intercollegiate football games. *Sport Marketing Quarterly, 14*, 43–53.

Ross, S. D. (2007). Segmenting sport fans using brand associations: A cluster analysis. *Sport Marketing Quarterly, 16*, 15–24.

Scott, D. K. (1999). A multiframe perspective of leadership and organizational climate in intercollegiate athletics. *Journal of Sport Management, 13*(4), 298–316.

Stevens, J. (1996). *Applied multivariate statistics for the social sciences* (3rd ed.). Mahwah, NJ: Lawrence Erlbaum Associates.

Straub, W. F., Martin, S. B., Williams, D. Z., & Ramsey, A. L. (2003). Pain perception of contact and non-contact sport athletes. *The Sport Journal, 6*(2). Retrieved March 31, 2008, from http://www.thesportjournal.org/article/pain-apperception-contact-and-non-contact-sport-athletes.

Tabachnick, B. G., & Fidell, L. S. (2001). *Using multivariate statistics* (4th ed.). Needham Heights, MA: Allyn and Bacon Company.

Thomas, J. R., & Nelson, J. K. (1996). *Research methods in physical activity* (3rd ed.). Champaign, IL: Human Kinetics.

Vermetten, Y. J. M. (1999). Consistency and variability of student learning in higher education Unpublished doctoral dissertation, Tilburg University, Netherlands.

Weaver, M. A., & Chelladurai, P. (2002). Mentoring in intercollegiate athletic administration. *Journal of Sport Management, 16*(2), 96–116.

Wells, D. E., Southall, R. M., & Peng, H. (2000). An analysis of factors related to attendance at Division II football games. *Sport Marketing Quarterly, 9*(4), 203–210.

Zhang, J. J., Smith, D. W., Pease, D. G., & Jambor, E. A. (1997). Negative influence of market competitors on the attendance of professional sport game: The case of a Minor League Hockey team. *Sport Marketing Quarterly, 6*(3), 31–40.

Zhang, J. J., Pennington-Gray, L., Connaughton, D. P., Braunstein, J. R., Ellis, M. H., Lam, T. C., & Williamson, D. (2003). Understanding women's professional basketball game spectators: Sociodemographics, game consumption, and entertainment options. *Sport Marketing Quarterly, 12*(4), 228–249.

Zikmund, W. G. (2000). *Business research methods* (6th ed.). Fort Worth, TX: Harcourt College Publishers.

CHAPTER 21

COMMUNICATING RESEARCH RESULTS: WRITTEN REPORTS AND ORAL PRESENTATIONS

OBJECTIVES FOR COMPLETING THIS CHAPTER ARE THAT STUDENTS WILL BE ABLE TO:

Appreciate the importance of effective communication in reporting research findings

Understand the methods of communicating research results

Appreciate the factors that affect the communication process in sport management

Understand the various types of research reports

Understand the components of research reports

Understand the requirements for poster and oral presentations

Understand the general rules in the development and use of tables, figures, and charts

Understand the nature of the three most popular writing styles used in communicating research results

WHEN THE RESEARCH PROJECT has concluded, the next step is to prepare to report the project, its results, and recommendations. This will involve either a written report or an oral presentation. This chapter will first present the types of written reports and their specific components, with examples in sport management to help illustrate the application of each of those components. In the next section, this chapter will present how to prepare an oral presentation.

COMMUNICATING RESEARCH RESULTS

An important aspect of reporting research is to remember that it is a form of communication. After spending weeks or even months on a research project, the researcher might feel that writing a report is a waste of time because all of the important work has been accomplished. However, communicating the project and its results is just as important as conducting the research. The researcher is communicating the arrangement of the project, the purpose, its objectives, the methods used, the logistics of collecting the data, how the data were analyzed, what the analysis means, what conclusions can be drawn, and what recommendations can be made based on the results. Therefore, the researcher should make every attempt to communicate effectively and efficiently.

There are different formats that can be used for communicating the research. This chapter explains how research is communicated in sport management.

Factors Affecting the Selection of a Communication Method

What communication method is best? The answer to this question is contingent upon a number of factors. Research is best communicated when consideration is given to factors that affect the communication process, including what kind of setting is involved, who is the audience, what standards of reporting should be followed, and how much time (if an oral report) or space (if a written report) is allotted for the report. Figure 21-1 illustrates these factors and a flowchart for making determinations about the best way to communicate the research project results.

The first decision that the researcher needs to make is determine if the research is being conducted for a *sports business setting*, or an *academic setting*. This decision will affect the determination of the type of communication method that will be used.

Type of audience refers to who will be receiving the communication of the research. In the sports business setting, there are different groups of individuals to whom the report will be targeted. Examples of those groups or individuals are executive management, marketing, production, operations, event management, grounds, game day crew, facility management, manufacturing plant, distribution staff, sales personnel, sales management, product design, and research and development. In the academic setting, the audience might be students, faculty, administrators, or researchers.

Further determination of audience includes understanding how much experience members of the audience have. In many cases, individuals in the business setting have less experience with research than those in the academic setting. Yet, some groups in the business setting have a lot of experience. For example, those who work in the research and development area will typically have experience in research.

The reason for determining how much experience the audience has with research is to guide the researchers in how technical they can be with the report. If they will be communicating with individuals with little or no research experience, then they will need to use lay terminology and simple methods of communication. If the audience has research experience, they can use greater detail and technicality in the communication.

To guide the researcher or the individual who will be developing a written report, there are *standards of writing style*. Some of the more common ones used in sports business and academia are presented later in this chapter. The reason for this step is to determine if there are required standards that must be followed. Secondarily, even if standards are not required, following a writing style manual offers an organized approach to putting the report together. If a writing standard is required, the researcher must follow that standard. If not, it would be helpful to choose one to follow.

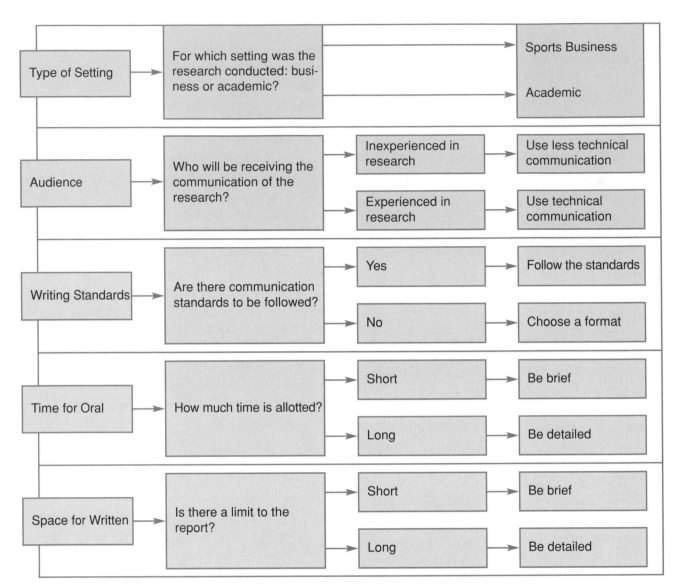

FIGURE 21-1. Factors Used to Determine the Best Method for Communicating the Research Project

The other factor to consider before planning the report is time or space. *Time allotted* for an oral presentation will dictate how detailed the report can be. *Space allotted* for a written report will influence how much information is included and how it will be presented. If time or space is short, the presentation must be brief and to the point. If there is more time or space allotted, the presenter should take the opportunity to include as much information as possible about each element of the research project.

Types of Reports

The basic types of reports are briefing, short, and long. Any of these may be used in the sports business or academic setting. In the sports business setting, the approach for the report is of a more practical analytical nature. In academia, the approach is usually of a more scientific nature, but results and recommendations should be practical. In some research, either sports business or academic, the nature is of a more theoretical approach. That is, the research and its results will be primarily used for information, or for a foundation upon which future research can be based. The report of the research is the organized presentation of the research, its results, conclusions drawn based on the findings, and recommendations for the application of the information. Figure 21-2 illustrates each type and their components.

Type → Sections Included ↓	Briefing	Short	Long
Preface/Foreword			✔
Cover Letter			✔
Title Page	✔	✔	✔
Executive Summary		✔	✔
Abstract			✔
Introduction	✔	✔	✔
Statement of Problem	✔	✔	✔
Purpose of Research			✔
Research Objectives			✔
Review of Literature			✔
Exploration for Information		✔	✔
Analysis of Existing Literature			✔
Methodology	✔	✔	✔
Sampling Design			✔
Research Design		✔	✔
Data Collection Method			✔
Data Analysis Method			✔
Limitations			✔
Findings/Results	✔	✔	✔
Conclusions & Discussion	✔	✔	✔
Recommendations	✔	✔	✔
References		✔	✔
Tables & Figures	✔	✔	✔
Appendix/Exhibits		✔	✔

FIGURE 21-2. Research Report Sections and Order of Inclusion for Written or Oral, Business or Academic Research Reports

Briefing. The briefing can be an oral, poster, or Power Point presentation, and consists primarily of three sections (preparing the oral presentation will be discussed in latter part of this chapter). In the briefing, the lengthy material is summarized down to the shortest, but most important, points of the project.

Time is a factor always to be considered in the oral presentation. The presenter should first find out how much time will be available so that the report will to fit into the amount of time allotted. A presenter should never go into a presentation without having first practiced so that the presentation is within the time limit. In the business setting, the individuals to hear the report will most likely not be interested in the logistical details of the research. They want to hear the results and recommendations for how to apply the results. One tip is to think of the presentation as containing five-fifths: the introduction will take one-fifth, while the other two sections should each be given two-fifths of the time. For example, if the presenter is given 25 minutes, then use only five minutes for the introduction, and 10 minutes each for the remaining findings and recommendations sections. The briefing should consist of the following parts:

1. Introduction. This should be kept to a bare minimum including coverage of the purpose and objectives of the research as a reminder of why this study was conducted.
2. Findings and conclusions. This can be done by presenting the findings and then conclusions afterward, or vice versa. In this part, the researcher should concentrate on presenting the results of the research along with conclusions that can be made based on these results.
3. Recommendations. The last part of the presentation should be spent giving recommendations about how to use the results. In the sports business, the presenter should spend this time talking about what the results mean and how they can be used as solutions to the original problem.

Short report. The short report includes more details and information than the briefing. The short report is appropriate when the problem is well defined, has a relatively simple methodology, and has findings, conclusions and recommendations that are uncomplicated and straightforward.

A short report is five to ten pages in length. It should include a brief introduction that presents the statement of the problem studied. Next a short summary of any existing information that could be used to help explain or solve the problem should be included. If answers were found in exploration, then the next section would be an explanation of how this information provides direction for solving the problem. If answers were not found, then the next section will be an overview of the research methodology utilized. The final portion of the report will contain the findings of the study, conclusions that can be formulated based on the findings, and recommendations about how to apply the information gained in the study.

Long report. The long report is one that includes extensive details of every aspect of the research project. For the sports business setting, this report will include great detail about each of the steps of the project with heavy emphasis on the findings and recommendations. For this purpose, the report will be written with a practical management style. For the academic setting, the report will follow a specific writing manual as required by the academic publication or organization and will be written in a formal academic language style.

In the sports business setting, often the individuals to whom the report will be presented have no background in research methodology. Therefore, every effort should be taken to present the information in non-technical language so that those individuals can understand the project and its uses. On the other hand, in the academic setting it is important to present the research according to standards set by research and scientific organizations. These standards exist to protect the integrity and validity of every aspect of research. For instance, there are specific standards and protections for research projects that will involve human subjects.

Often, practitioners (those in the business settings) believe that academics (those in academic settings) produce research that cannot be used in the "real world." These individuals believe that academics produce research geared for nothing more than to be published in an academic journal. Although this is true of some research projects, it is certainly not true of all academic research. Additionally, academic research that has a theoretical or scientific basis produces information that enhances or furthers the existing information on a topic.

Further, some academic research is conducted specifically for the academic setting. For example, academics study the aspects of the young field of sport management, such as growth, curriculum development, program development, accreditation standards, and even the growth of the research literature. The information from this research is important to guide the development of the field and thus has a practical nature for those in academia.

Categories of Written Reports

As pointed out earlier, written reports are based on the intended audience and setting. The categories of written reports include the sports business research report, the academic professional manuscript, the thesis, the dissertation, and the poster presentation. Any category can be used in either setting, but it is most common that the business report is used in a business setting, whereas the other four categories are used in an academic setting.

The business setting might include any type of sports business in which a researcher will be presenting the results of a research project. The academic setting might include submitting the manuscript to an academic journal for publication, submission of an abstract of a research project to be presented at an academic conference as an oral presentation or as a poster presentation, a thesis manuscript developed as a graduate student's academic program requirements, or a dissertation manuscript developed as a doctoral student's academic program requirements. Either setting may require a briefing, short, or long report. The following section of the chapter presents all of the components of the research report.

COMPONENTS OF THE RESEARCH REPORT

A report is developed based on its intended audience and use. Research being reported for a sports business management team will be put together and written in a format and a language appropriate for that purpose. Research that will be reported in academic literature will be written and formatted in a manner appropriate for that purpose. The more commonly used writing styles are presented in writing manuals that are presented later in this chapter in the section titled "An Introduction to Writing Style Handbooks."

The reporting of all research should be done with a typical ordering of each section. The sections generally include introduction, literature or information, methodology, findings, conclusions, and recommendations. Figure 21-2 illustrates the many possible sections of a report along with those sections that are typical in three different types of reports: briefing, short, and long. Additionally, these sections are used if the report is oral or written.

Preface/Foreword

In a report that is extensive, there may be a short preamble to the entire document. These sections are commonly used in academic works, especially in textbooks. The *preface* is a brief introduction to a document that explains its scope, intention, or background. The preface is usually written by the author.

The *foreword* is also a brief introduction to the document, but is usually written by a person other than the author. This piece usually compares the document to other works and offers an informal view of how valuable the document is.

Cover Letter

If the research report is presented in a formal manner, a cover letter can provide an introduction for the reader from the author. The cover letter can include a brief overview of the project, a explanation of how the informational document is organized, and a note of appreciation for the opportunity.

Title Page

The *title page* is a one-page cover sheet. It is typically presented in a stylized format that gives the document a pleasing look. The title page should include at least four items: the title, the date, to whom the report is presented, and by whom it was prepared. Other information might include author contact information. Figure 21-3 illustrates a typical format for the title page for a report in a business setting, and for an academic paper submitted to an academic journal.

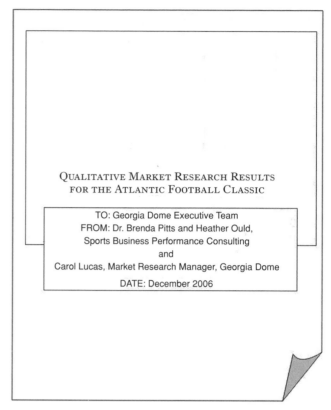

FIGURE 21-3. Examples of the Title Page: Top example is for a sports business setting. Bottom example is for an academic setting

Executive Summary

An *executive summary* is a miniature report of the research project, usually two to three pages in length (single spaced). The executive summary covers all the aspects of the body of the report in abbreviated form. This section is written after the full report is completed. Figure 21-4 presents an example of an executive summary.

Abstract

An *abstract* is a very brief overview of the study and usually is limited to 300 words or less. This amounts to approximately a long paragraph. It typically begins with a statement about the the purpose of the study, followed immediately by selected results and conclusions. The abstract gives the reader just enough information to get an idea of what the

---

Executive Summary

Many researchers involved in measuring sports event sponsorship have suggested that measuring levels of spectator awareness of sponsor company identities should involve more analysis of the long-term effects of sponsorship. However, the literature is overwhelmingly filled with studies of awareness levels at single (individual) events, while only a few studies are found that have measured awareness levels over a specific duration of time. In addition, stakeholder-based evaluation models have been suggested as a theoretical framework for this analysis in sponsorship. Therefore, it was the purpose of this study to examine the long-term effects of corporate sponsorship signage on awareness levels of high stakeholder spectators.

Specifically, the research questions that guided this study were: As high interest stakeholders, do season ticket holder spectators know who are the corporate sponsors of their athletic program? Will lengthened exposure to corporate sponsors increase the spectator's knowledge of the corporate sponsors? And, are season ticket holder spectators more willing to support the sponsors?

A sponsorship recall instrument was developed based on instruments in previous literature (Pitts, 1998; Singh & Rothschild, 1983). The survey instrument featured three main stadium sponsor categories as well as six company categories that advertised in surrounding areas. Also, three "dummy" categories were included to assess potential confusion between official sponsors and ambush companies. Subjects were asked to assess whether or not they noticed sponsor signs in or around the stadium (yes or no), and, if yes, fill in the blank for each category they believed to have a sponsor. Also measured were various demographic items and items related to history with the athletic program and involvement levels.

The findings of this study reveal some potential concerns for sponsors: these spectators did not have a high rate of awareness, awareness increased only slightly over the duration of the event (4 months), and

the majority was not willing to support the sponsors. The results showed that there were increases in the recall rates for eight of the nine actual sponsor companies used in the study from the beginning of the season to the end of the season. However, those recall rates for the nine sponsors ranged from zero to 81% in the preseason survey and zero to 88.6% in the post-season survey. The results of the Z Test for significant differences revealed that only three of nine Z Tests were significant for the change between pre-season and post-season tests.

The results of this study raise questions about the typical purposes of sponsorship. It has been noted in previous sponsorship literature that too much sponsorship advertising is creating an over-exposure effect. That is, there is so much sponsorship advertising and it has been a part of the sports event and venue for so long that spectators don't even notice it anymore. Moreover, there is a growing concern over "clutter"— there is so much sponsorship advertising at any given event that one's brain cannot discern between advertisers. In the current study, these factors could have had an effect. Indeed, in recent years, sponsoring companies are moving toward exclusive and title sponsorship contracts as a means of combating these effects.

The results of the current study have academic implications in relation to the current state of research involving sport sponsorship recognition and recall examination. First, they raise questions concerning theories and research into spectator involvement levels in relation to sport sponsorship. There has been only minimal research in sport sponsorship utilizing involvement or social judgment theories. As a result of the findings of the current study, we believe that there is a need for attention to and increased research using these theories in sport sponsorship.

Source: Slattery, J., & Pitts, B. G. (2002). Corporate sponsorship and season ticket holder attendees: An evaluation of changes between pre and post season sponsorship recall. *International Journal of Sports Marketing & Sponsorship, 4*(2), 151–174.

FIGURE 21-4. Example of an Executive Summary

A good abstract is

- **accurate:** Ensure that the abstract correctly reflects the purpose and content of the manuscript. Do not include information that does not appear in the body of the paper. If the study extends or replicates previous research, note this in the abstract, and cite the author (initials and surname) and year. Comparing an abstract with an outline of the paper's headings is a useful way to verify its accuracy.
- **self-contained:** Define all abbreviations (except units of measurement) and acronyms. Spell out names of tests and drugs (use generic names for drugs). Define unique terms. Paraphrase rather than quote. Include names of authors (initials and surnames) and dates of publication in citations of other publications (and give a full bibliographic citation in the article's reference list).
- **concise and specific:** Make each sentence maximally informative, especially the lead sentence. Be as brief as possible. Abstracts should not exceed 120 words. Begin the abstract with the most important information (but do not waste space by repeating the title). This may be the purpose of thesis or perhaps the results and conclusions. Include in the abstract only the four or five most important concepts, findings, or implications. (pp. 12–13)

FIGURE 21-5. How to Write a Good Abstract, from the *APA Manual*

Abstract

The purpose of this study was to assess the media preferences and consumption behaviors of attendees at an action sports event, with a specific focus on comparing members of Generation Y (Gen-Y) to Generation X (Gen-X). Research participants were event attendees at the Gravity Games (N = 2108). A series of chi square analyses indicated some differences between the generations. In general, Gen-Y participants, when compared to Gen-X, watch more television, were more likely to (a) watch action sports (i.e., Gravity Games & X Games) on television, (b) play video games more often, and were less likely to watch traditional sports like the NFL and NBA on television. Clearly, Gen-Y action sports consumers use and prefer media differently than their Gen-X counterparts. Marketing implications and future research directions are discussed.

Source: Bennett, G., Sagas, M., & Dees, W. (2006). Media preferences of action sports consumers: Differences between Generation X and Y. *Sport Marketing Quarterly, 15*, 40-49.

Abstract

Following Super Bowl XXXVIII, which was held in Houston in 2004, criticism and controversy arose concerning the selection of talent as well as the execution of the event's halftime show. Given the increasing emphasis and investment of the entertainment aspect of sporting events, this study set out to explore Super Bowl viewers' perceptions on a number of ancillary entertainment elements of the event, as well as those elements' relative importance to viewers' enjoyment of the broadcast. A computer-based survey was developed and administered to two different groups: a purchases list of Super Bowl viewers (N = 892) and a random sample of NFL database subscribers (N = 209). Results from analysis on the whole groups of respondents (N = 1,101) showed that the competitiveness of the game and the teams competing were the two most important elements affecting viewers' enjoyment of the Super Bowl broadcast. The third highest rated item was the commercials. The halftime show, which rated sixth in its perceived contribution to the enjoyment of the broadcast, received marginally positive ratings relating to its overall importance of the entertainment value of the Super Bowl. Respondents were then grouped into two categories based on their self-reported level of fan avidity. Analysis of variance results indicated statistically significant differences between the two fan groups on 16 of the 19 items analyzed, indicating that self-identified "avid sports fans" were more interested in core game elements, while those respondents who identify themselves as "low/moderate sports fans" seemed to have more positive opinions of the ancillary or entertainment aspects of the broadcast.

Source: Apostolopoulou, A., Clark, J., & Gladden, J. M. (2006). From H-Town to Mo-Town: The importance of Super Bowl entertainment. *Sport Marketing Quarterly, 15*, 223–231.

FIGURE 21-6. Examples of Abstracts

full report is about so that the reader can decide whether or not reading the whole report will be beneficial. See Figure 21-5 for the APA guidelines on what should go into a well-written abstract. See Figure 21-6 for two examples of the abstract.

Introduction

The introduction section in a full report can be comprised of components that describe the parts of the project: the problem statement, purpose of the research, research objectives, and background information. In many projects, the introduction section may be taken directly from the proposal with some editing.

Statement of problem. The problem statement is comprised of the stated need for the research. This is the original question that began as the reason for developing the research project. An example is: "After evaluating the annual analysis of the fans in attendance at the annual SuperCross events held at the Georgia Dome, it was determined research is needed to find out why attendance has been decreasing over a three-year period of time." It is then followed by a stated purpose of the research and research objectives.

Purpose of research. The purpose of the research is a statement about the bottom line reason for the study. An example is: The purpose of this research was to examine the factors that affected attendance at the 2007 SuperCross event at the Georgia Dome.

Research objectives. In this section, the list of objectives of the research is outlined. The objectives address the purpose of the study in more specific terms. These may be a list of research questions or hypotheses. An example of this is: Based on the purpose of the study, the following questions guided this study: Why has attendance been dropping? What affects the attendance of current attendees? Are there factors such as pricing or promotions that can be changed in order to have a positive affect on attendance for future events? Let us use a real study to exemplify how

to raise research questions. This study was conducted to assess the data analysis of statistical techniques used in *Sport Marketing Quarterly* (*SMQ*) from 1992 to 2004, Quarterman, Pitts, Jackson, Kim and Kim (2005, p. 231) posited three research questions with respect to the quantitative studies in *SMQ*:

> What were the most frequently used quantitative statistical data analysis techniques that were primary to the research purposes, questions, and/or hypotheses appearing in SMQ from 1992 to 2004?
>
> What were the most frequently used quantitative statistical analysis techniques that were primary to the research questions or hypotheses appearing in SMQ from 1992 to 2004 when classified as descriptive, parametric inferential, and nonparametric inferential statistics?
>
> What were the trends in the use of statistical data analysis techniques used in SMQ from 1992 to 2004?

Review of Literature

In this section, the results of the search for existing information are presented. In a briefing, none of this is presented unless the answer to the research question is found in existing literature that could completely answer the research question, or have an influence on it, or serve as information that could greatly add to the resulting recommendations.

Exploration for information. The information that provided answers to the research questions, or solutions to problems, will be presented in this section. It should be presented in an organized manner. There is no truly right or wrong way to organize this information, except that it should be organized based on a logical manner that presents how and where the information search took place, what was found, what information was provided from the search, and how and why this information answers the research questions or provides solutions to the research problem.

Analysis of existing literature. This section includes a presentation of what was found in existing literature and the researcher's analysis. This should be presented in an organized manner with attention to what information offers help in answering questions or finding solutions. This section also puts historical (old) studies or information into context. As well, it demonstrates the connections between the informational pieces (articles, books, manuscripts, presentations, etc.) that the researcher is using.

The researcher should refer to the APA manual for help in developing this section. Also, it can be helpful for the researcher to study how authors of existing manuscripts presented their literature review sections.

Methodology

In this section, a description of how the study was conducted needs be presented in detail. This description should enable the reader to evaluate the methods the researcher used and their appropriateness. This section should also present enough information about the methods used in the study so that other researchers can replicate the study. To present information in this section, the researcher should identify the subsections with headings. The subsections usually include sampling design, research design, data collection methods, data analysis methods, and limitations of the study.

Sampling design or subjects. Identifying the subjects in a study is critical. The identification of the target population being included in the study should be first presented in this section. In addition, the specific method used to determine an appropriate sample of this population should also be included. Furthermore, the actual logistical methods used in appropriating the sample while data collection is in process should be reviewed as well. In a study to examine the effects of time on sponsorship recognition, Pitts and Slattery (2004) described their subjects in this way:

> The population selected for examination in this study was season ticket holders at a successful and nationally ranked university football organization. This population was selected because highly or nationally ranked collegiate football teams can have high interest, high involvement, and highly loyal fans. . . . A selective sampling technique was used to obtain a useful sample for the study. . . . From the resulting list of 10,958 season ticket holders, every 22nd name was selected using a computer program to reach a sample size of 500.

Research design. The research method, or design, selected for the study is presented in this subsection. The presentation should be accurate in describing each step in the execution of the plan. A description of the instrument, including how it was designed and tested for reliability and validity is a critical part of this subsection. In this subsection, the researcher should also justify why the design was appropriate for the study.

Data collection method. This subsection should give precise details about the method(s) used to collect the data, and a description of each step used and how this was controlled so that the collection was accurate and appropriate. For example, the following is how Dixon and Bruening (2007, p. 388) described how they collected the data for their study designed to examine the challenges of balancing work and family by NCAA Division I female head coaches:

> Participants were notified by email when the host site was functional and each was issued a login name and password. Instructions on how to maneuver the site were included in this informational email and were also included as a link on the host site. The participants were all instructed to read the information sheet and consent letter included on the site first and then to proceed with the study (assuming they agreed with the consent letter). From there each participant completed a brief (22-item) questionnaire to

provide basic demographic information (e.g., age, number of years in the profession, number of years as a head coach, number and ages of children, spouse or partner's occupation) without taking valuable time away from the online focus group format to answer these questions.

Data analysis method. In this section, the researcher should present and describe the details of the methods used to analyze the data. A justification of why these methods are appropriate for the study should also be provided.

Limitations. The limitations of the study need to be discussed in this section. The researcher must be precise and forthcoming. The following is an example of how the limitations of a particular study are presented:

> Three limitations for this study should be recognized. First, while explicit instructions for both sets of content analyses were provided, ambiguity and variability can still exist in the results. Set standards for what constituted being a "critical" part of the website were not in place; thus consistency across participants can be questioned. Second, some of the content categories indicated through the SII may be extremely difficult to communicate through a website and subjective to evaluate on a website. . . .The third limitation was the convenience samples in Studies 1 and 3 were different from the venue sample in Study 2.

The Concluding Sections

These concluding sections typically are the majority of the report. These sections present what was found in results of the study, what conclusions can be drawn from the results, and what recommendations can be made based on the results.

Findings/results. In this section, the researcher presents the raw findings or results of the data analysis. This should be done without comment or discussion. Results should be organized in a logical manner, or in a way that follows the design of the study. Tables, charts, figures, or other illustrative aids are used in this section. The researcher should choose a medium that clearly and efficiently presents the data and other information.

Conclusions and discussion. This is the famous "So what?" section. That is, after a study is conducted, everyone asks "So what does this mean?" and "How can we use that?" After presenting the results, the researcher is now in a position to interpret what the results mean and what conclusions can be formulated. In this section, the researcher is free to interpret the results in relation to the original purpose, questions, hypotheses, and objectives of the study. The researcher may begin this section with discussing whether or not the results of the study answered the research question, supported the hypotheses, or met the objectives of the study, followed by a description of *how* the results answered the questions.

Recommendations. Recommendations are suggestions for how the research can be applied. These should be presented with detail for the action to be taken. In academic research to be published in journals, the recommendations often include ideas for future study that will broaden, enhance, or test understanding in the research area. In sports business, the recommendations will include suggestions for business actions. Justifications should be offered. Alternatives can be suggested. The following is an example of recommendations offered after completing a study:

> Finally, this study can also serve as a road map for future research studies. One suggestion is to replicate this investigation. Using a longitudinal approach would be useful with data collection taking place at different time intervals (for example, every two years). Conducting telephone and face-to-face interviews may assist in increasing the response rate of this type of investigation. Continuing the investigation over a 10-year period to observe

changes in challenges is also recommended. Another suggestion is to utilize quantitative measures in future research by developing and implementing a scale for rating and ranking the themes and responses solicited in the current investigation. Also future investigations of challenges confronting females as athletic directors need to examine the generalizability of the current findings of more diverse groups when categorized by such dimensions as race and age (Quarterman, Dupreé, & Willis, 2006, pp. 538–539)

References

This section contains a list of all of the sources cited within the study. The researcher should follow a standard from a writing manual so that citations will be easy to understand. Some of the more commonly used writing manuals are presented elsewhere in this chapter.

Tables, Figures, and Charts

In a manuscript, tables and figures as well as other illustrations should be presented following a writing manual format. Some manuals call for tables, figures, and charts to be placed within the report closest to where they are referenced. Other writing style manuals call for them to be printed one per page at the end of the manuscript, before the appendix or exhibits. Suggestions for formulating tables, figures, and charts are in a different section of this chapter.

Appendix/Exhibits

The appendix or exhibits section is the place to put a number of pieces of information that are not placed within the body of the report. Some of those include large tables, instructions, copies of surveys and questionnaires, detailed drawings, or other material important to be included.

THESIS AND DISSERTATION FORMAT VERSUS JOURNAL ARTICLE OR BUSINESS REPORT FORMAT

Some university academic programs in sport management require or allow the student to complete a thesis or dissertation. The thesis and dissertation format is much more detailed than other formats. The purpose for this detail is for the student to present every possible piece of information and material as evidence of their ability to conduct research and write a thesis or dissertation. The thesis or dissertation study is supervised by a committee of faculty, one of whom is designated as the student's "major advisor" for the project.

Every section as listed in the "Long" column in Figure 21-2 is included in the thesis and dissertation manuscript. Each section includes great detail and information about the topic of that section.

PREPARING POSTER AND ORAL PRESENTATIONS

The Poster Presentation Report

The poster presentation is used as a method of presenting the research project by posting the results—hence, the title of poster. That is, a briefly written report using several components will be produced for posting in an area designated for the poster. This is more typical for a setting in which a number of different types of presentations are given, such as at a convention, exhibition, or conference. At an academic conference, for example, there are be oral presentations along with workshops, seminars, round-table discussion groups, and symposia. An additional type of presentation is the poster presentation. Typically, a four-by-six-foot space on a professional display board is provided for the presenter. The poster presenter displays the research report within this space. The event designates a date and time for a session in which researchers display their posters. As individuals come to read and view the research projects, they may ask questions about the projects of the researchers, who are available for discussion next to their posters.

The preparation of a poster report should be done with the same attention to detail and content as any other type of report or presentation. There are a number of formats from which one can choose, or one can be creative and develop the display with a personal touch. Either way, the poster style report should include the basic components of the written report: introduction, methodology, results, conclusions and discussion, recommendations, and references. Additionally, because the poster report is a visual display, attention should be given to graphic presentation.

The Oral Presentation

Researchers often present their research projects and findings in an oral presentation. These presentations have some unique characteristics that make them somewhat different from public speaking. Typically, the presentation is made to a relatively small group of people (10 to 50, depending on the setting), the presentation is limited to details about the project, speaking time allotted can be as short as 15 minutes or as long as an hour, and there is time for questions and discussion following the presentation.

Preparation of the oral presentation. An oral presentation should include many of the same components as a written report. Usually, the length of each component is limited by the amount of time allotted for the presentation. Preparation should be given as much attention as preparation of the written report, with an emphasis on specific points to be made during the presentation.

Some researchers prepare an oral presentation by first writing the full report. After this, the researcher outlines the key components to include and points to be made. Then, the researcher develops the actual presentation using either brief notes or a fully written presentation.

A decision to make early in the planning stage is whether to give the presentation by memory, from notes, or by reading the paper. Giving a presentation by memorizing it can be risky. It is possible to forget certain points, or even whole parts of the report. In the end, questions could be asked that the researchers might not be able to answer because they will have no notes with them. Giving a presentation from notes is not as risky; however, it does require that the researchers still memorize some information that they include in their notes.

Giving a presentation by reading the manuscript is a good style to use if the researchers don't fall prey to the worst effect of this—putting the audience to sleep. If they choose this style, they need to be sure to practice what they have written so much that they don't have to look down at the paper constantly. They should look at the audience members so as to engage them in their presentation.

Setting can determine which style is used. It is highly advisable to use a relaxed, polished presentation with notes in a sports business setting. In an academic setting, it is more expected that a well-practiced and strictly straightforward presentation be given either from notes or by reading the paper.

Delivery and performance. The content of a research report is the primary concern in a presentation. However, the delivery and performance of this by the presenter can affect how the audience accepts the communication. Researchers should consider the audience and setting and prepare appropriately with appearance, demeanor, speech pattern, enunciation, gestures, and the like. Figure 21-7 offers good advice for preparing to present. Figure 21-8 offers good advice to consider during the presentation.

EFFECTIVE PRESENTATION WITH GRAPHICS: TABLES, CHARTS, FIGURES, AND MORE

Presentations of research, either written or oral, are enhanced and thus are more effective if they include graphics. These are typically tables, charts, figures, and other similar illustrations. This section of the chapter presents a general guide to the development and use of these so that the presentation will be enhanced.

Text Presentation

This is a common method of presenting data when the report includes a very small amount of results to present. However, there are guidelines that should be followed for expressing research results in written language. Each writing manual, as presented in the last sections of this chapter, offers specific rules and

1. Know who your audience is before preparing the presentation. That way, the presentation can be customized to the audience.

2. What expectations are there for your presentation? Should the presentation be formal or informal? Should you have a Power Point presentation? Should you have handouts?

3. Outline your report for presentation and prepare the presentation according to this.

4. Prepare to deliver the presentation clearly and succinctly. The written report will provide greater detail of your research.

5. Choose graphic aids that are easy to understand and are simple, not cluttered.

6. Check out the presentation room and equipment well before the presentation day and time.

7. Practice, practice, practice. Practice your presentation enough times that you are comfortable with the material you must cover and can deliver the presentation in the exact time allotted. Use a watch to time yourself and where you should be in your presentation at certain points in time.

8. Come to the presentation room well in advance of the presentation time to set up. Have everything set up and ready to start presenting on time; don't waste your presentation time to get organized and get equipment set up.

9. Bring back-up media with your presentation saved in several formats in case the equipment doesn't read the media you brought, or in case of equipment failure. For example, bring your presentation files saved on two or three flash drives and a CD. It is even advised to bring your own laptop and connector cables as a back-up. In addition, bring paper copies of the presentation in case all equipment fails and in case you want the audience to have paper copies on which to take notes.

FIGURE 21-7. Preparing for the Presentation

1. Dress appropriately.

2. Arrive early and get everything set up and ready to go when the presentation time is supposed to start.

3. Be positive and confident; you are the authority; you know more about your topic than anyone else.

4. Acknowledge the audience. This will get their attention immediately.

5. Speak so that everyone can hear you. Enunciate clearly. Don't use or overuse "uh," "you know," or other distracting utterances.

6. Use a professional appearance; be aware of gestures, stance, eye contact, and other movements.

7. Use effective visual aids.

8. Stick to the presentation without wandering around topics.

9. Stick to your previously practiced time limits—be at certain places in the presentation at specific times as you practiced. If you don't make it, though, don't panic; just make an adjustment by speaking a bit faster to catch up, or skip a paragraph or two.

10. Stop on time and invite questions for discussion.

FIGURE 21-8. Delivering the Presentation

Tables, Charts, and Figures

The most common method for presenting data is through the use of illustrations: tables, charts, and figures. These allow the presenter to show large amounts of data in a small amount of space. However, there are specific guidelines for the presentation of these. Writing manuals provide detailed guidelines for developing and presenting tables, charts, and figures in a written manuscript. In this section, we provide a general overview of the use of tables, charts, and figures.

A table is an illustration of data in a tabular format—see Figure 21-9 for two examples. All other illustrations are considered figures. Usually in the form of charts, models, diagrams, and other illustrations, figures present numerical information in a visual form. Figure 21-10 presents some of the many different types of charts and graphs available for the researcher to use in depicting data.

guidelines for writing research results into the text of the document. For example, the *APA Publication Manual* (2001) states that titles of tests should be capitalized; names of factors should be capitalized; an abbreviation should be used only after the first presentation of the complete term is presented; figures should be used to express all numbers of 10 and above; and any number under 10 or that begins a sentence shoud be spelled out.

TABLE 4
Top Ten Countries of Olympic Games Medal Count

Nation	Gold	Silver	Bronze	Total
United States	974	772	661	2,407
USSR	473	376	355	1,204
Italy	218	178	198	594
France	209	220	250	679
Germany	205	210	227	642
Great Britain	197	245	247	689
East Germany	193	167	164	524
Sweden	185	186	217	588
Hungary	156	138	161	455
Norway	149	141	125	415

TABLE 6
Factors That Affected Attendance at the 2003 Women's Final Four Championships in Atlanta, Georgia

Factors	Mean
To attend a Championship tournament	4.73
Entertainment value of the games	4.31
Support of the teams playing in the tournament	3.93
Tournament location	3.69
Availability of tickets to purchase	3.53
The Georgia Dome as a venue	2.98
Price of tickets	2.93
Dates games are scheduled	2.92
Promotion of the event	2.75
Days of the week games are scheduled	2.74
Other activities taking place in the city	2.73

Note: Likert Scale of 1 to 5 with 5 being most affect.
Source: Pitts, B.G., Lu, D., Ayers, K., & Lucas, C. (2004). Factors affecting spectator attendance at the 2003 NCAA Women's Final Four Basketball Championship. Paper presented at the 2005 European Association for Sport Management, Belgium, 2004.

FIGURE 21-9. Examples of Two Tables

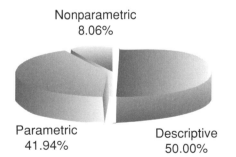

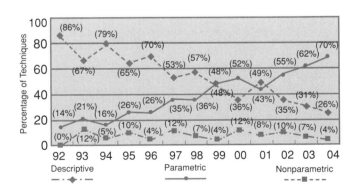

FIGURE 21-10. Examples of Common Charts and Graphs

Source: Quarterman, J., Pitts, B. G., Jackson, E. N, Jr., Kim, K., & Kim, J. (2005). Statistical data analysis techniques employed in *Sport Marketing Quarterly*: 1992 to 2004. *Sport Marketing Quarterly*, *14*(4), 227–239.

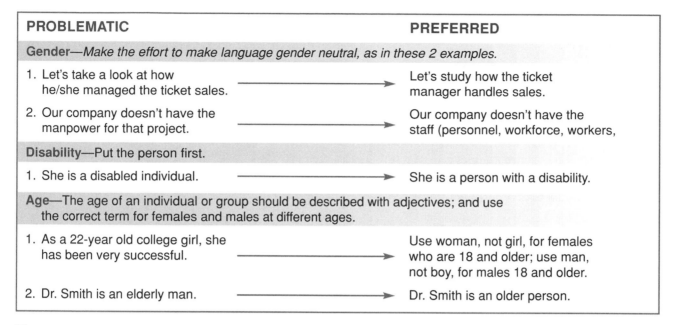

PROBLEMATIC	PREFERRED
Gender—*Make the effort to make language gender neutral, as in these 2 examples.*	
1. Let's take a look at how he/she managed the ticket sales. →	Let's study how the ticket manager handles sales.
2. Our company doesn't have the manpower for that project. →	Our company doesn't have the staff (personnel, workforce, workers,
Disability—Put the person first.	
1. She is a disabled individual. →	She is a person with a disability.
Age—The age of an individual or group should be described with adjectives; and use the correct term for females and males at different ages.	
1. As a 22-year old college girl, she has been very successful. →	Use woman, not girl, for females who are 18 and older; use man, not boy, for males 18 and older.
2. Dr. Smith is an elderly man. →	Dr. Smith is an older person.

FIGURE 21-11. A Few Examples of Problematic Language and Preferred Uses

SUCCESSFUL PRESENTATION WITH BIAS-FREE LANGUAGE

All researchers are expected to use language free of bias in preparing their research reports. In fact, the *APA Publication Manual* (2001) requires it. This writing manual stipulates that it is "committed . . . to the fair treatment of individuals and groups, and this policy requires authors of APA publications to avoid perpetuating demeaning attitudes and biased assumptions about people in their writing" (p. 61).

As such, the researchers should make a habit of checking their work for biased language just as they check it for spelling and grammar. The APA manual provides excellent guidelines and examples of avoiding biased language. These include such topics as labels, participation, gender, sexual orientation, racial and ethnic identity, and disabilities, as well as using language that is positive, appropriate, puts people first, and uses emotionally neutral expressions. Figure 21-11 provides some examples of problematic language and preferred uses.

It is imperative to take the time to learn about how to use bias-free language, practice using it, and practice writing with it. Sport management professionals come into contact with numerous diverse individuals; it is their responsibility to treat individuals as they want to be treated—with utmost respect.

AN INTRODUCTION TO WRITING STYLE HANDBOOKS

There are many handbooks that contain guidelines for writing. These handbooks are popular within and adopted as official manuals by different fields of study or organizational areas. For the academic field of sport management, the vast majority of academic journals and textbooks follow the APA manual. The following gives a brief introduction to three of the most popular writing manuals.

The American Psychological Association Publication Guidelines

The American Psychological Association (APA) sponsors guidelines for the preparation of formal manuscripts and presentations. These include very specific details about every aspect of the paper or presentation. The purpose of these guidelines is to offer recommendations to standardize the format of the paper or presentation. The foreword of the fourth edition of the APA Publication Manual, commonly referred to as "the APA Manual," states the following:

> The *Publication Manual* presents explicit style requirements but acknowledges that alternatives are sometimes necessary; authors should balance the rules of the *Publication Manual* with good judgment (p. iii).

And the Introduction of the fifth edition includes this statement:

> Rules for the preparation of manuscripts should contribute to clear communication. These rules introduce the uniformity necessary to convert manuscripts written in many styles to printed pages edited in one consistent style. They spare readers a distracting variety of forms throughout a work and permit readers to give full attention to content. (p. xxiii)

The APA offers an Internet site dedicated to continuous help for the writer—http://APAstyle.apa.org. This site contains information about all APA manuals and help guides. It also provides answers for up-to-date questions regarding format. For example, the current edition of the manual was published in 2001. Many changes have been made in the world of technology regarding publishing, reference citation, and literature. The site carries the most up-to-date information regarding changes and recommended writing style guidelines to accommodate those changes.

The APA website also offers information about their other publications that are helpful to the writer. One of these, *Displaying Your Findings: A Practical Guide for Creating Figures, Posters, and Presentations* (2003), offers easy-to-follow instructions and examples for using illustration in a paper or presentation. Figure 21-12 presents the table of contents of that book. Figure 21-13 shows the table of contents of the main manual.

The MLA Style of Writing

The Modern Language Association (MLA) style is most commonly used to develop papers and cite sources within the liberal arts and humanities fields. The style recommended by the association for preparing scholarly manuscripts and student research papers concerns itself with the mechanics of writing, such as punctuation, quotation, and documentation of sources. MLA style has been widely adopted by schools, academic departments, and instructors for nearly half a century.

- Content and Organization of a Manuscript
- Expressing Ideas and Reducing Bias in Language
- APA Editorial Style
- Reference List
- Manuscript Preparation and Sample Paper
- Material Other Than Journal Articles
- Manuscript Acceptance and Production
- Journals Program of the American Psychological Association
- Bibliography
- Checklist for Manuscript Submission
- Checklist for Transmitting Accepted Manuscripts for Electronic Production
- Ethical Standards for the Reporting and Publishing of Scientific Information
- References to Legal Materials
- Sample Cover Letter

FIGURE 21-12. Table of Contents of *Publication Manual of the American Psychological Association: Fifth Edition* (2001)

- Figures
- Bar Graphs
- Line Graphs
- Plots
- Scatter Plot
- Group Centroids Plot Multidimensional Scaling
- Drawings
- Apparatus
- Maps
- Questionnaires
- Stimuli
- Hand-Drawings and Handwriting
- Combination Graphs
- Pie Graphs
- Miscellaneous Graphs
- Dendrogram
- Stem-and-Leaf Plots
- Charts
- Photographs
- Posters
- Slides and Overheads for Presentations

FIGURE 21-13. Table of Contents of *Displaying Your Findings: A Practical Guide for Creating Figures, Posters, and Presentations*

MLA guidelines are also currently used by over 125 scholarly and literary journals, newsletters, and magazines with circulations over one thousand; by hundreds of smaller periodicals; and by many university and commercial presses. MLA style is commonly followed not only in the United States but in Canada and other countries as well; Japanese translations of the *MLA Handbook for Writers of Research Papers* appeared in 1980, 1984, and 1988, and a Chinese translation was published in 1990.

In a 1991 article on style manuals, *Booklist* cited MLA documentation style as one of the "big three," along with the guidelines published by the American Psychological Association and the University of Chicago Press (Modern Language Association, 2007).

The MLA produces two handbooks. One is for high school and undergraduate students and is titled the *MLA Handbook for Writers of Research Papers.* The other, which targets graduate college students,

scholars, and professional writers, is the *MLA Style Manual and Guide to Scholarly Publishing.* Look for more information about this writing style and its handbooks at its website www.mla.org.

The Chicago Manual of Style

The Chicago Manual of Style (15th edition) is another of the most used writing style manuals. In Figure 21-14, the history of this well-known manual shows that it is just over one hundred years old! Published by the University of Chicago Press originally in 1906 as a guide to writers for articles and other works to be published by the Press, these guidelines also have been modified over time as techniques and technologies have changed. The *Chicago Manual* is also published as an online book. Look for information about this manual at the website http://www.chicagomanualofstyle.org.

The History of *The Chicago Manual of Style*

The history of *The Chicago Manual of Style* spans more than one hundred years, beginning in 1891 when the University of Chicago Press first opened its doors. At that time, the Press had its own composing room with experienced typesetters who were required to set complex scientific material as well as work in such exotic fonts as Hebrew and Ethiopic. In that distant time, professors brought their handwritten manuscripts directly to the compositors, who did their best to decipher them. The compositors then passed the proofs to the "brainery"—the proofreaders who corrected typographical errors and edited for stylistic inconsistencies. To bring some order to the process, the staff of the composing room drew up a style sheet, which was then passed on to the rest of the university community. Even at such an early stage, "the University Press style book and style sheet" was considered important enough to be preserved in the cornerstone of the (then) newly constructed Press building in 1903, along with other items from the Press's early years.

That sheet grew into a pamphlet, and by 1906 the pamphlet had become a book: *Manual of Style: Being a compilation of the typographical rules in force at the University of Chicago Press, to which are appended specimens of type in use*—otherwise known as the

first edition of the *Manual.* (See a facsimile of the first edition in PDF format.) At 200 pages, the *Manual* cost 50 cents, plus 6 cents for postage and handling. Now in its fifteenth edition, *The Chicago Manual of Style* has evolved into a 984-page (and $55.00) reference book, known as the authoritative voice for authors, editors, proofreaders, indexers, copywriters, designers, and publishers.

This hundred-year evolution has taken place under the ongoing stewardship of Chicago's renowned editorial staff. Suggestions and requests from users have always played a role in revisions of the *Manual.* In adapting to the needs of its users as well as to developments and technological advances in writing, editing, and publishing, the *Manual* has undergone more than a dozen substantial revisions.

One of the most significant was begun in 1968, led by the editorial team of Catharine Seybold and Bruce Young, who rearranged, expanded, and updated the eleventh edition to produce the twelfth edition. The 20,000-copy first printing sold out before the publication date even arrived. By 1969, the *Manual* was an industry leader. Sales of the twelfth edition totaled more than 150,000 copies—the same number as total sales for the first eleven editions.

FIGURE 21-14. A history of one writing style manual

Continued on next page

The History of *The Chicago Manual of Style (continued)*

The publication of the thirteenth edition in 1982 was another notable moment in the history of the *Manual*. It was at this point that *A Manual of Style* became *The Chicago Manual of Style*, a change that reflected the title most often used by the book's audience. The thirteenth edition incorporated the new United States copyright regulations that became law in 1978, and the production and printing sections of the *Manual* were revised to include the phototypesetting technology that replaced lead type as well as the Linotype and Monotype metal-casting machines of the 1970s. Nearly 200 pages longer than its predecessor, the thirteenth edition addressed, for the first time, the effects of personal computers and word processors, which authors were just beginning to use in preparing their manuscripts.

Although the thirteenth edition briefly touched on this new and radical technology, the personal computer was still a novelty in 1982, and few understood the far-reaching effects it would have on the lives of writers, much less on the publishing industry. But by 1993, eleven years later, computer word processing was becoming the norm, and the *Manual* began to address more systematically the role of computers in writing and editing. The fourteenth edition weighed in at 936 pages and sold for $40.00. It reflected significant changes in style, usage, procedure, and technology, and contained new and more extensive editing examples based on requests from editors, authors, indexers, and teachers of publishing courses. The fourteenth edition also offered an expanded glossary that included words unfamiliar to publishers just a decade earlier, as well as an updated chapter on copyrights and permissions. New technologies for composition, design, printing, and binding were described, including the preparation of jackets and covers and the process of obtaining and displaying ISBNs and bar codes for the expanded group of self-publishers created by the computer age. Nearly half a million copies of the fourteenth edition have been sold since its debut, helping to bring the grand total of all *Manual of Style* sales to well over one million.

Summary

Reporting research results is done in different formats contingent upon the purpose of the research. Research conducted for use in a sports business setting will be reported in a format useful to the business. Research conducted for primary use in academic settings will be reported in a format in accordance with the various academic categories for its dissemination and function.

Typical components of a research report in academia will include an abstract, an introduction to the topic, a summary of the research previously conducted, a review of the research methodology used for the study, a detailed report of the findings of the study, a conceptual discussion of the findings, and conclusions based on the findings of the study. Additionally, a list of references cited and further information provided, such as tables, figures, and appendices, will be included as the last sections of the report.

There are guidelines to be followed for writing the report. One such set of guidelines is the *American Psychological Association Publication Manual*—commonly known as the APA writing manual. These guidelines provide information on all aspects of the organization of the research report. The APA manual also outlines guidelines on appropriate language in contemporary society. For example, there are guidelines and suggestions on how to write with gender-appropriate language.

STUDY QUESTIONS

1. What is the importance of effective communication in reporting research findings?
2. How many different methods can sport management professionals use to communicate the results of their research?
3. What are the factors affecting the communication process in sport management?
4. What are the different types of research reports? Explain.
5. How many components does a research report typically have and what are they?
6. What are the requirements on the preparation of a poster or oral presentation?
7. What are the general rules in the development and use of tables, figures, and charts? Explain these rules briefly
8. Differentiate the three most popular writing styles used in communicating research results.

LEARNING ACTIVITY

Select an article from one of the sport management journals, critique the article, and explain what you would do to improve the quality of the study.

References

Dixon, M. A., & Brunening, J. E. (2007). Work-family in coaching I: A top-down perspective. *Journal of Sport Management, 21*(3), 377–407.

Filo, K., & Funk, D. C. (2005). Congruence between attractive product features and virtual content delivery for Internet marketing communication. *Sport Marketing Quarterly, 14*(2), 112–122.

Modern Language Association. (2007). What is MLA style? http://www.mla.org/style.

Pitts, B. G., & Slattery, J. (2004). An examination of the effects of time on sponsorship awareness levels. *Sport Marketing Quarterly, 13*(1), 43–54.

Quarterman, J., Dupree, A. D.. & Willie, K. P. (2006). Challenges confronting intercollegiate female athletic directors of NCAA member institutions by division. *College Student Journal, 40*(3),

Quarterman, J., Pitts, B. G., Jackson, E. N., Jr., Kim, K., & Kim, J. (2005). Statistical data analysis techniques employed in *Sport Marketing Quarterly*: 1992 to 2004. *Sport Marketing Quarterly, 14*(4), 227–239.

INDEX

Ridinger, L. L., 308
Ridpath, B. D., 180
Riemer, H. A., 183
Robinson, M. J., 298, 312
Ross, S. D., 315, 318

S

sampling methods, 231, 238–240
  approaches to, 233
    convenience sampling, 234
    nonprobability sampling, 233
    probability sampling, 233
    purposive (judgmental) sampling, 234–235
    quota sampling, 234
  appropriateness of sampling design, 238
  determining sample size, 237–238
  nature and scope of, 231
  probability sampling procedures, 235
    random cluster sampling, 237
    simple random sampling, 235–236
    stratified random sampling, 236
    systematic random sampling, 236–237
  sampling process, 238
San Antonio, 255
Scale of Athletic Department Goals (SADG), 178
Scarborough Research, 114
Schneider, R. G., 253
Schultz, A. M., 175
Schumacher, S., 4
Schvaneveldt, J. D., 180
Scott, E. P., 103
secondary data, 25, 109, 117–118
  advantages of, 114–115
  case study of, 117
  limitations of, 115–116
  nature of, 109
  process of, 116
    evaluating data, 116–117
    gathering data, 117
  sources of, 111–114
    government publications, 114
    previous research, 114
    previous surveys, 114
    private internal data, 114
    private trade organizations, 113
    public records, 113

uses of, 109–111
  to answer research questions, 109–10
  to build a statistical model, 111
  to clarify situations, 110
  to help decision-making, 110
  to provide exploratory information, 110
  to verify primary research findings, 111
Seymour, D. T., 99
Seymour, S., 189
Shaw, S., 96
Sidewell, M. J., 252, 253
The SMART-Journal, 40
Smith, D. W., 300, 301
Soloman four-group experimental design, 149
Spearman-Brown split-half coefficient, 176, 178
Spearman's rank-order correlation (Spearman's *rho*), 177, 283
Spencer, N. E., 301, 310
The Sport Journal, 40
Sport Management Association of Australia and New Zealand, 13
sport management research, 3, 13
  characteristics of, 5–6
    interdisciplinary nature of, 5, 13
    quantitative nature of the research, 5–6, 13
    wide variety of specialty areas, 5, 13
  definition of, 4
  evolution and future of, 12–13
  philosophical approaches to, 7
    naturalistic paradigm, 8–9, 13
    positivist paradigm, 7–8, 13
  purposes of, 6–7
  value of for the practice of sport management, 5
  value of for students, 4–5
sport management research, approaches to, 9
  applied research, 9
  basic research, 9
  casual research, 11
  combined qualitative and quantitative approaches, 38–39
  descriptive research, 11
  exploratory research, 11
Sport Management Education Journal, 40
Sport Management Review, 12, 40
Sport Marketing Association, 13, 161

ABOUT THE AUTHORS

MING LI is the Director of the School of Recreation and Sport Sciences at Ohio University and a professor in sports administration. Before joining the faculty at Ohio University, he taught at Georgia Southern University for eleven years. Dr. Li's teaching and research interests are in financial and economic aspects of sport, international sport management, and research methods in sport management. He received his bachelor's degree in education from Guangzhou Institute of Physical Culture (PRC), his master's degree in education from Hangzhou University (PRC), and his Doctor of Education from the University of Kansas in Sport Administration. His professional affiliations include: American Alliance for Health, Physical Education, Recreation and Dance (AAHPERD), North American Society for Sport Management (NASSM), Sport Marketing Association, and International Council for Health, Physical Education, Recreation, Sport and Dance (ICHPER.SD). He has held offices as Member-at-Large on the Executive Council of NASSM, Chair of the Sport Management Council of the National Association for Sport and Physical Education (NASPE), and Director of the Sport Management & Administration Commission of ICHPER.SD. He was the recipient of the 1999 Taylor Dodson Award given by the Southern District AAHPERD. The award is presented annually to a young professional who has demonstrated strong leadership qualities in the field of health, physical education, and dance. Currently, Li is President of NASSM. He has actively participated in the NASPE-NASSM Sport Management Program Review process. In 2001, he finished his three-year term serving on the Sport Management Program Review Council (SMPRC). He has served as a consultant to several institutions in program evaluation and development in sport management. Li has memberships on the editorial boards of several professional journals, including *Journal of Sport Management*, *International Journal of Sport Management*, and *Sport Marketing Quarterly*. In 1996, he worked for the Atlanta Committee for the Olympic Games (ACOG) as an Olympic Envoy. The Envoy appointment was awarded as a result of Li's leadership ability, decision making and communication skills, and ability to work in a multi-cultural environment. For the contribution he has made to his profession, the institution, and the community, he was given the 2000–2001 Award for Excellence in Service by Georgia Southern University. Li has published more than 25 articles in refereed journals, two books (*Economics of Sport* and *Badminton Everyone*), and a number of book chapters. Presently, he is working on a book project, *International Sport Management* as a co-editor. In addition to publications, Li also made numerous refereed presentations at state, national, and international conferences. He is an Honorary Guest Professor of two institutions in China, Guangzhou Institute of Physical Education and Sun-Yat Sen University.

BRENDA G. PITTS, internationally renown in sport business management, particularly in sport marketing and in sport management program development, is currently professor of sport management, director of the Dr. R. Cooter Sport Business Research Center, and program director at Georgia State University in Atlanta, Georgia. Additionally, she works as a sport marketing consultant.

In research, Dr. Pitts is distinguished as a Dr. Earle F. Zeigler Scholar and one of the first research fellows of the North American Society for Sport Management (NASSM). She is author/coauthor of six sport marketing textbooks, editor of and an author in three Sport Marketing Association's books of papers, and author of numerous publications and presentations. Her work has been published in several scholarly journals such as the *Sport Management Education Journal, Journal of Sport Management, Sport Marketing Quarterly, Journal of Vacation Marketing, International Journal of Sports Marketing and Sponsorship, Women in Sport and Physical Activity, Sport Management and Related Topics Journal,* and the *International Journal of Sport Management.* Her research foci include: (1) sport marketing with emphases in consumer behavior, fan and spectator analysis, sport sponsorship and brand awareness measurement, and economic impact and visitor spending; and (2) sport management education with emphases in program design, curriculum standards and accreditation, instructional methodology, and examination and analysis of the body of literature (research journals and books) in sport management.

Dr. Pitts was an editorial board member (1991–1998) and later co-editor-in-chief of *The Sport Management Library* (1998-2000), a project that produced more than 20 textbooks in sport management. She serves on the review boards of the *Sport Marketing Quarterly,* the *Sport Management and Related Topics Journal,* and the *Sport Management Review* (Australia); she previously served on the review board of the *International Journal of Sport Management.* She has served as a guest editor for papers for the *Journal of Sport Management* and the *Women in Sport and Physical Activity Journal.*

Dr. Pitts received the 2004 Dr. Garth Paton Distinguished Service Award from NASSM in recognition of meritorious service. Some of Dr. Pitts's service accomplishments have included serving as co-chair of the committee that wrote the first *Sport Management Curriculum Standards* (published in 1993); serving on the first Sport Management Program Review Council (1993-1996), of which she is a continuing reading member; acting as program chair of 2 NASSM conferences; hosting (as co-director) the 1990 NASSM Conference; hosting (as executive director) the 2004 NASSM Conference; fulfilling the roles of council member, president-elect, president, and past-president of NASSM (1990-1995); serving as vice-president of academic affairs of the new Sport Marketing Association; acting as founder and co-director for the first scholarly conference on lesbian and gay sport studies; and helping establish the Sport Management Council under NASPE so that there could be more research outlets for faculty in sport management.

Dr. Pitts has served as a consultant in sport marketing for various sport businesses, including the Georgia Dome in Atlanta (with clients such as the Professional Bull Riders, Inc., SuperCross, and the Atlanta Falcons), Tallahassee Soccer Association, and the NCAA.

Her research, consulting, and services work have taken her around the world; her international stops include Sweden, South Africa, Hong Kong, Singapore, Malaysia, Spain, France, Australia, Germany, Hungary, England, The Netherlands, Japan, Canada, Taiwan, Portugal, Scotland, Cyprus, and China.

Dr. Pitts enjoys all kinds of sports, more recently soccer, golf, boating, volleyball, jogging, tennis, and softball. Her outstanding career in basketball has brought her such awards as the retirement of her high school basketball uniform number; membership in the "A" Club of the University of Alabama; induction into the Huntsville (Alabama) Sports Hall of Fame; induction into the Women's Basketball Hall of Fame, Knoxville, Tennessee; and a nomination for the Alabama Sports Hall of Fame. Recently, Dr. Pitts has won a couple of golf tournaments but has wisely decided to keep her day job.

JEROME QUARTERMAN, Ph.D., is an associate professor in Health, Human Performance and Leisure Studies and Coordinator of Sport Management Studies at Howard University in Washington, D.C. Previously, he was a full-time faculty member in sport management studies at Florida State University and at Bowling Green State University in Ohio. Of his 34 years of teaching, 18 have involved teaching students in sport management courses in undergraduate and graduate courses at both the master's and doctoral levels. His research interest includes assessments of the managerial roles and skills of practicing managers in sport organizations,

barriers and choices confronting student athletes, and research of research methods applied to sport management studies. He has published over forty articles in physical education, intercollegiate athletics, sport management, and sport marketing journals. His research has appeared in the *International Journal of Sport Management, Sport Marketing Quarterly, Journal of Sport Management, the Academic Athletic Journal, Journal of Teaching Physical Education*, and *the Journal of Physical Education, Recreation and Dance*. He is also a co-editor of a leading textbook in sport management studies, entitled *Contemporary Sport Management* (third edition).

He is also a reviewer for the *International Journal of Sport Management, Academic Athletic Journal*, and *The SMART ON LINE Journal*. He teaches students in a variety of courses including Research Methods in Sport Management Studies, Organizational Theory in Organizations of the Sport Industry, Intercollegiate Athletic Administration, Ethics in Organizations of the Sport Industry, Organizational Behavior in Organizations of the Sport Industry, Managing Human Resources in Organizations of the Sport Industry, Leadership and Management in Organizations of the Sport Industry, Introduction to Facilities in Organization, and Introduction to Sport Management Studies. He has also served as department chair at Southern, Alabama State, Kentucky State, and Hampton universities. Dr. Quarterman earned an undergraduate degree from Savannah State University, a master's from Kent State University and a doctoral degree from The Ohio State University. He is the proud parent of Terrance and Michele.